TRADE AND DEVELOPMENT REPORT, 1997

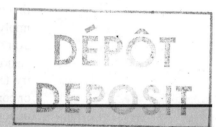
Report by the secretariat of the
United Nations Conference on Trade and Development

UNITED NATIONS
New York and Geneva, 1997

Note

- Symbols of United Nations documents are composed of capital letters combined with figures. Mention of such a symbol indicates a reference to a United Nations document.

- The designations employed and the presentation of the material in this publication do not imply the expression of any opinion whatsoever on the part of the Secretariat of the United Nations concerning the legal status of any country, territory, city or area, or of its authorities, or concerning the delimitation of its frontiers or boundaries.

- Material in this publication may be freely quoted or reprinted, but acknowledgement is requested, together with a reference to the document number. A copy of the publication containing the quotation or reprint should be sent to the UNCTAD secretariat.

UNI
TD
T62

UNCTAD/TDR/17

UNITED NATIONS PUBLICATION
Sales No. E.97.II.D.8
ISBN 92-1-112411-5
ISSN 0255-4607

FOREWORD

The 1997 *Trade and Development Report* examines trends in the international economy with particular reference to developing countries, comparing current and past performances and assessing prospects for future development. It sheds light on the pressing policy issues facing developing countries and the wider international community.

Drawing upon themes set at the ninth session of the United Nations Conference on Trade and Development (UNCTAD), as well as on the work of the United Nations Regional Commissions and of the Specialized Agencies, this year's report focuses on the growing income gaps among and within countries.

Achieving more equitable growth remains a central aim of the work of the United Nations on development. This *Report* illuminates the key role played by investment in achieving rapid growth, as well as the contribution that appropriate government policies can make. A partnership between the United Nations, national governments and civil society can, and will, achieve the twin objectives of faster growth and greater income equality.

Kofi A. Annan
Secretary-General of the United Nations

Contents

Part One

GLOBAL TRENDS

Chapter I

Chapter II

Annex to Part One

List of text tables

List of boxes and charts

Classification by country or commodity group

The classification of countries in this Report generally follows that of the UNCTAD *Handbook of International Trade and Development Statistics 1994*.[1] It has been adopted solely for the purposes of statistical or analytical convenience and does not necessarily imply any judgement concerning the stage of development of a particular country or area. As noted in the Foreword to the *Handbook*, the classification differs from that used previously, in particular as regards regional and total aggregates for developing countries.

The term "country" refers, as appropriate, also to territories or areas.

References to "Latin America" in the text or tables include the Caribbean countries unless otherwise indicated.

Unless otherwise stated, the classification by commodity group used in this Report follows generally that employed in the *Handbook of International Trade and Development Statistics 1994*.

Other notes

References in the text to *TDR* are to the *Trade and Development Report* (of a particular year). For example, *TDR 1996* refers to *Trade and Development Report, 1996* (United Nations publication, Sales No. E.96.II.D.6).

The term "dollar" ($) refers to United States dollars, unless otherwise stated.

The term "billion" signifies 1,000 million.

The term "tons" refers to metric tons.

Annual rates of growth and change refer to compound rates.

Exports are valued f.o.b. and imports c.i.f., unless otherwise specified.

Use of a hyphen (-) between dates representing years, e.g. 1988-1990, signifies the full period involved, including the initial and final years.

An oblique stroke (/) between two years, e.g. 1990/91, signifies a fiscal or crop year.

Two dots (..) indicate that the data are not available, or are not separately reported.

A dash (-) or a zero (0) indicates that the amount is nil or negligible.

A dot (.) indicates that the item is not applicable.

A plus sign (+) before a figure indicates an increase; a minus sign (-) before a figure indicates a decrease.

Details and percentages do not necessarily add to totals because of rounding.

---

[1]   United Nations publication, Sales No.E/F.95.II.D.15.

Abbreviations

ACP	African, Caribbean and Pacific (group of States)
ACR	accumulation/concentration ratio
ASEAN	Association of South-East Asian Nations
BIS	Bank for International Settlements
CEPAL	Economic Commission for Latin America and the Caribbean (Comisión Económica para América Latina y el Caribe)
CEPR	Centre for Economic Policy Research (London)
CFA	Communauté financière africaine (franc zone)
CIS	Commonwealth of Independent States
c.i.f.	cost, insurance and freight
DAC	Development Assistance Committee (of OECD)
DRF	Debt Reduction Facility (of IDA)
EC	European Community (or Communities)
ECA	Economic Commission for Africa
ECAs	export credit agencies
ECE	Economic Commission for Europe
ECGD	Export Credits Guarantee Department (United Kingdom)
ECLAC	Economic Commission for Latin America and the Caribbean
ECU	European currency unit
EEC	European Economic Community
EFTA	European Free Trade Association
EMS	European Monetary System
EMU	Economic and Monetary Union
ERM	Exchange Rate Mechanism of EMS
ESAF	Enhanced Structural Adjustment Facility (of IMF)
ESCAP	Economic and Social Commission for Asia and the Pacific
EU	European Union
EXIM	Export-Import Bank (United States)
FAO	Food and Agriculture Organization of the United Nations
FDI	foreign direct investment
f.o.b.	free on board
FY	fiscal year
GATS	General Agreement on Trade in Services
GATT	General Agreement on Tariffs and Trade
GDP	gross domestic product
GNP	gross national product
GSP	generalized system of preferences
HIPCs	heavily indebted poor countries
HS	Harmonized Commodity Description and Coding System (Harmonized System)
IBRD	International Bank for Reconstruction and Development (World Bank)
IDA	International Development Association
IDB	Inter-American Development Bank
IFAD	International Fund for Agricultural Development

IFC	International Finance Corporation
ILO	International Labour Organisation
IMF	International Monetary Fund
LDC	least developed country
LIBOR	London Interbank Offered Rate
MBs	marketing boards
MERCOSUR	Southern Cone Common Market
MFA	Multi-Fibre Arrangement
MFI	multilateral financial institution
MFN	most favoured nation
MTAs	Multilateral Trade Agreements
MVA	manufacturing value added
NAFTA	North American Free Trade Agreement (Canada-United States-Mexico)
NBER	National Bureau of Economic Research (United States)
NGO	non-governmental organization
NIEs	newly industrializing economies
NIESR	National Institute of Economic and Social Research (London)
NRI	Nomura Research Institute (Tokyo)
NTMs	non-tariff measures
ODA	official development assistance
OECD	Organisation for Economic Cooperation and Development
OPEC	Organization of the Petroleum Exporting Countries
PPP	purchasing power parity
R&D	research and development
SAF	Structural Adjustment Facility
SAP	Structural Adjustment Programme
SDR	special drawing right
SITC	Standard International Trade Classification
SPS	Sanitary and Phytosanitary
SSA	sub-Saharan Africa
TBT	technical barriers to trade
TNCs	transnational corporations
TRIMs	trade-related investment measures
TRIPs	trade-related intellectual property rights
UNCTAD	United Nations Conference on Trade and Development
UNDP	United Nations Development Programme
UNIDO	United Nations Industrial Development Organization
UNU	United Nations University
VAT	value added tax
WIDER	World Institute for Development Economics Research
WIPO	World Intellectual Property Organization
WTO	World Trade Organization

OVERVIEW

Global trends

The world economy is continuing to grow slowly. Despite the success in reducing inflation almost everywhere, expectations of faster growth have not been fulfilled so far. Since the beginning of the decade, world output growth has averaged about 2 per cent, compared to the roughly 3 per cent attained during the turbulent years of the 1980s. Since the economic recovery that started in 1993, in no year has world output growth exceeded 3 per cent, 1996 included. The prospects are for a continuation of this slow growth.

The slowdown in developed countries from an average growth of 2.8 per cent in the 1980s to 1.8 per cent since the beginning of the 1990s has affected all the major countries, including the United States, where growth averaged 2.3 per cent in the 1990s, against 2.7 per cent in the previous decade. The contribution of individual industrial countries to global growth has varied over time as business cycles have become increasingly desynchronized. In 1993-1994 expansion was faster in the United States than in the European Union (EU) and Japan; in 1995 it was faster in EU than in the United States and Japan; and in 1996 it was fastest in Japan.

A certain pattern of growth can be observed in the developing world since 1990, where growth has averaged 4.8 per cent including China, and 3.9 per cent if China is excluded. Much of this growth has been due to East Asia, where expansion has been both fast and stable. In Latin America growth has been not only more unstable but also on average much lower - less than 3 per cent annually. In Africa the fall in real per capita income that began in the 1980s continued in the early 1990s, but there has been a marked improvement over the past two years, when output rose faster than population for the first time in many years.

A significant development in 1996 has been the slowdown in world trade. While world merchandise exports had grown at rates 3-4 times that of world output in the previous two years, in 1996 the difference was much smaller, a tendency which can be expected to continue in coming years, as the initial effects of widespread trade liberalization, particularly in developing countries, taper off. This recent slowdown in world trade has also been associated with a weakening of commodity prices. After two years of sustained increases, many non-oil commodity prices began to decline in 1996, particularly those of interest to developing countries.

Improved governance and strong commodity prices have been among the most important factors accounting for a broad-based recovery in sub-Saharan Africa, others being the substantial improvement in weather conditions as well as diminished civil strife. However, some of these factors are of a one-off character. Sustainability of recovery depends on the expansion of exports of non-traditional products so that higher export earnings can finance the imports needed for investment. It also depends on utilizing existing capacity more fully. But many countries of the region have a competing claim on export earnings, namely the payment of their mounting arrears on external debt. Thus, external debt relief and the transfer of new resources, as well as continued domestic policy efforts, are the key to sustained recovery in Africa.

In this respect the Highly Indebted Poor Countries (HIPCs) Debt Initiative of the World Bank and IMF is a major step forward and could play an important role. A speedy and flexible implementation of the Initiative is, however, crucial; and completion dates must be such that relief is available in good time. If, as is feared in some quarters, the eligibility and sustainability criteria prove too restrictive, some countries in need of immediate relief may not be eligible at all. Increased flexibility in the application of certain conditions determining country eligibility, as well as promptness in implementation, are essential for ensuring a lasting and rapid solution to the debt crises of the HIPCs not only in Africa but also in other regions.

In Latin America, growth averaged 3.3 per cent in 1996, with recovery in Mexico and Argentina and continued strong expansion in Chile. Exports continued to be the main demand impetus for most countries of the region, particularly on account of increasing intra-regional trade. However, at about 10 per cent in 1996, the rate of growth of the value of merchandise exports for the region as a whole was less than half that of the previous year. Most countries continue to face serious policy dilemmas in attaining both growth and price stability. Control over inflation depends largely on the stability of the nominal exchange rate, while even modest growth is often associated with a rise in deficits on current account. Reconciling external equilibrium and competitive exchange rates with growth and price stability remains the basic challenge for most Latin American countries.

Asian economies continued to perform well in 1996, but even there growth slowed with the weakening of exports. Policies in a number of East and South-East Asian countries have been reoriented towards curbing rising deficits on current account and holding back inflationary tendencies, and in some cases towards dealing with weaknesses in the financial sector. China succeeded in bringing down inflation to a single digit, while nevertheless growing at an impressive rate of almost 10 per cent. In some countries the slowdown reflects difficulties in sustaining export expansion now that the relatively easy stages of labour-intensive production for export have been completed. It also highlights the importance of technological upgrading and productivity growth in maintaining the export momentum.

Growth experience continued to vary among the transition economies of Europe. In the region as a whole output fell by 2.8 per cent, a repeat of the previous year. Output continued to decline on average in the CIS area, most markedly in the Russian Federation and Ukraine, but in some other member countries there was at last a resumption of growth. In Central and Eastern Europe only a few countries managed to sustain steady growth. However, their current-account balances generally deteriorated as a result of currency appreciations brought about by surges in capital inflows, tariff reductions and a slower growth of exports to Western Europe.

The economies of Central and Eastern Europe, East Asia, and Latin America all continue to depend, to an important extent, on private capital inflows to finance current-account deficits. During 1996 and early 1997 there was a substantial expansion in the major categories of external financing for many countries in these regions, whose integration into the global network of financial markets is now well established. For these countries the one-off capital inflows associated with the process of integration are becoming less important, and they are now experiencing the effects of more differentiated changes in international investors' perceptions, in both favourable and unfavourable directions. For example, some of them have recently had to confront large capital outflows and periods of strong downward pressure on their currencies as a result of investors' reactions to the current-account deficits or to increased fragility of domestic financial systems. These events suggest that sustainable current-account balances may be lower than recent levels. Policies concerning exchange rates and capital accounts, as well as monetary policy more generally, must now increasingly take into account their impact on market perceptions and of the need to manage financial inflows and outflows.

Among the major industrial countries the United States has enjoyed a more persistent expansion than most forecasters had predicted. After six years of continuous expansion, unemployment and inflation have both fallen to historically low levels, below 5 per cent and 3 per cent, respectively, belying the widespread belief that a drop of unemployment below 6 per cent would trigger accelerated inflation. Indeed, while monetary policy allowed unemployment to fall to as little as 4.8 per cent in early 1997, inflation continued to abate. In this connection it may be recalled that in *TDR 1995* the view was expressed that the unemployment problem in the North could not be solved unless central banks acted boldly and tested their theories about the level of unemployment compatible with stable inflation.

The United States recovery has been driven primarily by investment, which has brought about a significant increase in productivity, particularly in manufacturing. However, much of the resulting gain has been captured by profits. After six years of expansion, average gross weekly earnings in real terms in 1996 were below the level of 1991 (itself below that of 1987), while the share of profits in gross value added in the non-financial business sector rose by 3.5 percentage points from 1992 to 1996.

Japan finally reaped the benefits of its fiscal packages, growing at 3.5 per cent in 1996 after a prolonged recession. Recovery has also been greatly helped by the depreciation of the yen against the dollar. However, the growth stimulus of the emergency budget measures is now largely exhausted, and current plans are to reduce the budget deficit. Thus, the performance of the economy will increasingly depend on exports and hence on the exchange value of the yen.

The widely expected recovery has not materialized in continental Western Europe, where unemployment has reached record levels. As foreseen in *TDR 1996,* efforts to meet the Maastricht targets for fiscal deficits prevented automatic stabilizers from coming into play, thereby strengthening the deflationary forces and raising unemployment. Growth fell to under 1.5 per cent in both France and Germany, while in Italy the decline was even stronger, from 3 per cent to under 1 per cent. In contrast, thanks largely to a rise in private domestic spending, expansion continued in the United Kingdom.

However, political developments in the European Union suggest that governments are increasingly being confronted by a major challenge: how to reconcile growth and employment with the objective of meeting fiscal targets. The underlying rationale for setting fiscal targets was to attain conditions conducive to monetary and exchange rate stability. In the event, there has been a remarkable convergence of inflation and interest rates among the major EU countries, and exchange rates have also been stable, even though fiscal deficits generally remain above the targets. By contrast, the debate over the targets is creating conditions that can provoke greater volatility in financial and currency markets. Consequently, perhaps the best way for generating the right conditions for growth and employment without sacrificing stability would be, as suggested in *TDR 1994*, to cut the Gordian knot of fiscal convergence and proceed to monetary union as soon as possible.

Differing contributions by the major industrial countries to global demand, combined with the appreciation of the dollar, have started to produce global trade imbalances similar to those experienced in the 1980s, with a growing deficit in the United States and growing surpluses in Western Europe and Japan. While domestic demand has expanded rapidly in the United States, most other industrial countries have continued to rely on exports for growth.

The experience of the 1980s illustrates the difficulties that can be posed by mounting trade imbalances and misalignments in exchange rates for both the international trading system and international monetary stability. These imbalances cannot be blamed on the United States fiscal deficits - as they could in the 1980s - since expansion in that country has been associated with falling rather than rising deficits. The burden of adjustment consequently has to be borne by surplus countries. A return to a more sustainable pattern of global demand and trade balances therefore requires an expansion of demand in Europe and Japan rather than monetary tightening in the United States.

Furthermore, if monetary policy is tightened in the United States, its effects may not be limited to widening the global deflationary gap. If accompanied by upward pressure on the dollar, the effect might well be to increase, rather than to reduce, trade imbalances. History shows that a combination of slow growth, rising unemployment and increased trade imbalances can make it difficult to resist protectionist pressures and avoid trade frictions. Moreover, the consequences of a combination of such frictions, dollar appreciation, and a hike in international interest rates would today be more serious and widespread for developing countries than in the 1980s, in view of the increased integration of many of them into the global trading and financial system and of their greater dependence on highly liquid capital inflows.

Globalization, growth and distribution

Inequality: the record

The big story of the world economy since the early 1980s has been the unleashing of market forces. The deregulation of domestic markets and their opening up to international competition have become universal features. The "invisible hand" now operates globally and with fewer countervailing pressures from governments than for decades. Many commentators are optimistic about the prospects for faster growth and for convergence of incomes and living standards which greater global competition should bring.

However, there is also another big story. Since the early 1980s the world economy has been characterized by rising inequality and slow growth. Income gaps between North and South have continued to widen. In 1965, the average per capita income of the G7 countries was 20 times that of the world's poorest seven countries. By 1995 it was 39 times as much.

Certainly, a number of developing countries have been growing faster than industrial countries, but nevertheless not fast enough to narrow the absolute per capita income gap. In Africa, where the gap has been widening over the last three decades, average per capita income is now only 7 per cent of that of the industrial countries. In Latin America, the change has been more abrupt: average per capita incomes have fallen from over one third of the northern level in the late 1970s to one quarter today. Only a handful of East Asian economies have managed to sustain growth rapid enough to narrow the gap, or even in some cases to catch up, with the North. However, as these economies have graduated into the high-income club, few developing countries have been able to step into their place; the middle strata of developing countries, with incomes between 40 per cent and 80 per cent of the average in advanced countries, are thinner today than in the 1970s.

Polarization among countries has been accompanied by increasing income inequality within countries. The income share of the richest 20 per cent has risen almost everywhere since the early 1980s, in many cases reversing a postwar trend. In more than half of the developing countries the richest 20 per cent today receive over 50 per cent of the national income. Those at the bottom have failed to see real gains in living standards, and in some cases have had to endure real losses. In many countries, the per capita income of the poorest 20 per cent now averages less than one tenth that of the richest 20 per cent. But the increase in the shares of the latter has invariably also been associated with a fall in the share of the middle class. Indeed, this hollowing out of the middle class has become a prominent feature of income distribution in many countries.

The trend towards a widening of gaps between income groups is apparent in both more and less successful developing countries, and is associated with export-oriented as much as with inward-oriented strategies. In East Asia, inequality has increased, albeit to different degrees, in both the first- and second-tier NIEs during the past two decades. With the exception of the Republic of Korea and Taiwan Province of China, inequality in East Asian economies today is as high as or even higher than in other developing countries. In Latin America, while the debt crisis of the early 1980s and the economic slowdown led to a worsening of income distribution, the subsequent recovery has failed to turn this around. In Africa, rising rural inequality is widespread.

These trends are rooted in a common set of forces unleashed by rapid liberalization that make for greater inequality by favouring certain income groups over others:

- Growing wage inequality between skilled and unskilled workers is not just a problem for the North. It is becoming a global one. In almost all developing countries that have undertaken rapid trade liberalization, wage inequality has increased, most often in the context of declining industrial employment of unskilled workers and large absolute falls in their real wages, of the order of 20-30 per cent in some Latin American countries;

- Capital has gained in comparison with labour, and profit shares have risen everywhere. In four developing countries out of five, the share of wages in manufacturing value added today is considerably below what it was in the 1970s and early 1980s. In the North there has been a remarkable upward convergence of profits among the major industrial countries. The rate of return on capital in the business sector of the G7 countries taken together rose from 12.5 per cent in the early 1980s to over 16 per cent in mid-1990s. This is again the counterpart to declining wage shares;

- Financial liberalization has given rise to a rapid expansion of public and private debt. A new rentier class has emerged worldwide with the substantial expansion of international capital flows and the hike in real interest rates. In some developing countries interest payments on private and public debt have reached 15 per cent of GDP. Where asset holding is concentrated and the tax system regressive, as is often the case in developing countries, government debt is serving to redistribute income from the poor to the rich, in a manner that is proving even more regressive than "taxation" through inflation. Much of the rise in business revenues in both the North and the South has been absorbed by increased interest payments;

- Agricultural price liberalization has not always removed the urban bias or boosted incomes of farmers, as is particularly evident in Africa. In many countries that have implemented reforms, expected improvements in the domestic terms of trade for agriculture have not materialized and farm-gate prices for export crops have remained well below border prices. The benefits of liberalization have been reaped mainly by traders rather than by farmers.

Does inequality matter?

It is possible that these international and national divisions reflect merely temporary adjustments to a rapidly changing world economy. Helping the rich to get richer may indeed be a prelude to rapid growth and the trickling down of income gains to all other socio-economic groups. But evidence is mounting that slow growth and rising inequalities are becoming more permanent features.

Over the past decade, the world economy has settled down to an average rate of growth of around 3 per cent per year - some 2 percentage points lower than that achieved during the "Golden Age" of 1950-1973. Such a relatively modest rate can solve neither the North's labour market problems nor the

South's poverty problem; nor will it allow for a narrowing of the North-South divide. Past issues of the *Trade and Development Report* have examined some of the underlying causes of this slowdown. What is especially disturbing is that the increased concentration of national income in the hands of a few has not been accompanied by higher investment and faster growth. In the North, profits are at levels not seen since the 1960s, but in the main they now generate much less investment and employment than previously. In the South, the rich often receive more than half of the national income, but private productive investment is rarely sufficient to generate a significant increase in per capita income.

It is this association of increased profits with stagnant investment, rising unemployment and re-duced pay that is the real cause for concern. What matters is not inequality *per se*, but the manner in which incomes of the rich are used. Profits accrue to a small minority of the population whose spending behaviour has wider economic and social implications. For owners of capital, investment acts as a social tax on profits which justifies concentration of income in the hands of a few. Affluent groups that invest a large share of their incomes and generate a general improvement in the standard of living will acquire greater legitimacy than those that do not. In some successful late industrializers in East Asia, where the rich receive less than 50 per cent of national income, private savings and investment reach one third of GDP. By contrast, in many developing countries where the share of the rich in national income exceeds 50 per cent the share of private savings and investment in GDP barely exceeds 15 per cent.

Some of the factors making for greater inequality in a globalizing world at the same time deter investment and slow down growth. The fast pace of financial liberalization has delinked finance from international trade and investment. Higher interest rates brought about by restrictive monetary policies have raised the cost of capital formation and encouraged large segments of the industrial and commer-cial classes to concentrate their energies on buying and selling second-hand assets. The premium that global finance places on liquidity and the speedy entry into and exit from financial markets in search of quick gains have undermined the "animal spirits" needed to make longer-term commitments to invest-ment in newly created productive assets. The greater exit options enjoyed by capital, combined with slow demand growth and excess supply of labour, have been instrumental in raising global profits, often without encouraging investment. Corporate restructuring, labour shedding and wage repression in this world of sluggish growth have thus become the order of the day, generating increased job and income insecurity.

If this situation continues, there is a real threat of a political backlash that may wipe out several of the benefits of recent economic reforms in developed and developing countries alike, and perhaps even roll back some of the achievements of economic integration. The 1920s and 1930s provide a stark and disturbing reminder of just how quickly faith in markets and openness can be overwhelmed by political events. Nor should there be any doubt that the burden of such international economic disinte-gration would once again be borne by those who can least afford it.

What is to be done?

Concern about income inequalities has in the past led some countries to establish institutional arrangements that severely restrict the role of markets and private property. Such arrangements have often successfully limited income disparities for quite long periods. But the result has in many cases been a loss of dynamism and eventual stagnation. Most countries now agree that this is too high a price to pay and that a certain degree of income inequality is necessary to provide the resources and incen-tives for activities that bring more general prosperity.

The basic policy challenge in the South is how to translate rising profits into investment at a pace sufficient to underpin a social contract whereby initial inequalities can be justified - and eventually reduced - by the resulting rise in incomes and living standards of the mass of population. To meet this challenge, some awkward truths must be faced. In the first place, no economic law exists that will make developing economies converge automatically towards the income levels of developed countries. Second, growth and development do not automatically bring about a reduction in inequality. Even the fast-growing economies of East Asia have been confronted with distributional challenges.

The good news, however, is that where convergence has occurred, there are by now clear explanations for it in terms of the development strategy pursued. Moreover, various episodes in the East Asian development experience suggest that governments have an important role to play in reconciling rapid growth with distributional objectives.

If speculative talk about converging incomes and living standards is to cede place to a realistic policy agenda, it is necessary to have a firm grasp of what drives economic growth in a market economy. That role belongs to profits. What distinguishes the successful late industrializers from other developing countries is the high animal spirits of their business class, reflected in exceptionally high rates of saving and investment from profits. This experience shows that policies designed to manage profits so as to accelerate growth can also serve to manage distribution:

- **Managing profits:** A strong profit-investment nexus does not emerge spontaneously from greater global competition. Certain basic conditions such as political stability and secure property rights must indeed be fulfilled. But this is not enough. Policies must be actively pursued that are designed to provide incentives to private firms to retain profits and invest them in the enhancement of productivity, capacity and employment. Fiscal instruments, both taxes and subsidies, can be important tools in this respect. But there is also an array of trade, financial and competition policies that can help raise profitability and investment in key industries above what might be attained under free market conditions. Closing unproductive channels of wealth accumulation and discouraging luxury consumption are essential ingredients of such a strategy.

- **Managing integration:** The quality and quantity of investment can be improved by means of closer linkages with the world economy through trade and capital flows, including FDI. But these external linkages must be complementary to, and not a substitute for, the domestic forces of growth through capital accumulation and technological capacity building. This can be achieved only through a carefully managed and phased integration into the world economy, tailoring the process to the level of economic development in a country and capacity of existing institutions and industries. Such a strategy contrasts sharply with the "big bang" liberalization adopted by some countries in recent years.

- **Managing distribution:** A necessary condition for strengthening the forces making for greater equality in the South is the rapid absorption of surplus labour. Where it is in the rural sector, land reform, agricultural policies and public investment can check the rising inequality typical of the growth process in economies with surplus labour. The challenge, however, is more daunting if the surplus labour simply shifts to urban areas. As countries move along the development path, industrial policies to support upgrading become vital for sustaining rises in real wages. It is at this stage that an adequate supply of educated labour is particularly important to prevent skill shortages leading to wider wage differentials. Throughout the process, taxes designed to discourage distribution of profits as personal incomes, as well as to restrain luxury consumption, serve not only to accelerate investment and job creation, but also to reduce inequalities in personal incomes. Profit-related pay, which has been widely used in East Asia, can also help strengthen the social fabric surrounding the profit-investment nexus.

The policy efforts of developing countries should be accompanied by an accommodating global environment. However, among the asymmetries of globalization is the fact that liberalization of the world economy has proceeded so far in a lopsided way that tends to prejudice the growth prospects of developing countries by discriminating against areas in which they can achieve comparative advantage. Liberalization of trade in goods has proceeded more slowly in those sectors where developing countries are more competitive. Thus, free trade in textiles will be achieved only in the first years of the next century and the major trading blocs continue to protect their agricultural sectors. New forms of protection against exports of manufactures from the South are being sought as a remedy for labour market problems in the North. While many restrictions have been lifted on the freedom of capital and skilled labour to move to where it is best remunerated, no attention has been paid to abolishing the many restrictions on the freedom of movement of unskilled labour. Progressive redressing of these biases remains an important challenge facing the international community if an enabling global environment is to be created.

Global efforts to help developing countries could still come to naught if the slowdown in economic growth in the North is not reversed. Thus, a return to faster growth and policies of full employment is not only a prerequisite for resolving the twin evils of high unemployment and increasing wage inequality in the North, but is also essential for defusing the threat of a popular backlash against globalization, which might put the gains of global economic integration at risk.

Rubens Ricupero
Secretary-General of UNCTAD

GLOBAL TRENDS

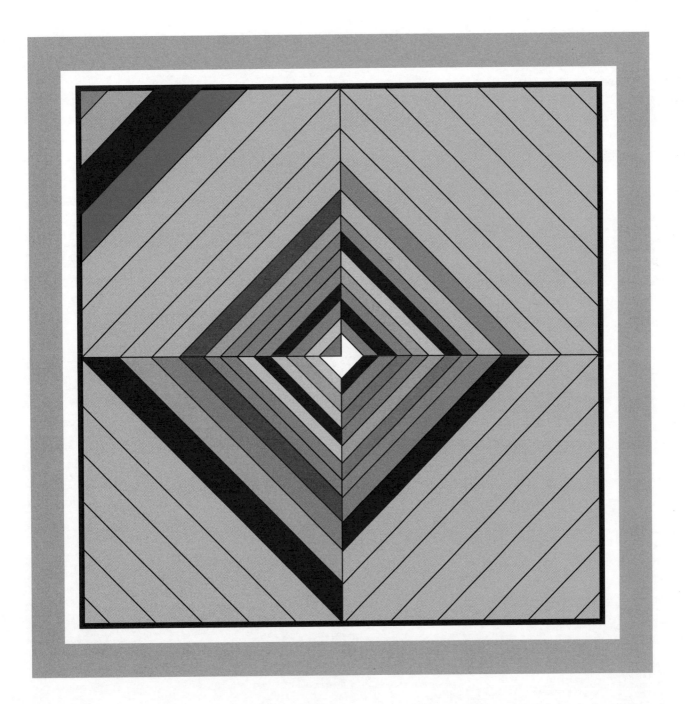

Part One

Chapter I

THE WORLD ECONOMY: PERFORMANCE AND PROSPECTS

A. Overall trends

1. World output

The economic recovery that began in 1993 continued throughout 1996, when world output grew by 2.8 per cent (table 1). However, as foreseen in *TDR 1996*, growth has again failed, for the third consecutive year, to fulfil expectations that the world economy would embark on a new era of sustained growth in excess of 3 per cent, which would allow unemployment in the North to be lowered and average per capita income in the South to rise. Current short-term prospects are for neither faster growth nor reduced unemployment.

Growth in the developed market economies as a whole has continued to remain below the rates of the 1980s. At 2.3 per cent in 1996, the growth rate was slightly above the previous year but slower than had earlier been expected. Expansion in the United States has been more persistent than most forecasts had predicted, and Japan has finally reaped the benefits of its fiscal packages and attained a recovery faster than expected. But the widely expected recovery in continental Western Europe, where unemployment has reached record levels, has not yet materialized. Policy in the European Union has continued to focus on the requirements of introducing a single currency in 1999, rather than on employment and growth.

Developing countries (including China) grew twice as fast as developed countries in 1996, as in the previous year. However, growth in the developing world was uneven and fragile. Latin America has recovered from the depressed conditions of the post-Mexican crisis, but its growth remained at a modest 3.3 per cent. East Asia continued to be the brightest spot in the world economy, but even there growth slowed down with the weakening of exports, and policies in some countries have been reoriented towards curbing rising external deficits and price levels and, in some cases, towards coping with difficulties in the financial sector. Growth in both regions continues to depend, to an important degree, on capital inflows to finance increasing current account deficits.

Economic recovery in Africa, which began in 1994, gathered further momentum in 1996 as the growth of regional output accelerated to 3.9 per cent from 2.8 per cent in the previous year, exceeding population growth and reversing the decline in real per capita income that had persisted for almost a decade. Furthermore, the expansion in output was widespread among all subregions and countries. Favourable commodity prices, much improved weather, diminished civil strife in several instances, and greater domestic policy efforts have played an important role in the recovery. However, many of these factors are of a one-off

Table 1

WORLD OUTPUT, 1993-1997

(Percentage change)

Country/region	1993	1994	1995	1996[a]	1997[b]
World	1.4	2.8	2.4	2.8	3.0
Developed market-economy countries	1.0	2.9	2.0	2.3	2.3
of which:					
United States	3.4	4.1	2.0	2.5	2.9
Japan	-0.2	0.5	0.8	3.5	1.9
European Union	-0.6	2.8	2.4	1.5	2.0
of which:					
Germany	-1.2	2.9	1.9	1.4	2.2
France	-1.5	2.7	2.2	1.3	1.9
Italy	-1.2	2.2	3.0	0.7	1.2
United Kingdom	2.2	3.8	2.4	2.0	2.5
Central and Eastern Europe	-8.1	-10.3	-2.7	-2.8	0.7
Developing countries[c]	5.0	4.8	4.8	5.6	5.6
of which:					
Latin America	3.9	4.5	0.5	3.3	4.0
Africa	-0.6	1.4	2.8	3.9	3.9
Asia[c]	6.7	5.6	7.3	6.9	6.7
of which:					
China	14.0	11.8	10.2	9.7	9.0
Other countries	5.0	3.9	6.5	6.1	6.0
Memo item:					
Developing countries excluding China	3.9	3.7	4.0	4.9	5.1

Source: UNCTAD secretariat calculations, based on data in 1990 dollars.
   a Estimate.
   b Forecast.
   c Including China.

character and cannot be expected to lift output indefinitely. Commodity prices are already levelling off, weather is changeable, and there is a limit to gains from a peace dividend. Sustained growth in Africa, as in poor countries elsewhere, ultimately depends on combining policy efforts with adequate external financing.

In 1996, output in the transition economies of Central and Eastern Europe as a whole declined by 2.8 per cent, as in the preceding year. However, divergence in economic performance has continued to widen. A number of countries in Central Europe have sustained strong growth, whereas in many other countries there were further economic setbacks, leading to further falls in output and even to social and political chaos.

2. World trade

Growth in the volume of world merchandise exports slowed down sharply in 1996, reaching only 4.6 per cent, against 10.0 per cent in the preceding two years (table 2), and falling more than had been expected at the beginning of the year. Since output continued to grow more or less at a constant pace, the divergence between trade and output growth, which has been increasing since 1990, was greatly reduced. Only a modest acceleration of growth in world trade is expected in 1997.

An important factor in the slowdown of world trade was a sharp deceleration of import growth in developed economies, which together account for about two thirds of world import demand, from 11.0 per cent in 1994 to only 5.2 per cent in 1996 (table 2). Particularly drastic was the drop in both the United States and Japan. In Western Europe imports remained sluggish because of slower GDP growth, whereas other factors were at play in the United States and Japan. In those two countries the income elasticity of imports (i.e. the ratio of the percentage change in import volume to that of GDP from 1995 to 1996) dropped respectively from 4.0 to 2.6 and from 15.6 to 1.0, whereas it increased from 2.8 to 3.1 in Western Europe. In Japan, slower import growth coincided with a depreciation of the yen, after a surge during 1991-1995 associated with a substantial appreciation of the currency. In the United States the rise in imports of capital goods, especially computers and related equipment, which had loomed large in earlier years, slowed dramatically in 1996.

In East Asia export growth declined significantly, falling below the growth of output for the first time in many years. A major factor was a drastic fall in the prices of certain electronic and information equipment, particularly semiconductors, largely on account of market saturation. In China a reduction in export tax rebates in late 1995 had prompted enterprises to rush their exports as much as possible, including those planned for 1996. By contrast, in Latin America, particularly among the members of MERCOSUR, the rate of acceleration of exports achieved in 1995 was maintained or even slightly exceeded in 1996.

Table 2

EXPORTS AND IMPORTS BY MAJOR REGIONS AND ECONOMIC GROUPINGS, 1994-1996

(Percentage change in volume over previous year)

	1994	1995	1996[a]
Exports			
World	10.4	10.0	4.6
Developed market-economy countries	9.6	7.4	4.2
of which:			
Japan	1.7	3.3	0.8
North America	10.0	9.4	5.7
Western Europe	11.3	7.4	4.0
Developing countries	13.5	16.2	6.1
of which:			
Africa	4.3	8.3	8.1
Latin America	9.2	9.9	9.3
South and East Asia	14.8	18.0	5.8
West Asia	7.1	16.9	7.3
China	31.0	20.7	0.7
Imports			
Developed market-economy countries	11.0	7.6	5.2
of which:			
Japan	13.6	12.5	3.5
United States	12.0	8.0	6.4
Western Europe	9.1	6.7	5.3

Source: *World Economic and Social Survey 1997* (United Nations publication, Sales No. E.97.II.C.1), table A.19 and (for the United States) *OECD Economic Outlook*, June 1997, p. 43.
a Preliminary.

In value terms the slowdown in world exports in 1996 was even sharper than in volume, growing by only 4.1 per cent as compared to 19.6 per cent in 1995. The average dollar prices of globally traded goods stabilized in 1996 after having increased by 10 per cent in the previous year, due partly to the appreciation of the dollar vis-à-vis the currencies of several major trading countries, particularly France, Germany, Japan and the Republic of Korea.

The picture is similar for the value of world exports of commercial services, with growth decelerating to 5 per cent in 1996 from 14 per cent in the preceding year. The slowdown in this trade (for both exports and imports) was particularly pronounced in Western Europe and Asia, whereas North America maintained the pace of expansion of the previous year. Financial and insurance services, royalties and licence fees, construction services and other business services continued to be more dynamic than transportation or travel. By and large, the slowdown in growth in the value of world trade in commercial services can be attributed to the appreciation of the dollar against a number of major currencies and to the stagnation of trade in continental Western Europe, which alone accounts for one half of world trade in commercial services.

3. Commodity prices

After two consecutive years of substantial increases, non-oil primary commodity prices started to decline in 1996 and for the year as a whole were over 4 per cent lower than in the previous year. This decline affected all major commodity groups except temperate foodstuffs. Slow growth in industrial countries, as well as oversupply and turmoil in metals markets, contributed to the downward pressure on prices during the year. Thus, after a more or less stable first quarter, prices started to weaken steadily for major non-oil commodity groups of export interest to developing countries. On an annual basis, prices of tropical beverages fell by over 15 per cent, and those of minerals and agricultural raw materials by more than 12 per cent (table 3). Most commodities were affected in the latter two groups whereas the average for tropical beverages reflected mainly the steep decline in coffee prices during the year.

Expectations of a large coffee crop in Brazil weakened prices during the year in spite of a tight supply situation. *Coffee* prices declined on average by some 26 per cent in 1996, but on the whole prices proved less volatile than expected thanks to low stocks, especially in consuming countries, and also to the export ceiling adopted by the Association of Coffee Producing Countries (ACPC). There

was a sharp recovery in the early months of 1997 because first estimates of the Brazilian crop were well below last year's level of output and also because of labour unrest in Colombia. With stocks at very low levels and a tight supply-demand situation, the expectation is for fluctuations around a rising trend in coffee prices in 1997. Concern over continued low earnings has encouraged a number of producers to explore more thoroughly the gourmet market, which has grown quite noticeably, especially in the United States.

Prices of other tropical beverages held up much better during 1996. *Cocoa* prices, in particular, remained firm during the year, in view of concerns about a possible tightening of supplies, even though crops in Côte d'Ivoire and Ghana turned out to be quite large. *Tea* prices recovered somewhat from the declines recorded in 1995, thanks mainly to increases in global demand, especially in Eastern Europe, and despite plentiful supplies from plantations in northern India and Kenya. *Banana* prices were on average 7.5 per cent higher than in 1995; after a sharp rise early in the year they dropped significantly thereafter. *Sugar* prices fell by 10 per cent from the 1995 level. By contrast, despite a drop in the latter part of 1996, *wheat* prices averaged a 13.7 per cent increase and *maize* prices one of 25 per cent. Since stocks are still relatively low, the risk of some rebound in grain prices, due to unforeseen increases in import demand or an unfavourable crop outlook, still exists. The *rice* market seems to be more or less well balanced, with price fluctuations much weaker than for other commodities.

Among agricultural raw materials, *rubber* and *cotton* prices weakened considerably in 1996, as did those of minerals. *Copper* prices were particularly volatile in 1996, sometimes plunging abruptly in a matter of hours. The uncertainties surrounding the losses by a major Japanese company due to unauthorized trading compounded the already weak market trends caused by oversupply and moderate demand growth. Expectations of large stock disposals added pressures to the prevailing sluggish market trends. Despite some recovery towards the end of the year, on account of improved consumption and lower stocks, prices were on average almost 22 per cent lower than in 1995 and could well fall further in the coming months. *Aluminium* prices also fared badly and lost much of the gains recorded in 1995; consumption growth was particularly sluggish in both North America and Japan, and consumption may even

Table 3

WORLD PRIMARY COMMODITY PRICES, 1994-1997

(Percentage change over previous year)

Commodity group	1994	1995	1996	Feb. 1997[a]
All commodities[b]	**17.6**	**10.5**	**-4.2**	**5.8**
Food and beverages	**19.4**	**4.6**	**2.3**	**9.6**
Tropical beverages	74.4	0.7	-15.7	29.3
Coffee	118.2	2.9	-26.3	35.4
Cocoa	24.8	2.7	1.6	-6.9
Tea	-4.4	-10.3	8.8	-1.4
Food	10.1	5.7	6.9	5.6
Sugar	19.6	10.8	-10.0	0.7
Beef	-10.9	-18.3	-6.4	2.8
Maize	1.4	23.5	25.1	-6.7
Wheat	4.8	30.4	13.7	8.8
Rice	33.6	-10.2	5.2	10.5
Bananas	-0.5	0.1	7.5	32.1
Vegetable oilseeds and oils	**25.5**	**10.2**	**-4.5**	**3.0**
Agricultural raw materials	**14.6**	**16.9**	**-12.2**	**-3.3**
Hides and skins	30.3	4.1	-23.7	1.6
Cotton	28.0	15.4	-7.9	0.0
Tobacco	10.4	-11.1	15.6	0.0
Rubber	39.3	38.6	-11.9	-2.5
Tropical logs	2.9	5.4	-20.1	-7.3
Minerals, ores and metals	**13.5**	**20.6**	**-12.3**	**4.2**
Aluminium	29.6	22.3	-16.6	5.3
Phosphate rock	0.0	6.1	8.6	7.9
Iron ore	-9.5	5.8	6.0	1.1
Tin	5.9	13.7	-0.8	0.8
Copper	20.6	27.2	-21.8	6.1
Nickel	19.8	29.8	-8.8	17.5
Tungsten ore	24.1	49.6	-17.9	3.1
Crude petroleum	**-4.1**	**9.3**	**20.7**	**-13.5**
Memo item:				
Manufactures[c]	**2.6**	**7.0**	**1.2**	**1.4**

Source: UNCTAD, *Monthly Commodity Price Bulletin*, various issues; United Nations, *Monthly Bulletin of Statistics*, various issues.

a Change from December 1996.
b Excluding crude petroleum.
c Unit value index of exports of manufactures from developed market-economy countries.

have declined in both Western Europe and the countries members of CIS.

The major exception to this bleak picture was *petroleum* prices, which rose steadily throughout the year and by December were almost $6 per barrel higher than 12 months earlier. While low stocks and robust demand growth due to a long cold winter contributed to the buoyancy of oil markets, the steady rise in oil prices also reflected continued production restraint by OPEC members and shortfalls in supply from other exporters due to technical problems. The much-delayed resumption of oil exports from Iraq (under Security Council resolution 986) also led to speculative purchases and higher prices. Prices can be expected to weaken in the near future on account of oversupply (total OPEC production exceeded the quota in the last quarter of 1996). However, there is much uncertainty concerning non-OPEC members on account of continued possible technical constraints.

B. The world economy: growth and imbalances

Global imbalances reminiscent of the 1980s have recently started to emerge in the world economy, due in large part to disparities in demand growth in the major industrial countries. While growth of domestic demand in the United States has continued, and even accelerated, most other industrial countries have relied essentially on exports for growth in their economies. As in earlier periods of demand imbalance, these conditions have been accompanied by increased exchange rate variability. Since 1995 the yen has moved within a range of around 80 to 125 yen to the dollar and the corresponding variation in major European currencies has been around 30 per cent.

These disparities in demand growth, together with the appreciation of the dollar, have been the main factors behind a growing trade deficit in the United States and growing surpluses in Western Europe and Japan. However, unlike the 1980s, expansion in the United States has been associated with falling, rather than rising, fiscal deficits. A return to a more sustainable pattern of global demand and trade balances thus requires expansionary policies in the surplus countries, rather than a contraction in the United States. However, policy continues to be restrictive in most EU countries, especially those aspiring to be initial participants in the monetary union, since economic performance in 1997 will be the basis for determining eligibility. In Japan the current expansion is not based on permanent factors. The growth stimulus of the emergency budget packages is now largely exhausted, and current plans are to act aggressively to reduce the budget deficit through higher taxes. Thus, there is little prospect of a contribution by Europe and Japan to a more balanced pattern of global demand.

The effect of the tightening of monetary policy in the United States may not be limited to widening the global deflationary gap. Together with continued upward pressure on the dollar, its likely effect will be to widen, rather than to narrow, the trade imbalances. It could also lead to a generalized increase in interest rates, given the increasing integration of world financial markets.

Such developments can have serious consequences for the global economy in general and developing countries in particular. A combination of slow growth, rising unemployment and increased trade imbalances could make it more difficult to resist protectionist pressures in the developed world and to avoid trade frictions. Moreover, a generalized rise in interest rates and the appreciation of the dollar could compromise the ability of developing countries to continue as a major source of global demand expansion, since these countries are extremely susceptible to reversals of capital flows. In addition, many of the larger developing countries, which are the most dependent on world trade, tie their exchange rates to the dollar. Consequently, any sharp appreciation of the dollar could also lead to an appreciation of their currencies against third countries, worsening their trade balances and necessitating restrictive domestic monetary policies. Such an outcome would not only compress domestic demand, but also threaten the financial stability of those countries that are in the process of trying to restructure their banking systems.

1. Developed market-economy countries

(a) United States

The United States is now in its sixth year of continuous expansion since the recession of 1990-1991. Rather than declining, as might be expected in this relatively late stage in the cycle, growth has accelerated to 2.5 per cent, a rate which is marginally above the official estimate of long-term sustainable growth.[1] The most visible impact of this sustained growth has been the simultaneous decline in unemployment to levels below 5 per cent and inflation to rates below 3 per cent, the lowest levels since 1973 and approaching Golden Age averages. This decline in the unemployment rate has occurred despite an accelerated growth of the labour force due to higher participation rates. There has also been a rapid decline in the government deficit, to around 1.5 per cent of GDP, and a primary surplus (i.e. in the budget balance net of interest payments on government debt) since 1994. A decline in the deficit is appropriate during sustained expansion and should normally lead to a balanced budget as the economy achieves full employment. The elimination of the deficit and the reduction in interest payments as a major component of government expenditure should free fiscal policy to play a more active role and take off some of the pressure from monetary policy.

There is, however, still a debate on the level of employment and the rate of growth compatible with price stability. While a number of estimates put the non-accelerating inflation rate of unemployment (NAIRU) at above 6 per cent, unemployment has been below that rate continuously for over three years, and in early 1997 fell to 4.8 per cent, without any significant wage or inflationary price pressures. Indeed, most measures of inflation have continued to decline during this period. This lends support to the proposal made in *TDR 1995* that, in order to solve the unemployment problem central banks must be willing to allow their economies to test the validity of assumed potential growth rates. The Federal Reserve appears to be showing such a willingness, since it has responded much more slowly with a tightening of policy than in 1994.

This benign behaviour of prices and wages is in part due to the recovery in productivity growth, which has been strong in manufacturing. Inflation in the service sector has been subdued despite increasing employment, suggesting that there has been an increase in productivity in these sectors also. Since 1992, 12 million jobs have been created in services, while all other sectors produced only 1 million new jobs, almost all in construction. Low-paying, low-productivity jobs (which were analysed in *TDR 1995* as "disguised unemployment") fell as workers shifted into higher-skilled positions in the service sector. There has also been a marked decline in long-term unemployment.

Despite lower inflation and improved employment conditions, there has been little movement in money wages, with the result that average gross weekly earnings in real terms have fallen in almost every year of the recovery. Average hourly real earnings in the private non-agricultural sector declined from $7.73 in 1987 to $7.45 in 1991 and failed to recover subsequently, remaining at $7.43 in 1996. As a result, consumption has contributed little to domestic demand expansion, which has been driven primarily by investment accompanied by improving exports, although imports have remained high. The continued rise in productivity, particularly in manufacturing, has meant that profits have improved considerably. Profits as a share of non-financial corporate business GDP rose by around 3.5 percentage points from 1992 to 1996, in part because of the reduction in net interest costs as firms replaced debt at lower rates or tapped the stock market for funding. As a share of national income, profits have returned to levels not seen since the beginning of the 1970s. Wage earnings, however, started to rise during 1996. Most recent figures point to a rise of around 2.0 per cent on an annual basis in 1997, suggesting that private consumption will also make a contribution to sustaining expansion.

(b) Japan

The Japanese economy has finally emerged from a prolonged period of stagnation, in which the economy grew by a little over 2.6 per cent in all from 1992 to 1995. As explained in past *TDRs*, this was primarily the result of overinvestment in the previous boom, when capital spending rose by around 8 per cent per annum. As a result of the collapse of the financial bubble and the global recession, capital spending fell by 23 per cent from

1991 to 1994, forcing industry to rationalize and restructure. Further, the yen appreciated sharply from 1991 to 1995. To offset this adverse impact of falling investment and exports, from August 1992 to September 1995 six separate stimulus packages were implemented, primarily for public works, as a consequence of which the construction sector was the main area of expansion in the economy; employment in the sector rose by 32 per cent from 1991 to 1995, against 9 per cent for the rest of industry.

Investment recovered in 1995; together with rising exports due to yen depreciation and the cumulative impact of the fiscal packages, it brought about an output expansion of 3.5 per cent in 1996. Exports expanded by 10 per cent in the second half of FY 1996, while imports declined. Private consumption remained low until the end of the calendar year, when it began to recover. The recovery continued into the first quarter of 1997 as consumers attempted to bring forward expenditures in view of the increase in consumption taxes that was to take place in April.

To the extent that the recovery in investment and exports has been due to the recent depreciation of the yen, growth in Japan may simply revive the trade frictions which dominated its relations with the United States in the 1980s. The largest Japanese producers have hedged themselves against problems of market access and a reversal of exchange rate movements by expanding their existing production facilities in the United States, Mexico and Asia; in 1995 Japanese automobile producers built more cars abroad than they exported from Japan. To the extent that Japanese profits and growth remain centred on exports, and thus on the behaviour of the exchange rate, they will continue to be erratic.

As a result of rationalization and downsizing, unemployment has remained above 3 per cent. In the restructuring that took place in 1990-1995 many industries, including textiles, steel, and electrical machinery, not only sought wage reductions but also reduced their permanent employment levels by up to 5 per cent. This continued success of Japanese industry in restructuring to offset the impact of a constantly appreciating currency has been one cause of the delay in the introduction of structural and regulatory measures to reduce the country's dependence on exports. Despite several attempts to introduce supply-side policies to reduce domestic costs and liberalize the economy,

economic performance remains dependent on exports, and investment both at home and abroad continues to be undertaken with an eye to international competitiveness.

(c) European Union

The level of activity in continental Western Europe declined towards the end of 1996 and some of the major economies, such as Germany and Italy, touched recession. In the United Kingdom, by contrast, expansion has been sustained and lasted longer even than in the United States. Indeed, there was an acceleration towards the end of the year, resulting in a growth rate of 2.0 per cent for the year as a whole. Spain and a number of smaller EU economies also achieved growth above 2 per cent.

The continued weak performance of the continental EU economies is due in large part to the continued application of restrictive fiscal policies aimed at reducing government deficits to the 3 per cent of GDP reference value set out in the Maastricht Treaty. Pressure on fiscal policy has become particularly acute, given that the decision on qualification for entry into the third phase of EMU will be determined by national economic performance in 1997. This concentration of public expenditure reductions and tax increases in 1996 and 1997 has more than offset the relaxation of monetary policy during 1995-1996. Indeed, given the continued abatement of inflation, to around 2 per cent for members of the European Exchange Rate Mechanism (ERM), monetary policy has become somewhat more restrictive in some countries.

As discussed in last year's *Report*, budget deficits increase due to cyclical factors, so that when growth is slow, rising deficits act as an automatic stabilizer of demand. Raising taxes or reducing expenditures to meet a budget deficit target in such conditions eliminates the normal stabilization properties of deficits, depresses growth and simply serves to raise deficits further, necessitating additional budget retrenchment. The consequence is increasing pressure on social safety nets and living standards, leading eventually to popular resistance against such policies. The insistence of some governments that qualification for entry into the third phase of EMU depends on meeting the precise numerical reference values in the face of mounting evidence that none of the major economies will be able to do so creates conditions conducive to greater volatility in financial and foreign exchange markets at the very time when expectations should be converging on uniform interest rates and irrevocably fixed exchange rates.

As a consequence of these restrictive policies, the performance of the major European economies has depended on export growth. Increasing global competition has put greater pressure on costs, leading to labour shedding and holding down wages, thereby compressing domestic consumption demand. Exports have been stimulated by the depreciation of most continental EU currencies relative to those of stronger economies, namely the dollar and sterling. A large proportion of Western European exports is now directed towards developing countries, in particular in Asia, and transition economies in Central Europe. Since growth in the former countries is less rapid than in the past, and in the latter is highly erratic, Western European exports and hence growth have been highly variable.

Political developments in EU suggest that it will be difficult to sacrifice growth and employment for the sake of meeting the reference values of EMU. However, postponing the date of entry of the third phase of monetary union is not a real option. Further budgetary restrictions may not bring about any improvement in deficits, whereas they risk creating financial and labour market instability. By most measures of nominal and real economic variables, convergence of the EU economies has already taken place. With the exception of Ireland, the prospects for 1997 are that no country will grow at a rate which is more than 1 percentage point away from the EU average. Likewise no country (with the exception of Greece) has an inflation rate which is more than 1 point higher, and long-term interest rates and public sector deficits are, with a few exceptions, also within this range. Fiscal balances in most countries in 1997 will be within half a percentage point of each other, at an average slightly above 3 per cent of GDP. Finally, unemployment rates are also converging, albeit at levels as high as 11 per cent. Since these averages for inflation and interest rates are in the ranges which are considered acceptable for monetary stability and also appear to be sustainable, whereas the unemployment rates are converging around a rate which appears stable but politically unacceptable, it seems reasonable to move to a single currency as rapidly as possible. Delay may cause fiscal deficits to diverge even further from the reference values, making it even more difficult to comply with the Maastricht targets. It should

be recalled that the reference values were drawn up to provide a broadly similar economic environment in all countries that would allow uniform monetary policy and low and stable inflation, objectives which have now been achieved. The issue of fiscal balance compatible with stability may need to be redefined subsequently, and the required adjustment be carried out under better cyclical conditions.

2. Latin America

In Latin America the recovery of output in 1996 was chiefly due to an upturn in Argentina and Mexico and, to a lesser extent, Uruguay, together with robust growth in some other countries (table 4). The contrasting recent experiences of Argentina and Mexico, in particular, highlight the kind of policy dilemmas faced by many Latin American countries. In those two countries, which together account for over 40 per cent of regional GDP, output contracted sharply in 1995 as a consequence of a reversal of capital flows. In Argentina the burden of adjustment fell entirely on domestic absorption as the nominal exchange rate was kept constant. While inflation was thus kept at international levels, unemployment soared. In Mexico, by contrast, the sharp decline in the exchange rate, combined with tight monetary policy, gave a strong boost to exports, offsetting partly the adverse effects of external adjustment on employment, but inflation soared, exceeding 50 per cent.

The recovery of both Argentina and Mexico in 1996 was significant, albeit modest. In both cases growth was export-led. In Mexico, devaluation played a key role whereas in Argentina the rapid expansion of exports largely resulted from a sharp rise of the real exchange rate in Brazil. In both Brazil and Argentina the expansion assisted recovery in Uruguay.

In Brazil, consumption played a leading role in the recovery that followed from the success of the *Plano Real* in stopping hyperinflation. After a spurt in 1994, growth slowed down as monetary policy was tightened in order to check domestic demand in the face of a sharp deterioration in the trade balance associated with trade liberalization and currency appreciation. High interest rates encouraged portfolio inflows, allowing monetary authorities to rely on the exchange rate as an in-

Table 4

LATIN AMERICA: OUTPUT, AND EXPORT AND IMPORT VOLUMES, 1994-1996

(Percentage change over previous year)

	Output[a]			Exports			Imports		
	1994	*1995*	*1996[b]*	*1994*	*1995*	*1996[b]*	*1994*	*1995*	*1996[b]*
All countries	4.5	0.5	3.3	9.2	9.9	9.3	14.8	4.9	9.5
of which:									
Argentina	6.7	-4.6	3.5	18.5	20.3	7.1	25.4	-14.4	18.3
Bolivia	4.8	3.7	4.0	20.1	5.2	9.9	0.7	13.2	24.5
Brazil	5.7	3.9	3.0	4.5	-2.3	2.2	27.2	31.4	4.7
Chile	4.1	8.2	6.5	12.0	11.5	10.5	3.2	23.1	10.1
Colombia	6.3	5.7	3.5	2.4	2.2	5.5	20.9	6.8	1.0
Costa Rica	4.4	2.3	0.5	4.3	8.7	4.1	2.4	-2.9	1.8
Ecuador	4.7	2.7	2.0	10.6	7.1	4.2	25.1	14.5	-13.3
El Salvador	6.0	6.1	3.5	32.0	15.3	10.6	16.3	21.6	0.3
Guatemala	4.1	5.0	3.0	5.3	19.4	-1.8	8.0	10.7	0.6
Mexico	4.6	-6.6	4.5	11.8	24.4	19.4	15.7	-13.8	21.8
Paraguay	2.9	4.5	2.0	14.8	19.7	-6.5	31.3	20.2	-14.0
Peru	13.9	7.7	2.0	17.9	8.2	5.1	24.5	27.5	-0.1
Uruguay	6.9	-2.8	5.0	2.9	-0.7	14.5	21.5	-5.3	12.8
Venezuela	-2.5	2.3	-1.5	7.3	6.0	8.9	-26.5	24.9	-8.0

Source: Table 1 (for regional output totals), table 2 (for regional export totals) and ECLAC, *Preliminary Overview of the Economy of Latin America and the Caribbean 1996*, Santiago, Chile, 1996 (United Nations publication, Sales No. E.96.II.G.13), tables A.1, A.9 and A.10.

a Based on values at 1990 prices.

b Preliminary.

strument for price stability. However, the resulting currency appreciation added further to trade deficits. Measures initiated in 1995 to restrict financial capital inflows have been eased in recent months (see chapter II). A combination of relatively high budget deficits and monetary policy has continued to attract financial capital at the expense of investment and exports. Consequently, growth faltered further in 1996.

Peru has gone through similar phases of rapid expansion and slowdown. Growth was rapid after the success in taming hyperinflation in 1992, but concerns for the external balance led the authorities to adopt restrictive fiscal and monetary policies, which cut growth drastically after 1994.

In Chile, exports continued to grow faster than output. In spite of a 30 per cent reserve requirement on all foreign financial investments, strong capital inflows have continued, resulting in a sizeable real appreciation of the currency. Partly for that reason, real wages have risen, bringing about increases in consumption and so in aggregate demand that have necessitated restrictive monetary and fiscal policies.

In the external sector, with the exception of Argentina, which benefited from a rise in prices of temperate zone foodstuffs, gains in the terms of trade in 1996 were achieved only by oil exporters. Even so, domestic conditions and policies in the major oil-exporting countries of the region hindered them from capitalizing fully on favourable oil prices. In Mexico, a major exporter of manufactures, the terms of trade were unchanged, as they were also in Brazil, Costa Rica, Paraguay and Peru. In other countries, the terms of trade fell, in some cases substantially (for example, in Chile due to the drastic fall in copper prices noted above).

While exports continued as the main source of growth for most countries, for the region as a whole they increased in value by only 10.2 per cent in 1996, against nearly 21 per cent in the previous year. The deceleration was region-wide (with the exception of Venezuela, and to a lesser extent Bolivia and Uruguay) and was the result of stagnant or declining export prices, following an upsurge in 1995. Trade among countries of the region has grown rapidly, on account of both unilateral trade liberalization and the strengthening of trade groups, such as MERCOSUR,[2] the Andean Group, the Latin American Integration Association (LAIA), the Central American Common Market (CACM), and the Caribbean Community (CARICOM). During 1994-1996, intra-MERCOSUR exports grew on average by about 17 per cent per annum, compared to 9 per cent for exports of the member countries to the world. While exports to developed countries are heavily concentrated on raw materials and natural-resource-intensive goods, intra-regional trade has a much larger component of manufactures; in 1995, manufactures constituted 37 per cent of the region's exports to the world but 46 per cent of intra-regional trade. The strengthening of regional trade links and the opening up of broader economic spaces among the countries in the region has not only provided a means of diversifying exports, but also encouraged intra-regional investment flows; Argentine firms have been investing in Brazil and Brazilian firms in Argentina, while Chilean firms have made large investments in Argentina, particularly in agro-industrial sectors.

The growth of import volume for the region in 1996 was almost twice that of the previous year, primarily because of economic recovery in Mexico and Argentina, which together account for nearly half of the value of regional imports, and also because of a similar recovery in Uruguay. Among the countries where import volume growth was weaker than in 1995 special mention should be made of Brazil and Chile. Ecuador, Paraguay and Venezuela were prominent among countries where imports actually declined in volume.

The region continued to be dependent on substantial capital inflows. In 1996, they amounted to $50 billion, against $26 billion in 1995, with a larger proportion consisting of FDI and investment in long-term bonds. The existing structure of most of the economies in the region makes for low rates of growth, as they still rely on raw materials for their export earnings. Trade liberalization and the dismantling of import substitution regimes have not, by themselves, induced export diversification and a more dynamic integration of most Latin American countries into the international economy. Slow output growth has translated into growing unemployment and falling or stagnant real wages. A worsening of the labour situation, which was already evident in 1995 in a number of countries, such as Argentina, Mexico, Uruguay and Venezuela, continued in 1996. Only in Chile, Nicaragua and Peru was the unemployment rate lower than in 1995. At the same time, it is not at all certain that a new era of low inflation has been inaugurated. Real exchange rates continue to be very volatile, discouraging productive investment and reducing growth below its potential.

3. Developing Asia

An outstanding feature of events in developing Asia in 1996 was a significantly slower growth of output in a number of economies, which was accompanied by a sharp slowdown in exports (table 5) that was particularly pronounced for the first-tier NIEs (Hong Kong, Republic of Korea, Singapore and Taiwan Province of China), as well as in Malaysia, Thailand and China. The slowdown in exports obliged a number of countries to take measures to restore external balance by restricting aggregate demand.

The decline in export growth has given rise to a debate on the sustainability of rapid economic expansion in Asia, although it is now evident that the performance of the fast-growing economies of the region is not attributable to any single factor. The links between capital accumulation, technological progress and economic growth in the first-tier NIEs, and the interdependence of exports and investment and its role in accelerating structural change and industrial growth, were analysed in detail in *TDR 1996*. To remain competitive over the years, both governments and private entrepreneurs have managed to overcome such constraints as shortages of skills and expertise, rising labour costs and structural and infrastructure bottlenecks which had emerged as a result of rapid growth. With respect to what happened to exports in 1996,

Table 5

DEVELOPING ASIA: OUTPUT, AND EXPORT AND IMPORT VALUES, IN SELECTED SUBREGIONS AND COUNTRIES, 1994-1996

(Percentage change over previous year)

	Output[a]			Exports			Imports		
	1994	*1995*	*1996*	*1994*	*1995*	*1996*	*1994*	*1995*	*1996*
Newly industrializing economies	7.6	7.5	6.3	15.0	21.0	4.8	17.4	22.9	5.6
of which:									
Hong Kong	5.4	4.7	4.7	11.9	14.8	4.0	16.7	19.1	3.0
Republic of Korea	8.6	9.0	7.0	15.7	31.5	4.1	22.4	32.1	12.2
Singapore	10.5	8.8	7.0	25.8	21.5	6.7	19.8	21.6	6.0
Taiwan Province of China	6.5	6.0	5.7	9.4	20.0	8.2	10.3	21.0	2.0
South-East Asia	7.8	8.2	7.4	19.2	22.8	5.6	21.9	28.4	8.2
of which:									
Indonesia	7.5	8.2	7.8	9.9	13.1	8.8	13.9	23.0	11.8
Malaysia	9.1	10.1	8.8	23.1	25.9	4.0	28.1	29.4	1.3
Philippines	4.4	4.8	5.5	18.5	29.4	17.5	21.2	23.7	25.0
Thailand	8.9	8.7	6.7	22.2	24.7	0.1	18.5	31.6	4.1
South Asia	6.6	6.4	6.5	13.2	20.6	11.7	14.7	26.7	10.2
of which:									
Bangladesh	4.2	4.4	4.7	6.3	37.1	11.8	3.2	39.4	17.9
India	7.2	7.1	6.8	18.4	20.9	13.0	27.0	30.0	8.1
Nepal	7.9	2.9	6.1	-2.7	-9.6	2.0	14.6	21.9	9.3
Pakistan	4.5	4.4	6.1	-1.4	16.1	7.0	-13.6	18.5	16.2
Sri Lanka	5.7	5.6	3.8	15.2	18.4	12.0	21.7	9.0	8.0
China	11.8	10.2	9.7	35.6	24.9	1.5	10.4	15.5	5.1

Source: *Asian Development Outlook 1997 and 1998* (Hong Kong: Oxford University Press for the Asian Development Bank, 1997), tables A1, A11 and A13.

a Based on data in constant prices.

the key question is whether the outcome was due to temporary factors or reflected underlying forces of a longer-term nature.

To begin with, it should be recalled that both 1994 and 1995 were years of exceptional export growth because of the unusual coincidence of a number of factors, including the appreciation of the yen, a strengthening of efforts by Japanese corporations to relocate production overseas, and the large demand for electronic products. On the other hand, factors responsible for the decline in the value of exports in 1996 include a dramatic fall in the prices of some electronic and information equipment, particularly semiconductors, which had dire consequences for a number of countries in the region; in December 1996, the unit price of semiconductors had fallen by nearly 70 per cent from its level a year earlier. As a share of total exports, electronic products currently account for nearly 50 per cent in Singapore, almost 25 per cent in Malaysia and the Republic of Korea, and 10-15 per cent in Taiwan Province of China, Thailand and the Philippines. Furthermore, with the depreciation of the yen vis-à-vis the dollar by some 53 per cent between April 1995 and February 1997, a number of currencies linked to the dollar appreciated strongly. Finally, some countries lost competitiveness in a number of labour-intensive products. While some of these factors may be reversed over time, they nevertheless pose serious problems of adjustment.

China succeeded in 1996 in bringing down inflation to a single-digit rate and taking some heat off the economy, which nevertheless grew at an impressive rate of almost 10 per cent. On 1 December 1996, it formally gained the status of an IMF Article 8 country, which made the yuan convertible for the purposes of current account transactions. Improving the agricultural infrastructure and accelerating the reform of state-owed enterprises are objectives that continue to be given top priority in economic reform.

Unlike both the first-tier NIEs and South-East Asia, the growth momentum was maintained in South Asia (table 5), while in West Asia growth accelerated. Among the first-tier NIEs, growth fell significantly in the Republic of Korea in 1996 as the economy experienced both internal and external imbalances; the current account deficit was almost triple that of 1995. Hong Kong was directly affected by weaker export demand from China on account of the latter's own slower export growth, but nevertheless maintained the previous year's growth rate. In Taiwan Province of China, tensions with the mainland affected consumer and business confidence in the second half of 1995 and early 1996. Because of its relatively diversified export base, it was less affected than other economies by the slump in demand for electronics, so that the rate of GDP growth declined only marginally. In contrast, there was significantly slower growth in Singapore, due to a sharp deceleration in investment in machinery and equipment as a result of weaker exports and adjustments to bloated inventories.

In South-East Asia, output growth in 1996 slowed moderately in both Indonesia and Malaysia, exports slowed down and monetary and fiscal stance was tightened to counter inflationary pressure. In both countries, high interest rates triggered inflows of foreign funds, which in turn offset the impact of stringent monetary policy. Eventually, to reduce their current account deficits, the authorities had to resort to raising deposit reserve ratios. In Thailand, the 2-percentage point fall in the growth rate was the result of currency appreciation and rising real wages which eroded competitiveness in labour-intensive sectors. In addition, financial markets were disturbed by the sharp increase in non-performing assets of banks (see chapter II). By contrast, growth in the Philippines accelerated in 1996, while its balance of payments stayed at sustainable levels for the third consecutive year.

For South Asia as a whole the growth momentum has been unabated, but there was considerable variation among countries. Economic reforms in India implemented so far have enhanced its integration into the world economy, but stronger growth in 1996 was constrained by high domestic real interest rates and supply bottlenecks. In Pakistan, although growth accelerated significantly, the chronic budget deficit persisted and continues to threaten internal and external stability. Good weather played a key part in economic recovery in Nepal, whereas civil war and drought were responsible for the slowdown in Sri Lanka. In Bangladesh, the implementation of a comprehensive programme of structural reforms since the early 1990s has been associated with only a slight acceleration of the growth rate.

Economic performance in West Asia is dominated by developments in the oil sector and by political conditions in the subregion. The continued recovery in output in 1996, following a mild recession in 1994, was due largely to the rise in oil prices, which provided the oil-exporting countries of the subregion with much-needed revenues to ease fiscal and external imbalances as well as the means to repay some of the arrears to contractors and suppliers (Saudi Arabia) or reduce their external debt (Islamic Republic of Iran). For member countries of the Gulf Cooperation Council[3] as a whole, despite more than two decades of export diversification, the oil sector still accounts for 35-40 per cent of GDP, 80 per cent of government revenues, and 85 per cent of exports.

4. Africa

The economic recovery in Africa that set in in 1994 continued in 1996; moreover, it was broadly based. In all the subregions, with the

Table 6

AFRICA: OUTPUT GROWTH BY SUBREGION, 1990-1996

(Percentage change over previous year)[a]

	1990 -1995	1994	1995	1996
Central Africa	-2.5	-1.3	5.0	4.4
of which:				
Cameroon	-0.4	-1.5	6.0	4.0
Central African Republic	-0.1	5.7	1.1	1.3
Equatorial Guinea	7.5	0.6	11.0	16.2
Gabon	2.7	1.7	3.4	2.9
East Africa	2.9	4.5	4.9	4.3
of which:				
Ethiopia	2.5	2.2	3.2	3.6
Kenya	2.6	2.5	6.3	3.9
Madagascar	0.0	2.2	2.0	3.5
Somalia	-0.1	-21.0	2.3	3.9
Uganda	6.0	7.2	8.5	6.0
United Republic of Tanzania	3.0	2.9	3.5	4.6
North Africa	1.5	1.8	1.8	4.4
of which:				
Algeria	1.2	0.7	4.0	5.5
Egypt	1.9	2.7	2.6	3.2
Morocco	1.8	7.2	-5.0	5.9
Sudan	3.7	1.7	3.5	4.0
Tunisia	5.0	6.5	2.5	6.6
Southern Africa	0.9	2.5	2.5	3.0
of which:				
Botswana	4.4	2.5	3.1	4.9
South Africa	0.7	5.1	2.9	2.5
Zambia	-1.1	1.0	-4.9	4.9
Zimbabwe	0.2	4.6	-3.4	6.6
West Africa	2.4	2.5	3.4	4.2
of which:				
Côte d'Ivoire	-0.2	0.8	5.4	5.2
Ghana	4.5	8.0	4.5	5.0
Niger	0.6	2.9	3.8	2.6
Nigeria	3.3	2.1	2.3	3.8
Senegal	1.6	1.3	4.6	4.6

Source: ECA, "Report on the Economic and Social Situation in Africa, 1995" (E/ECA/CM.21/3), Addis Ababa, March 1995, statistical table 2; *ibid., 1997* (E/ECA/CM.23/3), Addis Ababa, March 1997, table I.5 and statistical table 2.

a Based on values at 1990 prices.

exception of East and Central Africa, growth was faster than in 1995 (table 6). In 11 countries it reached or surpassed the 6 per cent target set by the United Nations New Agenda for the Development of Africa in the 1990s (UN-NADAF), in 28 it ranged from 3 per cent to 6 per cent, in 12 it was still positive but below 3 per cent, and in only 2 did output decline abruptly.[4] The major factors behind this improved performance of Africa in 1996 were greater policy effort, favourable weather in most subregions, significantly higher export earnings (particularly by oil-exporting countries), and improved terms of trade.

The rise in agricultural output by 5.2 per cent in 1996, in contrast to no growth in the previous year, was the highest since the beginning of the decade and was the major factor behind the strong economic recovery in the region as a whole. At the same time, upturns in the prices of bananas, groundnuts, tea and tobacco, as well as crude oil, lead, iron ore and phosphates, more than compensated for the fall in the prices of beverages, metals and non-oil minerals and agricultural raw materials, so that there was an improvement of 4.6 per cent in the terms of trade and of 8.8 per cent in the purchasing power of exports. The value of exports increased by 8.7 per cent, on account of a 4.0 per cent rise in volume and a 4.7 per cent increase in prices. On the other hand, the value of imports grew more rapidly (9.3 per cent), almost entirely because of an increase in volume.

The North African economies rebounded strongly in 1996 following four years of modest to lacklustre growth. The major factors responsible for the surge in output included much better weather, spirited industrial growth, a rise in oil prices and recovery in the tourist trade. Most remarkable was the sharp swing in output in Morocco, which suffered from a severe drought in 1995 but enjoyed a record harvest in 1996 together with a recovery in the prices of potash. Agriculture also contributed much to the faster growth of output in Egypt and Sudan. In contrast, Tunisia was hit by drought for the second year running, resulting in severe output losses. Nevertheless, growth accelerated, largely thanks to industry. Despite the upturn in agriculture and vigorous industrial expansion by 8 per cent, North Africa continues to be overwhelmingly dependent on minerals, and on hydrocarbons in particular.

The growth momentum which began in West Africa in 1994 was sustained in 1996. Aided by high oil prices and improvements in the agricultural sector, the Nigerian economy grew by nearly 4 per cent, compared to 2 per cent or so in the previous two years. However, consumer spending remained weak because of the prevailing high unemployment and the inadequacy of public utility services. Indeed, many sectors other than oil and agriculture continued to suffer from severe recession. Countries of the franc zone (CFA) continued to reap the benefits of the economic reforms initiated since 1994. In Côte d'Ivoire, the largest of those economies, there was a recovery in agriculture, and also in the water, power and construction sectors, as well as a revival in manufacturing and services. Senegal maintained the improved growth rate of 1995; an expansion in construction, tourism and other service sectors, as well as in export-oriented industrial activities, more than compensated for the relatively poor performance in agriculture. Output growth in Niger, on the other hand, declined in 1996, on account of unfavourable weather and unprecedented declines in uranium prices. In Ghana, the 1995 growth rate was surpassed. Production and exports of cocoa, its major export earner, increased and in addition gold has become a major source of export revenue.

Average GDP growth in Central Africa in 1996 was slightly below the 5 per cent reached in the previous year, but performance varied considerably among countries. In the CFA countries growth was faster (at 4.8 per cent) than in 1995 (3.1 per cent). The best result was achieved by Equatorial Guinea, where GDP rose by more than 16 per cent as a result of a strong revival in mineral and oil output. Gabon continued on the path of recovery embarked on in the previous year. Performance in other countries of the subregion was affected in varying degrees by continuing social tension, civil and political instability and the associated burden of coping with very large numbers of refugees and displaced persons. GDP in Burundi declined by close to 6 per cent in 1996, due largely to economic sanctions by neighbouring countries, as a result of which huge stocks of unsold coffee and tea were accumulated. In Cameroon, the most important of the CFA countries in the subregion, growth slowed in 1996, after the strong upturn in 1995, due to reduced oil production and greater political instability.

Although the average growth rate in East Africa in 1996 exceeded that of the African region as a whole, it was slightly lower than in 1995, in spite of a significant improvement in industrial output.

It was largely Kenya, the largest economy in the subregion, that pulled down the average, due to a weak performance in agriculture and tourism. In Uganda also growth slowed down, whereas in the United Republic of Tanzania it accelerated. Both countries benefited from an increased inflow of FDI. While agricultural output rose by almost 50 per cent in Somalia in 1996, harvests were generally a third below the levels prevailing before hostilities broke out, and consequently the rise does not seem to have had a significant impact on the overall food situation. Ethiopia more than maintained its relatively high growth rate of 1995, owing to a combination of good weather and a revival in manufacturing.

Although output in Southern Africa grew on average in 1996 less than in Africa as a whole, the increase constituted a further improvement over the rates of the previous years. The primary cause was the return of favourable weather and higher export receipts. Economic recovery has also been aided by greater political stability and improved commodity prices. Outstanding was the turnaround in Zimbabwe, due to an improved performance in agriculture, manufacturing and mining, and also in Zambia, as a result of a significant recovery in copper production as well as in both agriculture and manufacturing. However, the Zambian economy is still beset with problems of declining export revenues and a resurgence of inflation. Economic performance was disappointing in South Africa, the most developed country in the subregion and which accounts for more than a quarter of Africa's total output. Growth slowed somewhat in 1996, having decelerated more markedly in the previous year, as the economy suffered from relatively high rates of inflation and unemployment.

While the African countries are highly dependent on foreign trade, export-led growth remains seriously constrained by the persistence of anachronistic production structures and heavy reliance on a narrow range of primary exports. Investment is considerably below the levels needed to attain and sustain a rate of growth that would have any appreciable or significant impact on the economies of the region. The need for greater mobilization of domestic resources and their efficient utilization is further dictated by declining inflows of ODA and the serious difficulties experienced in attracting FDI. The debt burden in many countries has become intolerable. Despite the many reschedulings and arrangements to reduce debt-service obligations to a more manageable level, the debt overhang has grown large enough to prejudice the success of the very reform efforts aimed at the restoration of economic and socio-political viability in many African countries. Accumulated arrears at the end of 1994 amounted to $54.9 billion, or 20 per cent of the total debt stock. Given that, of the 41 countries which have been identified as eligible under the HIPC Initiative, 33 are in Africa, the future performance of the region depends, *inter alia*, on how the initiative is implemented (see chapter II below).

5. Central and Eastern Europe

The European (and Central Asian) economies in transition continued to show a marked divergence between those which continued in 1996 to enjoy further growth and those which were still struggling to achieve economic stability and balance. All three Baltic States achieved faster growth than in the previous year (when it had been negative in Lithuania) and growth was positive in the majority of the CIS members.

For Central and Eastern Europe as a whole, growth in 1996 was significantly slower than in the previous year (table 7).[5] The general slowdown of growth in this subregion is attributable to internal and external imbalances, which called for more restrictive macroeconomic policies, as well as to major market failures in some countries.

With growth of 6.0 per cent in 1996, Poland became the first of the transition countries to reach a level of output exceeding that of 1989 (to the extent of over 4 per cent). Turkmenistan was virtually at the pre-transition level, while Slovenia had recovered to 7 per cent short of it, and in a number of other countries the shortfall was 10-20 per cent. Slovakia continued to maintain rapid growth in both 1995 and 1996. However, recovery so far has depended primarily on the expansion of non-manufacturing activity and government expenditures on infrastructure. The sustainability of growth in the Czech Republic, which is undergoing financial difficulties (see chapter II) is also open to question. Although GDP grew relatively fast in both 1995 and 1996, its industry is becoming increasingly uncompetitive.

Major macroeconomic adjustments were undertaken in Hungary following the implementation of a stabilization programme in May 1995. Fiscal

and current account deficits declined substantially in 1996, inflation slowed down and manufactured exports rose. The economy is now apparently poised for a much faster rate of growth. There was a marked recovery for the first time in Croatia in 1996. In Slovenia, large investment projects in infrastructure and services kept the growth rate above 3 per cent. Both economies benefited from the lifting of United Nations sanctions and the resumption of economic relations with the former Yugoslav republics.

In a number of other Central and Eastern European countries economic conditions worsened. Growth in Romania decelerated sharply in 1996 in the face of worsening macroeconomic imbalances, leading to radical policy changes by a new government. The social and political crisis in Bulgaria was the first case of a major upset in the transition process following a gradual recovery and disinflation; the drop in output of some 10 per cent in 1996 after modest growth in 1994-1995 was of much the same magnitude as in 1990, the year following the break-up of the USSR. In Albania, the collapse of large-scale fraudulent investment schemes brought political and social chaos. As in Bulgaria, major market failures led to a rapid and more general deterioration of the economic situation and to a serious political crisis.

Growth in the Baltic States accelerated in 1996. For the first time since their independence, there was positive growth in all three countries. Both Lithuania and Latvia seem to have largely recovered from the banking crisis of 1995. Indeed, in all three countries, there was improved macroeconomic stability, but it was accompanied by a widening of trade and current account deficits.

Growth in the CIS continued to be uneven. For the Commonwealth as a whole, output continued to fall, but there was positive growth in seven countries, compared to only two in 1995. The recovery was particularly marked in Belarus, Kyrgyzstan and Uzbekistan. In Azerbaijan, Kazakstan and Turkmenistan, the fall in output appears to have already bottomed out, while Armenia and Georgia continued the upturn of 1995. In contrast, output was further depressed in the Republic of Moldova and Tajikistan. The Moldovan economy, which is heavily dependent on agriculture, was badly affected by poor weather in 1996.

Contrary to earlier expectations, output in Ukraine and the Russian Federation continued to

Table 7

EUROPEAN ECONOMIES IN TRANSITION[a]: SELECTED ECONOMIC INDICATORS, 1994-1996

Country/region	GDP			Consumer prices			Current account balance		
	Change over previous year[b] (Per cent)						($ million)		
	1994	1995	1996	1994	1995	1996	1994	1995	1996[c]
Central and Eastern Europe[d]	3.9	5.6	4.0	..	..	..	..	-1389	-12935
of which:									
Bulgaria	1.8	2.1	-10.0	122.0	33.0	311.1	-25	-26	-34
Croatia	0.6	1.7	4.4	-3.0	3.7	3.5	103	-1711	-1129
Czech Republic	2.6	4.8	4.4	10.3	8.0	8.7	-50	-1362	-4476
Hungary	2.9	1.5	0.5	21.3	28.5	19.9	-3911	-2480	-1678
Poland	5.2	7.0	6.0	29.4	22.0	18.7	..	5455	-1352
Romania	3.9	7.1	4.1	61.9	27.7	56.8	-428	-1639	-2336
Slovakia	4.9	6.8	6.9	11.8	7.4	5.5	712	646	-1401
Slovenia	5.3	3.9	3.5	18.3	8.6	8.9	540	-36	47
Baltic States	-0.2	1.4	3.4	..	..	..	-67	-827	-908
of which:									
Estonia	-2.7	2.9	3.5	41.8	28.8	14.9	-178	-185	-223
Latvia	0.6	-1.6	2.5	26.1	23.3	13.2	201	-27	-273
Lithuania	1.0	3.0	4.0	45.0	35.5	13.1	-90	-614	-412
CIS	-14.5	-5.7	-5.3	..	..	..	9629[e]	7471[e]	8804[e]
of which:									
Belarus	-12.6	-10.0	3.0	1957.3	244.2	39.1	-506	-567	-752
Rep. of Moldova	-31.2	-3.0	-8.0	104.6	23.8	15.1	-82	-115	-134
Russian Federation	-12.7	-4.2	-6.0	214.8	131.4	21.8	11378	9305	10243
Ukraine	-22.9	-11.8	-10.0	401.1	181.7	39.7	-1161	-1152	-553

Source: ECE, *Economic Survey of Europe in 1996-1997* (United Nations publication, Sales No. E.97.II.E.1), table 3.1.1 and appendix table B.15.
  a Including also the economies of Central Asian countries members of CIS.
  b For consumer prices change from December to December.
  c January-September except for Slovakia (Jan.-Nov.) and Croatia, Czech Republic, Hungary, Poland, Romania, Slovenia and The former Yugoslav Republic of Macedonia (Jan.-Dec.).
  d Incorporating revision of Poland's balance of payments data.
  e Total for the four States listed.

decline, affecting all sectors in the latter country, where domestic demand was severely depressed by continued pursuit of monetary and fiscal austerity as part of the stabilization programme of February 1996. In Ukraine, where substantial progress was made in macroeconomic stabilization, output continued to fall.

One of the most encouraging developments in the region in 1996 has been the slowing down of inflation. By the end of the year consumer prices were 20 per cent or less than 12 months earlier in 15 out of 25 countries, with the notable exceptions of Bulgaria and Romania. By contrast, the balance of payments of most European transition economies worsened despite a reduction in debt burdens, as imports of goods and services increased more than exports. Exceptionally, however, the Russian Federation continued throughout 1994-1996 to achieve a substantial current account surplus.

In Central and Eastern Europe, and in Estonia and Latvia, the current account deficit widened, as a result of stronger output expansion, a rising real exchange rate due to an upsurge in capital flows, tariff reductions, and a slowing of exports to Western Europe. In several cases the deterioration proved much greater than had initially been expected. In most countries the current account has been in deficit since the beginning of the decade, but the imbalance in 1996 is the largest so far.

C. Short-term outlook and uncertainties

Since the tightening of monetary policy during 1994, the quarterly performance of the United States economy has been highly erratic. However, the accelerated expansion that started in the second half of 1996 continued in the first quarter of 1997. The very strong increase in consumer expenditure since the beginning of 1997 suggests that some of the productivity gains which have led to increased profits and investment during the current cycle are starting to translate into higher real personal incomes and generate greater consumer confidence. It is also possible that the impact on household wealth of the sustained increases in stock prices has produced some increase in discretionary expenditures. Because of faster demand growth than in its major trading partners and the recent appreciation of the dollar, the trade balance of the United States is unlikely to contribute to growth in the coming year, while the agreement recently reached on the budget suggests that fiscal policy will be neutral or at best provide only a slight stimulus. With unemployment below 5 per cent, fears of inflationary pressure are increasing. Yet, there has been no evidence of either rising wages or rising prices. The Federal Reserve has already taken measures with a view to forestalling such pressure; its intervention rate and long-term rates have again moved up to around 7 per cent. Interest rates are widely expected to increase during the year. The outcome for 1997 will thus depend on the behaviour of consumers, on the extent of monetary tightening, and movements of the exchange rate.

In Japan, performance in 1997 will also depend on consumer behaviour and the exchange rate, as well as on fiscal policy. The impact of the series of fiscal packages has now been absorbed, and the Government has announced its intention to introduce measures to reduce some of the accumulated outstanding debt created. Higher consumption taxes that came into force in April 1997 are expected to depress consumption in subsequent quarters. On the other hand, and barring any sharp reversal of the depreciation of the yen, both exports and investment should continue to expand. However, if the current recovery is judged to be a continuing one, interest rates may well be increased. Although the risk of financial instability seems to have lessened, any substantial increase in interest rates may put an end to the highly profitable financial operations whereby borrowed yen are swapped into dollars for investment in United States long-term Treasury bonds. Since such operations have been instrumental in bringing about yen depreciation, any rise in interest rates would lead to a sharp reversal of the movement. Growth during 1997 is likely to be uneven.

Prospects for EU countries are dominated by the fact that performance in 1997 is to be used as a yardstick for judging eligibility for membership of the EMU. Fiscal policies are thus expected to remain restrictive and monetary policies unchanged. Consumption is likely to stagnate, except in countries that have either chosen to delay entry or have not yet taken a final decision, while investment will be influenced primarily by exports and hence exchange rates. Most countries have benefited from the continued appreciation of the dollar, but exchange rates will also be influenced by the Maastricht process as markets attempt to gauge the relative position of the dollar against the future euro and the latter's initial currency basket.

In Germany, despite strong exports, growth in 1977 is unlikely to be much greater than 2 per cent. Given the extent of corporate restructuring under way, this will not be sufficient to reduce unemployment. France faces similar conditions, but without any investment response to increasing export sales. Unless these trends are reversed by a new economic package, growth is likely to be lower than in Germany. In Italy, fiscal retrenchment introduced in a last-minute-attempt to reach stage three of EMU will depress demand at the same time as the reentry of the lira has reduced the possibility of achieving greater competitiveness of exports, which remain the sole impetus in the economy. The growth rate in 1996 was below even the most pessimistic expectations, and 1997 is unlikely to be much better. The United Kingdom stands apart, with low and stable inflation, falling unemployment and a surprisingly stable current account, despite an appreciation of sterling and booming consumer demand. In the absence of any new fiscal measures, further increases in interest rates are likely, even though their impact may be felt little in the current year.

Recent trends are also expected broadly to continue in developing countries. For Latin America output growth is expected to further accelerate in 1997. In particular, activity may pick up moderately in Argentina, Brazil, and Colombia and more sharply in Peru. With resumed substantial inflows of foreign capital, most of the countries in the region will not face an external constraint to growth. However, vulnerability to swings in capital flows remains high in a number of countries with large external deficits. Moreover, in most countries the basic conditions for sustained rates of growth of 5 per cent or more have not yet been fulfilled. Questions also arise as to whether the export surge can be sustained. In Mexico, where much of the recent surge in exports was a one-off response to exchange rate alignment, a policy of taking the restoration of capital inflows as an opportunity to lower the rate of inflation by using the exchange rate as a nominal anchor can have serious adverse effects not only on exports but also on investment, and hence more generally on growth. In Brazil, where a combination of trade liberalization and currency appreciation in the context of an exchange-based stabilization programme has resulted in a substantial worsening of the current

account, there is very little room for domestic expansion or export growth without an exchange rate adjustment. For that country the challenge is how to move to more realistic and flexible exchange rates without triggering a financial crisis or inflation. Indeed, attaining exchange rate stability and sustainable payments positions while growing vigorously remains the most important challenge to most countries in the region.

For developing Asia, prospects for 1997 are for growth at a pace similar to, but in the first-tier NIEs below, that of 1996. Most countries in South-East Asia are expected to fare better in 1997, but large current account deficits and financial instability may render it difficult for some to accelerate or even maintain growth. Although no longer benefiting from a strong yen, exports are expected to continue to be an important source of growth in East Asia. More generally, the outlook for developing Asian countries will depend to a significant extent on developments in China and in the industrialized world, particularly Japan and Western Europe. Having been guided successfully to a soft landing in 1996 after a three-year austerity programme, the Chinese economy appears poised to enter a period of relative stability with mild inflationary pressure and sustained high rates of growth. Among the factors that may influence policies and economic performance in China is the forthcoming quinquennial party congress scheduled for the autumn of 1997, the first in the post-Deng era, as well as the resumption on 1 July 1997 of Chinese sovereignty over Hong Kong. In South Asia, growth is expected to further accelerate in 1997, while in West Asia it is likely to be more moderate because of a fall in oil prices.

Although the economies of most African countries remain fragile, the region can be expected to maintain its current growth trend in 1997. Non-oil commodity prices are expected to increase modestly on account of favourable movements in food and agricultural raw material prices on world markets. Oil prices, on the other hand, are likely to decline, to the advantage or disadvantage of different countries, depending on their net export positions. Central Africa is expected to continue the strong recovery of 1996 through improved performance in the mining sector and - it is hoped - greater political stability in Rwanda and Burundi. Prospects for East and Southern Africa are promising, in as much as weather conditions have been favourable in the first quarter of 1997 and the prices of minerals, particularly copper, gold and

Table 8

GDP GROWTH IN SELECTED OECD COUNTRIES IN 1996: COMPARISON OF ACTUAL GROWTH WITH FORECASTS BY VARIOUS INSTITUTIONS

(Percentage)

Country	LINK (May 96)	ECE (June 96)	OECD (Dec. 95)	EU (Dec. 95)	IMF (April 96)	NIESR (May 96)	NRI (May 96)	UNCTAD (June 96)	**Actual**
United States	2.0	2.0	2.7	2.3	1.8	2.2	2.0	2.2	2.5
Japan	2.0	2.0	2.0	2.3	2.7	2.4	1.5	2.1	3.5
Germany	2.0	1.0	2.4	2.4	1.0	1.0	0.8	0.5	1.4
France	0.9	1.5	2.2	2.4	1.3	1.6	1.2	0.9	1.3
Italy	2.2	2.0	2.5	3.0	2.4	1.4	2.1	1.5	0.7
United Kingdom	2.2	2.0	2.7	2.7	2.2	2.4	2.0	2.2	2.0

Source: Table 1 for actual growth rates; *TDR 1996*, table 5.

diamonds, have turned upwards. In addition, the revamping of the former East African Community, whose permanent Tripartite Commission was inaugurated in March 1996, is expected to exert a positive influence in the subregion through greater currency convertibility, increased demand, and better synchronization of standards for industrial goods. In West Africa, the expectation is for better prices of cocoa, coffee and gold, as well as an increase in industrial investment and capacity utilization. For North Africa, weather conditions are important, but much will also depend on prices of oil and potash as well as the extent of economic recovery in EU countries. Consequently, growth in the subregion may well be lower than in 1996.

Expectations for the transition economies in Central and Eastern Europe (and Central Asia) as a whole are for faster growth, but with much variation among countries. The fragility of the banking sector may be a crucial factor in a number of countries. In some of the more advanced economies, particularly the Czech Republic, Poland and Slovakia, slightly slower growth is expected, while in others (Croatia, Slovenia and the three Baltic States) growth is likely to accelerate. Hungary is expected to continue its recovery following the severe macroeconomic restructuring which began in early 1995. On the other hand, output is expected to decline significantly in Bulgaria and Romania as a consequence of the ongoing strong macro-

economic adjustment and restructuring programmes. For CIS members, prospects are for continued expansion in Armenia, Azerbaijan, Georgia, Kazakstan and Kyrgyzstan. Progress in Belarus and Moldova, respectively, will depend largely on whether energy imports from the Russian Federation continue and on how the weather treats the agricultural sector. Neither the Russian Federation nor Ukraine shows signs of emerging in 1997 from extended periods of declining GDP.

A caveat nevertheless needs to be entered in respect of short-term forecasts. As pointed out in previous issues of this Report, they are subject to varying degrees of uncertainty associated with a variety of factors, such as the evolution of economic policies, which can be subject to unexpected shifts as a result of political developments, and external influences that are transmitted through international trade, finance and investment. Trade policy has become particularly important, in the light of globalization of the world economy and the way in which multilateral Agreements reached in the Uruguay Round are implemented. (For trade disputes that have arisen regarding "national treatment" see the annex to Part One.)

The degree of uncertainty and hazards associated with short-term forecasting can be seen from table 8, which compares GDP forecasts for 1996 by various international organizations and research

Table 9

ALTERNATIVE FORECASTS OF GDP GROWTH IN 1997 FOR SELECTED OECD COUNTRIES

(Percentage)

Country	LINK	ECE	OECD	EU	IMF	NIESR	NRI	UNCTAD
United States	2.6	2.5	3.6	2.3	3.0	2.8	2.6	2.9
Japan	1.5	1.6	2.3	1.8	2.2	2.0	1.1	1.9
Germany	2.5	2.0	2.2	2.2	2.3	2.5	1.8	2.2
France	2.5	2.2	2.5	2.1	2.4	2.6	1.8	1.9
Italy	1.1	1.2	1.0	1.4	1.0	1.1	0.6	1.2
United Kingdom	3.2	3.0	3.0	3.0	3.3	3.0	2.7	2.5
Memo item:								
European Union	2.5	..	2.3	2.3	2.4	2.4	1.7[a]	2.0

Source: United Nations, University of Pennsylvania and University of Toronto, "Project Link World Outlook" (mimeo), post-LINK meeting forecast (May 1997); ECE, *Economic Survey of Europe in 1996-1997* (United Nations publication, Sales No. E.97.II.E.1); OECD, *Economic Outlook* (June 1997); Commission of the European Communities, *European Economy, Supplement A* (December 1996); IMF, *World Economic Outlook* (May 1997); National Institute of Economic and Social Research (London), *National Institute Economic Review* (April 1997); Nomura Research Institute (NRI), *Quarterly Economic Review* (May 1997); and table 1.

a Total OECD.

institutions for selected OECD countries with the actual outcome. All forecasters failed dismally to allow for the acceleration of recovery in Japan and all were overoptimistic for Italy, and to a lesser extent also the United Kingdom.

Forecasts for 1997 by the same institutions, on the other hand, appear to converge better than those made for 1996 (table 9). With the notable exception of Japan, all forecasts agree that growth in the selected OECD countries will be faster than in 1996. As regards individual countries, the spread in percentage points among the alternative forecasts is highest for the United States and Japan (1.3 and 1.2, respectively) whereas for the European countries it is only around 0.7-0.8.

Perhaps a major source of uncertainty surrounding short-term prospects is the possible evolution of politics and policies in the EU. Predicting how the EU will move in the fiscal and monetary fields in the second half of 1997 has been made particularly difficult as a result of the general elections held in May/June in the United Kingdom and France. In view of the importance of the EU in the world economy, any sudden shifts in policy can have serious repercussions for the rest of the world, including other major industrial countries and developing countries.

A second source of uncertainty relates to currency and financial markets. The persistence of trade imbalances may lead to large swings in exchange rates which, in turn, serve to redistribute overall demand and growth impulses, rather than eliminate disparities in demand generation. Deepening of imbalances and increased exchange rate instability could in turn lead to financial instability, with unfavourable consequences for global growth due to the depressing effect on expenditure and recourse in some countries to more restrictive macroeconomic policies.

Finally, there is uncertainty regarding the economic implications of the return of Hong Kong to China. It is not clear what the effects of resumed Chinese sovereignty will be either on the trade and investment links within the "Chinese Economic Area", consisting of China, Hong Kong and Taiwan Province of China, or on broader patterns of economic interdependence in East and South-East Asia. ∎

Notes

1 The Council of Economic Advisers, in *Economic Report of the President, 1997*, table 2.3 (p. 86), estimated the long-term growth rate of the United States economy for the period 1996-2003 at 2.3 per cent.

2 In January 1995, the Common External Tariff, which covers about 85 per cent of the value of trade among member countries, went into effect. Chile became an associate member in October 1996 and Bolivia reached a similar agreement with the Group in December.

3 The members are Bahrain, Kuwait, Oman, Qatar, Saudi Arabia and United Arab Emirates.

4 For country detail see the 1997 source cited for table 6.

5 For purposes of this chapter this group of countries corresponds to "Eastern Europe" as defined by the ECE secretariat in the source to table 7, i.e. Albania, Bosnia and Herzegovina, Bulgaria, Croatia, Czech Republic, Hungary, Poland, Romania, Slovakia, Slovenia, The former Yugoslav Republic of Macedonia, and Yugoslavia.

Chapter II

INTERNATIONAL FINANCIAL MARKETS AND THE EXTERNAL DEBT OF DEVELOPING COUNTRIES

A. Recent trends in private external financing

During 1996 there was a continuation of the previous year's expansion of most major categories of external financing from international financial markets. This is exemplified in table 10 for selected instruments involving international issuance or syndication, but a similar expansion also characterized cross-border transactions in domestically issued securities of several countries. An especially large increase was recorded by issues of external bonds, but it may well have been linked to some extent to the reduced recourse by borrowers to syndicated credits, which is also evident from the table. The shares of developing countries and transition economies in most categories of financing remain fairly small but have substantially risen since the early 1990s for issues of both external bonds and international equities. Moreover, as is illustrated by the remarks which follow, not only the financial markets but also the economies more generally of several such countries are increasingly experiencing effects of global financial integration.

In recent issues of *TDR* attention has been drawn to the way in which such integration has been accompanied by changes at the level of transactions, with implications for the categorization of different financial flows, and by the emergence of sources of private external financing for developing countries in emerging financial markets themselves. In *TDR 96*, for example, there was a discussion of the progressive blurring of the distinction between international bonds and Euro-medium-term notes (EMTNs), and attention was drawn to the growing importance to portfolio investment in developing countries of purchases of domestically issued instruments by mutual funds and of cross-border flows originating in other developing countries, mainly in East Asia. Both these trends continued to be evident in 1996. For example, the Bank for International Settlements (BIS) recently noted that over 60 per cent of drawings made under EMTN programmes consisted of international bonds.[1] Funds flowing directly into the stock markets of developing countries of East Asia, which already accounted for more than 60 per cent of total portfolio equity investment in the region in 1995, continued to increase in 1996.[2] Banks and individuals in Asian countries other than Japan have become significant purchasers of debt as well as equity instruments issued not only by Asian entities but also by Latin American ones. This trend is likely to be accelerated by the establishment of more mutual funds holding bonds in their portfolios (a recent phenomenon in Asia) and diversification of their portfolios by the institutions in the region managing pension schemes.[3] Similar developments are evident in Latin America, though they are at an earlier stage. For example, Chilean investments abroad during the last six years are estimated at $12 billion, of which much the greatest part is in other Latin American countries.[4]

Table 10

SELECTED CATEGORIES OF INTERNATIONAL FINANCING AND SHARES
OF DEVELOPING AND TRANSITION ECONOMIES THEREIN, 1992-1996

(Billions of dollars and percentage shares)

Category	1992	1993	1994	1995	1996
External bond offerings					
Total ($ billion)	333.7	481.0	428.6	467.3	710.6
Share of developing countries[a]	5.5	10.6	11.5	10.2	14.4
Syndicated credits					
Total ($ billion)	117.9	136.7	236.2	370.2	343.4
Share of developing countries[a]	16.4	16.4	10.3	11.5	12.0
Eurocommercial paper programmes					
Total ($ billion)	28.9	38.4	30.8	55.9	80.6
Share of developing countries[a]	11.8	7.8	6.5	15.9	3.8
Other non-underwritten facilities[b]					
Total ($ billion)	99.0	113.6	222.1	346.1	375.0
Share of developing countries[a]	4.6	6.2	5.4	5.1	6.2
International equity[c]					
Total ($ billion)	23.5	40.7	45.0	41.0	57.7
Share of developing countries[a]	15.3	18.9	23.6	25.1	24.1

Source: OECD, *Financial Market Trends*, March 1997; UNCTAD secretariat estimates.

a Including the transition economies of Eastern Europe.
b Non-underwritten syndicated borrowing facilities, including medium-term note (MTN) programmes but excluding Eurocommercial paper.
c Including international placements of equity for privatizations.

The internationalization of financial markets is also blurring distinctions between international and certain domestically issued bonds. The distinctions long used for this purpose, with some exceptions due to the peculiarities of certain countries' regulatory regimes, resulted in the traditional categorization of bonds issued by non-residents in a particular country's financial market and denominated in its currency as foreign bonds, and of bonds issued by residents or non-residents in foreign currency as eurobonds. International bonds consisted of foreign bonds and eurobonds. Other bonds (i.e. those issued by residents in domestic currency) were classified as domestic. This categorization fails to take account of other features shared by international and certain domestic bonds such as

an investor base consisting of non-residents as well as residents and arrangements for listing, issuing, trading and settlement - features whose importance has tended to increase with internationalization. As a result, bond issues in domestic currency, those by both non-resident and resident issuers which are targeted at non-resident investors, are now widely defined by major reporting organizations as eurobonds, while foreign bonds are defined as those issued by non-residents and targeted at residents and domestic bonds as those for which both the issuers and the targeted investors are residents.[5]

As shown in table 11, there was continued growth during 1996 (the first three quarters) for the third consecutive year in the total external

Table 11

EXTERNAL ASSETS OF BANKS IN THE BIS REPORTING AREA[a] VIS-A-VIS DEVELOPING AND TRANSITION ECONOMIES, 1994-1996

	Percentage increase[b]			Stock in Dec. 1996
	1994	1995	1996	$ billion
Total[c]	**7.4**	**14.4**	**13.0**	**845**
of which in:				
Latin America	0.9	7.1	8.8	267
Africa	-6.4	-8.8	-5.9	37
West Asia	-2.7	-5.3	5.3	93
East and South Asia	20.5	30.4	19.4	439
Central Asia	102.0	30.6	38.9	2
Eastern Europe	-15.5	3.9	11.9	93
Other Europe[d]	4.7	8.4	24.8	7
All borrowers[e]	4.2	9.6	6.2	8290

Source: BIS, *International Banking and Financial Market Developments*, various issues.

a Including certain offshore branches of United States banks.
b Based on end-year data after adjustment for movements of exchange rates.
c Excluding offshore banking centres, i.e. in Latin America: Bahamas, Barbados, Bermuda, Netherlands Antilles, Cayman Islands and Panama; in Africa: Liberia; in West Asia: Bahrain and Lebanon; and in East and South Asia: Hong Kong, Singapore and Vanuatu.
d Malta, Bosnia and Herzegovina, Croatia, Slovenia, The former Yugoslav Republic of Macedonia, and Yugoslavia.
e Including multilateral institutions.

claims on developing countries other than offshore centres of banks in the BIS-reporting area (after adjustment for the effect of fluctuations in exchange rates), and only Africa, of the regions specified, experienced a decrease. In the case of export credits, as shown in table 12, overall increases in net flows to developing countries and transition economies in 1995 and the first half of 1996 were accompanied by contractions for Africa and Latin America, and in 1995 for Eastern Europe.

As in other recent years, financing from the international capital markets was heavily concentrated on a limited number of developing countries, although 1996 and early 1997 were also notable for first-time or renewed access to the market for internationally issued debt instruments for several countries. For example, eight developing countries or territories of East and South-East Asia[6] accounted for almost two thirds of the exchange-

rate-adjusted increase during 1996 in external claims on developing countries (other than offshore centres) of banks in the BIS-reporting area. The same eight countries, except Taiwan Province of China, accounted for 40 per cent of net international debt issues by developing countries and economies in transition, while five Latin American countries were recipients of more than 50 per cent of net flows in this form.[7]

Since mid-1996 a number of countries have issued international bonds for the first time or returned to the market for such bonds after long absences. They include Jordan, Tunisia, Panama, Croatia, Estonia, Latvia, Lithuania, Poland, Romania, Russian Federation and Kazakhstan. Moreover, after an earlier small private placement of $10 million, Ecuador issued a eurobond of $400 million. The Russian issue was for more than $1 billion, and was followed by another for a still

Table 12

TOTAL EXPORT CREDITS[a] TO DEVELOPING AND TRANSITION ECONOMIES, BY REGION

A. Prevalence of negative flows

(Percentage of the number of countries in the region[b])

Region	1992 1st half	1992 2nd half	1993 1st half	1993 2nd half	1994 1st half	1994 2nd half	1995 1st half	1995 2nd half	1996 1st half
Total	**41**	**38**	**38**	**48**	**43**	**34**	**36**	**51**	**47**
of which in:									
Africa	42	48	52	58	64	42	52	56	56
Latin America	51	46	38	43	38	30	30	57	54
West Asia	57	36	14	50	57	36	36	57	14
East and South Asia[c]	17	17	30	45	27	21	30	42	36
Central Asia[d]	..	..	..	..	12	12	-	12	37
Eastern Europe[e]	43	29	43	29	29	43	36	50	50

B. Net flow and stock in mid-1996

(Millions of dollars)

Region	Net flow 1992	Net flow 1993	Net flow 1994	Net flow 1995	Net flow 1996 (first half)	Stock (end-June 1996)
Total	**25216**	**20903**	**17398**	**6466**	**3103**	**316189**
of which in:						
Africa	2583	2164	-65	-617	-1131	62365
Latin America	4641	3869	1740	-3562	-760	65648
West Asia	1687	2173	2042	1224	1815	45974
East and South Asia[c]	8348	6058	16404	10235	3047	88504
Central Asia[d]	..	..	532	345	40	1433
Eastern Europe[e]	8015	5929	-2704	-1552	187	48533

Source: BIS and OECD, *Statistics on External Indebtedness, Bank and Trade-related Non-bank Claims on Individual Borrowing Countries and Territories*, new series, various issues.
   a After adjustment for movements of exchange rates.
   b Excluding countries for which data are not available.
   c Including Oceania; and from 1993 also China, People's Democratic Republic of Korea, Mongolia and Viet Nam.
   d Armenia, Azerbaijan, Georgia, Kazakhstan, Kyrgyzstan, Tajikistan, Turkmenistan and Uzbekistan.
   e Up to 1993: the former socialist countries of Eastern Europe; 1994-1996: Bulgaria, Czech Republic, Hungary, Poland, Romania, the Baltic States and countries members of CIS (excluding those listed in note *d*).

larger amount ($2 billion). The initial Russian and Polish issues have been followed by municipal as well as corporate issues: for example, St. Petersburg recently raised $300 million.

These first-time issues and returns to the bond market were accompanied by the first-time assignment of credit ratings to the foreign currency debt of a number of countries by the major credit rating agencies as well as by several upward and downward movements in ratings of other countries. Amongst the countries receiving ratings from Moody's and Standard and Poor's for the first time were Egypt (whose rating from Standard and Poor's in January 1997 was of investment grade),[8] Kazakhstan, Lebanon, Panama, Republic of Moldova, Romania, Russian Federation, and Trinidad and Tobago. Hungary received a rating of investment grade from Standard and Poor's (after having earlier received such a rating from other agencies), Tunisia received such ratings from Moody's and Standard and Poor's, Uruguay such a rating from Moody's, and Lithuania from Standard and Poor's. An interesting development in April 1977 was the assignment by Standard and Poor's to a number of Argentine corporations of a rating higher than that of the country's sovereign entities. This was justified by the agency's belief that Argentina's monetary regime, whose linking of the money supply to foreign exchange reserves had withstood strains imposed by capital outflows in the aftermath of the Mexican crisis in 1995, had reduced the importance of country risk[9] sufficiently for borrowing entities in both the public and the private sector to be evaluated purely for their credit risk.[10] Other major rating agencies have yet to depart from the more traditional approach which, for the great majority of loans, assigns to sovereign entities a rating which sets a ceiling to those accorded to other borrowers.

B. Capital flows and policy responses in selected developing countries

1996 and early 1997 witnessed significant shifts in capital flows to emerging financial markets and in recipient countries' policies towards such flows. With the exception of the period following the crisis of Mexico's external payments at the beginning of 1995, policies in these countries during the 1990s have been directed more to overcoming the problems caused by large capital inflows than to the traditional preoccupation of earlier years, namely the attraction of inflows adequate to cover deficits on current account, while none the less ensuring that investment in certain activities or sectors was reserved partly or wholly for residents.[11] The inflows were largely the effect of the changes in the portfolios of institutional investors associated with the process of integrating selected developing countries and transition economies into the global network of financial markets. Now that this integration has become well established (though the number of countries affected is likely to continue to increase in future), all the financial markets involved can expect to experience the effects of changing perceptions among international investors in both favourable and unfavourable directions. Developments in international financial markets since mid-1996 exemplify this situation: unfavourable shifts in investors' perceptions regarding countries only recently in receipt of large inflows, in response partly to substantial current account deficits but also to domestic developments (especially, in one case, the proliferation of the financial sector's non-performing loans), have led to large outflows and periods of strong downward pressure on exchange rates. Policy reactions in the countries affected have included measures directed at the balance of payments as well as others with a primarily internal focus. Elsewhere, policy towards the capital account has included both restrictive measures and more accommodating stances, depending on whether the primary concern of the country in question was to moderate or to sustain capital inflows.

Table 13

EXTERNAL FINANCING FOR SELECTED DEVELOPING AND TRANSITION ECONOMIES
BY MAJOR CATEGORIES, 1991-1995

| Country | Cumulative total | Loans[a] | Internationally issued portfolio investments | | Net FDI |
			Debt[b]	Equity[c]	
	($ billion)	(Per cent of total)			
Latin America					
Argentina	46.4	10	45	12	33
Brazil	37.7	20	49	9	22
Chile	13.5	36	5	21	38
Colombia	10.5	36	17	5	43
Mexico	74.4	19	28	18	35
Peru	5.0	23	0	3	74
East and South Asia					
China	152.6	23	4	7	65
India	11.9	24	2	51	24
Indonesia	26.3	30	8	17	45
Malaysia	27.8	33	-4	7	64
Philippines	8.9	-19	27	38	54
Republic of Korea	74.6	68	28	10	-6
Thailand	91.8	84	4	5	7
Eastern Europe					
Czech Republic	11.0	30	36	0	33
Hungary	12.3	-35	50	6	79

Source: BIS, *International Banking and Financial Market Developments*, various issues; IMF, *International Capital Markets*, World Economic and Financial Surveys (Washington D.C.: IMF), various issues; World Bank, *Global Development Finance*, Vol. 1 (Washington D.C.: World Bank, 1997); and UNCTAD, *World Investment Report, 1996* (United Nations publication, Sales No. E.96.II.A.14).

a Estimated exchange-rate-adjusted changes in the external positions of assets of BIS-reporting banks vis-à-vis individual countries.
b Net issues of international debt securities by country of residence, including euronotes and international bond issues.
c International equity issues and the change in the year-end net asset value of international emerging market equity funds.

During the first half of the 1990s, there was substantial variation in both the scale and the character of recipient developing countries' dependence on major categories of debt and non-debt external financing from the international financial markets, as shown in table 13. For example, for the Latin American countries in the table bank lending tended to be less important as a share of such financing than for the Asian countries, with the outstanding exception of the Philippines. This reflected the continuing effects of the debt crisis of the 1980s, which included restraints on new lending by banks and reductions in their outstanding exposure resulting from restructuring agreements. The relatively high shares of internationally issued bonds and other debt instruments for some Latin American countries is a result of their recent return to international financial markets.[12] Two Asian countries (China and Malaysia), one Latin American country (Peru), and one Central European country

(Hungary) depended to an exceptional extent on FDI in comparison to the other countries in the table.[13] In Hungary and the Czech Republic (as well as in Poland, which is not shown in the table) substantial shares of the FDI were associated with the purchase by external investors of shares in privatized enterprises, and relatively small shares (only about 20 per cent according to OECD estimates) were associated with "green field" operations involving the creation of new facilities from scratch.[14]

Since 1996 net flows of FDI and of debt securities to both Latin America and East and South-East Asia have continued to increase. Figures for debt financing in 1996 and early 1997, however, point to improvements in the perceptions of international investors regarding the position of the main borrowing countries of Latin America but greater caution regarding some of the Asian recipients. Thus, whilst there was an acceleration of the growth in the exposure of banks in the BIS-reporting area (after adjustment for changes in exchange rates) to Latin America ($16.4 billion in 1995 and $21.8 billion in 1996), the growth in exposure to East and South Asian countries slackened from $86.3 billion to $72.3 billion.[15] Moreover, the greater caution noted above probably also contributed to depressing issues of debt instruments by East and South-East Asian entities in the first quarter of 1997.[16]

Table 14 makes possible a preliminary review of trends in the external financing of selected developing countries from the international financial markets. One country shown (Venezuela) ran a surplus on current account in 1996. As in other recent years, the shares of external financing in the form of net FDI (generally regarded as being associated with a more durable commitment by investors to recipient economies) varied widely, as did the proportions of deficits on current account covered by such inflows. The deficit on current account of China, which, as in other recent years, was the largest recipient of FDI,[17] was covered eight times by its net inflow in this form. Other countries whose current account deficits were covered by net FDI were Mexico (more than three times), Poland (three times), and Hungary (for which the ratio of net FDI to the deficit was one). For the remaining countries other than the Republic of Korea (which was a net provider of FDI) the proportion of the deficit covered by net FDI ranged from above 75 per cent (Malaysia: 98 per cent, Peru: 94 per cent, Chile: 88 per cent, and Indone-

sia: 78 per cent) through 50-70 per cent (Colombia: 54 per cent, and Argentina: 50 per cent) to below 40 per cent (Czech Republic: 31 per cent, Brazil: 23 per cent, and Thailand: 21 per cent).[18]

Other, more disaggregated, data concerning the external financing in 1996 and early 1997 from the international financial markets of the countries shown in table 14 provide additional information as to the context of the policy measures associated with their capital inflows and outflows (discussed below). As can be seen from table 15, in 1996 all the Asian countries except Thailand increased their net borrowing (after adjustment for changes in exchange rates) from banks in the BIS-reporting area and the Republic of Korea replaced Thailand as the largest net borrower, the decrease in the figure for the latter amounting to $30 billion. Moreover, all these countries (including Thailand) increased their net issues of international debt securities. For all the Latin American countries in table 14 except Venezuela the growth in the (exchange-rate-adjusted) exposure of BIS-reporting banks was positive in 1996, but not always at levels higher than in 1995. However, with the exception of Venezuela and Peru, these countries were recipients of greater amounts of money through net issues of international debt securities, Argentina, Brazil and Mexico all being net borrowers of more than $10 billion in this form.[19] As regards the countries of Central and Eastern Europe the (exchange-rate adjusted) exposure of BIS-reporting banks increased during 1996 for the Czech Republic and Hungary but contracted for Poland (which, however was the recipient of $0.4 billion in net issues of international debt securities).

As in other years since the beginning of the 1990s, borrowing during 1996 in the form of both bank loans and debt securities by the countries in table 14 was driven partly by arbitrage operations of banks in the recipient countries, for onward lending domestically at higher interest rates of funds raised in international markets. Countries for which such arbitrage was particularly important (and for which indications of the differentials between domestic interest rates and those in major OECD countries are given in table 16) included Brazil, for which 64 per cent of the increase in its (exchange-rate-adjusted) liabilities to BIS-reporting banks and almost 30 per cent of its net issues of international debt securities were inter-bank, the Republic of Korea (for which the corresponding percentages were 76 per cent and 56 per cent),

Table 14

FEATURES OF THE BALANCE OF PAYMENTS AND EXTERNAL FINANCING OF SELECTED COUNTRIES IN IN ASIA, EASTERN EUROPE AND LATIN AMERICA, 1994-1997

(Billions of dollars, unless otherwise indicated)

ASIA

	China				Indonesia				Republic of Korea				Malaysia			
	1994	1995	1996	1997[e]	1994	1995	1996	1997[e]	1994	1995	1996	1997[e]	1994	1995	1996	1997[e]
Current account balance	6.9	1.6	-5.3	..	-2.8	-7.0	-7.4	..	-3.9	-8.3	-23.5	-6.3	-4.1	-6.8	-6.3	..
Per cent of GDP	*1.3*	*0.2*	*-0.7*	..	*-1.6*	*-3.5*	*-3.3*	..	*-1.0*	*-1.8*	*-4.8*	..	*-5.9*	*-7.7*	*-6.5*	..
Net direct investment	31.8	33.8	42.3	..	1.5	3.7	5.8	..	-1.7	-1.8	-1.8	..	4.3	5.8	6.2	..
Net portfolio investment[a]	-3.5	0.8	..	..	3.9	4.1	..	..	6.9	10.8	..	..	-1.6	..	..	..
Short-term debt[b]	29.1	31.8	31.0	..	14.0	16.2	17.9	..	28.1	45.4	62.0	..	7.6	7.5	8.5	..
Import cover *(months)*[c]	5.7	6.7	7.7	9.9	3.3	3.1	3.4	4.0	2.6	2.5	2.3	2.0	4.8	3.5	3.7	3.6
Short-term debt plus current account deficit *(percentage of reserves*[d]*)*	*42*	*40*	*35*	..	*139*	*169*	*138*	..	*125*	*164*	*251*	..	*46*	*60*	*55*	..
Interbank debt *(percentage of total bank debt*[b]*)*	*73*	*76*	*78*	..	*41*	*43*	*39*	..	*78*	*78*	*78*	..	*73*	*70*	*73*	..

ASIA (cont.)   EASTERN EUROPE

	Philippines				Thailand				Czech Republic				Hungary			
	1994	1995	1996	1997[e]	1994	1995	1996	1997[e]	1994	1995	1996	1997[e]	1994	1995	1996	1997[e]
Current account balance	-3.0	-2.0	-2.9	..	-8.1	-13.6	-13.8	..	-0.1	-1.4	-4.5	-1.1	-4.1	-2.5	-1.7	0.5
Per cent of GDP	*-4.6*	*-2.7*	*-3.5*	..	*-5.6*	*-8.2*	*-7.5*	..	*0.4*	*4.6*	*-8.6*	..	*-9.8*	*-5.7*	*-3.9*	..
Net direct investment	1.3	1.1	..	..	0.9	1.2	2.9	..	0.8	2.5	1.4	..	1.1	4.5	1.7	..
Net portfolio investment[a]	0.3	1.2	..	..	2.5	4.1	..	..	0.8	1.4	0.9	..	2.5	2.2	..	..
Short-term debt[b]	9.7	11.0	12.0	..	29.2	41.1	44.0	..	1.2	1.2	1.2	..	2.4	3.2	3.1	..
Import cover *(months)*[c]	2.8	2.3	3.1	2.9	5.5	5.3	5.3	5.1	3.8	5.5	5.9	4.5	5.7	7.7	5.3	4.3
Short-term debt plus current account deficit *(percentage of reserves*[d]*)*	*212*	*203*	*149*	..	*127*	*152*	*153*	..	*21*	*19*	*46*	..	*96*	*47*	*49*	..
Interbank debt *(percentage of total bank debt*[b]*)*	*58*	*61*	*70*	..	*82*	*86*	*86*	..	*63*	*68*	*73*	..	*75*	*69*	*69*	..

Table 14 (concluded)

EASTERN EUROPE (cont.) / **LATIN AMERICA**

	Poland				Argentina				Brazil				Chile			
	1994	1995	1996	1997^e	1994	1995	1996	1997^e	1994	1995	1996	1997^e	1994	1995	1996	1997^e
Current account balance	-2.6	-4.2	-1.4	-1.5	-9.4	-2.4	-4.0	..	-1.2	-18.1	-24.3	-6.8	-0.6	0.2	-2.5	..
Per cent of GDP	-2.8	-3.6	-1.0	..	-3.3	-0.9	-1.4	..	-0.2	-2.5	-3.3	..	-1.2	0.2	-3.3	..
Net direct investment	1.8	3.6	4.2	..	0.5	1.2	2.0	..	2.0	3.5	5.5	..	0.8	1.0	2.2	..
Net portfolio investment^a	-0.6	1.2	..	..	3.7	4.7	11.5	..	44.7	9.4	10.5	..	0.9	-	3.1	..
Short-term debt^b	0.2	1.1	1.2	..	12.2	14.5	15.9	..	36.4	43.7	46.5	..	3.9	3.5	3.3	..
Import cover *(months)*^{c}	3.1	5.2	5.0	4.9	6.7	7.2	7.9	6.7	10.2	9.4	10.5	9.9	11.5	9.4	8.9	9.2
Short-term debt plus current account deficit *(percentage of reserves)*^{d}	48	36	14	..	151	118	110	..	101	124	121	..	34	23	39	..
Interbank debt *(percentage of total bank debt)*^{b}	21	24	32	..	29	31	32	..	38	45	48	..	43	37	31	..

LATIN AMERICA (cont.)

	Colombia				Mexico				Peru				Venezuela			
	1994	1995	1996	1997^e	1994	1995	1996	1997^e	1994	1995	1996	1997^e	1994	1995	1996	1997^e
Current account balance	-3.2	-4.1	-4.8	..	-29.4	-0.7	-1.8	0.4	-2.2	-4.2	-3.6	..	2.5	2.3	7.4	..
Per cent of GDP	-4.7	-5.1	-5.7	..	-7.0	-0.2	-0.5	..	-4.3	-7.2	-5.8	..	2.8	1.4	11.4	..
Net direct investment	1.5	2.2	2.6	..	11.0	7.0	6.4	0.9	2.9	1.9	3.4	..	0.1	0.6	1.4	..
Net portfolio investment^a	0.4	-	..	..	7.6	-10.8	20.6	2.8	0.6	0.2	1.0	..	0.3	0.3	..	..
Short-term debt^b	3.6	4.6	5.0	..	59.7	43.1	45.0	..	3.9	4.5	4.9	..	2.1	2.8	3.2	..
Import cover *(months)*^{c}	6.7	6.0	7.2	..	0.8	2.5	2.4	4.3	11.8	10.2	12.9	..	7.3	4.6	9.2	11.7
Short-term debt plus current account deficit *(percentage of reserves)*^{d}	87	107	102	..	900^f	267	241	..	87	106	80	..	-5	8	-32	..
Interbank debt *(percentage of total bank debt)*^{b}	24	24	28	..	32	26	24	..	29	38	44	..	15	17	16	..

Source: BIS, ECLAC, IMF, World Bank, J.P. Morgan, Union Bank of Switzerland, and UNCTAD secretariat estimates. For more details see the notes to this chapter.

a Externally issued bonds, other securitized debt instruments and equities.
b At end of year.
c Import cover is reserves divided by imports times the number of months in period. Reserves are international reserves minus gold at the end of the period (end of February 1997 for Indonesia, Malaysia and Peru).
d For reserves see note c.
e First quarter.
f Based on a mid-December estimate of reserves.

Table 15

INTERNATIONAL BANK LENDING AND OTHER DEBT FINANCING FOR SELECTED COUNTRIES, 1995 AND 1996

(Billions of dollars)

Country	Internationally issued debt securities[a]		Change in outstanding bank loans[b]	
	1995	1996	1995	1996
China	0.3	1.5	10.2	13.4
Indonesia	0.1	1.9	6.9	8.1
Republic of Korea	8.6	17.2	22.5	25.9
Malaysia	1.4	4.6	3.2	7.2
Philippines	0.5	3.1	1.5	5.4
Thailand	1.3	4.4	38.8	8.9
Czech Republic	..	..	3.6	1.9
Hungary	1.9	-0.8	-0.3	0.8
Poland	0.2	0.4	0.2	-0.4
Argentina	7.6	11.5	1.9	3.3
Brazil	6.0	11.8	12.0	10.0
Chile	0.1	2.3	1.4	0.5
Colombia	0.7	1.8	1.5	3.1
Mexico	0.9	14.1	-4.2	1.0
Peru	..	..	1.6	2.6
Venezuela	-0.4	-0.4	-1.7	-0.8

Source: BIS, *International Banking and Financial Market Developments*, May 1997, tables 5A and 10A.
 a Net issues of euronotes and international bonds.
 b Change in exchange-rate-adjusted exposure of BIS-reporting banks to the country.

Malaysia (80 per cent and 4 per cent), and Thailand (82 per cent and 42 per cent).[20]

The problems for policy caused by large capital flows (inward and outward) have led since mid-1996 to various responses from the governments of countries affected by them. In Latin America these responses continue to be character-ized by markedly different degrees of interventionism. Argentina, for example, has opted for a largely non-interventionist approach. Its principal policy measure directed towards the capital account of its balance of payments has been the establishment of a stand-by financing facility of more than $6 billion from private international banks for the purpose of helping to avoid a liquidity crisis in the event of major capital outflows. Under Argentina's currency regime the money supply is closely linked to foreign exchange reserves, and the central bank's capacity to operate as lender of last resort is correspondingly limited. In 1995 an outflow of about $8 billion (or approximately 20 per cent of bank deposits) put a severe strain on the financial system, and the new facility is designed to provide protection against such difficulties in the event of large outflows in future.[21] Chile and Mexico introduced measures which increased central-bank flexibility regarding intervention in the currency markets. Chile adjusted the band within which its currency floats, in order to allow for further appreciation of the peso. Mexico established a scheme designed to enable reserves to be accumulated without putting upward pressure on the exchange rate during periods when its currency is strong. Under the scheme the central bank periodically auctions to banks options whereby they can sell to it dollars for pesos at the exchange rate of the previous day but on conditions permitting exercise of the options only if the exchange rate is at a premium to its 20-day moving average.[22]

In Colombia and Brazil, where policy approaches to capital inflows (as in Chile) have been interventionist and involved a number of different measures of control, changes were made in the tax and regulatory regimes for international capital transactions, designed in Colombia to reduce upward pressure on the exchange rate and in Brazil to facilitate the financing of the persistent deficit on current account (and, through one measure, to reduce this deficit). Colombia imposed a tax on foreign borrowing at a rate which varies with the difference between domestic interest rates and international inter-bank interest rates after allowance for the extent of devaluation of its currency during the previous 12 months.[23] Brazil reduced taxes on foreign borrowing in the form of both securities and bank loans,[24] and relaxed restrictions on the use by foreigners for hedging of derivatives traded on Brazilian exchanges - restrictions which had originally been introduced to prevent foreign investors using the creation of synthetic financial instruments to avoid taxes previously imposed as

Table 16

REPRESENTATIVE SHORT-TERM INTEREST RATES IN SELECTED COUNTRIES, 1995-1997

(Period average in per cent per annum)

Country	1995	1996 First quarter	1996 Second quarter	1996 Third quarter	1996 Fourth quarter	1997 First quarter
United States[a]	6.0	5.4	5.5	5.6	5.5	5.6
France[a]	6.7	4.5	4.0	3.9	3.5	3.4
Germany[a]	4.5	3.4	3.4	3.3	3.2	3.2
Japan[a]	1.3	0.7	0.7	0.7	0.5	0.6
United Kingdom[a]	6.7	6.3	6.0	5.8	6.3	6.3
Republic of Korea[b]	14.0	11.1	12.7	16.9	14.1	12.6
Malaysia[c]	6.8	7.1	7.2	7.4	7.3	7.4
Thailand[d]	11.5	11.5	10.2	9.3	10.5	12.9
Brazil[e]	38.8	31.0	26.7	25.5	24.1	22.1

Source: United States, France, Germany, Japan and United Kingdom: IMF, *International Financial Statistics*; Republic of Korea, Malaysia, Thailand, and Brazil: J.P. Morgan, *Emerging Markets: Economic Indicators*, 6 June 1997.

  a For the United States, France, Germany, Japan and the United Kingdom, the interest rate is the London interbank offered rate (LIBOR) on three-month deposits.
  b Overnight call money rate.
  c Three-month interbank rate.
  d One-month interbank rate.
  e Overnight interbank rate.

a disincentive to capital inflows.[25] It also introduced selective controls on import financing in order to reduce its trade deficit, with exemptions for imports from MERCOSUR countries.[26]

When last year's *TDR* was under preparation, it seemed that some Central European countries might increasingly have to face problems for macroeconomic policy caused by large capital inflows similar to those recently experienced in East and South-East Asia and Latin America.[27] In the event, capital inflows into two of the countries principally affected, the Czech Republic and Poland, slowed. The deficit on current account of the first of those two countries has been increasing since 1994, and in 1996 reached 8.6 per cent of GDP. According to preliminary estimates, the deficit remained above $1 billion in the first quarter of 1997,

and was eventually associated with a series of speculative attacks on the currency. As a result, the central bank abandoned the fluctuation band for the koruna of 15 per cent vis-à-vis a basket of five currencies, which had been widened as recently as February 1996 in response to large capital inflows, and substituted a managed float in which it appears that intervention will in future be designed to keep the exchange rate against the Deutsche mark within a target range.[28]

Countries of East and South-East Asia have been the recipients of very large capital inflows since the beginning of the 1990s. The flow has been not only to countries or territories which ran surpluses on current account during much or all of this period (such as China, Singapore and Taiwan Province of China) but also to those which ran deficits (such as Indonesia, Malaysia, Philippines and Thailand). As in Latin America, both the extent and the nature of the policy response to these inflows has varied, among countries and through time. In the Philippines, for example, where the central bank intervenes to maintain the stability of the exchange rate with the dollar, heavy reliance is placed on the sterilization of capital inflows. Sterilization has also been an important feature of the response of Thailand and Indonesia. But in the latter case it has been combined with a currency band which has varied in width with the strength of the inflows, and in Thailand with a number of ad hoc measures intended to reduce the influence of such inflows on domestic short-term interest rates. Malaysia's response also initially relied heavily on sterilization, but as the scale of the capital inflow increased, the Government resorted to various more direct controls, which have been gradually relaxed as the inflows diminished after 1995. The Republic of Korea, which has traditionally maintained a restrictive regime for capital transactions and has in recent years been a net supplier of FDI to other countries (including some members of OECD), has relaxed a number of its controls over inflows since mid-1996. This relaxation is partly due to commitments made in the context of its accession to OECD but also reflects the need to finance an increased deficit on current account.[29]

In the countries mentioned above, where capital transactions continued to be characterized by large net inflows, policy has since mid-1996 followed broadly the lines already described.[30] However, Thailand has experienced periods of substantial capital outflows and downward pressure on the exchange rate, which were accompanied by a series of policy packages directed at both internal and external economic difficulties.

The concerns leading to the capital outflows appear to have focused on the combination of a number of unfavourable developments in both the domestic and the external sectors, such as the worsening of the balance of payments on current account (due partly to a slowdown of export growth), an increase in short-term external debt in 1996 (both shown in table 14), and the proliferation of non-performing loans of banks and finance companies, particularly due to their exposure to the property sector. The weaknesses of financial firms are concentrated above all among finance companies,[31] many of which had in June 1996 outstanding loans amounting to between 20 per cent and 40 per cent of the total to a property sector characterized by high vacancy rates, and of which no less than 25 per cent did not meet internationally recognized capital standards in early 1997.[32] The position of major banks was stronger, with lower percentages of outstanding non-performing loans (though there remains some uncertainty as to the extent of their exposure to affiliated finance companies).[33] The Government's policy packages have been directed at the financial and property sectors as well as the balance of payments. In May 1997 it introduced a programme of export incentives and increased tariffs on imported consumer goods. Its initiatives in respect of the financial sector include a credit line of more than 8 billion baht to troubled institutions, attempts to rationalize the sector's existing structure through the encouragement of mergers, and tighter enforcement of the provisions which financial institutions have to make against loan losses. In order to reduce the property sector's vacancy rates, in April 1997 the Government lifted restrictions on foreign ownership of condominiums and loosened those on foreign ownership of land for residential purposes. During early 1997 there has been some improvement in Thailand's major economic indicators such as the trade balance and the amount of short-term external debt.[34] But at the time of writing the economy remained vulnerable to imbalances in the markets for financial and non-financial assets, and to the consequent loss of confidence among domestic and foreign investors.

Thailand's current difficulties appear to be of a primarily domestic origin, although the speculative boom in asset prices was fuelled to a significant extent by capital inflows.[35] In this context various indicators of Thailand's external financial position in table 14 are of interest: while the current deficit increased slightly from 1995 to 1996, certain other indicators were relatively favourable. For example, the ratio of short-term debt plus the deficit to reserves, a figure to which some analysts attribute special importance as a pointer to the likelihood external payments problems, stood at a level of only 150 per cent (compared to about 900 per cent for Mexico in 1994). However, the shift in investors' sentiment is capable of putting severe pressure on the external payments position if sales of assets and withdrawals of bank deposits by non-residents are sufficiently large.[36] The resulting situation could have implications for the capital accounts of other countries in East and South-East Asia. Booms in property prices with speculative components in this region have not been limited to Thailand, and since mid-1996 there has been some dumping by foreigners of shares in the Philippines owing to reports of banks' high property exposure.[37] Other countries in the region have demonstrated their awareness of the dangers of speculative property financing: Malaysia and the Philippines, for example, have introduced various measures designed to restrict lending to the sector and to tax capital gains therein. Moreover, currency intervention in support of the baht by other central banks of certain East and South-East Asian countries is an indication of their determination to contain the threat that difficulties in one country will generate destabilizing capital flows in the region.[38] This support appears to have been motivated partly by concern that currency misalignments and the other problems of macroeconomic policy which such flows might cause could have unfavourable effects on economic prospects more generally.

C. The terms of export credits and trade financing arrangements

As noted in section A, net flows of export credits to developing countries increased in 1995 and the first half of 1996 but not all regions shared in this expansion. Net flows to Africa and Latin America were negative throughout this period, as were those to Eastern Europe in 1995. The relative importance of export credits as a source of external financing varies among recipients. However, the conditions on which this category of external financing is made available are of more general interest as an indicator of countries' creditworthiness, and the same is true of the conditions attached to credit insurance from the private market. Thus, for example, these conditions are generally correlated with the costs of financing and payments arrangements other than credit insurance for imports, such as charges on letters of credit. The prevalence of high costs and restrictive conditions on credit insurance for developing countries serves to bring out in another way the general point already made in section A that, in spite of the recent revival of external financing for certain developing countries and economies in transition, access to such financing is unevenly distributed, and for the great majority of these countries remains restricted.

The level of net flows of private export credits[39] is influenced by both supply and demand, and the official insurance provided by ECAs generally covers only part of the transactions with which the credits are associated (for large, complex contracts sometimes only a limited part). Thus these flows respond not only to costs but also to economic conditions in recipient countries, and in particular to the pace of investment, given the role of export credits in the financing of capital goods. The discussion which follows focuses on the cost side and its relation to financing and payments arrangements more generally.

The costs of private export credits consist of interest, premiums on official insurance, and various other transaction costs associated with restrictive conditions on which such insurance cover is made available (of which examples are discussed below). The interest rates on the financing of exports to developing countries are either commercial rates (linked to the rates at which the providers of the finance can borrow) or minimum rates for lending in different currencies under the OECD Arrangement on Guidelines for Officially Supported Export Credits, the so-called OECD Consensus. The insurance premiums typically consist of a basic rate, which varies with characteristics of the credit such as the payments arrangements used and the maturity of the loan, supplemented by additional premiums that vary according to a country's creditworthiness, particularly its recent record of making international payments. Maximum and minimum levels for these so-called Commercial Interest Reference Rates for different currencies in 1996 and the first five months of 1997 are shown in table 17.

For less creditworthy borrowers official insurance is generally provided only subject to various restrictive conditions relating to the pro-

Table 17

COMMERCIAL INTEREST REFERENCE RATES[a]

Currency		1996		1997 (up to May)	
		High	Low	High	Low
Australian dollar		9.6	8.0	8.6	7.9
Austrian schilling		6.9	6.0	5.9	5.5
Belgian franc		7.7	6.9	6.8	6.4
Canadian dollar	(1)[b]	7.6	5.9	6.5	5.4
	(2)[c]	8.1	6.7	7.1	6.2
	(3)[d]	8.5	7.2	7.5	6.8
Danish krone		7.5	6.6	6.7	6.2
Finnish markka		7.8	6.2	6.1	5.8
French franc		7.5	6.1	6.0	5.6
Deutsche mark		6.7	6.0	6.0	5.7
Irish punt		8.1	7.0	7.0	6.6
Italian lira		10.8	7.5	7.3	6.2
Japanese yen		3.4	2.4	2.5	2.3
Korean won[e]		.	.	12.5	12.5
Netherlands guilder	(1)[b]	6.2	5.6	5.7	5.3
	(2)[c]	7.0	6.3	6.3	6.0
	(3)[d]	7.8	7.3	7.1	6.7
New Zealand dollar		10.0	8.1	8.9	7.9
Norwegian krone		7.3	6.7	6.4	5.6
Spanish peseta		11.6	8.0	7.6	6.8
Swedish krona		9.7	7.3	7.2	6.3
Swiss franc		5.3	4.8	4.8	4.3
Pound sterling		8.6	7.9	8.4	7.9
United States dollar	(1)[b]	7.5	6.1	7.4	6.6
	(2)[c]	7.7	6.4	7.5	6.8
	(3)[d]	7.8	6.5	7.7	6.9
ECU		7.2	5.8	5.8	5.3

Source: OECD press releases and publications.

    a Minimum interest rate for officially supported export credits denominated in specified currencies or weighted averages of currencies advanced by participants in the OECD Arrangement on Guidelines for Officially Supported Export Credits (the OECD Consensus). New rates are set on a monthly basis, and highest and lowest of these rates during specified years are shown.

    b Maturity of less than five years.

    c Maturity of from five to eight-and-a-half years.

    d Maturity of more than eight-and-a-half years.

    e Included only as from 15 May 1997.

portion and amount of the credit for which cover is available, the limit on the amount of money below which the exporter or bank can exercise discretion in granting insured credits, the length of the period after the occurrence of non-payment before claims are met (the claims-waiting period), and the types of security required (which may consist of a guarantee from a national public entity in the importing country or a letter of credit issued by one of its banks and confirmed by a bank in an

Table 18

TERMS*a* OF INSURANCE COVER TO SELECTED REGIONS
FROM SELECTED EXPORT CREDIT AGENCIES*b*

*(Number of instances*c* in which EXIM or ECGD applied specified terms)*

Region/period	Normal terms*a*		No cover*a*		Restrictive conditions*a*	
	Short-term*d*	Medium- and long-term*e*	Short-term*d*	Medium- and long-term*e*	Short-term*d*	Medium- and long-term*e*
Africa						
Late 1996/early 1997	9	13	16	45	11	14
Latin America						
Early 1997	8	14	5	16	13	22
East and South Asia*f*						
Early 1997	11	19	4	11	11	22
Eastern Europe						
Late 1996	2	3	6	13	4	8

Source: Payments and credit surveys in *Project and Trade Finance*, various issues.

a Normal terms apply when cover is available to a borrower subject to no restrictive conditions. Such conditions include surcharges and restrictions on the availability of insurance cover and reflect mainly the perceived riskiness of the provision of financing to the borrower in question. The number and stringency of the conditions vary. For some borrowers cover is not available on any terms.

b The Export-Import Bank (EXIM) of the United States and the Export Credits Guarantee Department (ECGD) of the United Kingdom.

c Each country for which information is available corresponds to one instance for the terms on its insurance for short-term credits from EXIM, and to two instances for the terms on its insurance cover for medium- and long-term credits, one for EXIM and one for ECGD.

d Insurance cover for credits with maturities up to 180 days, except in the case of credits from EXIM for certain equipment goods and bulk agricultural commodities, for which maturities up to 360 days are also classified as short-term.

e Insurance cover for credits other than short-term.

f Including Oceania.

OECD country). Although the effect on the costs of export credits may be hard to quantify, such restrictions all entail increases. If perceptions of a country's creditworthiness become sufficiently unfavourable, export credit insurance may cease to be available even at high premiums and with extremely restrictive conditions. The availability of official export credit insurance, on the one hand, and interest rates, on the other, should not be regarded as independent determinants of the cost of export credits. The risk premiums included in interest rates on trade financing, which can represent a substantial proportion of total rates, may well be significantly reduced for credits carrying official insurance or guarantees.[40]

The data on terms of export credits in tables 18 and 19 refer to those available from EXIM and ECGD (the latter for medium- and long-term credits only). The terms of export credit insurance vary substantially among the agencies of OECD countries. This variation is evident, for example, in the average premiums charged for credit insurance by a sample of 10 such agencies in 1996, which are shown in table 20. The range of these premiums was frequently large, sometimes exceeding by sub-

Table 19

CHANGES IN TERMS[a] ON INSURANCE COVER AVAILABLE TO SELECTED REGIONS FROM SELECTED EXPORT CREDIT AGENCIES[b]

(Number of instances)

	From late 1995/early 1996 to late 1996/early 1997	
Region	More favourable terms[a]	Less favourable terms[a]
Africa	2	0
Latin America	2	2
East and South Asia[c]	0	2
Eastern Europe	0	2

S*ource:* Payments and credit surveys in *Project and Trade Finance*, various issues.

a All instances in which there has been a change in the terms of export credit insurance available from EXIM or ECGD between the categories, "normal cover", "no cover", and "restrictive conditions". (For "instances" and these three categories see notes **a** and **c** to table 18.) Such changes are recorded separately for short-term and for medium- and long-term credits.

b The Export-Import Bank (EXIM) of the United States and the Export Credits Guarantee Department (ECGD) of the United Kingdom.

c Including Oceania.

Table 20

PREMIUMS OF PRINCIPAL ECAs FOR SELECTED DEVELOPING AND TRANSITION ECONOMIES, 1996

(Percentage points)

Economy	Average premium	Range
Algeria	9.2	6.9-12.1
Argentina	7.7	4.3-12.5
Brazil	8.6	5.7-12.9
Bulgaria	10.3	6.2-16.3
Chile	2.9	1.1-3.9
China	2.9	1.7-4.7
Colombia	4.3	2.8-5.7
Côte d' Ivoire	10.8	9.0-12.1
Cuba	10.8	9.0-12.1
Czech Rep.	3.0	1.1-4.6
Egypt	10.8	7.8-16.3
Estonia	6.8	3.1-11.7
Ghana	8.4	6.9-10.0
Hong Kong	2.0	1.1-3.9
Hungary	5.8	3.7-9.3
India	5.3	3.6-9.6
Indonesia	4.6	3.6-6.4
Kenya	10.2	7.8-12.1
Malaysia	2.3	1.1-3.9
Mexico	6.3	3.7-12.2
Morocco	6.6	4.3-10.7
Nigeria	10.8	9.0-12.1
Pakistan	7.7	4.5-17.5
Peru	10.2	7.3-12.1
Philippines	7.5	4.6-11.5
Poland	6.6	4.6-9.6
Romania	9.0	6.0-14.0
Russian Federation	11.2	6.9-16.2
South Africa	4.8	2.8-6.9
Slovakia	6.2	3.6-9.3
Slovenia	5.0	2.8-6.9
Thailand	2.5	1.1-3.9
Venezuela	9.7	5.9-14.6
Viet Nam	10.0	7.4-14.0

Source: R.Kelsey, "Getting better terms from EKN", *Project and Trade Finance*, October 1996.

stantial amounts the means of those charged by the different agencies included in the table.[41] In spite of such variation the data on terms, on which tables 18 and 19 are based, do give broadly representative indications as to the perceptions of countries' creditworthiness affecting the costs and other terms of financing and payments arrangements for their imports.

As is shown in table 18, for the majority of developing countries and economies in transition credit insurance cover from EXIM and ECGD continues to be available only on restrictive conditions or not at all. Even for the countries of East and South Asia, the region which has had the greatest concentration of creditworthy countries in recent years, cover was available on normal terms (i.e. without restrictions) in only 42 per cent of instances[42] for short-term credits and in only 37 per

Table 21

**PROPORTION OF EXPORT CREDIT AGENCIES[a] IN SELECTED OECD COUNTRIES[b]
THAT INCURRED CASH-FLOW DEFICITS, 1987-1996**

(Percentage)

	1987	1988	1989	1990	1991	1992	1993	1994	1995	1996
Proportion:	83	65	65	71	83	83	54	33	27	26

Source: Information supplied by the Berne Union.

　a 1987-1989: 23 agencies ; 1990-1991: 25 agencies ;1992-1994: 24 agencies; 1995: 26 agencies; 1996: 27 agencies.

　b Some of these countries have more than one export credit agency.

cent of instances for medium- and long-term credits; for Latin America the corresponding proportions were 31 per cent and 27 per cent, for Eastern Europe 17 per cent and 13 per cent, and for Africa 25 per cent and 18 per cent. Total unavailability of insurance cover continued to apply to medium- and long-term credits more frequently than to short-term credits, the proportion being 63 per cent for Africa (as opposed to 44 per cent for short-term credits), 54 per cent for Eastern Europe (50 per cent for short-term credits), 31 per cent for Latin America (19 per cent for short-term credits), and 21 per cent for East and South Asia (15 per cent for short-term credits).

Generally, the conditions associated with the availability of official credit insurance are characterized by a fairly high degree of inertia, and this is evident for 1996 in the small number of changes shown in table 19. The terms associated with the provision of private credit insurance also shift slowly, and here 1996 was no exception either.[43]

The prevalence of restrictive conditions for both official and private credit insurance cover reflects not only perceptions of borrowers' creditworthiness but also restrictions on supply due to operating constraints of the institutions writing the insurance. For private insurers the effects of such constraints are not easy to document. For ECAs they reflect partly the agencies' long-term obligations to be self-supporting in their commercial operations. Widespread interruptions of debt service had a strongly adverse effect on the profit performance of ECAs during much of the 1980s and the early 1990s, but table 21 shows that this performance has been improving since 1992. Thus it is reasonable to assume that pressures on ECAs from this source to impose restrictive conditions have begun to diminish, although this shift may now to some extent be offset by greater emphasis on profitability as an objective for public-sector institutions.

Perceptions of borrowing countries' creditworthiness and their relation to transactions costs in their trade are also evident from data other than the conditions associated with official export credit insurance, such as the preferred payment terms in the export credit and collection surveys in the biweekly *Financial Times* newsletter, *International Trade Finance*. The preferred payment terms in these surveys are "open account", "sight draft" or "cash against documents (CAD)", "unconfirmed letter of credit", "confirmed letter of credit", and "cash in advance" (see box 1).

As shown in table 22, for developing countries and economies in transition the greatest concentration of preferred payments terms is to be found in the categories of confirmed and unconfirmed letters of credit, the proportions being 90 per cent or more for Africa, Eastern Europe and Latin America and 76 per cent for East and South Asia.[44] By contrast, for a group of 21 OECD countries preferred payments terms for all but two (90 per cent) were "open account" and "sight draft" or "cash against documents", the others being assigned to "unconfirmed letter of credit".[45] As might

Box 1

PRINCIPAL PAYMENT TERMS IN INTERNATIONAL TRADE

Under *payment on open account* an invoice is sent to the importer at the same time as the shipping of the goods, payment being specified within a predetermined period. This arrangement requires no intermediary, so that the associated transaction costs are at a minimum. However, it is also based on trust and is used mainly in trade between entities (such as inter-related companies) with a history of satisfactory transactions.

The terms *sight draft* and *cash against documents (CAD)* refer to transactions in which the documents conferring title to goods are released to the importer only against payment by sight draft or on his acceptance of a time draft. A sight draft or bill of exchange is an unconditional order addressed by one party to another, requiring the latter to pay a specified sum on demand or at a fixed future date. Since such a bill is a negotiable instrument (which can be turned into cash immediately), the exporter thus obtains greater security than in the case of payment on open account. This arrangement does not require the interposition of a bank, and the associated costs are low. In the case of a time draft, payment is to be made at a specified time in the future (so that there is an additional risk that the accepted draft may not be paid at maturity).

A *letter of credit* is a written undertaking by a bank in response to the instructions of the applicant (the importer) to make payment to the beneficiary (the exporter) against prescribed documents. It provides the exporter with insurance against the commercial risk of non-payment by the importer since its validity is independent of the underlying transaction. However, especially when the bank issuing the letter of credit is a local institution in the importer's country, the exporter is not protected from political risk resulting from events in the importer's country such as the unavailability of foreign exchange or the imposition of foreign exchange controls which make fulfilment of the contractual obligation impossible. This risk can be removed by a *confirmed letter of credit* under which another bank, typically in the exporter's country, adds its commitment to pay to that of the issuing bank. Confirmation of the letter of credit results in charges by the confirming bank additional to those of an unconfirmed letter of credit (which consist of the fees of the issuing bank and others associated with arranging for the payment to be made).

In the case of *cash in advance*, delivery of the goods is authorized by the exporter only after actual receipt of money from the importer. This arrangement is used for transactions with a particularly high risk of non-payment.

The first two of the preferred payment terms in the surveys of *International Trade Finance* are appropriate for transactions carrying low degrees of payments risk, and the latter three for successively greater degrees. See, for example, D. Briggs and B. Edwards, *Credit Insurance: How to Reduce the Risks of Trade Credit* (New York, etc.: Woodhead Faulkner, 1988), pp. 25-26.

---

be expected, the correspondence between rankings of individual countries' creditworthiness on the basis of recommended payments terms in *International Trade Finance*, on the one hand, and the restrictiveness of conditions associated with official credit insurance, on the other, is far from perfect. Nevertheless, the distribution of countries according to the former provides a further indication of differences in perceptions of creditworthiness, and helps to explain the prevalence in the majority of developing countries and economies in transition of the relatively high costs of financing and payments arrangements for their imports.

Table 22

RECOMMENDED PAYMENT ARRANGEMENTS[a] **FOR SELECTED DEVELOPING AND TRANSITION ECONOMIES**

(Number of countries)

Region	Open account	CAD[b]/ sight draft	Unconfirmed letter of credit	Confirmed letter of credit	Cash in advance
Africa	0	0	14	13	3
Latin America	0	2	21	2	0
East and South Asia	1	3	7	6	0
Eastern Europe	0	0	5	6	1

Source: *International Trade Finance*, 28 February 1997.
   a Data refer to the situation in early 1997. For explanation of these arrangements see box 1.
   b Cash against documents.

D. Renegotiation and reduction of bank debt

Restructuring of developing countries' bank debt due to the difficulties that started in the 1980s continued to decline in importance, and agreements since those discussed in last year's *TDR* included a number of economies in transition and African countries. Among the agreements reported in last year's *TDR* that have progressed or reached final conclusion,[46] mention should be made of the following: Panama and Peru, which concluded agreements to restructure $3.9 and $8 billion, respectively; the Russian Federation, which is moving slowly toward conclusion of its earlier agreement in principle to restructure $33 billion; and The former Yugoslav Republic of Macedonia, which reached agreement in principle to restructure $280 million. Viet Nam will conclude its restructuring of $750 million of debt this summer. There have only been two new London Club[47] agreements since mid-1996. In early 1997, Côte d'Ivoire reached an agreement with its creditors to restructure debt

of $7.2 billion, and Senegal an agreement to restructure debt of $118 million. Two low-income countries concluded debt buyback agreements with assistance from the IDA Debt Reduction Facility,[48] namely Mauritania in August 1996 and Senegal in December 1996. In operations intended to improve the structures of their liabilities, Mexico, the Philippines and Brazil completed swaps of uncollateralized long-term bonds for Brady bonds.

In April 1996, Panama finalized its earlier agreement to restructure $2 billion of principal and $1.9 billion of past-due interest. Under the menu of options, principal was exchanged for $88 million in 45-per-cent discount bonds, $268 million in par bonds and $1,612 million in front-loaded interest-reduction bonds. The discount and par bonds are collateralized by 30-year United States Treasury zero-coupon bonds, and the interest payments on all three bonds are collateralized on a rolling basis. For the restructuring of the past-due interest, $130 million was paid at the conclusion of the agreement, $590 million was forgiven (by the recalculation of interest and the waiving of penalties) and the remaining $1,248 million was exchanged for past-due interest bonds. The cost of the cash payments and bond collateral was $226 million, of which 60 per cent was funded by Panama and the remainder by the Inter-American Development Bank, the World Bank and IMF.

In November 1996, Peru finalized its earlier agreement to restructure $4,181 million in principal and $3,809 million in past-due interest. Under the menu of choices, Peru bought back $1,266 million of the principal at 38 cents per dollar of the debt's face value, and the remainder was exchanged for $947 million in 45-per-cent discount bonds, $189 million in par bonds and $1,779 million in front-loaded interest-reduction bonds. As for Panama, the discount and par bonds are collateralized by 30-year United States Treasury zero-coupon bonds and the interest payments on all three bonds are collateralized on a rolling basis. For the restructuring of the past-due interest, $308 million was paid at the conclusion of the agreement, $1,217 million was repurchased at 38 cents per dollar of face value, and the remaining $2,284 million was exchanged for past-due interest bonds. The cost of the cash payments, buybacks and bond collateral was $1.4 billion. Peru itself financed 45 per cent of the cost, Eximbank-Japan funded 7 per cent and the remainder was equally shared by the Inter-American Development Bank, the World Bank and IMF.

As reported in last year's *TDR*, in November 1995 the Russian Federation agreed in principle with its creditors to repay $25.5 billion of eligible principal and $7.5 billion in past-due interest. The agreement followed lengthy negotiations over the status of the country's commercial bank debt following the breakup of the USSR. At the time of writing final conclusion of the agreement was still pending, but the likely terms are as follows: the $25.5 billion of eligible principal will be paid back over 25 years, with a seven-year grace period at an interest rate linked to LIBOR. In late December 1996, the Russian Federation completed the upfront payment of $2 billion for past-due interest into an escrow account, and the remaining past-due interest is to be paid by interest notes over 14 years.

There has been progress in the difficult negotiations over the sharing out of the commercial bank debt of former Yugoslavia. Slovenia and Croatia recently concluded agreements with the commercial banks involved. In October 1996, The former Yugoslav Republic of Macedonia agreed in principle to restructure its 5.4 per cent share of the principal and 3.7 per cent share of the past-due interest owed by former Yugoslavia - a total amount of $280 million. In exchange for principal and past-due interest, it will issue 15-year bonds, paying fixed rates of interest in the first four years and a rate of interest linked to LIBOR thereafter.

Viet Nam's debt renegotiation is nearly concluded: more than 90 per cent of its creditor commercial banks have accepted the proposed agreement on its debt of $750 million. Of the menu of options, most banks have selected the 30-year par bond, which was issued in June.

Côte d'Ivoire reached agreement with its creditors to restructure $2.6 billion in principal and $4.6 in past-due interest. In the menu of options, principal is to be bought back at 24 cents per dollar of its face value (with past-due interest cancelled) or exchanged for either 30-year discount bonds (collateralized by United States Treasury or French Treasury zero-coupon bonds at a below-market rate of interest for the first 10 years) or 20-year front-loaded interest reduction bonds (at a below-market rate of interest). To restructure past-due-interest, the Government is to issue 20-year past-due interest bonds (at a below-market rate of interest for the first 16 years). The agreement is expected shortly to be signed and will reduce the present value of the country's commercial bank debt by 79 per cent.

In August 1996, Mauritania concluded an agreement with its commercial banks to restructure $92 million of debt, of which $37 million in past-due interest was written off and $55 million was bought back at 10 cents per dollar of its face value. Much of this debt was assumed by the Government following the privatization of a development bank. The total cost was $5.3 million, of which the World Bank paid $3.2 million through the IDA Debt Reduction Facility.

In December 1996, Senegal concluded an agreement with the assistance of the Debt Reduction Facility to restructure $118 million of debt, of which $75 million consisted of principal and $43 million of past-due interest. The two options were a buyback at 16 cents per dollar of its face value or exchange for a long-term zero-coupon bond issued by the Government and collateralized by United States Treasury zero-coupon bonds with a similar maturity. Total costs are estimated to be $13.4 million, of which the World Bank would pay $7.7 million through the Debt Reduction Facility and the remainder would be funded by the Netherlands and Switzerland.

Mexico and the Philippines made offers to swap uncollateralized long-term bonds for outstanding Brady bonds during 1996. They would thus be able to benefit both from access to the collateral required for the Brady bonds and from the discounted price of the bonds to be retired, though the former holders of the Brady bonds would receive higher interest on the uncollateralized long-term bonds. In May and September Mexico retired $3.6 billion of Brady bonds at an average discount of 24 per cent, thus also freeing $0.4 billion in collateral. In September the Philippines issued a $0.7 billion eurobond in exchange for Brady bonds as a first step in a series of swaps. In the spring of 1997 Brazil used part of a bond issue of $3 billion to retire $2.7 billion of Brady bonds, also freeing $0.6 billion in collateral. Argentina and Venezuela are reported to be considering similar operations.

E. Official debt

1. The HIPC Initiative: first steps

The external debt situation of developing countries has improved. A rise of 7.2 per cent in their debt stock in 1995 was more than offset by a strong increase in their exports and combined GNP[49]. The ratio of debt-to-exports for developing countries as a whole declined from nearly 180 per cent in 1993 to 170 per cent in 1994 and 151 per cent in 1995.

However, the debt problem of low-income countries is still a matter of concern. The debt-to-exports ratio of the severely indebted low-income countries remains high. In 1995, it stood at 421 per cent, while for countries classified by the World Bank as heavily indebted poor countries (HIPCs) it was 447 per cent. The ratio of actual debt service payments to exports in 1995 was respectively 17.0 per cent for developing countries as a whole, 18.6 per cent for the severely indebted low-income countries and 20.4 per cent for the HIPCs. Over the period 1985-1994 actually paid debt service on long-term debt for the last group of countries averaged about one third of their scheduled debt service (see table 23).

Almost the entire debt of the HIPCs is owed to official creditors, bilateral and multilateral. While Paris Club bilateral official creditors have gradually improved the terms of debt rescheduling and increased the percentage of debt reduction, the remaining official debt, namely debt owed to non-OECD bilateral official creditors and to multilateral financial institutions, has not been tackled in any formal framework[50]. The gravity of the debt problem of the HIPCs has attracted increasing attention from the international community, and in 1996 a proposal was put forward by IMF and the World Bank to alleviate their burden in a comprehensive way. The HIPC Initiative, which was endorsed by the Interim and Development Committees in September 1996, represents an important contribution towards resolving the debt problems of HIPCs and helping these countries to exit from the vicious circle of debt reschedulings (see box 2).

The total cost of the Initiative was tentatively estimated by the Fund/Bank staff between $5.5 billion and $8.4 billion. The World Bank established the HIPC Trust Fund in November 1996, and has subsequently allocated $500 million from its IBRD surplus to this Trust Fund as an initial

Table 23

MAIN DEBT INDICATORS FOR HEAVILY INDEBTED POOR COUNTRIES, 1985-1994

(Percentage)

Country	Debt to exports ratio[a] Nominal value	Debt to exports ratio[a] Present value	Per capita GDP growth rate	Gross resource flows[b]/ exports	Paid debt service/ exports	Paid debt service/ government revenue[c]	Government revenue[c]/ GDP	Paid debt service/ scheduled debt service	Reserves/ imports (Months)
					(Annual average)				
Angola	302	278	-3.7	33.1	7.0	14.2^d	27.4^d	28.7	..
Benin	272	142	-0.7	38.9	7.4	13.8^d	12.0^d	28.2	2.0
Bolivia	457	332	1.2	71.8	37.3	39.4	15.3	59.7	4.7
Burkina Faso	201	104	0.1	57.8	8.1	11.9^e	12.4^e	42.9	4.5
Burundi	891	388	-1.1	166.0	32.0	21.3	16.4	84.8	4.4
Cameroon	303	250	-6.9	31.5	20.8	14.1^f	18.5^f	54.8	0.3
Central African Rep.	464	243	-2.3	83.8	12.5	15.7^g	11.9	36.4	4.0
Chad	400	195	0.9	108.0	5.9	12.2^g	8.4^g	18.4	2.1
Congo	434	370	-2.3	32.9	32.1	..	..	34.6	0.1
Cote d'Ivoire	557	486	-4.4	34.6	34.4	..	..	40.2	0.2
Dem. Rep. of Congo	706	594	-7.6	30.6	15.7	43.1	10.8	15.5	1.2
Equatorial Guinea	435	308	1.2	103.2	11.4	8.5^h	18.5^h	9.9	0.5
Ethiopia	608	383	-12.2	126.3	23.6	15.8	17.1	54.3	2.4
Ghana	392	242	1.4	93.1	34.1	41.0^f	13.6^f	64.6	3.9
Guinea	402	255	0.5	49.0	15.3	35.7^i	13.4^i	26.0	0.8
Guinea-Bissau	1934	1280	2.0	252.8	26.1	28.8^e	13.6^e	8.5	1.4
Guyana	479	345	1.0	48.3	35.0	49.6	39.9	22.9	2.3
Honduras	347	271	0.5	55.0	30.5	45.2	18.2	47.5	0.9
Kenya	307	225	0.5	56.4	34.8	34.2	21.8	78.6	1.5
Lao P.D.R.	791	214	2.2	131.5	9.1	9.5^h	13.7^h	77.7	1.2
Liberia	374	339	-3.2	16.5	3.7	12.5^j	17.1^j	2.5	0.1
Madagascar	694	495	-1.9	85.4	34.3	58.1^k	9.2^k	28.0	1.9
Mali	523	288	0.6	80.1	14.6	19.2	15.5	31.0	2.4
Mauritania	469	327	-0.1	56.7	23.4	55.0^j	23.1^j	32.2	1.1
Mozambique	1367	1039	4.0	286.1	23.8	37.2^d	16.7^d	7.1	1.2
Myanmar	600	442	-1.3	44.6	24.7	6.3	9.0	35.5	3.6
Nicaragua	2879	2579	-1.3	198.3	32.9	19.4	29.5	3.3	1.3
Niger	544	322	-2.4	97.5	31.4	22.4^d	8.5^d	61.0	4.8
Nigeria	277	250	1.5	18.7	23.9	50.5	12.6	57.0	2.6
Rwanda	1142	533	-2.4	171.1	14.1	8.2^l	10.6^l	61.0	2.7
Sao Tomé & Princ.	2085	1101	-1.2	324.5	26.0	28.0^l	19.8^l	13.7	0.0
Senegal	253	166	-0.7	49.5	21.2	..	..	76.2	0.3
Sierra Leone	835	637	-0.3	80.9	24.0	51.4	6.9	6.6	0.7
Somalia	4711	3745	-0.4	544.5	21.8	..	..	1.1	0.6
Sudan	3384	3057	-0.4	78.5	10.7	2.6^m	14.5^m	1.2	0.3
Togo	1285	733	-3.0	34.7	16.0	37.7^a	28.4^a	62.3	5.2
Uganda	1005	719	2.9	187.1	52.9	74.8^g	4.7^g	32.7	1.3
U.. R. of Tanzania	367	226	1.8	163.8	32.7	29.7	16.7	10.3	1.0
Viet Nam	638	524	4.1	21.7	12.4	..	..	33.7	0.0
Yemen	239	189	..	28.5	8.1	8.8^f	52.6^f	18.8	1.8
Zambia	592	465	-2.4	66.8	26.5	61.4	15.7	12.8	1.3
All HIPCs	540	..	-0.9	103.4	22.2	28.8	17.0	34.7	1.8

Source: UNCTAD secretariat calculations, based on World Bank, *World Debt Tables*; IMF, *International Financial Statistics;* United Nations, *National Accounts* database.

Note: All debt and debt service figures relate to public and publicity guaranteed long-term debt.

a 1992-1994.
b Net resource flows plus principal repayments plus IMF purchases.
c Excluding grants.

d 1990-1994.	*g* 1985-1992.	*j* 1988-1994.	*m* 1991-1994.
e 1986-1992.	*h* 1985-1988.	*k* 1986-1994.	
f 1985-1987.	*i* 1985-1993.	*l* 1989-1994.	

contribution. The IMF established the ESAF-HIPC Trust Fund for financing special ESAF operations under the HIPC Initiative. Until resources are secured to finance the full costs of the Initiative and the continuation of ESAF, it has been decided that an amount of up to SDR 180 million[51] can be transferred from the ESAF Trust Reserve Account to be used for ESAF operations. Bilateral donor countries will also make contributions to the Trust Fund, in amounts as yet unknown.

In April 1997, the Executive Boards of IMF and the World Bank agreed, in principle, to extend debt relief to Uganda, the first country to complete the first stage of the debt relief process and thus reach its decision point (see box 2). The total relief package in present-value terms would amount to $338 million, of which the World Bank would contribute $160 million. IDA has agreed to advance a portion of this relief during the next 12 months through the provision of $75 million in the form of IDA grants. The IMF will be providing in present value the equivalent of $70 million, which will reduce Uganda's nominal debt service to the Fund by about $90 million over the next nine years. The remaining debt relief will have to be shared by other multilateral creditors (up to 40 per cent) and bilateral creditors, including the Paris Club.

Three other countries are likely to have their decision points determined in 1997: Bolivia, Côte d'Ivoire and Burkina Faso. Three more countries (Benin, Guyana and Mali) have agreed stock-of-debt operations on Naples terms with Paris Club creditors and can be considered to have established the first three-year track record.

Within the debt relief package for Uganda alone, the World Bank share represented about one third of the Bank's total contribution to the HIPC Trust Fund, and the IMF share about 27 per cent of the resources allocated to ESAF operations (as mentioned above). As the three other possible candidates for debt relief (Bolivia, Côte d'Ivoire and Burkina Faso) had a combined external debt at the end of 1995 more than seven times that of Uganda[52], the resources made available so far to the HIPC Trust Fund seem likely to fall short of the debt relief required by these countries. Should that prove to be the case, there could be a delay in the provision of debt relief. In this context, the issue of the partial sale of IMF gold to finance the Initiative again deserves to be given careful consideration.[53]

2. Framework issues and modifications

The HIPC framework in its original form called for a six year time-frame, strict criteria concerning eligibility and debt sustainability, and strong performance conditionalities. Over the past year, a more flexible stance has evolved as a result of the application of exceptional treatment to some HIPCs, in particular Uganda, Bolivia and Côte d'Ivoire. Framework modifications to date include the addition of other debt indicators, such as debt-to-fiscal revenue, to determine eligibility; a shorter time-frame for countries with a strong track record; extension of the one-year export calculation to a three-year export average; and a combination of debt reduction and additional interim financing by the World Bank to compensate through cash flow savings for a delay in the completion point.

There is also discussion about the possibility of introducing an additional conditionality, related to social and human development. However, while social and human development concerns are well justified, these concerns should not be encapsulated in an additional set of conditionality criteria linked to the implementation of the Initiative. This could deny many HIPCs the benefit of timely access to debt relief, if they are unable to meet these criteria because of limited resources and weak institutional capacity.

As regards increased framework flexibility, one change that has been introduced concerns the number of years necessary to reach the completion point. The Initiative now allows for flexibility in regard to countries which have already demonstrated a strong track record of adjustment. For Uganda and Bolivia, for example, the time frame for the provision of debt relief has been shortened from three years to one, or at most, two years.

Another example of flexibility is the recent broadening of the criteria for HIPC eligibility for assistance. Previously, debt sustainability was to be primarily measured in relation to a country's export base, so that HIPCs with relatively large export sectors were less likely to qualify for debt relief than less outward-oriented economies with similar debt burdens. As relatively high export receipts could conceivably coexist with inadequate budgetary revenues, eligibility criteria have been expanded to include fiscal constraints as an indicator of ability to meet external debt obligations (see box 3). ■

Box 2

THE HIPC INITIATIVE: KEY FEATURES

The HIPC Initiative provides a very useful framework for implementing a strategy of burden-sharing among all creditors to reduce the debt of the HIPCs to a sustainable level. The objective is to help them achieve overall debt sustainability, on a case-by-case basis, thus providing an exit from the rescheduling process. Debtor countries will have to show a track record of good policy performance as monitored by IMF and the World Bank. The six-year performance period under the Initiative consists of two stages of implementation.

First stage

During this first three-year stage (corresponding roughly to the duration of an ESAF agreement), the debtor country will have to establish a track record of good performance and the Paris Club will provide flow rescheduling on Naples terms (67 per cent reduction of Paris Club eligible debt on a present-value basis). Other bilateral and commercial creditors will provide at least comparable treatment. Bilateral donors and multilateral institutions will continue to provide support in the framework of World Bank/IMF-supported adjustment programmes. The end of the first phase is the **decision point**, reached after a three-year track record of good performance. A few months before the decision point, a debt sustainability analysis will be undertaken to determine whether the debtor country is eligible for further debt relief. Three alternative situations can occur:

- If a Paris Club stock-of-debt operation on Naples terms is sufficient to achieve debt sustainability within three years (i.e. by the completion point - see below), the country would be able to exit from the debt rescheduling process;

- If such a stock-of-debt operation is not sufficient to achieve debt sustainability, the country would be eligible for further debt relief;

- In borderline cases, where there is doubt about whether sustainability would be achieved by the completion point, the country would receive further flow rescheduling under Naples terms, with the assurance of additional action at that point, if needed.

Second stage

If the country is deemed eligible for support under the Initiative, it will go through a second stage, of normally three years[1], during which the Paris Club will provide more relief through flow rescheduling (up to 80 per cent of the present value of Paris Club debt). Other bilateral and commercial creditors will provide at least comparable treatment. The country will have to establish a second track record of good performance under World Bank/IMF programmes. The performance criteria during this second stage include macroeconomic indicators and progress on structural reforms and social reforms. Donors, bilateral creditors and multilateral institutions

Box 2 (concluded)

will also provide enhanced support in the form of grants and concessional loans. The end of the second stage is the **completion point**.

At the completion point, provided that the country has met the performance criteria under the Initiative, Paris Club creditors will provide a stock-of-debt operation of up to 80 per cent reduction in present-value terms. Other bilateral and commercial creditors will provide at least comparable treatment. Multilateral institutions will provide the committed reduction in present-value terms of their claims necessary for the total debt to reach a sustainable level. The World Bank, for instance, would provide assistance for this purpose through the HIPC Trust Fund, while IMF would provide assistance through a special ESAF grant or loan that would be paid into an escrow account and used to cover debt service to the institution.

Eligibility criteria

To qualify for exceptional assistance under the Initiative, countries will have to be ESAF-eligible and IDA-only. The debt sustainability analysis (DSA) will determine the eligibility of debtor countries, and eventually the amount of debt relief necessary for the country to achieve a sustainable level of debt, on the basis of the following criteria:

(i) The ratio of the present value of debt to exports should fall within a range of 200-250 per cent or below, by the completion point;

(ii) The debt-service-to-exports ratio should fall within a range of 20-25 per cent or below, at the completion point;

(iii) Within the prescribed ranges, debt sustainability would be determined on the basis of various measures of vulnerability, including the burden of external debt on the government budget, the diversity of the country's export base, its reserve coverage, its resource balance and other relevant factors;

(iv) In April 1997, the Executive Boards of IMF and the World Bank approved the introduction of an additional sustainability criterion, captured by a ratio of the present value of debt to fiscal revenue of 280 per cent, provided that two other criteria are met: an export-to-GDP ratio of at least 40 per cent and a minimum threshold ratio of fiscal revenue to GDP of 20 per cent.

---

[1] Exceptionally, the second stage could be shortened for countries that have demonstrated a record of sustained strong performance.

Box 3

DEBT SUSTAINABILITY CONCEPTS

The implementation of the HIPC Initiative rests on the debt sustainability analysis of debtor countries. The sustainability criteria are based on concepts of debt overhang[1] and foreign exchange constraint. The debt overhang is captured by the ratio of the present value of debt to exports, while the foreign exchange constraint is reflected in the debt service to exports ratio. More recently, a fiscal constraint, measured by the ratio of the present value of debt to fiscal revenue, is also being taken into account.

In the HIPC Initiative, the calculation of the present value of debt is a determining factor in fixing the amount of debt relief granted. The present value of debt is obtained by taking all future debt service obligations (including interest payments at the original rate of the loan and amortization payments) until full repayment of the debt, and dividing them by a factor based on a given discount rate. If the discount rate is equal to the original interest rate of the loan, the present value will be equal to the face value of debt. If the discount rate used is higher than the original interest rate of the loan, the present value will be lower. The present value can be used to measure the grant element of a concessional loan - i.e. a loan with a rate of interest below the prevailing market rate. In that case, the debt service flow is calculated at the concessional rate but is discounted at the higher market rate. The present value of the debt is lower than its face value, and the difference is the grant element.

However, the concept is less useful when calculating the debt burden of debtor countries. Indeed, the present value of debt, if obtained by discounting the flow of debt service by the market rate of interest prevailing in creditor countries, does not truly reflect the debt servicing burden of debtor countries[2]. The prevailing market rate of interest has no bearing on the amount of actual debt service because the loans made to HIPCs invariably carried concessional interest rates. Applying a discount rate which is higher than the original rate on a loan gives a present value which is lower than the face value of the loan, thus understating the true burden of debt for debtor countries.

It is, therefore, necessary to reconcile the concepts of debt overhang and cashflow constraints to determine a level of debt which debtor countries will be able to service. One possibility would be to use the debt stock as a target for reduction, instead of the present value. The stock of debt would be reduced to a level which would produce a stream of future debt service payments commensurate with the cashflow constraints. For the purpose of burden sharing, the present value calculations would then be used to make debt service reductions equivalent to the desired reduction of the stock of debt, when some creditors provide relief through debt stock reduction while others do it through interest rate reduction. In this case, the flow of debt service should be calculated at the new interest rate, i.e. after relief, while the discount rate should be the original, higher, interest rate of the loan. The difference between the face value and the present value of the debt will give the right measure of the relief provided.

A similar problem appears, in the framework of the HIPC Initiative, in connection with the fiscal constraint, which is measured by the ratio of the present value of debt to fiscal revenue. This ratio might not, however, accurately reflect the fiscal constraint, which is more in the nature of a cashflow constraint. In the same way as the foreign exchange constraint is measured by the ratio of debt service to exports, the fiscal constraint would be more appropriately measured by the ratio of debt service to government revenue (excluding grants). There is, therefore, a justification for using threshold values of these two debt-service ratios to reflect the capacity of debtor countries to service their debt through export earnings and fiscal revenue.

---

[1]   The literature on the debt overhang provides evidence of the negative effect of a large amount of debt on economic growth. A high level of debt creates uncertainty about the country's capacity to service its debt and discourages private (domestic and foreign) investment. Furthermore, high debt service is perceived by investors as a form of "tax" on the future income of the country, thus dissuading new investment. A high level of debt can also be an obstacle to economic reforms and high debt service may crowd out productive expenditures (public and private). The debt overhang argument, therefore, supports explicit debt reduction, as opposed to continuous debt reschedulings.

[2]   See *TDR 1995*, p.36, for a critique of the present value concept.

Notes

1   BIS, *International Banking and Financial Market Developments*, August 1996, p. 17.

2   World Bank, *Global Development Finance 1997*, Vol.1: *Analysis and Summary Tables* (Washington, D.C.: The World Bank, 1997), p. 104. ("East Asia" in that volume comprises Cambodia, China, Fiji, Indonesia, Lao People's Democratic Republic, Malaysia, Mongolia, Myanmar, Papua New Guinea, Philippines, Solomon Islands, Thailand, Tonga, Vanuatu, Viet Nam, Samoa, Kiribati and Democratic People's Republic of Korea.)

3   G. Evans, "Asian investors: growing appetite", *Euromoney*, Feb. 1997.

4   *Latin American Economy and Business*, April 1997, p.2. (According to these estimates, Argentina accounted for 48 per cent of these investments, Peru for 14 per cent, and Colombia for 8 per cent.)

5   BIS, *International Banking and Financial Market Developments*, Feb. 1997, pp. 21-22.

6   China, India, Indonesia, Republic of Korea, Malaysia, Philippines, Taiwan Province of China and Thailand (*ibid.*, May 1997, table 5A).

7   *Ibid.*, table 10A. The Latin American countries are Argentina, Brazil, Chile, Colombia and Mexico.

8   Debt instruments of less than investment grade are not permitted to be held by certain institutional investors under the regulatory regimes of some countries.

9   Country risk refers to the risk of failure to meet the obligations on a loan for reasons other than the solvency of the borrowing entity (which is covered by credit risk). In particular, it includes risk due to the actions of the government of the country of the borrowing entity (such as the imposition of foreign exchange controls which impede or delay the meeting of these obligations) or to the legal regime.

10   Standard and Poor's new approach was also extended to a Panamanian bank which received a rating higher than that of the country's sovereign entities *(International Insider*, 28 April 1997).

11   For typical pre-1990 policies in developing countries towards capital inflows see *TDR 1994*, Part Two, annex to chap. II, sect. B.2.

12   International investors have also become large buyers and sellers of the domestically issued short- and long-term debt instruments of some developing countries.

13   Two of the countries included in table 14 (Venezuela and Poland) are not covered by table 13. For the first total external financing was a small negative figure (-$0.1 billion), and for the second the total was dwarfed by a large contraction in banks' exposure partly due to a debt restructuring agreed with its creditors.

14   See D.M. Sobol, "Central and Eastern Europe: financial markers and private capital flows", *Federal Reserve Bank of New York Research Paper* No. 9629. FDI associated with privatization has generally been a smaller share of total FDI in Asia and Latin America, figures for which during the period 1991-1994 can be found in UNCTAD, *World Investment Report 1996* (United Nations publication, Sales No. E.96.II.A.14), table I.3.

15   BIS, *International Banking and Financial Market Developments*, May 1997, table 5A.

16   Net issues of international debt securities by East and South-East Asian countries fell from $14.3 billion in the last quarter of 1996 to $6.3 billion in the first quarter of 1997, while net issues by Latin American countries rose from $9.5 billion to $10.3 billion (*ibid.*, table 10A.)

17   Figures for net FDI in China are generally considered inflated by flows which are misreported, often thanks to opportunities available to investors owing to the close integration of its economy with that of Hong Kong (which is the source of more than 50 per cent of the country's FDI). Thus, for example, some of the FDI is believed to consist of funds sent out of the country and then reinvested in ways that take advantage of preferences available only to certain enterprises which are recipients of foreign investment. Moreover, Chinese enterprises' foreign borrowing is apparently sometimes repackaged as FDI in order to circumvent controls on their accumulation of foreign debt. See J.P. Morgan, *Emerging Markets Data Watch*, 31 Jan. 1997, p. 3.

18   Alternative recent estimates of net FDI in 1996 for some of the countries covered in table 14 are preliminary and show considerable variation. For example, estimates for Argentina vary between $2 billion and $3.2 billion, for Brazil between $5.5 billion and $10.5 billion, and for Chile between $6.4 billion and $7.6 billion.

19   There was an increase from 1995 to 1996 in the share of total Latin American issues of international debt securities accounted for by private-sector entities (financial and non-financial enterprises) as opposed to public-sector ones (governments and state

agencies) from a little over 25 per cent to almost 40 per cent. This increase was due mainly to private-sector issuers in Brazil and Chile (BIS, _op. cit._, tables 10A, 10B, 10C, 10D, and 14).

20   _Ibid._, tables 5A, 5B, 10A, and 10B.

21   See J.P. Morgan, _Emerging Markets Data Watch_, 23 August 1996, p. 8, and K. Warn, "Argentina to expand $6 bn loan facility", _Financial Times_, 21 May 1997.

22   J.P. Morgan, _Emerging Markets Data Watch_, 2 Aug. 1996, p. 14.

23   _Ibid._, 24 January 1997, p. 19.

24   _Ibid._, 1 Nov. 1996, p. 10; 25 April 1997, pp. 9-10; and 2 May 1997, p. 7.

25   J. Wheatley, "Brazil lifts hedge restrictions", _Financial Times_, 26 May 1997, and "Deregulation delights BM&F", _ibid._, 4 June 1997.

26   _Latin American Economy and Business_, April 1997, p. 2.

27   See _TDR 1996_, Part One, chap. II, sect. B.2.

28   J.P. Morgan, _Emerging Markets Data Watch_, 30 May 1997, p. 33.

29   For example, the raising of the ceiling on foreign equity investment in the shares of individual firms to 23 per cent (part of the planned liberalization of the country's capital account associated with its OECD accession) was implemented as of 1 May 1997 and is to be followed by an additional accelerated raising of the ceiling to 25 per cent in the second half of the year. The increase of 1 May was accompanied by an opening to foreign investors of the market for non-guaranteed convertible bonds and a relaxation of the limits on borrowing abroad for state banks.

30   China's central bank, too, engages in a policy of the partial sterilization of the expansion of the money supply due to its purchases of the foreign exchange associated with capital inflows through reductions in its loans to commercial banks.

31   Finance companies are the most important non-bank financial institutions in Thailand, accounting for rather less than 20 per cent of the total assets of such institutions in the early 1990s. See United States Department of the Treasury, _National Treatment Study 1994_ (Washington, D.C., 1994), p. 488.

32   Concerning the high exposure of Thai finance companies to the property sector see T. Bardacke, "Thai property crisis leaves banks exposed", _Financial Times_, 7 Feb. 1997; and concerning the capital of such companies see J.P. Morgan, _Emerging Markets Data Watch_, 7 March 1997, p. 1.

33   For example, at the end of 1996 non-performing loans as a proportion of total loans amounted to between 4.3 and 8 per cent for five of Thailand's largest banks and to 7.7 per cent for all banks (_ibid._, 28 Feb. 1997, p. 24).

34   By the beginning of 1997, according to the Bank of Thailand, the country's short-term external debt was falling and amounted to only 44 per cent of total external debt, in comparison to 50 per cent at the beginning of the previous year (_ibid._, 31 Jan. 1997,

p. 22). On estimates indicating a narrowing of the trade deficit in the first quarter of 1997 see the same source, 23 May 1997, p.26.

35   Much of this external financing was in the form of interbank borrowing from Thailand's offshore banking sector (the Bangkok International Banking Facility).

36   Liabilities to non-residents as a proportion of total domestic credit of the Thai banking system are estimated at more than 45 per cent in early 1997 (_ibid._, 25 April 1995, p. 1).

37   Concerning the longer-term origins of the property boom in selected East and South-East countries, which is associated with major cities' mutually competitive objectives to become commercial or financial centres and involve luxury and middle-class housing as well as offices, see E. Paisley, "Asia's property perils", _Institutional Investor_, Jan. 1996.

38   Concerning support for the baht by central banks of other East and South-East Asian countries see T. Bardacke, "Singapore joins Thailand in the defence of the baht", _Financial Times_, 15 May 1997, and P. Montagnon and J. Ridding, "Asian central banks may bolster links", _ibid._, 26 May 1997.

39   The export credits in table 12 include not only the private lending that carries insurance or guarantees from an export credit agency (ECA.), which is discussed in the present section, but also direct lending by OECD Governments, the determinants of which are not discussed here. It is customary to define credits carrying "official" insurance or guarantees as "private export credits". "Official" insurance in this context is in some cases provided by privately owned institutions with officially recognized mandates.

40   The difference which official insurance cover can make to the interest costs of international loans can be exemplified by the Birecik hydroelectric dam project in Turkey initiated in 1995. Of two loans used to finance the project, the one for DM 400 million without official guarantees carried a rate of interest of 230 basis points over LIBOR, while the second, for DM 1.4 billion, which was supported by guarantees from the Austrian, Belgian, French and German ECAs, carried a rate of interest of only 100 basis points over LIBOR. See World Bank, _Global Development Finance 1997_, Vol. 1 (Washington, D.C.: The World Bank, 1997), p. 24. (In comparison of the net cost to the borrower of the two loans account would need to be taken not only of the rates of interest but also of the charges associated with the guarantees.)

41   The ECAs upon which the figures in table 20 are based are the Compagnie Française d'Assurance pour le Commerce Extérieur (COFACE) of France, Hermes of Germany, the Export Development Corporation (EDC) of Canada, the Compañia Española de Seguros de Crédito a la Exportación (CESCE) of Spain, ECGD, the Sezione Speciale per l'Assicurazione del Credito all'Esportazione (SACE) of Italy, the Office National du Ducroire

(OND) of Belgium, EXIM, the Export-Import Insurance Division of the Ministry of International Trade and Industry of Japan, and Exportkreditnämmden (EKN) of Sweden. Figures are not available for the premiums charged by each of these ECAs to all the countries in the table. See R. Kelsey, "Getting better terms from EKN", *Project and Trade Finance*, Oct. 1996.

42   The concept, "instance", is explained in note c to table 18.

43   The same sources used for tables 18 and 19 indicate no change in such terms during the year.

44   The country coverage for the four regions for which preferred payments terms are given in *International Trade Finance* is smaller than that in the Payments and Credit Surveys in *Project and Trade Finance* on which tables 18 and 19 are based.

45   The 21 countries are Australia, Austria, Belgium, Canada, Denmark, Finland, France, Germany, Iceland, Ireland, Italy, Japan, Luxembourg, Netherlands, New Zealand, Portugal, Spain, Sweden, Switzerland, United Kingdom, United States.

46   The various stages involved in the negotiation of an agreement to reduce debt and debt-service obligations to commercial banks are described in *TDR 1995*, Part One, ch. II, note 46.

47   The London Club is the forum in which commercial banks renegotiate external debt with debtor countries.

48   Under the IDA Debt Reduction Facility (established in 1989) money is made available to low-income countries for reduction of their external debt in the form of obligations to commercial banks and suppliers through buybacks at large discounts on face value. The financing is contingent on programmes acceptable to IDA for medium-term adjustment and the management of external debt. Other donors may provide cofinancing in the form of grants in support of individual debt-reduction operations under the Facility.

49   See World Bank: *Global Development Finance 1997*, Vol. 1, Appendix 2 "External debt trends in 1995".

50   The UNCTAD secretariat has repeatedly highlighted the heavy burden represented by the multilateral debt and debt owed to non-OECD creditors of the low-income countries, notably in *TDR 1993, TDR 1995* and *TDR 1996*.

51   At an exchange rate of $1.44 per SDR at the end of 1996, this amounted to $258 million.

52   The stock of debt of Bolivia, Burkina Faso, Côte d'Ivoire and Uganda at the end of 1995 amounted respectively to $5.3 billion, $1.3 billion, $19 billion and $3.6 billion (see World Bank, *Global Development Finance 1997*), Vol. 1.

53   See, *TDR 1995*, p.45 and *TDR 1996*, p.54 on the proposal to sell a portion of IMF gold reserves.

Sources for table 14
Current account balance and GDP: 1994-1995 were taken from IMF, *International Financial Statistics* and 1996-1997 were taken from J.P. Morgan, *Emerging Markets: Economic Indicators*, except for Malaysia in 1995, where the item was taken from the latter source. **Net direct investment:** 1994-1995 were taken from IMF, *International Financial Statistics* and 1996 was taken from World Bank, *Global Development Finance, 1997*, except for Hungary in 1995 and Mexico in 1996, where the item was taken from World Bank, *Global Development Finance, 1997*, for Republic of Korea and Czech Republic in 1996, and Mexico in 1997, where the item was taken from J.P. Morgan, *Emerging Markets Data Watch*, and for Colombia, Peru and Venezuela in 1996, where the item was taken from ECLAC, *Preliminary Overview of the Latin American and Caribbean Economy 1996*. **Portfolio investment:** 1994-1995 were taken from IMF, *International Financial Statistics*; Argentina, Brazil, Czech Republic and Mexico in 1996 and Mexico in 1997 were estimated from J.P. Morgan, *Emerging Markets Data Watch* and BIS, *International Banking and Financial Market Developments*, and Chile and Peru in 1996 were estimated from ECLAC, *Preliminary Overview of the Latin American and Caribbean Economy* and BIS, *International Banking and Financial Market Developments*; **Short-term debt:** all data were from Union Bank of Switzerland (UBS). **Import cover:** imports for 1994-1995 were taken from IMF, *International Financial Statistics,* for 1996 were made available by UBS, and for 1997 were taken from J.P. Morgan, *Emerging Markets Data Watch*, except for Malaysia in 1995, for which the item was made available by UBS, and for Poland and Argentina in 1996, where it was taken from IMF, *International Financial Statistics;* reserves for 1994-1996 were taken from IMF, *International Financial Statistics* and for 1997 were taken from J.P. Morgan, *Emerging Markets: Economic Indicators*, except for China, Malaysia and Poland in 1996, where the item was also taken from the latter source. **Short-term debt plus current-account balance as per cent of reserves:** based on the data in sources cited above. **Interbank debt as per cent of total bank debt:** both interbank debt and total bank debt for 1994-1996 were taken from BIS, *International Banking and Financial Market Developments*.

ISSUES INVOLVED IN TRADE DISPUTES THAT HAVE ARISEN CONCERNING THE NATIONAL TREATMENT PROVISION OF THE WTO AGREEMENT

Globalization and liberalization are modifying the relative impact of trade measures. With the entry into force on 1 January 1995 of the Marrakesh Agreement Establishing the World Trade Organization (WTO), some are losing their importance as trade barriers and as instruments of trade policy. The Agreement on Agriculture and the Agreement on Safeguards, for example, make it virtually impossible to resort to quantitative restrictions and voluntary export restraints, in both agriculture and industry. On the other hand, the Agreement on Agriculture gives prominence to the tariff quota[1] as a liberalizing measure, but this, as discussed below, has given rise to a number of disputes concerning implementation. The liberalization of border measures and increased penetration of markets by investors have also served to focus attention on internal measures designed to protect domestic production, explaining to some extent the preoccupation of the WTO dispute settlement mechanism with issues relating to the national treatment principle.[2]

The strengthening of the GATT dispute settlement mechanism is one of the major achievements of the Uruguay Round.[3] Since the WTO Multilateral Trade Agreements (MTAs) entered into force on 1 January 1995, the number of disputes referred to the new dispute settlement mechanism has increased dramatically compared to the situation under the former GATT. As of 2 July 1997, the WTO Dispute Settlement Body had received 88 requests for consultations, involving 63 separate matters. Seven of the panels constituted have completed their work, and in five cases both the Panel Report and the report of the Appellate Body have been adopted. In almost half

of these disputes, the question of conformity with the national treatment provisions of GATT article III has been at issue.

Article III aims at ensuring that the benefits of tariff concessions are not frustrated by measures of internal taxation and regulation which could be applied in a discriminatory fashion against imported products. Its disciplines include the following broad elements: (i) the imported product must not be subject to internal taxes or other internal charges in excess of those applied to "like domestic products"; (ii) the imported product must be accorded treatment no less favourable than that accorded to like domestic products in respect of rules and requirements affecting the sale, purchase, transportation, distribution or use of the product; (iii) regulations relating to the mixture, processing or use of products may not specify that a certain amount or proportion must come from domestic sources; and (iv) internal taxes or other internal charges or internal quantitative regulations may not be applied in a manner so as to afford protection to domestic production. While elements (i), (ii) and (iii) relate to the rate of taxes, regulations and the compulsory utilization of domestic products, respectively, element (iv) is about "the manner of application" of taxes, regulations, etc. Its purport is that even if the taxes or charges are applied at the same rate on the imported and like domestic products, the manner of application should not be such as to afford protection to domestic production. Thus, both *de jure*, and *de facto* discrimination is prohibited. Similarly, internal quantitative regulations, even other than those mentioned above, cannot be applied in a manner which affords protection to domestic production either of a particular product or of directly competitive or substitutable products.

The observation that as tariff barriers to trade are reduced or eliminated, non-tariff measures become of greater importance has been repeated so often it has almost become a cliché. However, it is evident that globalization of production and trade liberalization have led to greater attention being paid to the effects of internal measures that discriminate against imports. Thus, it is no accident that the large number of complaints brought before the WTO Dispute Settlement Body have included allegations of contravention of the national treatment provision of GATT article III mainly through: (a) discriminatory internal taxes; (b) local content requirements; (c) allocation of tariff quotas among supplying countries; (d) measures relating to technical standards and the environment; (e) measures aiming at the preservation of cultural identity; (f) the limitation of access to distribution channels.

A. Discriminatory internal taxes

Some disputes have involved complaints over certain traditional forms of discrimination For example, in many countries domestic production of alcoholic beverages has benefited from a variety of protective measures, including fiscal privileges (such as taxes) and state trading. In the so-called "beer war" between the United States and Canada during 1990-1991, each country had filed a case against the other with respect to domestic (or internal) measures affecting the sales of certain imported alcoholic beverages in the other's market. The United States challenged Canada's monopoly of import and distribution by provincial liquor boards and restrictions on the size of the package in which imported beers could be sold. In the retaliatory complaint filed by Canada, the United States measures (both state and federal) on taxation and sale of alcoholic beverages were claimed to discriminate against imports.[4]

The Uruguay Round succeeded in achieving considerable trade liberalization in this sector, and exposed internal barriers that permitted the continuation of protection. For example, Japanese taxes on alcoholic beverages were recently challenged by the European Communities (EC), Canada and the United States on the alleged grounds that they discriminated against imports of vodka, whisky, cognac and white spirits by imposing substantially lower taxes on the domestic product *shochu*. They argued that *shochu* and the imported products were "like products".

The definition of the term "like product" has been the subject of dispute on many occasions. The general practice has been to interpret it on a case-by-case basis. But certain essential features have often been recognized as relevant in this context, e.g. the end-use of the product in a given market, the tastes and habits of consumers, and the properties, nature and quality of the product. Both the WTO Panel, in July 1996, and the Appellate Body, in October 1996, concluded that *shochu* and vodka were like products and that Japan, by taxing imported products in excess of like domestic products, was in violation of GATT article III:2, first sentence.

As noted above, the requirement of "no less favourable treatment" applies not only to the rate of a tax but also to the manner in which it is applied; and "domestic production" refers not only to like products but also to directly competitive or substitutable ones. What is a directly competitive or substitutable product has been the subject of intense consideration. Here again the practice has been to proceed case by case. For example, in the dispute on alcoholic beverages, it was concluded that *shochu* and other distilled spirits and liqueurs listed in HS tariff heading 2208, except for vodka, were "directly competitive or substitutable products", and that Japan, in the application of the Liquor Tax Law, did not tax imported and directly competitive or substitutable domestic products in the same way and afforded protection to domestic production in violation of article III:2, second sentence. It was the view of both the Panel and the Appellate Body that the term "directly competitive or substitutable product", in accordance with its ordinary meaning, should be interpreted more broadly than the term "like product".[5] The European Communities and the United States are similarly contesting taxes on alcoholic beverages by the Republic of Korea, and a similar case is being brought by several countries against Chile.

B. Local content requirements

The Agreement on Trade-Related Investment Measures (TRIMs), drawing upon earlier GATT panel decisions, prohibits investment measures which contravene GATT article III, notably local content requirements. It in effect codifies the finding in the complaint brought by the United States in 1984 against Canada's administration of the local content provisions of the Foreign Investment Review Act (FIRA).[6] The TRIMs Agreement has encouraged WTO members to challenge measures such as local content requirements which are prevalent in certain sectors, notably the automotive sector.

For example, complaints have recently been made by Japan, EC and the United States against Indonesia concerning its "National Car Programme". Under that programme, the Government designated "PT Timor Putra National" as the only "national car" manufacturing company eligible for exemption from customs duties and luxury taxes on condition that it achieved specified minimum local content ratios (20 per cent by the end of the first year of production, 40 per cent by the end of the second year and 60 per cent by the end of third year). Furthermore, the Government permits complete vehicles produced abroad by the Korean Kia Motors Corporation to be imported tariff-free as "national" cars so long as Indonesian workers participate in the foreign production of the vehicle and Korean Kia Motors Corporation counter-purchases from Indonesia parts worth 25 per cent of the value of the vehicles to be imported thereunder.

Complaints have also been filed by Japan, EC and the United States against Brazil concerning certain measures affecting trade and investment in the automotive sector. These measures require that companies must maintain a government-established ratio of net exports (by value) of certain goods, such as complete vehicles, to imported auto parts receiving duty preferences. They consider that the local content requirements in Brazil's automobile investment incentive measures constitute a prohibited TRIM, inconsistent with GATT article III:4.

C. Allocation of tariff quotas

Another area where it is perceived that breaches of the national treatment principle are being used to frustrate the liberalization achieved in the Uruguay Round is in the administration of the tariff quota system under the Agreement on Agriculture. For example, in the complaint filed by the United States against the Philippines concerning the latter's tariff quotas for pork and poultry, the United States considered that the implementation of these tariff quotas, in particular the delays in permitting access to these quantities and the licensing system used, appeared to be inconsistent with the relevant WTO provisions, including those under GATT article III. In the case of complaints by Ecuador, Guatemala, Honduras, Mexico and the United States against the European Communities in relation to the importation, sale and distribution of bananas, the WTO Panel found that the allocation to Category B[7] operators of 30 per cent of the licences allowing the importation of third-country and non-traditional ACP bananas at in-quota tariff rates was inconsistent with the requirements of GATT article III:4. The ruling was based on the conclusion that the design, architecture and structure of the EC measure indicated that this measure was applied so as to afford protection to EC producers.[8] Despite the fact that its exports are negligible, the United States took a leading role to protect the interests of United States banana corporations operating in Central America. The Panel felt that under the Understanding on Rules and Procedures Governing the Settlement of Deputes, the United States had a right to advance the claims it had raised, even if it did not have actual trade or a potential export interest, since its internal market for bananas could be affected by the EC regime and by that regime's effect on world supplies and prices. The case also set a precedent for interpreting the legal meaning of the provisions in the General Agreement on Trade in Services (GATS) and its Schedule of Commitments, in particular with respect to those related to national treatment as provided for in article XVII of that Agreement.[9]

D. Technical standards

Many of the measures for which conformity with GATT article III is being challenged relate to those imposed for social and other non-economic reasons. The Agreement on Technical Barriers to Trade (TBT) was originally negotiated during the Uruguay Round with a view to ensuring that standards and technical regulations did not contravene the national treatment principle. It was recognized that the application of such standards and technical regulations required that foreign products meet domestic standards and be subject to conformity assessment procedures (e.g. testing) but that neither the technical regulations nor the related procedures should be applied so as to result in unnecessary restriction of trade. The Agreement on the Application of Sanitary and Phytosanitary Measures (SPS) applies the national treatment principle to the extent possible in the application of measures intended to protect human, animal and plant life and health.

The increased scope and application of measures aimed at environmental protection has also increased the possibilities of circumventing the national treatment principle by imposing more stringent conditions for foreign products. The first case resolved in the WTO dealt with a challenge by Venezuela and Brazil to environmental protection regulations in the United States relating to standards for gasoline, which they claimed allowed greater flexibility to domestic than to foreign refiners in conforming to special regulations for reformulated gasoline in major urban centres. The complaining countries were successful in demonstrating that the United States "Gasoline Rule" imposed more stringent criteria for foreign refiners. They argued that, by imposing less favourable standards for imported gasoline from certain countries than those applied to domestic products, the United States violated several provisions of the MTAs, including GATT article III.[10] They also claimed that the Gasoline Rule had nullified and impaired benefits under the non-violation provision of GATT article XXIII:1(b). The European Communities and Norway made submissions to the Panel as interested third parties, expressing concern that the gasoline rule could justify the fears of many countries about the use of purported environmental measures as disguised restrictions on international trade. Venezuela stressed that it was not seeking to avoid legitimate regulations for environmental protection, but merely wanted its gasoline to be subject to the same rules as gasoline produced in the United States.

Under GATT article III.4, the Panel found that imported and domestic gasoline were like products and that under the regulation imported gasoline was effectively prevented from benefiting from sales conditions as favourable as those afforded to domestic gasoline. It rejected the United States argument that the requirements of article III:4 were met because imported gasoline was treated similarly to gasoline from similarly situated domestic parties. Such an interpretation, it said, would be contrary to the ordinary meaning of article III:4, and would mean that imported and domestic goods could no longer be treated on the objective basis of their likeness as products, but rather on the basis of a "highly subjective and variable treatment" according to extraneous factors. It would create great instability and uncertainty in the conditions of competition as between domestic and imported goods in a manner fundamentally inconsistent with the object and purposes of GATT article III. In its concluding remarks the Panel noted that it was not its task to examine generally the desirability or necessity of the environmental objectives of the United States' Clean Air Act or the Gasoline Rule; WTO members were free to set their own environmental objectives, but were bound to implement those objectives through measures consistent with the provisions of GATT 1994, notably on the relative treatment of domestic and imported products.

One of the notable characteristics of such disputes is the high degree of technical competence required to prepare evidence in support of a complaint. The cases under the Agreement on the Application of Sanitary and Phytosanitary Measures mentioned above have to be based on "scientific evidence" (e.g. that beef from hormone-fed cattle endangers human health); under the Agreement on Technical Barriers to Trade there is provision to call upon technical expert groups to assist panels in disputes. However, the need for such technical expertise is not confined to interpretations of these Agreements. For example, in order to successfully challenge the decision of the French Government to restrict the use of the term "coquille Saint-Jacques", Canada, Peru and Chile were required to demonstrate that molluscs harvested in the Pacific Ocean were in fact "like products". The complainants claimed that the French decision would reduce competitiveness of their exports of scallops in the French market as they would no longer be able to be sold as "coquilles Saint-Jacques" although there was no difference between their scallops and French scallops in terms of colour, size, texture, appearance and use.

E. Preservation of cultural identity

Other measures imposed for health, environmental, cultural and social reasons are currently being challenged. A dispute brought by the United States against Canada involves measures by the latter, motivated by considerations of cultural identity, imposing an 80 per cent tax on revenue from advertisements placed in the Canadian editions of periodicals sold both in Canada and abroad (the so-called "split-run" periodicals). The United States also complained about Canada's disallowing an income tax deduction to Canadian firms which advertise in "split-run" periodicals and applying favourable postage rates to its own periodicals

F. Distribution channels and related provisions of the General Agreement on Trade in Services

In the "Kodak/Fuji" case currently before the Dispute Settlement Body, the United States is challenging a series of Japanese laws, regulations, requirements and measures which it considers effectively exclude the firm Eastman Kodak from the Japanese market for consumer photographic film and photographic paper. According to the United States, these Japanese measures are "liberalization countermeasures"; they include measures to restructure the distribution system for photographic products, as well as the Premiums Law and the Large Stores Law and related measures aimed at preventing Kodak and other foreign firms from obtaining adequate access to the Japanese film distribution network and retail outlets.[11] The United States considers that these measures by Japan, including the measure to provide protection to the domestic production of consumer photographic film and paper, nullify or impair its benefits and violate GATT provisions within the meaning of GATT article III:1. It claims that they also conflict with GATT article III:4 since they affect the conditions of competition for the distribution, offering for sale and internal sale of consumer photographic film and paper in a manner which accords less favourable treatment to imported film and paper than to comparable products of national origin. The United States has also alleged that these measures nullify or impair its benefits (a "non-violation" claim) in as much as the Japanese Government's ineffective enforcement of its competition law was not foreseen when the concessions were negotiated on this product.

The United States has also filed a separate case under the GATS concerning Japan's measures affecting distribution services (not limited to the photographic film and paper sector referred to above) through the operation of the Large Stores Law, which regulates the floor space, business hours and holidays of supermarkets and department stores. In its view, the Large Stores Law has the effect of limiting the establishment, expansion and business operations of large stores in Japan by foreign investors and exporters. It further argues that by impeding the business operations of large stores, the Law reduces productivity in merchandise retailing, raises costs, discourages new domestic capital investment and ultimately limits the selection and quality of goods and services.

One of the driving forces of globalization has been the recognition by enterprises of the importance of obtaining access to domestic distribution systems, or of setting up their own distribution systems in the importing country. The major developed countries pressed for commitments in GATS for market access and national treatment in this sector. During the Uruguay Round, 35 countries made commitments related to distribution services, in particular with respect to wholesale and retail trade. It should be noted that while GATT article III deals only with goods, GATS article XVII contains a national treatment provision for service suppliers. National treatment, however, is not an obligation, as it is for trade in goods, but a concession that can be extended on a sectoral or subsectoral basis. In the Uruguay Round, countries were not prepared to accept that any enterprise or natural person which gained access to the domestic market would have the automatic right to engage in all activities on the same basis as domestic suppliers. The GATS differs from the GATT in the sense that market access and national treatment are both seen as negotiable. Accordingly, market access for services does not automatically imply national treatment, which is also subject to negotiation. Some countries considered that the two concepts should be merged into a single discipline. Such an approach was subsequently adopted for the basic NAFTA obligation on investment, in which the national treatment provision is broadened to subsume the market access concept, i.e. including the right of establishment. The national treatment provision in the draft OECD Multilateral Agreement on Investment virtually reproduces the equivalent NAFTA text.

* * * * *

With the significant reduction of tariffs and liberalization of non-tariff measures at the border, the discriminatory application of domestic taxes and regulations to protect national production, often reflecting protectionist pressures from domestic producers, has become more prominent as a barrier to trade. National treatment, as defined by GATT article III, alongside MFN treatment, is one of the central principles of the multilateral trading system. The main purpose of the national treatment rule is to eliminate or reduce "hidden"

domestic barriers to trade and to increase transparency and predictability. In other words, GATT article III is designed to impede the adoption of policies and measures that have domestic protection as their purpose. As a result of the Uruguay Round, the idea of national treatment has been extended from trade in goods to trade in other areas, such as services, though in a limited manner. In this context, the intention to multilateralize the rules and disciplines relating to government procurement practices can be viewed as another step towards strengthening the application of the national treatment rule. However, with increasing interactions between trade, investment and competition policies, an analysis is often drawn between the elimination and/or reduction of "hidden" domestic barriers to trade and the peeling away of the layers of an onion. As formal import restrictions have been removed, "embedded" barriers have come to light, such as domestic regulatory measures and inter-firm trading relationships. Thus, as the process of trade liberalization gathers momentum, the application and enforcement of competition policy at the national level assumes greater importance. ■

Notes

1 Under a tariff quota a fixed quantity of a given product may be imported at a special tariff rate; for quantities in excess of the quota the general, higher, tariff rate is applied.

2 Under this principle, WTO members are required to accord treatment to imported products no less favourable than that accorded to like domestic products (article III of GATT 1994).

3 See UNCTAD, *The Outcome of the Uruguay Round: An Initial Assessment. Supporting Papers to the Trade and Development Report, 1994* (United Nations publication, Sales No. E.94.II.D.28), chap. IX.

4 See GATT documents DS17/R and DS23/R reproduced in GATT, *Basic Instruments and Selected Documents, Supplement No. 39* (Geneva, Dec. 1993).

5 See the reports of the Panel and the Appellate Body in WTO document series WT/DS8, WT/DS10 and WT/DS11.

6 Under the Canadian FIRA, foreign investors are required to give preference to purchase of Canadian goods over imported goods and to meet certain export performance requirements. The GATT panel found that Canadian requirements were inconsistent with GATT article III:4, which stipulates that imported products shall be accorded treatment no less favourable than that accorded to like products of national origin in respect of requirements affecting their internal sale, purchase, transportation, distribution or use.

7 Under the EC's operator category rules set out in article 19 of Council Regulation (EEC) 404/93 (as amended), import licences are distributed among three categories of operators, based on quantities marketed during the latest three-year period for which data are available. Category A refers to operators that have marketed third-country and/or non-traditional ACP bananas, who are given a 66.5 per cent allocation of import licences allowing imports at in-quota rates. Category B refers to operators that have marketed EC and/or traditional ACP bananas, given a 30 per cent quota allocation. Category C refers to operators who started marketing bananas other than EC and/or traditional ACP bananas in 1992 or thereafter ("newcomer category"), given a 3.5 per cent allocation.

8 See also the Report of the Appellate Body (WTO document WT/DS8/AB/R), p. 29.

9 See WTO documents in the series WT/DS27/R/... of 22 May 1997.

10 See the reports of the Panel and the Appellate Body in WTO document WT/DS2/9, 20 May 1996. Venezuela did not make any claim based on article 12 of the TBT Agreement (Special and Differential Treatment of Developing Country Members), rejecting the notion that it was seeking privileges for its own gasoline. Brazil stated that it, too, was not asking for a ruling under article 12, but wished to point out that the discriminatory treatment affecting its gasoline was particularly objectionable in the light of the provisions of that article.

11 See United States Trade Representative (USTR), *1997 National Trade Estimate Report on Foreign Trade Barriers* (Washington, D.C.), pp. 225-227.

Part Two

GLOBALIZATION, DISTRIBUTION AND GROWTH

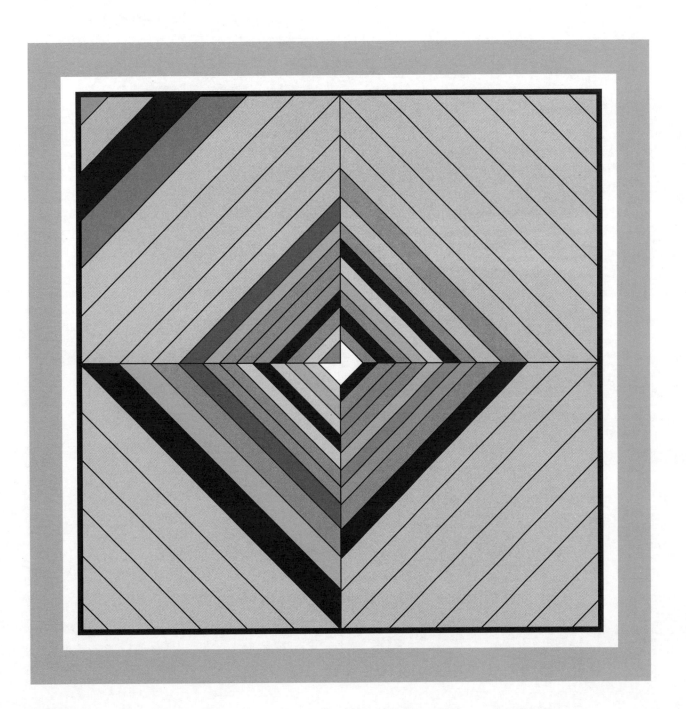

Chapter I

THE ISSUES AT STAKE

Since the late 1970s there has been a fundamental change in economic policy, first in the industrial countries, and then in the developing countries. In the latter this change has affected not only macroeconomic policy, but also development strategy. Emphasis has increasingly been placed on a minimal role for the State, greater reliance on private initiative and market forces, and increased openness and greater integration into the world economy. It was thought that such a reorientation of policy was needed not only to attain a stable macroeconomic environment, but also to accelerate growth and more generally to raise living standards. Price distortions due to government interventions and resistance to opening up were assumed to be responsible for slow growth, unequal income distribution and widespread poverty. Growth based on global market forces, it was thought, would thus be more rapid and widely shared, allowing developing countries to catch up with the industrial countries, and the poor with the rich.

The world economy is in many respects more closely integrated today than at any time in history. However, integration has not proceeded at a uniform pace on all fronts. Among the asymmetries of globalization is the fact that liberalization of the world economy has proceeded so far in a lopsided way. For example, trade liberalization has proceeded more slowly in products where developing countries are more competitive. By contrast, many restrictions have been removed on the freedom of movement of capital, where industrialized countries have a comparative advantage. Likewise, unskilled labour where the South has comparative advantage, has far fewer employment options than labour embodying capital (i.e. skilled labour).

The outcome of unleashing market forces in combination with asymmetries in liberalization raises a number of concerns. There are a number of trends suggesting that in many respects national economies are polarizing rather than growing closer together. Marginalization and poverty are perhaps the most evident feature, but the tendency towards polarization affects more deeply the socio-economic fabric:

- Taken as a whole, the world economy is growing too slowly to generate sufficient employment with adequate pay or to alleviate poverty;

- This has accentuated longstanding tendencies for divergence between developed and developing countries. Moreover, greater gaps between them have been accompanied by widening gaps within the South as a handful of newly industrialized economies have pushed ahead of other developing countries;

- Finance has been gaining an upper hand over industry, and rentiers over investors. Trading in existing assets is often a much more lucrative business than creating wealth through new investment;

- Capital has gained in comparison with labour, and profit shares have risen in developed and developing countries alike;

- Growing wage inequality between skilled and unskilled labour is becoming a global problem;

- The hollowing out of the middle class has become a prominent feature of income distribution in many countries;

- There is almost everywhere increased job and income insecurity.

These seven "stylized facts", documented and analysed in the following chapters, pose a serious challenge for policymakers. Some of these features of the global economy may simply represent temporary dislocations associated with a rapid shift towards market forces and closer integration. Others may be of a more permanent nature. However, unless action is taken to counter these tendencies for a widening of gaps between poor and rich countries, and between the poor and the rich within countries, there is a risk of a serious political backlash that may nullify the gains from several positive elements of recent economic reforms in developed and developing countries alike. History shows that growing inequality under conditions of stagnation is a recipe for socio-political instability. The challenge at the close of the 20th century is thus, to paraphrase the Austrian economist Joseph Schumpeter, not to allow the destructive forces of modern capitalism to gain an upper hand over its creative forces.

The increasing gap between the poor and the rich cannot be bridged unless growth is accelerated. Recent experience has demonstrated that there are limits to redistribution without growth. Capital accumulation must consequently be put at the top of the policy agenda. The association of increased profits with stagnant investment, rising unemployment and reduced pay is already widely resented and threatens to raise questions about the acceptability of placing an ever-increasing share of national product in the hands of a few. Unless incomes of this minority are used to create more general prosperity, they may lose their social justification.

The idea that unfettered global market forces will generate a process of catching up by developing countries which is accompanied by improved income distribution has little historical or theoretical support. A much greater role needs to be played by governments in the South in accelerating growth and reconciling it with greater equality. This role should be fundamentally different from the kind of misguided interventions that pervaded many developing countries in the past. Despite increased pressures arising from the advent of new technologies, transnational corporations and global market forces, there remain many options for governments to influence accumulation and growth as well as the distribution of their benefits. Significant disparities in economic performance among developing countries today indeed reflect, in part, differences in how these policy options are exercised.

A realistic discussion of growth, distribution and development should start from the recognition that, in a market economy based on private property, most resources are concentrated in the hands of a minority, whose spending behaviour determines capital accumulation and growth. The main policy challenge in the South is how to translate rising profits into investment at a pace sufficient to underpin a wider social contract in which inequalities are justified by the extent to which they result in rising living standards for the mass of the population, leading eventually to reduced inequality. The challenge is particularly daunting in the many countries where the rich take more than half of the national product, but spend very little on activities contributing to general prosperity. In meeting this challenge it will be necessary for most developing countries to phase carefully integration into the world economy, tailoring the process, in each case, to the level of economic development and the capacity of existing institutions and industries. In these respects, governments of developing countries can draw valuable policy lessons from the experience of the successful late industrializers in East Asia.

However, if biased patterns of liberalization and globalization continue to prejudice growth prospects in developing countries by discriminating against sectors where they can build comparative advantage, the task will be a very difficult one. It would also be difficult to redress the balance between labour and capital, industry and finance, skilled and unskilled labour, or the poor and the rich. Attaining greater symmetry in liberalization remains a major challenge for the global community.

An essential concomitant of a more open world economy is the resolution of labour market problems in the major industrial countries. As examined in detail in *TDR 1995*, without faster growth policymakers are faced with an unpalatable choice between high and rising unemployment and growing wage inequality, or between open and disguised unemployment. Thus, faster growth in the North is essential not only to address these domestic problems, but also to remove systemic biases in the current process of liberalization.

Solution of these problems depends on the acceleration of investment through both demand and supply-side measures.

****

The next chapter examines global growth and convergence dynamics in a historical context, drawing on the experience before the First World War, when similar globalization pressures were at work, as well as the more recent trends. Evidence shows that divergence and polarization have been the dominant trends in the world economy over the past 120 years, and that convergence has taken place only within a small group of industrial economies. Global market forces do not spontaneously create the pattern of differential growth rates needed to achieve economic convergence between poorer and richer countries. Catching up by the former depends on the success of national policies in accelerating accumulation and growth, and on the management and phasing of integration into the world economy, a task which is greatly facilitated when the world economy grows faster. However, the considerably increased mobility of capital that characterizes the current process of globalization has not resulted in higher investment and faster growth, but rather in higher profit shares at the expense of labour.

Chapter III turns to income inequality within countries. It reviews the evidence on patterns and trends in income distribution, examines factors accounting for differences therein among countries, and analyses why growth is associated sometimes with rising and sometimes with falling inequality. It concludes that it is very difficult to generalize about how income distribution changes in the course of economic development. The crude stereotype of East Asia as a region of low and decreasing inequality is a misleading description, not only because some countries of the region have relatively high levels of inequality, but also because even in more successful cases, inequality increased during various episodes of their industrialization. Two tendencies have been identified regarding the more recent trends in income distribution in developing countries. First, there has been an increased concentration of income in the hands of the richest

20 per cent of the population at the expense of the middle class. Second, the growth-inequality relationship appears to have changed in the 1980s in most developing countries in ways which imply that growth now is more unequalizing. However, successful experiences of postwar industrialization show that government policies can shift the balance of forces towards those making for lesser inequality.

Chapter IV discusses the impact of trade and financial liberalization in developing countries on income distribution. Attention is focused on the evolution of wage differentials between skilled and unskilled workers, the distribution of manufacturing value added between labour and capital, the impact of agricultural price reforms on domestic terms of trade and agricultural incomes, and the sources of increases in the share of interest and other financial incomes. The evidence suggests that the "big bang" approach to liberalization has shifted the balance of forces towards those making for greater inequality without always generating additional stimuli for growth.

Chapter V reviews the effects of income distribution on accumulation and growth. It is first argued that unequal income distribution can slow both human capital formation, by reducing the capacity of the poor to invest in education, and physical capital formation, by generating social and political instability and uncertainty. The proposition is then examined that unequal income distribution is essential for rapid growth because the rich save and invest a greater proportion of their incomes than the poor. It is shown that the relationship between inequality and growth is greatly influenced by the extent to which profits are saved and invested. High reinvestment of profits fosters growth with lower inequality in terms of personal income distribution. Indeed, what distinguishes the East Asian NIEs from other developing countries is a considerably higher propensity to save and invest from profits.

The final chapter draws on the East Asian experience and examines how governments have influenced the emergence of a dynamic capitalist class with high "animal spirits". It first discusses the key policy instruments and institutions used in animating the investment-profits nexus - that is, the dynamic interactions between profits and investment whereby profits constitute simultaneously an incentive for investment, a source of investment and an outcome of investment. This is followed by a discussion of policies aiming at discouraging luxury consumption by the rich. The chapter concludes with an examination of the role of profit-related payments to labour in reconciling distributional and growth objectives. While some of the policies reviewed in the chapter were introduced at a time when globalization forces were less dominant, they nevertheless hold lessons which remain relevant and in varying degrees applicable to many developing countries today. ■

Chapter II

GLOBALIZATION AND ECONOMIC CONVERGENCE

A. Introduction

The gap between the richest and the poorest countries in the world is vast. Average per capita income in the richest countries is some 50 times that in the poorest. The persistence of very low standards of living for much of the world's population should be seen as among the most pressing challenges facing policymakers at both the domestic and the international level. Recent trends also suggest that it is not only those developing countries on the lowest rungs which are finding it difficult to raise living standards for the majority of their citizens. With the notable exception of the newly industrializing East Asian economies, growth in most developing countries slowed significantly in the late 1970s or early 1980s, often involving an absolute drop in per capita income. Although some countries have recovered quite strongly since the late 1980s, many have continued to experience slow and fragile growth which has further widened the gap between their average living standards and those of the richest countries.

This picture contrasts with much economic thinking which holds that the economic profile of developing countries in terms of their resource endowments and distance from the technological frontier should give rise to a very fast pace of economic growth and a reduction of income gaps across the world economy. While a variety of explanations have been offered for why economic theory and reality diverged in such a striking way, emphasis has increasingly been placed on the resistance of many developing countries to integration into the global economy. On this view, only a swift and complete removal of restrictions on flows of goods and factors of production across borders can reverse decades of under-performance and close income gaps among countries. This conclusion is often given added weight by reference to the 19th century globalization experience.

This chapter surveys global growth and convergence dynamics. It begins (in section B) by introducing the concepts of "globalization" and "convergence" and considers how globalization can be expected to accelerate growth in developing countries. A brief review of convergence trends before the First World War is then made, followed by a more detailed account of the trends since World War II (sections C and D). In the light of this discussion, sections E and F examine the impact of increased trade and greater capital mobility on growth and convergence, drawing on recent experience. Particular attention is paid to how these international economic forces interact with such traditional elements of economic growth as a fast pace of investment and technological upgrading, and whether globalization has altered fundamentally the issues facing policymakers in developing countries.

B. Globalization and convergence

The concept of globalization refers both to an increasing flow of goods and resources across national borders and to the emergence of a complementary set of organizational structures to manage the expanding network of international economic activity and transactions. Strictly speaking, a *global economy* is one where firms and financial institutions operate transnationally - i.e. beyond the confines of national boundaries. In such a world goods, factors of production and financial assets would be almost perfect substitutes everywhere and it would no longer be possible to consider nation States as distinct economic identities with autonomous decision-making power in the pursuit of national objectives. Those public goods that are needed to maintain an open market system, such as secure property rights and a stable monetary system, would become a global responsibility. Overall economic performance would depend upon the response of firms to global market incentives and the effectiveness of global regulations.

The world economy is far from such a supranational paradigm. A more apt description of the current situation is *global economic interdependence*, where cross-border linkages between markets and among production and financial activities are now so strong that economic developments in any one country are influenced to a significant degree by policies and developments outside its boundaries. Nevertheless, resource endowments, institutional arrangements and policy choices matter very much to national economic performance, as well as to the way international forces influence that performance.

Over the past two decades growing cross-border linkages have exerted powerful influences on the shape of the world economy (table 24). From 1973 to 1994, the volume of world exports grew at an average annual rate of around 4.5 per cent. However, since 1985 the difference between the growth of exports and that of world output has increased significantly. As a consequence, world exports of goods and services in relation to world output rose from 12.1 per cent to 16.7 per cent over this period. Although this increase in aggregate trade flows has been no faster than in the period before 1973, there have been qualitative changes in the pattern of trade which have strengthened global economic integration. These include the rise of manufactured exports from low-wage to high-wage economies and the growth of intra-firm trade accompanying a finer geographical separation of production activities.

Notwithstanding, international trade has not been the main catalyst for accelerating global economic integration. That role has been played by international capital. Cross-border financial flows have risen spectacularly over the past two decades, and the scope and depth of financial integration has far outpaced that in goods markets. The abandonment of fixed exchange rates in the early 1970s opened the flood gates to short-term capital flows; average daily trade in the global foreign exchange market has risen from $15 billion in 1973 to $880 billion in 1992 and over $1,300 billion in 1995. From 1980 to 1993, cross-border sales and purchases of financial assets rose from less than 10 per cent of GDP in the United States, Germany and Japan to 135 per cent, 170 per cent and 80 per cent, respectively. International banking has also, over this period, grown considerably faster than world trade or output. The increase in flows has been accompanied by a series of more qualitative changes, including a shift in the composition of private capital flows from bank lending to equity and portfolio investments, particularly in respect of capital flows to developing countries. Moreover, the holding of foreign securities in the portfolios of institutional investors from the advanced economies has been accompanied by a tremendous pace of financial innovation designed to reduce investors' exposure to credit, liquidity and exchange risks.[1]

Direct investment flows have also made a significant contribution to global economic integration in the sphere of production, and at a pace considerably faster than trade in goods and services. During the 1970s, annual flows of foreign direct

Table 24

INDICATORS OF THE GROWTH OF INTERNATIONAL ECONOMIC ACTIVITY, 1964-1994

(Average annual percentage change)

Period	World export volume	World FDI flows	International bank loans	World real GDP
1964-1973	9.2	..	34.0	4.6
1973-1980	4.6	14.8	26.7	3.6
1980-1985	2.4	4.9	12.0	2.6
1985-1994	6.7	14.3	12.0	3.2

Source: J. Perraton, D. Goldblatt, D. Held and A. McGrew, "The Globalisation of Economic Activity", *New Political Economy*, Vol. 2, No. 2, July 1997.

investment (FDI) averaged $27.5 billion, rising to $50 billion in the first half of the 1980s and $166 billion in the second half. Following a dip in the early 1990s, they reached $318 billion in 1995. There has been a steady shift towards FDI in services, which now accounts for well over half of the total stock of FDI. In addition, there has recently been an increase in the flow to developing countries (accounting for over one third of total inflows in 1993-1996), much of it linked to export-oriented manufacturing. These trends have increasingly been associated with a more elaborate system of intra-firm flows of goods and services as well as inter-firm alliances of various kinds, thereby adding a deeper layer of integration than was previously incorporated in international trade or financial capital flows.

The reach and effects of these cross-border flows have been greatly influenced by the pace at which various legal and political obstacles to trade and factor movements have been removed (openness), the ability of domestic producers to establish a strong position in the international division of labour (competitiveness), and the extent to which rules, institutions and technologies have been standardized internationally (harmonization). Whether greater openness, competitiveness and harmonization will ever lead to a truly global economy in the sense described above is very much open to question. However, there is a growing expectation that they will generate income convergence in the world economy by pushing growth rates in developing

countries above those in the advanced countries through a combination of efficiency gains, faster capital accumulation and rising productivity (see box 4).

The contribution of trade to accelerated growth in developing countries should come through the familiar efficiency gains associated with greater uniformity in prices for internationally traded goods as well as more dynamic gains linked to heightened international competitiveness and the advantages of specialization. Moreover, according to traditional trade theory, even in the absence of capital and labour mobility, convergence of factor prices should accompany greater openness; workers of comparable skill will be paid the same in the developed and developing worlds and owners of capital will likewise obtain the same rate of return on their investments.

Capital mobility strengthens considerably the role of international trade in bringing about convergence by linking international economic forces more directly to economic growth. Free capital movements should allow savings to be pooled and allocated globally, improving the international allocation of resources and equalizing rates of return on capital (adjusting, of course, for differences in risk), as capital moves from low-return locations in the North to high-return locations in capital-scarce developing countries. Simultaneously with these gains, capital mobility, particularly in respect of direct investments, should further accelerate

Box 4

MEASURES AND CONCEPTS OF ECONOMIC CONVERGENCE

Economic convergence concerns the gaps in living standards between countries: are they closing or widening, and at what speed? Posing this question immediately raises that of the variable (or variables) that need to be considered. Some studies concentrate on real GDP per head, per worker or per worker-hour, others look at total factor productivity (TFP), while yet others focus on factor prices, such as real wages or rates of return on capital. Each measure provides different information and can behave quite differently over fairly long periods. Consequently, the ranking of countries depends on the particular measure used.

Still, labour productivity remains as good a measure of convergence trends as any other. Productivity not only links the long-run competitiveness of domestic firms and sectors in international markets to rising living standards but also provides a basis for establishing economic leadership among countries. Although productivity and per capita income measures are not identical because of differences in demographic and employment trends, a sustained improvement of incomes is unlikely without an increase in productivity.[1]

It is now customary to distinguish between two types of convergence; *beta* convergence and *sigma* convergence. *Sigma* convergence is concerned with the dispersion around the mean of per capita income, or a related variable in a group of economies, the dispersion typically being measured by the standard deviation or the coefficient of variation. Other measures used include the Gini coefficient, the ratio of the highest to the lowest income or of the average relative to the highest.

Beta convergence is concerned with the relative growth performance of rich and poor countries. Convergence occurs when there is an inverse relationship between the initial value of a given variable (such as per capita income or productivity) and subsequent GDP growth. Thus, if countries with lower initial values of this variable grow faster, they can be said to be catching up with richer countries. However, even if poorer countries grow faster, their absolute income gap with the richer countries can increase for quite sometime, if there is a large initial inequality. Indeed, unless the ratio of growth rates between a poor and rich country equals or is greater than the ratio of their starting incomes, the absolute income gap will first increase, reach a maximum, and subsequently decline.

Two approaches to *beta* convergence are usually distinguished. The traditional approach involves the argument that there is an inherent tendency for the poorer countries to grow faster than the richer ones since, on the conventional analysis of growth economics, greater effort is needed to raise output at higher levels of income.[2] Thus, poor countries should grow faster than wealthy ones as long as their savings rates and technology are identical. Convergence on a common level of income is then only a matter of time.

In the alternative approach ("conditional convergence"), however, poorer countries have the potential to grow faster than advanced countries, but only if they satisfy certain conditions. If these conditions are not satisfied, their growth rate may be below their potential, or even below that of richer countries. Because conditional convergence is closely related to policies needed for catching up, it takes up many of the traditional concerns of development economists.

Early empirical research on differences in long-term growth performance among countries found little support for unconditional convergence. In response, more recent growth models have allowed for conditioning influences and a larger role for economic policy.[3] However, much of this literature has focused on whether developing countries are below their own long-run potential growth rate as determined by labour force growth, savings and technological progress. Because these factors are thought to be beyond the influence of policymakers, the scope to influence convergence is limited to reaching their potential growth rate. As a consequence, it has largely avoided the central question concerning the best policy and institutional arrangements for accelerating economic growth at different levels of development. After a comprehensive survey of this recent literature, one prominent contributor has concluded that "policymakers who want to promote growth would not go far wrong ignoring most of the vast literature reporting growth regressions. Basic theory, shrewd observations, and common sense are surely more reliable guides for policy".[4]

[1] For a discussion of why productivity matters and the different ways of measuring it, see W. Baumol, S. Blackman and E. Wolf, *Productivity and American Leadership: The Long View* (Cambridge, MA: MIT Press, 1989).

[2] R. Solow, "A Contribution to the Theory of Economic Growth", *The Quarterly Journal of Economics*, Vol. 70, 1956.

[3] See, for example, N. Mankiw, D. Romer and D. Weil, "A contribution to the empirics of economic growth", *The Quarterly Journal of Economics*, Vol.107, 1992; and R. Barro and X. Sala-i-Martin, "Convergence", *Journal of Political Economy*, Vol. 100, 1992. For a general review of these studies, see J. Fagerberg, "Technology and international differences in growth rates", *Journal of Economic Literature*, Vol. XXXII, Sept. 1994.

[4] G. Mankiw, "The Growth of Nations", *Brookings Papers on Economic Activity*, 1995 (Washington, D.C., The Brookings Institution, 1995), pp. 307-8.

growth through higher rates of accumulation and the transfer of technology and organizational skills.

In an interdependent world economy the fundamental issue is not whether these global forces bring potential benefits to developing countries, which they clearly can do. Nor is it only a matter of weighing the costs against the benefits from a full and swift subordination of the domestic economy to global market forces. Rather, it is how to best manage the interaction of domestic and international economic forces so that it leads to faster economic growth and rising living standards, particularly in developing countries.

C. Lessons from the 19th century

Assessing the impact of contemporary globalization trends is made difficult by the fact that they have been in operation over relatively few years. Most accounts accept that the mid-1970s mark a turning-point in international economic relations, although a noticeable acceleration in globalization trends only appears from the mid-1980s. However, globalization pressures are not unique to the late 20th century. Indeed, there are enough features in common between the past two decades and the half century before 1913 for some observers to interpret contemporary trends in the world economy as a return to this earlier episode of globalization, following a long interregnum of inward-looking, nationally-oriented development strategies in most developing countries.[2]

Like the current period, the late 19th century was characterized by a steady, but not spectacular, expansion of international trade. According to one recent estimate, the share of exports in world GDP rose from 5 per cent in 1870 to 8.7 per cent in 1913.[3] Also, as in the current period, cross-border capital flows assumed a much more prominent role in shaping the world economy. By 1913, the annual flow of international capital had reached 5 per cent of the GNP of the capital-exporting countries, notably the United Kingdom but also France and Germany.[4] The typical investment involved government bonds with long maturities, often of many decades, but FDI appears to have accounted for one third of the total stock of overseas investment by 1913.

These expanding trade and capital flows were closely interlinked. The growing demand for food and raw materials in Europe and North America encouraged FDI in primary sector activities; commodity exports accounted for over 60 per cent of world trade at both the beginning and the end of the period, and 55 per cent of the stock of FDI in 1914 was in this sector.[5] Complementary portfolio investment flows financed infrastructure projects, particularly railway construction, in the same primary-exporting countries.[6] In addition, because many of the resource-rich economies were also labour-scarce economies, the emerging growth opportunities attracted large inflows of unskilled workers, particularly from the poorer European fringe.[7]

Expanding cross-border linkages in the 19th century were, in part, driven by and reinforced with the help of new technologies in transport (railways and steamships) and communications (the telegraph and telephone) as well as new organizational arrangements to harmonize standards and reduce cross-border transaction costs. The most significant of these was the gold standard, which was adopted by a number of countries during the 1870s and provided a stable international monetary and payments framework for the growing volume of trade and financial transactions. But other public organizations (such as a rudimentary international patents system[8] and the Universal Postal Union), as well as the emergence of the multinational enterprise[9], were integral features of the globalization process during this period.

In line with much conventional thinking on globalization in the late 20th century, this earlier period has been described as one where international trade and capital flows strongly biased growth in favour of poorer economies, accelerating convergence in living standards in the world economy. At best, this is a very one-sided assessment of the period, concentrating on trends in its most dynamic subregion, where a large part of cross-border flows was concentrated.

To a very large extent the growing volume of cross-border flows of goods, capital and labour did not bring together a rich North and poor South in a new international division of labour, but rather helped to integrate the emerging industrial economies of Western Europe and North America with a small group of rich primary-producing economies elsewhere in the Americas and in Oceania.[10] To varying degrees this dynamic core also established links with a diverse collection of peripheral countries struggling to modernize their economies. Large parts of the developing world, by contrast, were forcefully integrated into the world economy through colonial ties.

From recently published OECD data it is clear that divergence was the dominant trend for the world economy during the period 1870-1913 (chart 1). A group of core countries did converge during this period, but the pace was slow. Indeed, if the two fastest-growing outliers, Argentina and Canada, are taken out, core convergence switches to divergence. Even in this core, the absolute income gap between the top and the bottom, in terms of per capita income, increased significantly. Moreover, during this period the United States embarked on its own successful industrial take-off which allowed it not only to overtake Great Britain as the world's leading economy but also to forge ahead of even the most successful industrializing economies of Europe (chart 2). A stronger convergence trend did occur in Western Europe, where initial starting conditions were broadly similar and the leading industrial nations were being chased by a larger group of late industrializers, among which the star performers were Germany and some Scandinavian economies.[11] However, even in this case the trend to convergence became strong only after 1900,[12] and if Eastern and Southern European countries are included the trend switches to divergence.

International economic forces were certainly a factor accounting for rapid growth in some of Western Europe's high-performing economies. However, the links between globalization and convergence were neither simple nor direct. According to a recent estimate, European migration accounted for all the real wage convergence, almost three quarters of the GDP per worker convergence, and perhaps one half of the GDP per capita convergence.[13] Among the countries where there was wage convergence only a few achieved a rapid increase in output and productivity growth in the late 19th century. For example, at the beginning of the period 1870-1913 Sweden, Italy and Ireland had

Chart 1

INCOME CONVERGENCE AND DIVERGENCE AMONG COUNTRIES IN 1870-1913

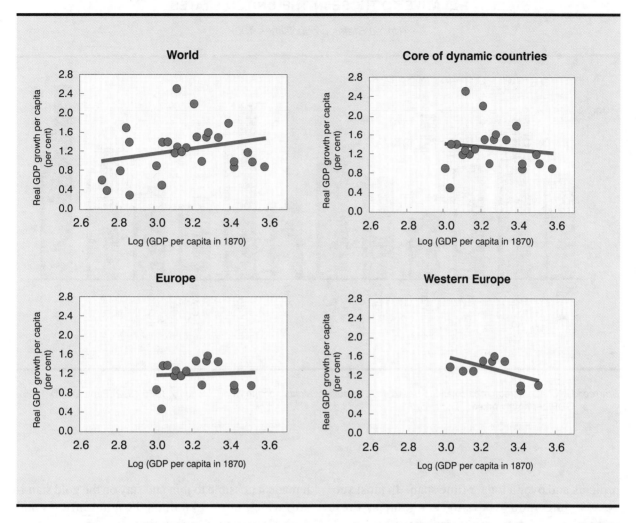

Source: UNCTAD secretariat calculations, based on A.Maddison, *Monitoring the World Economy, 1820-1992* (Paris: OECD, 1995).

Note: Growth rates of GDP per capita are annual averages for the period. The country groupings are as follows: *Western Europe:* Austria, Belgium, Denmark, Finland, France, Germany, Italy, Netherlands, Norway, Sweden, Switzerland, United Kingdom. *Europe:* Western Europe plus Czechoslovakia, Hungary, Ireland, Portugal, Russia, Spain. *Core of dynamic countries:* Europe plus Argentina, Australia, Canada, New Zealand, United States. *World:* core dynamic countries plus Brazil, China, India, Indonesia, Japan, Mexico.

comparable levels of per capita income, and in all three countries real wages had converged towards those of higher-wage economies by the end of the period. However, only Sweden exhibited strong output growth that was accompanied by a genuine process of catching up linked to successful industrial take-off. While international trade and capital movements certainly played a part in this process, they were not the handmaidens of Sweden's industrial growth (see box 5). Indeed, in that country, as in the other most dynamic economies of North America and Europe, industrial output grew faster than trade during this period while the expansion

of industry was itself a stimulus to trade through a growing demand for raw materials (see table 25).

The difference between success and failure during this earlier period of globalization rested on a series of domestic institutional reforms, including the strengthening of property rights and commercial laws, improvements to the educational system, the creation of more efficient and nationally integrated markets, and the emergence of new forms of financial intermediation, which helped nurture an industrial entrepreneurial class willing to commit their resources to larger investment

Chart 2

PRODUCTIVITY LEVELS[a] IN WESTERN EUROPEAN COUNTRIES IN 1870 AND 1913 RELATIVE TO THOSE IN THE UNITED STATES

(United States productivity = 100)

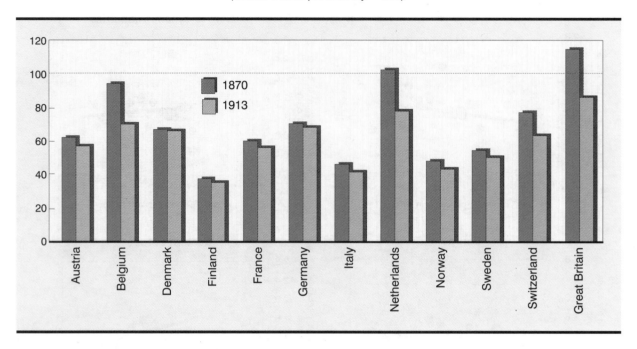

Source: UNCTAD secretariat calculations, based on A. Maddison, *Monitoring the World Economy, 1820-1992* (Paris: OECD, 1995).
a GDP per hour worked.

projects and over a longer time span. In most successful late industrializing economies, these institutional reforms were carried out by a modernizing State.[14] However, governments, through guarantees, loans and cash grants, also assumed a more active role in creating new markets and initiating and coordinating large infrastructure projects. Technology and industrial policies were also used to nurture infant industries. In all the successful late industrializers tariff levels on imported manufactures rose - in some cases, such as the United States, from already high levels.[15] But more active industrial policies were also used to support upgrading, particularly in the emerging engineering and chemical industries, including through publicly funded training and industrial research.[16]

Successful industrial take-off at home provided the basis for entry into the international economy in a way which reinforced growth and development. It also helped attract the foreign capital needed to finance growing import requirements and large-scale infrastructure development and to gain access to modern technologies. Furthermore,

it made it possible to join and stay on the gold standard, which in turn facilitated capital inflows and raised investment expectations.[17]

Elsewhere in the world economy the impact of international factor flows was very different. In some land-rich economies, mobile factors chased each other into primary sector activities, sometimes generating rather spectacular growth, as in Argentina and Mexico, and also, towards the end of the period, Russia. But in these cases, a class of strong industrial entrepreneurs failed to develop, capital remained quite footloose and speculative investment was widespread. There consequently tended to be a more unstable growth path than in the industrializing economies of the period.[18] Finally, in economies under colonial rule there were limited growth opportunities. In many cases, dependence on raw material exports was associated with enclave economies, often dominated by food products, which constitute the least dynamic and most volatile sector of world trade. At the same time, these economies became markets for manufactures from the industrial core, and although these markets were

Box 5

SWEDEN'S PATH FROM THE PERIPHERY

In the period 1870-1913 Sweden was among the fastest-growing countries in the world, breaking its reliance on traditional commodity exports and rapidly upgrading its industrial capacity. Although Sweden maintained close links with the international economy during this period, its rapid growth cannot be explained as the spontaneous outcome of globalization forces. Rather, institutional reforms, new types of policy intervention and measured integration with the world economy were at the heart of its successful industrialization process.

Sweden's modernization began in the early 19th century with a series of institutional reforms in agriculture, trade liberalization, a tightening of property rights and improvements to its educational system.[1] These marked a break with an earlier mercantile tradition and encouraged a fledgling domestic entrepreneurial class to build on established industrial traditions, such as in iron, as well as to move into new activities such as timber. As late as 1880 iron and timber still accounted for 56 per cent of total exports and 45 per cent of industrial employment. However, new and more sophisticated industries subsequently emerged, including pulp and paper, chemicals and steel, that employed large-scale modern manufacturing methods. Most importantly, a capital goods sector emerged with close links to agriculture and to the timber and metals industries. By 1914 these newer industries accounted for over 60 per cent of total exports.

The share of exports in GDP rose modestly from 18 per cent in 1870 to 22 per cent in 1913, and industrial output grew faster than exports. While export growth was made possible, in part, by the low tariff barriers in leading markets, particularly the United Kingdom, it was rapid productivity growth through the introduction of more capital-intensive production methods that allowed Sweden to enter new markets (Germany and North America).

Efforts to upgrade the industrial base relied heavily on collaboration between the public and private sectors. Typical of such collaboration was infrastructure development, initially in railways, but subsequently in other areas, such as telegraph and telephone services and power supply. In this process, the State sought not only to provide key ingredients for fast growth, but also to facilitate entry of domestic producers into new markets, particularly in the more demanding capital goods sector. Moreover, the need to raise capital abroad was instrumental in deepening Sweden's financial structures and, under close government supervision, establishing closer links between finance and industry along the lines of the German banking system.[2]

Significantly, the effectiveness of the State in this respect was helped by a series of reforms during this period, removing cumbersome procedures and overlapping responsibilities, creating new agencies with better links to emerging industrial activities and introducing new recruitment procedures to ensure a more professional bureaucracy.[3] New types of industrial policy were also introduced. As in most of Western Europe and North America, infant industry protection was an important component of late industrialization in Sweden; although they were not as high as in some other countries, average tariffs on manufactured products rose from around 4 per cent in 1875 to 20 per cent in 1913. These measures were accompanied by various subsidies to support rationalization and the adoption of new technologies, particularly in the newly emerging engineering industries, where R&D was critical to maintaining competitiveness.

---

[1] The role that education played, however, is controversial; see L. Sandberg, "The case of the impoverished sophisticate: Human capital and Swedish economic growth before World War 1", *Journal of Economic History*, Vol. XXXIX, 1979; K. O'Rourke and J. Williamson, "Around the European periphery 1870-1913: Globalization, schooling and growth", *NBER Working Paper*, No.5392 (Cambridge, MA: National Bureau of Economic Research, 1995).

[2] Sweden's long-term borrowing abroad represented about 50 per cent of its gross domestic investment at its peak in the 1880s, much of it for public infrastructure; see M. Panic, *European Monetary Union: Lessons From the Gold Standard* (London: Macmillan, 1992), table 3.2 and 3.3; A. Lindgren, "Long-term contracts in financial markets: Bank-industry connections in Sweden, illustrated by the operations of the Stockholm Enskilda Bank", in M. Aoki *et al.* (*eds.*), *The Firm as a Nexus of Treaties* (London: Sage, 1990); and I. Nygren "Transformation of bank structures in the industrial period: The case of Sweden 1820-1913", *Journal of European Economic History*, Vol 12, No. 1, 1983.

[3] R. Torstendahl, *Bureaucratization in Northwestern Europe, 1880-1985* (London: Routledge, 1991).

Table 25

GROWTH OF TRADE AND INDUSTRY IN SELECTED COUNTRIES, 1870-1913

(Annual average volume change in per cent)

Country/region	Exports	Manufacturing industry[a]	Per capita GDP
Western Europe	3.2	3.0	1.3
Germany	4.1	4.5	1.6
Sweden	3.1	3.5	1.5
Denmark	3.3	3.4	1.6
Switzerland	3.9	3.1	1.5
Italy	2.2	2.6	1.3
Belgium	4.2	3.2	1.0
Great Britain	2.8	2.0	1.0
Netherlands	2.3	3.0	0.9
United States	4.9	5.7	1.8
Canada	4.1	5.3	2.2
Russia	..	3.0	0.9
Japan	8.5	3.0	1.4

Source: UNCTAD secretariat calculations, based on A. Maddison, *Monitoring the World Economy, 1820-1992* (Paris: OECD, 1995). Output of manufacturing industry is from Paul Bairoch, "International Industrial Levels, 1750-1980", *Journal of European Economic History*, Vol. 11, No. 2, Fall 1982.
a 1860-1913.

small by world standards, imports could prevent the emergence of domestic industries or, worse still, could lead to deindustrialization.[19]

The evidence from the last century does not suggest that global forces will spontaneously cre- ate the pattern of differential growth rates needed to achieve income convergence. Rather, the lesson to be derived from the globalization episode before 1913 is that there is still an important role for ac- tive government policy if poorer countries are to benefit from international market forces.

D. Contemporary convergence trends

1. Global trends

Since 1950 there has been a steady process of economic integration which has continued even against the growing uncertainties and intermittent crises of the 1970s and 1980s. Indeed, in certain respects, the process of integration has accelerated recently and drawn in many more developing coun- tries and economies in transition. Table 26 provides some broad economic indicators for the leading industrial economies over these four decades. The Bretton Woods era, ending in the early 1970s, achieved an unprecedented degree of growth and

Table 26

INDICATORS OF ECONOMIC PERFORMANCE IN THE G7 COUNTRIES UNDER VARIOUS INTERNATIONAL MONETARY REGIMES

Indicator	Gold standard (1881-1913)		Bretton Woods[a] (1946-1958)		(1959-1970)		Floating rates (1974-1989)	
	Mean	Variation[b]	Mean	Variation[b]	Mean	Variation[b]	Mean	Variation[b]
Real growth per capita[c]	1.5	2.5	4.3	0.5	4.5	0.4	2.2	1.1
Inflation[c]	1.0	3.4	3.9	1.5	3.9	0.5	7.2	0.5
Real long-term interest rate	3.5	0.7	2.0	2.0	2.7	0.4	2.7	1.6
Change in real exchange rate[d]	0.9	0.9	5.8	1.5	2.0	1.0	8.2	0.8

Source: D. Felix, "Financial globalization versus free trade: The case for the Tobin Tax", *UNCTAD Review, 1996* (United Nations publication, Sales No. E.97.II.D.2), table 1.

a By December 1958, all European G7 countries had removed all exchange controls on current account transactions.

b Relative dispersal of annual observations around each period's mean value, as measured by the coefficient of variation.

c Average annual percentage change.

d Average year-to-year absolute rate of change.

stability, leading some observers to dub it a "Golden Age". As noted in section B, rapid growth in this period was accompanied by expanding trade and capital flows. Growth was also rapid in many developing countries during the 1960s and 1970s, often accompanied by profound economic, political and social changes associated with increasing industrial activity. However, the benefits were partly offset by relatively fast population growth, especially in Latin America and Africa. This "Golden Age", too, ended abruptly with a "growth meltdown" in many developing countries in the late 1970s and early 1980s.[20]

For this period as a whole, poorer countries grew on average more slowly than richer ones, giving rise to a trend of divergence in the world economy.[21] Taking real per capita GDP growth in OECD countries as a benchmark, over the past four decades strong economic catch-up has been a feature of a small group of newly industrializing economies in Southern Europe. Some developing countries, particularly in East Asia, have also sustained growth rates well in excess of the wealthiest nations (table 27). However, for most other developing countries per capita growth rates have either lagged behind, or been only marginally above, those of the advanced countries. This pattern did not

fundamentally change as growth slowed down in the North; since the early 1980s growth also slowed down in much of the developing world, particularly Latin America and Africa.

As a consequence of these trends income gaps have widened. From 1965 to 1995 average per capita income (in terms of purchasing power parity) in Africa fell from 14 per cent of that of the industrialized countries to a mere 7 per cent. In Latin America, while there was little change up to the late 1970s, the gap in income has widened considerably since then, with a dramatic drop from 36 per cent of the level in industrial countries in 1979 to around 25 per cent in 1995. By contrast, the rapid growth of the East Asian NIEs has secured them a per capita income increase from 18 per cent of the industrial countries' level in 1965 to 66 per cent in 1995.[22]

Productivity gaps have followed much the same pattern (see chart 3). Moreover, they appear to be closely linked to widening structural gaps in the world economy. Although the share of the advanced countries in world industrial output fell significantly from 1970 to 1995, while that of the developing countries has risen, the rise in the latter is almost exclusively a reflection of rapid indus-

Table 27

GROWTH IN THE WORLD ECONOMY: CATCHING UP BY DEVELOPING ECONOMIES ON OECD, 1960-1990

GDP growth differential with OECD[a]	1960-1990	1960-1973	1973-1990
More than 3 per cent	Republic of Korea Singapore Hong Kong Taiwan Province of China	Singapore Hong Kong	Hong Kong Indonesia Republic of Korea Singapore Taiwan Province of China
1 - 3 per cent	Botswana Malaysia Thailand	Republic of Korea Taiwan Province of China Botswana Gabon Lesotho Namibia Swaziland Barbados	Botswana Cape Verde Mauritius Seychelles Bangladesh China Malaysia
0 - 1 per cent	Indonesia Barbados Lesotho Morocco Tunisia Seychelles	Nigeria Jordan Malaysia Thailand Brazil Panama	Cameroon Lesotho Morocco Tunisia India Pakistan Syrian Arab Republic Myanmar Barbados
Memo item: Annual average growth of real GDP in OECD *(Per cent)*	3.2	4.4	2.2

Source: UNCTAD secretariat calculations, based on the Penn World Tables (see text, note 22).
a   Excess of average annual real GDP over the OECD average in percentage points.

trial growth in East Asia. Particularly since 1980, the share of Latin America and Africa has fallen sharply (table 28). Without entering the long-standing debate on the precise role of industry in development, these trends do suggest a strong association between structural change, productivity growth and living standards.

Differential growth trends have also had a direct influence on the relative position of countries in world income distribution, as can be seen from chart 4 and table 29, which show the trend in world income distribution during 1965-1990, classifying countries into five groups, each representing 20 per cent (a quintile) of world population.[23] Income divergence and increasing inequality in the world's population has been a persistent feature over this period, but with a noticeable worsening in the 1980s (chart 4). The increase in the income share of the richest 20 per cent of the world population

PRODUCTIVITY LEVELS[a] **IN SELECTED DEVELOPING COUNTRIES, 1950-1992,
RELATIVE TO THOSE IN THE UNITED STATES**

(United States productivity = 100)

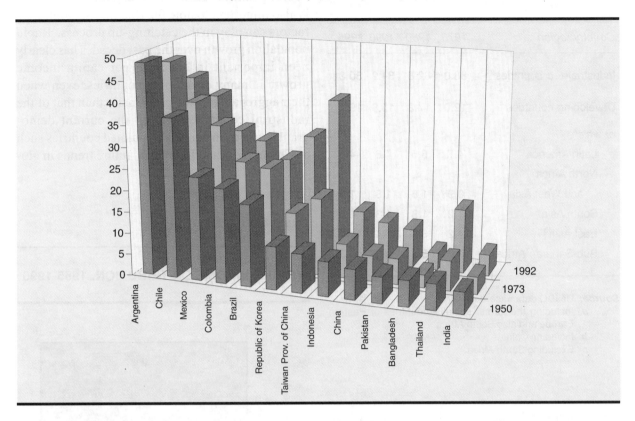

Source: As for chart 2.
   a GDP per hour worked.

was significant; it rose by 14 percentage points from 1965 to 1990, to reach over 83 per cent of world GNP. Much of this increase occurred in the 1980s and was concentrated in the countries with the richest 10 per cent of the world population (as measured by per capita income). The Gini coefficient, commonly used as a measure of inequality (see chapter III, box 6), stood at 0.66 in 1965, rose slightly to 0.68 in 1980 and reached 0.74 in 1990. Perhaps more striking has been the enormous increase in the income gap between the richest and poorest quintiles of world population. In 1965 average GNP per capita in the poorest quintile was $74 and in the highest $2,281, a ratio of 31:1. By 1990 the figures were respectively $283 and $17,056, yielding a ratio of 60:1. There is little evidence to suggest that this tendency towards greater dispersion has since been reversed.[24]

Table 29 shows which countries belong to the different quintiles in world income distribution.

While the majority of developing countries remained in the same quintile over the period 1965-1990, the table does show some significant movements. All the first-tier East Asian NIEs have moved into the highest quintile, the most impressive performance having been by the Republic of Korea and Taiwan Province of China, which moved up from the third quintile in 1965.[25] Their fast growth allowed them not only to overtake many developing economies which remained stuck in the second quintile throughout the period, but also to catch up with the advanced industrial economies and even overtake some of them. Moreover, their success meant that some countries in Latin America moved down from the first to the second quintile. Also, a large group of countries moved from the third to the second quintiles during this period, including a number of African middle-income ones, a feature which should not be overlooked in the context of a generally unsatisfactory performance of the region. Indeed, the most impressive leap of

Table 28

SHARE OF DIFFERENT REGIONS IN WORLD MANUFACTURING OUTPUT SINCE 1970

(Percentage)

Country/region	1970	1980	1990	1995
Industrialized countries[a]	88.0	82.8	84.2	80.3
Developing countries	12.0	17.2	15.8	19.7
of which:				
Latin America	4.7	6.5	4.6	4.6
North Africa and West Asia	0.9	1.6	1.8	1.9
South Asia	1.2	1.3	1.3	1.5
East Asia[b]	4.2	6.8	7.4	11.1
Sub-Saharan Africa[c]	0.6	0.5	0.3	0.3

Source: UNIDO data base.
    a Including the former socialist countries of Eastern Europe and also South Africa.
    b Including China.
    c Excluding South Africa.

any economy in this period was by Botswana, which moved from the bottom quintile in 1965 to the second quintile in 1990. Many African countries, however, remained in, or dropped down to, the ranks of the poorest countries (bottom quintiles).

The combination of income divergence, the strongly rising share of income going to the top quintile, particularly since 1980, and the fact that average per capita income in that quintile has risen not only relative to the lowest quintile but also to all other quintiles, points to a clustering of countries around higher and lower growth poles. Indeed, on some accounts the landscape of the world economy has already become polarized. Of the 98 developing countries for which data are available, 40 countries had income levels over 20 per cent of the average per capita income of the G7 countries in 1960 and 14 countries over 40 per cent. By 1990, the figures had fallen to 29 and 11, respectively. More generally, failure to catch up in this period is confirmed by the fact that the number of developing countries with per capita incomes over 80 per cent, 60 per cent and 40 per cent of the average per capita income of the G7 countries all decreased between 1960 and 1990.

However, a number of points should be borne in mind when evaluating the increasing dispersion of global income. As already noted, given the large differences among countries at the beginning of the period, absolute gaps could widen even when the poorer countries grew faster than the rich ones. It is also important to note the role that demographic factors can play in the catching-up process. Rapid population growth over the past decades has clearly been important in lowering per capita income growth in many developing countries, even when their aggregate income grew faster than that of the industrial countries. Given the current demographic trends in densely populated countries such as China, India and Indonesia, future trends in glo-

Chart 4

WORLD INCOME DISTRIBUTION, 1965-1990

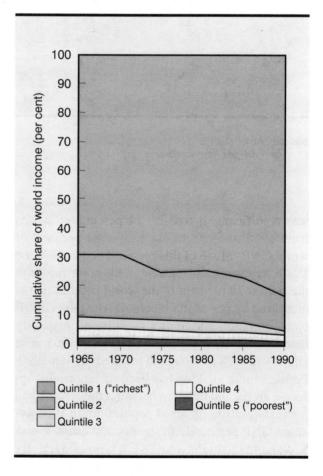

Source: As for table 29.
  Note: The five quintiles each represent 20 per cent of the world population. The country populations included in each quintile are determined by the ranking of countries according to per capita income. The methodology underlying the chart is the same as that for table 29. For further explanations, see that table and the text.

Table 29

POSITION OF COUNTRIES IN WORLD INCOME DISTRIBUTION, 1965 AND 1990

	Quintile 1 1965	Quintile 2 1965	Quintile 3 1965	Quintile 4 1965	Quintile 5 1965
Quint. 1 1990	Australia Italy Austria Kuwait Bahamas Luxembourg Belgium Netherlands Canada N. Zealand Denmark Norway Finland Sweden France Switzerland Germany[a] UK Iceland USA Israel USSR (1)	Barbados Seychelles Gabon Singapore Hong Kong Spain Ireland Japan Libyan Arab Jam. Malta Portugal Puerto Rico Saudi Arab.	Oman Republic of Korea Taiwan Province of China		
Quint. 2 1990	Argentina Venezuela	Belize Mexico Brazil(1) Panama Chile Peru Colombia Poland Costa Rica Romania El Salvador South Africa Fiji Suriname Guatemala Trinidad & T. Iraq Turkey Jamaica Uruguay Malaysia USSR (2) Mauritius Yugoslavia	Algeria Papua N. G. Brazil (2) Paraguay Cameroon Philippines (1) Congo St. Vincent C.d'Ivoire Swaziland Dominica Syrian A. R. Domin. Rep. Thailand Morocco Tunisia		Botswana
Quint. 3 1990			Bolivia Philippines (2) China (1) Senegal Comoros Sri Lanka Egypt Sudan Honduras Togo Liberia Zambia Mauritania Zimbabwe	Central African Republic	Indonesia Haiti Lesotho Myanmar
Quint. 4 1990			Benin Ghana Kenya Pakistan	China (2) India (1)	
Quint. 5 1990		Guyana Nicaragua	Gambia Madagascar Niger Nigeria Dem. Rep. of Congo		Bangladesh India (2) Burkina Malawi Faso Nepal Burundi Rwanda Chad U. Rep. of Ethiopia Tanzania

Source: UNCTAD secretariat calculations, based on R. Korzeniewicz and T. Moran, "World Economic Trends in the Distribution of Income, 1965-1992", *American Journal of Sociology*, Vol. 102, 1997; *World Bank Atlas* tape; World Bank, *World Tables* tape; Penn World Tables (see text, note 22); I. Borenstein, *Comparative GDP Levels*, ECE Economic Studies No. 4 (United Nations publication, Sales No. GV.E.93.0.5), New York, 1993; *Statistical Yearbook of the Republic of China, 1987*, Taipei; Central Bank of China, *Annual Report, 1995*, Taipei; United Nations Population Division database.

a Excluding the eastern Länder.

Note: The table shows the relative position of countries in world income distribution, i.e. to which of the five population quintiles of chart 4 they belong, and changes in their relative position from 1965 to 1990. The table (as well as the chart) was derived by (i) dividing the total population of the countries covered (representing 93.6 per cent of world population) into five groups of equal size (in 1990, for example, each quintile accounts for slightly less than 1 billion people), (ii) ranking countries in the relevant years according to their per capita income in current dollars, and (iii) allocating countries to the different quintiles in the order of their ranking. Countries with the highest per capita incomes are thus allocated to quintile 1 ("the richest") and those with the lowest to quintile 5 ("the poorest"). For some countries, their large population had to be distributed over two quintiles, in line with each quintile's cumulative population total. Such countries are indicated by the suffix (1) or (2). For example, in the case of China in 1965, 25 per cent of the population are included in quintile 3 and 75 per cent in quintile 4. All countries that were in the same quintile in 1965 and 1990 fall into the diagonally placed boxes of the table. For countries below the diagonal the relative position worsened between the two years, and for those above it improved. For example, the position of Argentina worsened (moving from quintile 1 in 1965 to quintile 2 in 1990), whereas Indonesia moved up from quintile 5 to quintile 3.

bal income dispersion could be quite different from those of the past if these countries succeed in maintaining the kind of income growth they have achieved in recent years. Finally, past trends in the distribution of income among countries say very little about the opportunities open to individual countries in terms of rapid growth and catch-up. Indeed, the increase in global dispersion has taken place while a number of poorer countries joined the ranks of the richest countries, in part because they have successfully exploited the opportunities presented by integration with the global economy.

2. Economic convergence in the OECD countries

Over the last four decades, convergence has been confined to a small group of industrialized economies, notably those of OECD. Prior to 1950, the United States outstripped Western Europe, opening up a large productivity and income gap with that region. Much of this gap was closed during the long postwar boom, when the poorer members grew more quickly; from 1950 to 1992, the countries in the bottom half of the list of OECD countries (ranked by per capita income) grew on average 1.4 percentage points faster each year than those in the top half; and, more strikingly, those in the bottom quarter grew 2.4 percentage points faster than those in the top quarter.[26] As a result, the dispersion of income halved; the coefficient of variation of per capita income, which stood at 0.48 in 1950, had fallen to 0.25 by 1992. The trend towards convergence for productivity has been even faster.[27]

The most striking example of rapid catching up in this period is Japan, where per capita income is now similar to that of the United States. In some industries, such as transport equipment and metal products, Japan has already overtaken the United States in terms of labour productivity, although it lags far behind in others, such as clothing.

This experience of OECD countries can provide a useful basis for understanding any wider process of economic convergence. First, it shows that if convergence indeed takes place, it is not an automatic process. Although various studies have traced accelerated productivity growth in OECD countries back to the late 19th century, a particularly fast pace of convergence was achieved only after 1950, when economic growth became a specific target of policymakers.[28] Even so, the absolute

income gap increased for a number of countries; over the period 1950-1992, Australia, United Kingdom and New Zealand failed to catch up with the United States (or fell further behind) and in the process were overtaken by other, more rapidly growing, economies such as those of Germany, France, Norway and, most impressively, Japan. On the other hand, extrapolating growth trends over the same period for the poorest OECD members, during which their average per capita income rose from under a quarter to over one half that of the United States, it would still take between 30 and 50 years for those same countries to eliminate the remaining income gap.

Second, while convergence is underpinned by a fast pace of capital accumulation in poorer countries, it is also closely linked to structural shifts in economic activity. In all OECD countries productivity growth in manufacturing has consistently been faster than in agriculture or services. Consequently, in most of the poorer members large movements of labour out of agriculture and into manufacturing have contributed to catching up, even though their productivity gap in manufacturing remained quite high.

Finally, there appears to be a close relationship between convergence and overall growth. For the OECD countries in 1950-1973 strong growth coincided with strong convergence. Since then, however, slower growth, weaker investment and sharper macroeconomic shocks have slowed productivity growth in all the member countries. In general, however, the poorer countries have suffered relatively more from this slowdown, and the convergence process has decelerated; indeed, on some measures it has actually gone into reverse.[29]

3. Economic convergence in the European Union

The conclusions outlined above concerning the industrialized (OECD) countries in general have particular validity for the countries of the European Union, where economic integration has been fastest. Since 1972, some less industrialized countries, with distinctly lower per capita income levels, have joined the Union. Until the early 1970s, convergence was strong among the 12 countries, more so for productivity than for income. After 1973 productivity convergence continued, but at a slower pace, while there was divergence for income.

During 1986-1990 convergence in income was reestablished, albeit against a backdrop of much slower average growth.[30]

Behind these convergence figures lies strong growth in the four peripheral economies that became EEC members after 1972.[31] A closer examination of sectoral trends also shows that a faster pace of convergence has been linked to strong growth in manufacturing, notably in Spain and Ireland. However, in Greece, Portugal and Spain, the fastest period of growth occurred prior to joining the Community. Moreover, the acceleration of growth in the second half of the 1980s which followed their accession failed to be sustained thereafter. Indeed, from 1990 to 1995 average annual growth in those three countries fell back to or below the EEC average.

As discussed in greater detail in the next section, trade has tended to play a supportive rather than a leading role in this convergence experience,[32] and the same also appears to hold for capital flows, including FDI. The one possible exception is Ireland, where growth since the end of the 1980s has not only exceeded that in the 1970s, but has been fast enough to suggest that the country has embarked on a dynamic catching-up process. In this respect, the large inflows of FDI seem to have played an important role, given the size of the Irish economy. However, as a share of overall investment inward FDI has been no more important in Ireland than in the other three peripheral countries, where growth performance was weaker. Moreover, there had been an even larger inflow of FDI during the 1970s, with no such growth. Large transfers from EEC, which exceeded 5 per cent of GNP in the 1990s, as well as selective industrial policies aimed at linking FDI to the development of indigenous industrial capabilities, with emphasis on technology and exports, have played a particularly important role in the growth performance of the Irish economy in this more recent period.[33]

4. *Divergence within the developing world*

As noted above, over the past three decades the developing countries as a whole have failed to move closer to the developed countries. Simultaneously, there has been a strong divergence within the developing world itself whereby countries with low initial per capita incomes have fallen further

Chart 5

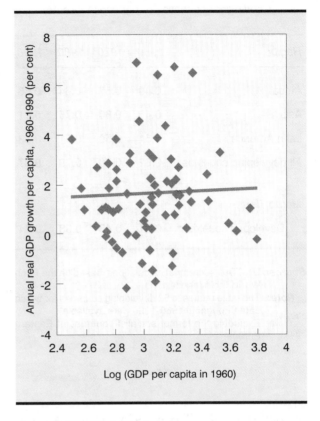

INCOME CONVERGENCE AND DIVERGENCE AMONG DEVELOPING COUNTRIES IN 1960-1990

Source: UNCTAD data base.

behind the others (chart 5). Increased dispersion has been accompanied by a significant increase in the absolute income gap between the richest and poorest developing countries. In 1960 the richest developing economy, in terms of purchasing power parity, was Venezuela, with a per capita income of $6,338, and the poorest was Lesotho, with only $313. By 1990 the richest was Hong Kong ($14,849) and the poorest Chad ($399). The ratio of maximum to minimum per capita income thus rose over this period from 20:1 to 37:1. Growing polarization since 1965 among developing countries is illustrated by recent data of IMF, which classifies developing countries (excluding major oil exporters) into five income brackets, each defined in relation to the per capita income (in purchasing power parity terms) of the richest developing country. There were considerably fewer developing countries with income levels ranging from 40 per cent to 80 per cent of the income of the richest country in 1995 than in 1965 and a much larger number

Table 30

INCOME CONVERGENCE AMONG DEVELOPING COUNTRIES, BY REGION, 1960-1990

(Coefficient of variation of per capita income)

Region	1960	1970	1980	1990
Africa	0.49	0.57	0.64	0.68
Asia	0.46	0.60	0.75	0.81
Latin America	0.51	0.50	0.51	0.53
All developing countries	0.62	0.70	0.79	0.87
Memo item:				
Developed countries[a]	0.51	0.43	0.38	0.34

Source: UNCTAD secretariat calculations, based on the Penn World Table (see text, note 22).
Note: The table relates to 82 developing countries for which data throughout 1960-1990 were available.
a Excluding the former socialist countries of Eastern Europe.

of countries had fallen by 1995 into the category of the poorest 20 per cent. These forces of polarization that prevailed throughout the period were intensified in the early 1980s.[34]

Among Latin American countries the dispersion of income was quite high in 1960 and has changed little since; after some narrowing until the late 1970s dispersion has increased in the 1980s (table 30). Brazil, Colombia and Mexico all experienced per capita growth rates in excess of the wealthiest Latin American economies, although only Brazil came close to the OECD average. In all three countries growth has slown down sharply since the early 1980s. By contrast, since the mid-1980s Chile, one of the region's richest economies, has achieved growth rates well in excess of the regional average and high enough to enable it to catch up with the industrialized countries of the world.

In Africa there has been a gradual widening in the dispersion of incomes throughout the past three decades, particularly in the 1970s. Only Botswana, Morocco and Tunisia, among the larger economies, have been able to narrow the gap with the industrial countries over the entire period, al-

though only in Botswana was growth significantly faster. As a consequence, these countries have reduced their income gap with the richest African countries. Since 1973 growth in Egypt, Cameroon and Cape Verde has been faster than the regional average, although the most impressive performance over this more recent period has been by Mauritius, which has always been one of the wealthiest African countries.

In Asia, where, unlike the two other developing regions, average per capita growth has exceeded that of OECD countries during the past three decades, there are considerable intra-regional differences, particularly between the rapidly growing East Asian economies and the slow-growing South Asian ones. Consequently, income divergence has increased sharply. In South Asia there was not a single economy with an average per capita growth rate in excess of the OECD average during 1960-1990, although some have emerged since 1973, in part due to the slowdown in OECD.

In East Asia growth has been spectacularly fast, beginning with Japan and then in the first-tier NIEs (Hong Kong, Republic of Korea, Singapore, and Taiwan Province of China). Japan, Hong Kong and Singapore have already graduated to the ranks of the richest economies and the other two economies have crossed the convergence threshold. However, with the exception of Japan, these are all small economies, with a combined population of less than 70 million. There are none the less signs of a wider dynamism emerging in this subregion, which shares some of the characteristics of the convergence process described above for the OECD countries.

As examined in detail in *TDR 1996*, a number of economies (Indonesia, Malaysia and Thailand) in South-East Asia have experienced sustained growth in excess of the world average for over four decades, with a strong acceleration over the past decade or so which has been accompanied by a very fast pace of capital accumulation and large structural shifts from resource-based to industrial activities. A third tier of rapidly growing developing countries has emerged in the subregion over the past two decades. Among this group of countries, China has had perhaps the most impressive performance, with double-digit growth rates. As a result of strong growth in these poorer economies and the slowdown in Japan and the first-tier NIEs associated with industrial maturity, greater income convergence is likely to be experienced in East Asia.

E. Trade, growth and convergence

The discussion above shows that income divergence has been the dominant trend in the world economy over the past 120 years, and that convergence has taken place only within a small group of industrial economies, particularly since the early 1950s. At various times since the second World War a number of countries, both in Latin America and in Central and Eastern Europe, managed to achieve very high growth rates, but they proved unsustainable, and in most cases the catching up process came to an end or the economies actually fell further behind. Only the first-tier NIEs of East Asia have exhibited a strong and sustained tendency to catch up with the industrial world.

This experience contrasts sharply with the prediction of traditional growth theory that poor economies have an inherent tendency to catch up, through faster growth, with the more advanced economies. An increasingly popular explanation of the postwar experience emphasizes the resistance of developing countries to full integration into the global economy. On this view, only those developing economies which remained open during the past three decades were able to outperform the more advanced industrial economies, while those that stayed closed fell further behind.[35]

Some studies of the determinants of economic growth found evidence in support of this explanation, but of the 50 variables that have been considered as determinants of growth, perhaps the only one on which there has been broad consensus is investment.[36] This consensus rests on the familiar principle that the direct contribution of investment to productivity growth, and the strong complementarities with other elements in the growth process, such as technological progress and skill acquisition, make investment a natural point of departure for policymakers seeking to formulate a robust development strategy. This was the conclusion already reached in the earlier convergence literature and has always been the focus of much of the historical literature on industrialization and economic development.

In a more open and integrated world economy both the quantity and the quality of investment are increasingly influenced by external factors. However, the forces driving capital accumulation retain strong domestic roots, and an economy that leaves development to global market forces alone is likely to be disappointed. Experience shows that carefully managed and phased integration is the key to success.

The remainder of this chapter addresses these issues. This section considers the possible contribution of international trade to growth and convergence in developing countries, and is followed by an examination of the impact of capital mobility on accumulation.

1. Trade and growth

Analysis of the links between trade and economic growth has long been hampered by ambiguities surrounding the categorization of national trade policies. Two concepts, openness and outward orientation, have often been used interchangeably for this purpose. In common parlance, however, openness refers to a situation characterized by the absence of restrictions on flows of goods across national borders, notably on imports. By contrast, outward orientation usually depicts a strategy of emphasizing world markets as an outlet for domestic producers, and is often synonymous with export promotion. A number of countries which are described as outward- or export-oriented in the above sense have often had important, but selective, restrictions on imports, even though such barriers tended to be lower than in countries emphasizing domestic rather than world markets.

The tendency to equate these two concepts in describing and assessing trade policy has its roots in the conventional trade theory that policies that combine protection with export promotion produce the same result as those relying on full-scale import liberalization, because they are equivalent in terms of incentive structure - a proposition that is valid only under very special conditions. This tendency has also given rise to a confusing proliferation of empirical indicators which are used interchangeably in connection with trade policy. However, findings of a recent survey examining six common measures of trade policy indicate that countries can be very differently ranked according to the measure used, and there are few significant cross-country correlations between these measures.[37] These findings raise obvious questions about the reliability of the various indicators in capturing some common aspects of trade policy, and about the interpretation of the empirical evidence on the relation between trade and economic performance.

Even when agreement can be reached on the appropriate concepts, the role of related measures within a broader development strategy can raise difficult issues. For example, if, as in some studies, an economy is considered open when its average tariff rate is less than 40 per cent and non-tariff barriers cover less than 40 per cent of trade, then on this criterion the first-tier East Asian NIEs would be classified as having been consistently open over the past 30 years or so, and their strong growth performance would bias the empirical results in cross-country regressions in favour of a link between openness and growth and convergence. Indeed, much of the evidence on the causation between high and rising shares of imports and exports, on the one hand, and rapid economic growth, on the other, hinges on the performance of a small number of East Asian NIEs which account for as much as three quarters of the increase in the share of developing countries in world manufactured exports from 1970 to 1990. However, a careful examination of these economies, notably the Republic of Korea and Taiwan Province of China, shows that while they were outward-oriented in the above sense, their trade policies were not liberal. They were not designed to align domestic prices to those in world markets so as to capture static efficiency gains. Indeed, there is ample evidence that price distortions in these economies were pervasive, even more so than in many other developing countries with a much less impressive economic performance. Rather, trade policies were designed to attain dynamic gains from linking trade to capital accumulation and technological change.[38]

In *TDR 1996* the UNCTAD secretariat introduced the idea of an export-investment nexus to capture the wider and mutually reinforcing set of growth-enhancing linkages between trade and investment. Exports enable domestic savings to be raised and balance of payments constraints on capital goods imports and accumulation to be overcome. But since export expansion depends on the creation of productive capacity in industry as well as on productivity growth, a sustainable growth process requires mutually reinforcing interactions between investment and exports. These interactions perhaps explain why an extensive body of research has long confirmed a strong correlation between trade and economic growth, but has been unable to establish causation.[39]

The extensive intervention of governments in East Asia in animating an export-investment nexus is by now well documented.[40] They pursued vigorous trade and industrial policies designed to stimulate local industry, applying export incentives and protectionist measures for industries at different stages of maturity. Export promotion through subsidies for certain industries was combined with protection for infant industries, rendering the conventional dichotomy between the two meaningless. Since tight restrictions on some imports were accompanied by low or zero tariffs on others, the average tariff rate and overall coverage was quite low. Measures of openness which conceal these facts conveniently ignore the central policy issues arising from this experience. To say that countries will suffer if they have an average tariff or quota coverage of more than 40 per cent says very little about the impact that selective trade and industrial policies might have on economic growth.

Trade policies would not have by themselves been sufficient to animate a dynamic growth process without the very rapid pace of investment. As examined in greater detail in chapter VI below, none of the governments in East Asia, with the possible exception of Hong Kong, left the pace or direction of investment to market forces; they employed a variety of fiscal and financial measures to foster reinvestment of profits and accelerate capital formation. In this context, trade was used to complement and enlarge the benefits of a fast pace of capital accumulation.

An examination of specific liberalization episodes in industrial countries to ascertain the impact on subsequent growth rates and the timing of income convergence also confirms this conclusion. The most commonly cited case of a direct relationship between the timing of trade liberalization and income convergence concerns the countries of the former European Economic Community (EEC) following the reduction of tariffs and the elimination of quotas initiated in 1959.[41] However, tariffs were still quite high in 1963 when the rapid convergence came to an end, and most of the spectacular increase in intra-EEC trade took place thereafter. Intra-EEC imports rose from 4 per cent of the combined GDP of the six countries in 1951 to only 6 per cent in 1963. It is difficult to believe that such a modest increase in trade, mostly concentrated towards the end of the period, could have been a major factor behind the impressive convergence of incomes which occurred during this period. A more convincing argument is that rapid growth in all the countries and income convergence among them led to a mood of optimism and created the political conditions required to dismantle trade barriers, which in turn led to a rapid expansion of trade and a virtuous growth circle. In all these countries, a very rapid pace of capital accumulation since the early 1950s, particularly in manufacturing, provided the basis of the convergence process, a process which was reinforced by closer integration through the growth of intra-industry trade.[42]

2. Trade and the convergence of wages

Because the immediate impact of trade liberalization is to change relative prices in line with a country's resource endowments, a general move towards greater openness in the world economy should be reflected in narrowing wage gaps among countries. Demand for labour should shift towards less-skilled workers in the South and more highly skilled workers in the North, raising relative wages of the unskilled in the former and of the skilled in the latter. Over time, wages of all similarly skilled workers should fully converge in the context of overall gains from increased trade.[43]

Despite the emphasis on the growth opportunities created by trade, there is growing concern in the North that trade with developing countries is bringing down wages of unskilled workers towards those in the South. However, as discussed in greater detail in *TDR 1995*, although such a tendency is consistent with the experience of growing wage differentials between skilled and unskilled labour in a number of advanced industrial economies, it is difficult to reconcile the actual size, scope and timing of wage movements in the North with shifts in North-South trade. So far, less attention has

been paid to the impact of trade liberalization on wage differentials between skilled and unskilled labour in the South itself, an issue which is addressed in chapter IV. This section focuses on wage gaps between similar workers in developed and developing countries.

The body of accumulated evidence, from both developed and developing countries, does not show any long-run wage convergence trend in the world economy.[44] From samples of countries at similar levels of development there is some evidence of wage convergence, but it is less evident the greater the number of countries included in the sample. A number of studies focusing on the former EEC have found some support for wage convergence among those countries.[45] The evidence is less clear when other OECD countries are also considered. Up to the early 1980s, growing trade among those countries was associated with wage convergence. Thereafter, however, no clear convergence pattern emerges, and average real wages of production workers in a number of countries, including the United States and the United Kingdom, diverged from the highest-wage countries such as the then Federal Republic of Germany.[46] As regards developing countries, a comparison of wage trends in 16 high-income and 8 middle-income countries at the industry level shows a statistically significant convergence of relative wages towards the world-wide mean due to greater international trade. However, convergence is modest and limited to the high-income economies.[47]

Over the past two decades most developing countries have experienced rising wage gaps with the North, sometimes either because real wages have declined in absolute terms (as in Latin America and much of Africa in the 1980s) or because they have risen less than in the developed countries (as in much of South Asia). The exception is the first-tier of East Asian NIEs, where manufacturing wages have converged on those of the North quite rapidly.

These general trends hold for all skill levels. Table 31 shows changes in the wage gap between various developing countries and the United States for a number of low, medium and high-skill industries from 1980 to the early 1990s. In all these countries except Kenya, the share of exports and imports in GDP rose sharply over this period. However, in most countries, and for all skill levels, there has been a strong decline in the wage of developing countries relative to the United States.

Table 31

WAGES AND PRODUCTIVITY PER EMPLOYEE IN SELECTED DEVELOPING COUNTRIES AND INDUSTRIES RELATIVE TO THE UNITED STATES, 1980 AND 1993[a]

(Ratio to the United States level)

A. Annual wage per employee

Country	Textiles 1980	Textiles 1993	Clothing 1980	Clothing 1993	Transport equipment 1980	Transport equipment 1993	Printing and publishing 1980	Printing and publishing 1993
Mexico	0.43	0.21	0.49	0.24	0.37	0.17	0.38	0.21
Chile	0.37	0.23	0.45	0.26	0.25	0.15	0.50	0.35
Colombia	0.23	0.11	0.19	0.10	0.13	0.07	0.16	0.09
Hong Kong	0.38	0.57	0.52	0.64	0.29	0.45	0.30	0.44
Republic of Korea	0.21	0.51	0.23	0.61	0.18	0.45	0.28	0.52
Malaysia	0.10	0.17	0.07	0.19	0.10	0.13	0.12	0.19
Indonesia	0.04	0.04	0.06	0.05	0.07	0.03	0.07	0.04
Turkey	0.21	0.33	0.24	0.24	0.26	0.27	0.28	0.33
India	0.08	0.05	0.08	0.05	0.06	0.04	0.07	0.05
Kenya	0.13	0.03	0.14	0.03	0.07	0.03	0.24	0.04
Morocco	0.24	0.13	0.14	0.14	0.30	0.14	0.32	..
Memo item:								
Germany	1.24	1.32	1.31	1.45	0.97	1.08	1.30	1.32

B. Value added per employee

Country	Textiles 1980	Textiles 1993	Clothing 1980	Clothing 1993	Transport equipment 1980	Transport equipment 1993	Printing and publishing 1980	Printing and publishing 1993
Mexico	0.43	0.25	0.84	0.22	0.50	0.35	0.40	0.22
Chile	0.57	0.32	0.72	0.34	0.55	0.20	0.84	0.44
Colombia	0.48	0.27	0.29	0.13	0.25	0.17	0.26	0.20
Hong Kong	0.35	0.43	0.42	0.41	0.23	0.29	0.28	0.33
Republic of Korea	0.29	0.63	0.28	0.65	0.24	0.54	0.29	0.57
Malaysia	0.16[b]	0.20	0.12[b]	0.14	0.13[b]	0.19	0.16[b]	0.20
Indonesia	0.08	0.07	0.05	0.07	0.17	0.16	0.07	0.08
Turkey	0.40	0.40	0.34	0.41	0.27	0.33	0.27	0.46
India	0.07	0.03	0.07	0.08	0.05	0.03	0.05	0.03
Kenya	0.14	0.02	0.13	0.03	0.05	0.01	0.15	0.03
Morocco	0.20	0.11	0.10	0.09	0.23	0.13	0.19	..
Memo item:								
Germany	0.94	1.19	1.26	1.33	0.86	0.83	0.95	0.82

Source: UNIDO, *Handbook of Industrial Statistics 1988* and *International Yearbook of Industrial Statistics, 1996.*
  a Or most recent year available.
  b 1975.

The exception to this trend has been the Asian NIEs, particularly those in the first-tier, such as the Republic of Korea, where wages for all skill levels have converged on the United States.

These widening wage gaps in manufacturing, both between developed and developing countries and also among developing countries, have coincided with a period of greater openness in the developing world. However, it is difficult to explain these trends simply in terms of differences in factor endowments, including differences in educational attainment. Rather, for most developing countries, strong growth in wages depends upon industrial expansion and upgrading so as to achieve higher levels of employment and rapid productivity growth in the economy as a whole, as well as in specific industrial sectors. A recent study of real wage growth in manufacturing in 32 developing countries for 1973-1990 confirms that the impact of trade on wages cannot be divorced from investment and productivity performance, and that greater openness to trade in this group of countries in the 1980s did not coincide with stronger wage growth.[48] As table 31 shows, those countries in East Asia which exhibited strong wage convergence also exhibited strong productivity convergence. This result has been attained in the context of the investment-export nexus described above, rather than as a result of spontaneous global market forces.

F. Capital mobility, growth and convergence

As noted above, the clearest sign of globalization has been the rapid increase in international flows of capital. It is precisely this aspect of globalization that is expected to yield the greatest benefits for developing countries. These benefits should arise from the contribution of capital flows to the two principal determinants of the catching-up process, namely capital accumulation and technology transfer.

This section first examines these propositions against the background of the historical evidence. It is argued that greater capital mobility can bring significant benefits to developing countries but that these benefits depend crucially on how a country manages its integration with global capital markets. It then examines to what extent increased capital movements help accelerate global growth by responding to opportunities for investment in physical assets, thereby equalizing rates of return on investment everywhere. It is found that there is an upward convergence of profits in OECD countries, where capital markets are much more closely integrated, but that higher profits are not associated with increased investment and faster growth. Rather, they have been brought about by the stronger bargaining power of capital against labour associated with globalization.

1. Foreign direct investment

The recent acceleration of flows of FDI has renewed interest in the role of transnational corporations (TNCs) as engines of economic growth, particularly in developing countries. Indeed, this role has been given prominence in many recent accounts of the contemporary globalization process, primarily for three reasons. First, unlike most other capital flows, FDI does not represent a fixed charge on foreign exchange reserves; second, it is a less volatile source of financing for the accumulation process; and third, it can have more direct links to economic growth than other cross-border flows, particularly because it facilitates the transfer of technology and generates spillovers into other sectors.

All these reasons carry considerable weight. The experience with FDI before 1913 suggests that it can indeed bring about a transfer of real resources internationally. Likewise, United States investment in Europe after the second World War was important in diffusing new technology. The success of some East Asian NIEs in attracting FDI with a strong export orientation also helped compensate for deficiencies in domestic technological and organizational skills during critical periods of their industrialization. However, there are a number of aspects of the current globalization experience that suggests that the impact of FDI on growth and convergence requires careful assessment before designing policies which aim to maximize the benefits from hosting TNCs.

Assessing the impact of recorded increases in FDI flows is especially difficult because they include a number of different types of investment activity with different effects. Greenfield FDI, which involves a firm constructing a new production facility abroad financed by capital raised in the home country, clearly makes a positive contribution to capital formation in the host country. The acquisition of a controlling interest in an already existing firm is likely to have a different impact from greenfield investment, and seems to correspond more to shorter-term capital flows. This may also be true for retained earnings. Although it is often presumed that these earnings are automatically reinvested in physical capital, existing statistical measures cannot distinguish between their use for such a purpose and their investment in financial assets.

Many of the changes in global financial markets that have facilitated capital mobility and the increase in FDI flows have also made it more difficult to evaluate their stability. Evidence suggests that even when FDI is governed by long-term considerations, such as real rates of return and securing market shares, aggregate FDI flows can respond rapidly to changes in short-term economic conditions. This is particularly true for non-repatriated earnings on existing stocks of FDI, which have constituted in recent years a more important source of asset acquisition abroad by United States and United Kingdom firms than capital outflows from those countries. As recognized by a recent World Bank study, even those forms of FDI that make the greatest contribution to host-country investment may involve unstable financial flows:

> Because direct investors hold factories and other assets that are impossible to move, it is sometimes assumed that a direct investment inflow is more stable than other forms of capital flows. This need not be the case. While a direct investor usually has some immovable assets, there is no reason in principle why these cannot by fully offset by domestic liabilities. Clearly, a direct investor can borrow in order to export capital, and thereby generate rapid capital outflows.[49]

These considerations suggest that a developing country that relies on FDI rather than portfolio inflows is not necessarily protected against external financial instability. It thus still needs to pay attention to the management of its balance of payments and to macroeconomic stability.

Any examination of the impact of FDI on economic growth and convergence must also bear in mind a number of other considerations. Although evidence suggests a positive association between FDI and growth, it is difficult to determine causation.[50] A realistic interpretation of the evidence suggests that there is a threshold level of income which needs to be crossed before FDI can make a significant contribution to overall growth performance.[51] Such a conclusion is also broadly consistent with the finding that technology and other spillovers from TNCs become significant only when there is already in place an appropriate level of local capabilities.[52]

It appears that FDI is attracted to economies with a proven growth record, be it to seek markets or cost advantages, in which case it can become part of a virtuous growth circle. However, much of the developing world remains outside this universe of international production because cost advantages alone do not offset low productivity levels or the absence of productive assets needed t complement firm-specific plant and equipment. Furthermore, risks associated with investment tend to be inversely related to the stage of development reached. While incurring these risks may be justified by the expectation of monopolistic profits associated with the exploitation of a particular natural resource in a poor developing country, there will be no such exceptional or monopolistic elements in manufacturing or services. Any attempt in these countries to improve cost advantages by easing their entry conditions for FDI, or by reducing wages further, will almost certainly fail to offset other disadvantages which cause the risk premiums to be high.

These considerations explain why the recent rapid surge in FDI flows to the South has remained heavily concentrated among a handful of developing countries. In 1993 the 10 largest host developing countries accounted for 79 per cent of the total FDI flow to the South; seven of them were in East Asia and alone accounted for close to two thirds of the total inflow. However, it should be kept in mind that in many developing countries FDI is unlikely to play the same role as in some East Asian countries. Malaysia is often cited as an ex-

Table 32

COMPARATIVE INFLOW OF FDI INTO MALAYSIA AND OTHER DEVELOPING COUNTRIES

(Average annual FDI inflow in 1991-1993)

	Total ($ billion)	Per capita ($)	Percentage of 1990 GDP
Malaysia	12.8	241.8	10.0
Developing countries[a]			
Actual inflow	136.8	16.5	1.4
Hypothetical inflow (I)[b]	2007.8	241.8	20.9
Hypothetical inflow (II)[c]	957.7	115.3	10.0

Source: R. Rowthorn, "Replicating the Experience of the NIEs" (mimeo), Cambridge, United Kingdom, 1996.
   a Excluding the first-tier NIEs.
   b Assuming the FDI inflow per capita to be the same as for Malaysia.
   c Assuming the FDI inflow as a percentage of GDP to be the same as for Malaysia.

ample of how to sustain rapid growth by attracting very large inflows of export-oriented FDI. Indeed, on both a per capita basis and relative to GDP, Malaysia had one of the largest stocks of inward FDI in the developing world in 1990 and inflows have continued to be substantial, constituting a major source of external financing. However, even if all other developing countries had the domestic prerequisites which would allow them to replicate Malaysia's experience, substantial increases in total FDI flows to the South would be required. As table 32 shows, even a modest replication of the Malaysian experience throughout the developing world implies a level of FDI outflows from the North that it would be totally unrealistic to expect. If all developing countries other than the first-tier NIEs received from OECD countries the same amount of FDI as a proportion of GDP as did Malaysia in 1991-1993, total FDI outflows from those countries would amount to about 27 per cent of their spending on investment. If, on the other hand, they received the same per capita FDI as Malaysia, the proportion would rise to 56 per cent.

In any event, the contribution of FDI to growth and industrialization depends very much on the degree of control that the foreign firm retains over its assets. The general body of evidence suggests that the nature and extent of any spillovers to domestic firms is industry-specific and depends on how domestic policymakers manage FDI, including its role in the export-investment nexus. Indeed, the role of policy is now even greater, given that the determinants and organization of FDI flows have become more complex. Rather than pursuing cost-reducing and/or market-seeking strategies aimed at raising corporate profits in a particular location, TNCs are increasingly seeking to combine these objectives around a tightly organized intra-firm division of labour where the choice of location for a specific activity is made in the context of the overall profitability of the firm. By widening the choice of possible locations in this way the advantages for the firm can be numerous. However, and particularly in developing countries, the consequence may well be that FDI becomes more footloose than in the past, relying heavily on imported inputs from other affiliates and with fewer linkages with and technological spillovers to the host economy.[53]

In this context it is important to recognize the different ways in which FDI has been attracted to and used in East Asian economies. While Hong Kong took a more laissez-faire approach, the attitude toward FDI was much more selective in the Republic of Korea and Taiwan Province of China and also, though to a lesser extent, in Singapore.

A larger array of policy measures could consequently be brought to bear on FDI to ensure that it made a positive contribution to economic growth. To date, the successful second-tier NIEs have taken a middle way. However, as discussed in *TDR 1996*, concern over heavy reliance on imported intermediate goods and over weak supply and technology linkages between the TNC-dominated export sectors and the domestic economy has already triggered more active industrial and technology policies in these countries, including the use of local content agreements and more selective incentives to attract higher-valued added activities and generate FDI spillovers in the areas of training and R&D.

2. Financial flows

An important difference between the current process of integration of global markets and that of the 19th century lies in the nature of financial flows. As noted above, in the earlier period greater integration of financial markets and increased flows of financial capital were complementary to international trade. In the more recent period, by contrast, finance is not simply a lubricant to real economic activity. The role of international finance has extended well beyond the coordination of international trade and investment. It has gained a life of its own independent of the international flow of goods and investment.

This is not to say that global linkages of finance with trade and FDI have been totally severed. The recent expansion of world trade and of TNC activities could not have taken place without a corresponding expansion of the global operations of financial institutions. Increased international trade in goods has necessitated an expansion of financial services; intermediaries now operate in each market to provide foreign exchange services and trade financing. The increased need for firms to secure foreign exchange cover in respect of both export earnings and foreign investment has added momentum to this process by providing a major role for international banks.[54]

However, this global financial deepening has occurred while the link between financial flows and foreign investment has considerably weakened. These financial flows are rarely associated with the flows of real resources - i.e. capital equipment embodying best-practice production techniques and other resource inputs seeking the highest available rates of return in the production of goods and services. Rather, they are primarily related to the purchase and sale in secondary markets of liabilities created for the financing of already existing real assets. As discussed in previous *TDRs*, a large proportion of these flows consists of liquid capital attracted by short-term arbitrage margins and prospects of speculative capital gain, rather than by long-term yields on productive investment. They are extremely volatile and subject to bandwagon effects, capable of generating gyrations in security prices, exchange rates and trade balances. They make little contribution to the international allocation of savings or diffusion of technology and hence to a reduction in international disparities in per capita income.

It is increasingly argued that financial globalization is creating systemic effects that undermine global stability and growth. Large swings in exchange rates and current account balances brought about by the volatility of capital flows tend to create considerable uncertainty regarding prospective yields on investment, particularly in traded goods sectors. This raises the minimum expected rate of return that will induce investors to undertake long-term investment, thereby slowing output growth. The problem is particularly serious for developing countries, where firms cannot always hedge against such risks by allocating their activities globally and through financial operations. Their outward-oriented strategies can consequently be endangered as investment in traded-good industries is depressed.

Experience shows that the factors that encourage inflows of liquid capital can also impede investment in productive physical assets. Circumstances can arise when the short-term return on financial assets and the return on productive capital investment move in opposite directions. When domestic short-term interest rates are raised relative to rates abroad in order to stabilize the economy or reduce the pace of expansion, they can attract liquid capital, placing upward pressure on the exchange rate. At the same time they may depress investment. For one thing, the slowdown of home demand, together with loss of competitiveness due to currency appreciation, can reduce the expected real return on capital assets. For another, the increase in the real return on financial assets can raise the cost of financing productive investment. As a result, the liquid capital inflows attracted by high interest rates are not used for productive investment; on the contrary, such investment may contract as short-term funds flow in.

This has indeed been the experience of a number of countries during the past two decades. In the 1980s capital flowed primarily from countries with high investment rates (e.g. Japan) to countries with low investment rates (e.g. the United States), and served to finance consumption rather than investment. Similarly, a very large part of the flows to Latin America in the first half of the 1990s financed consumption rather than investment and growth.

However, as examined in last year's *TDR*, a number of developing countries have been able to manage financial flows successfully. They have resorted not only to conventional methods, such as intervention in foreign exchange markets or adoption of more flexible exchange rate policies, but also to more direct controls, including quantitative restrictions on holding and issuing foreign currency assets and the composition of non-interest-bearing reserve requirements. Successful management of capital flows has depended on a flexible and pragmatic approach designed to maintain stable and sustainable exchange rates and current account positions without impeding capital flows related to trade and investment.

3. Capital mobility, accumulation and convergence of profits

As noted above, greater capital mobility is expected to sever the link between national savings and investment so that individual countries can save more than they invest, or invest more than they save. It should also lead to a greater equalization of the real rate of return on capital among countries. This section examines the available evidence, concentrating on the major OECD countries, where capital markets are much more closely integrated. Recent trends in profits in developing countries are discussed in chapter IV below.

The evidence for the OECD countries for the 1960s and 1970s shows a broad balance between national savings and investment. A seminal study relating the shares of gross domestic investment and gross national savings in GDP in those countries for 1960-1974 concluded that national savings tended to be invested in the country where they originated.[55] Moreover, this close link between national savings and investment holds even when a number of other factors are taken into account. Although the link is somewhat weaker in the 1980s, the evidence still confirms the existence of substantial imperfections in international capital markets.[56] These results are incompatible with the idea that over the long term international capital flows can exert a significant influence on national investment and growth rates.

However, these studies do not distinguish between the effects of FDI and of portfolio investment on capital accumulation, and there is little direct evidence on the effect of inward or outward FDI. However, according to a study relating to OECD countries, each dollar of outward FDI reduces investment in the home country by approximately one dollar and is not compensated by an inflow of portfolio investment.[57] Accordingly, portfolio investment cannot be lumped together with FDI in analysing the impact of international capital mobility on accumulation. It is indeed argued that while financial flows do not alter the dependence of domestic investment on domestic savings, this is not necessarily the case for FDI:

> ... an extra dollar of national saving would remain in domestic portfolio assets unless it is used by a multinational corporation to finance a cross-border direct investment. ... If the portfolio investments were completely segmented into national markets in this way, the effect of the outbound FDI on domestic available funds would not be offset by an international flow of portfolio capital and the aggregate domestic investment would be reduced by the full amount of the direct investment outflow.[58]

Thus, according to this evidence, over the long term financial flows do not reduce the dependence of capital accumulation on domestic investment. By contrast, FDI alters the domestic savings-investment balance; while outward FDI reduces investment in the home country, it appears to add to domestic investment in the host country. It follows that, to the extent that capital flows equalize rates of return on investment in different countries, they do so for FDI rather than for short-term capital.

The evidence shows a remarkable convergence of rates of return on capital among the OECD countries in the past 15 years. As can be seen in chart 6, the coefficient of variation in the rate of return on capital for the business sector among the G-7 countries fell significantly after the recession of

Chart 6

RATE OF RETURN ON CAPITAL IN THE BUSINESS SECTOR OF G7 COUNTRIES AND INTER-COUNTRY VARIATIONS[a], 1980-1996

(Per cent)

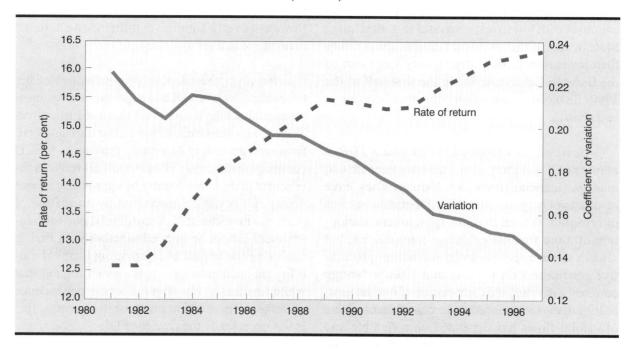

Source: *OECD Economic Outlook*, No. 61, June 1997.
   Note: The chart depicts three-year moving averages. Underlying data for 1997 and 1998 are projections.

1980-1982. A similar tendency is also observed for rates of return earned by United States companies on their investments abroad.[59] For the EU countries, the decline in variation has been more marked since the late 1980s.

This decline in variations in rates of return has occurred while the trend rate of return has been strongly upward. In other words, there has been an upward convergence of rates of return on capital in the major OECD countries. This upward trend in profits is also reflected in the increased share of capital income in the business sector (chart 7) - a tendency that is also to be found in developing countries (see chapter IV). However, the rise in profits has not been associated with a corresponding increase in the aggregate share of private investment in output in those countries, although the same period has witnessed a surge in outward and inward investment in the major industrial countries. It thus seems that increased FDI has served, at least partly, to redistribute, rather than to add to, aggregate global investment.

The tendency for investment shares to decline may have been linked to the other aspect of increased integration in financial flows, namely portfolio flows. As financial engineering has increased the scope to trade long-term fixed income securities for short-term gains, the integration of developed country bond markets has increased. This, along with the convergence in inflation rates which has occurred in recent years, has brought about a marked tendency towards convergence in long-term real rates of return, which are often considered as the most important determinant of investment financing costs. However, the increasing volume of trading in these instruments has tended to increase the volatility of bond prices to the point that in the 1990s they exceeded the volatility of equity prices. The result has been to increase the risk premium and raise long-term rates, which have also been pushed up by monetary policy. Thus, the impact of increased integration and financial flows in such markets has meant upward convergence in real long-term interest rates at historically high levels. The increase in profits is thus absorbed, at least partly, by increased interest charges on corporate debt, resulting in a downward pressure on investment in the developed economies.

This disparity between the evolution of profits and investment is not new. It is a tendency that emerged in the early 1980s, and that was noted a decade ago by the UNCTAD secretariat:

> The medium-term financial strategies adopted by the major developed market economies at the end of the 1970s sought to reverse the decline in profit shares and rates of return which had occurred in the course of the decade, and which were believed to be responsible for slow growth and unemployment. Thanks to falling raw material prices and wage costs, business profitability has been restored. However, this has not triggered the investment boom that policymakers were expecting. The main reasons are: slow demand growth; continued high real interest rates; and uncertainties regarding the key macroeconomic variables and the trading system. Unless these problems are resolved, investment and growth are likely to remain subdued.[60]

While profits are currently very close to their pre-1970 levels, they generate much less investment than previously. As discussed in greater detail in *TDR 1995*, the main reason for sluggish investment is the low-growth hysteresis created by monetary policy that tends to lock most major industrial economies into growth rates of around 2.5 per cent. By contrast, investment now generates higher profits than before. The evidence invariably points to rising unemployment and falling wage costs as the principal factors behind the surge in profits.[61]

Sluggish demand also generates excess supply in the product market, leading to fierce competition among firms. However, since investment is sluggish and the pace of capacity creation slow, the pressure on profits and prices is more than offset by the dampening effect of increased unemployment on wage levels. Consequently, real labour costs and inflation are reduced as profits rise.

The combination of increased mobility of capital, slow demand growth and excess supply of labour thus appears to be an important element in the rising profits in OECD countries. This process, while putting pressure on real wages does not necessarily lead to a convergence of real wages

Chart 7

PROFITS AND INVESTMENT IN THE G7 COUNTRIES, 1980-1995

(Per cent)

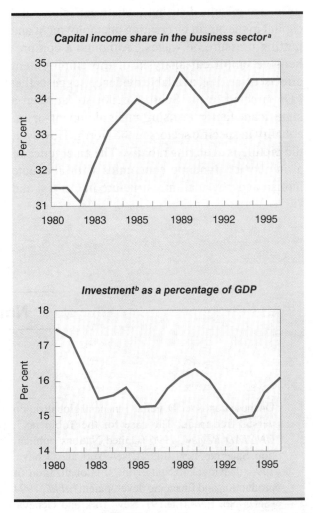

Source: *OECD Economic Outlook*, No.61, June 1997.
  a Gross operating surplus of enterprises, i.e. the difference between value added calculated at factor cost (i.e. excluding net indirect taxes) and labour income.
  b Gross fixed non-residential capital formation.

because of differences in labour market conditions. Those countries which have adopted "flexible" labour market policies tend to retain investment at home and even attract FDI inflows, adding to jobs at relatively low wages in productive sectors. As shown in *TDR 1995*, the policies also lead to the creation of large numbers of low-productivity, low-wage jobs in services sectors, transforming open unemployment partly into disguised unemployment. In countries where wages remain relatively rigid, labour market conditions are reflected in high rates of open unemployment, rather than low wages or disguised unemployment. Thus, as noted above, there has been no tendency for wages to converge in the OECD area since the early 1980s, despite increased trade and FDI flows.

Moving production facilities to developing countries through FDI in order to lower costs can influence income distribution between labour and capital in the North by creating unemployment and putting pressure on wages. Although a comprehensive empirical analysis of the employment effects is lacking, available evidence suggests that FDI directed to the South has not so far been a significant factor in rising unemployment or inequality in specific sectors in the North. However, the picture is changing rapidly. The emergence of a number of dynamic economies with adequate human and physical infrastructure in Central and Eastern Europe and Asia has certainly widened the options of capital to choose among alternative locations in both labour and skill-intensive production. Furthermore, in many industries it is becoming increasingly possible for TNCs to locate specific activities in the production chain in different countries according to their skill endowments, thereby allowing developing countries to enter more easily into the global system of production. These forces can certainly work towards a greater convergence between developing and developed countries and bring benefits to labour in the South. However, they can also reinforce the global tendency for the share of profits to rise at the expense of wages - something that is unlikely to be reversed as long as global demand is deficient and too much labour chases too little capital. ∎

Notes

1   On these trends see D. Felix "Financial globalization versus free trade: The case for the Tobin tax", *UNCTAD Review, 1996* (United Nations publication, Sales No. E.97.II.D.2), New York and Geneva, 1996; J. Kregel, "Capital flows: Globalization of production and financing development", *ibid., 1994* (Sales No. E.94.II.D.19), New York and Geneva, 1994; Y. Akyüz, "Taming International Finance", in J. Michie and G. Grieve Smith (eds.), *Managing the Global Economy* (Oxford: Oxford University Press, 1995).

2   See, for example, J. Sachs and A. Warner, "Economic Reform and the Process of Global Integration", *Brookings Papers on Economic Activity*, No. 1, 1995 (Washington, D.C.: The Brookings Institution, 1995); J. Williamson, "Globalization, Convergence and History", *The Journal of Economic History*, Vol. 56, No. 2, 1996; *Global Economic Prospects and the Developing Countries 1996* (Washington, D.C.: The World Bank, 1996); IMF, *World Economic Outlook*, May 1997.

3   See A. Maddison, *Monitoring the World Economy* (Paris: OECD, 1995), table 2.4.

4   In 1914, the United Kingdom accounted for 41 per cent of the gross nominal stock of overseas investment, France for 20 per cent and Germany for 13 per cent (Maddison, *op. cit.*, table 3.3).

5   The figure rises to perhaps as much as two thirds when related infrastructure and service activities are included. On the sectoral breakdown of FDI in this period, see J. Dunning, "Changes in the level and structure of international production: The last one hundred years", in M. Casson (ed.), *The Growth of International Business* (London: Allen and Unwin, 1984).

6   The expansion of the great British merchant banking houses, for example, that engineered the globalization of trade in the British Empire in the 19th century was based on their ability to integrate the provision of financial services with their trading activities in primary commodities. They soon extended their activities to the underwriting of international bond issues to provide the financing for foreign investments comprised of the export of British manufactured goods, in particular capital goods, thus serving to coordinate the international allocation of financial capital and capital goods throughout the Empire.

7   An estimated 32 million people emigrated from Europe during 1881-1915. During this period, Southern Europe overtook Northern Europe as the main source of emigrants and while the "Western offshoots" (North America and Australasia) remained the leading host nations, Latin America also became an increasingly important destination. There was also large-scale emigration from India and China during this period, although it was to a much greater extent of a temporary nature: see

A.G. Kenwood and A.G. Lougheed, *The Growth of the International Economy, 1820-1990* (London: Routledge, 1992 (third edition)).

8   The Paris Convention for the Protection of Industrial Property was negotiated in 1883 and the Berne Convention for the Protection of Literary and Artistic Works three years later.

9   See M. Wilkins, "Multinational Corporations: An Historical Account", in R. Kozul-Wright and R. Rowthorn (eds.), *The Transnational Corporation and the Global Economy* (London: Macmillan, 1997).

10 In 1870 Britain was among a group of "super-rich" core economies which included the other early industrial economies (Belgium and Switzerland), the Netherlands (an established trading and financial centre) and a group of wealthy primary-producing economies (Australia, New Zealand and the United States) with strong political, economic and cultural links to Britain. But adopting a cut-off per capita income of $1,000, this core in 1870 also included most European economies as well as Canada and Argentina.

11 The initial income gap between leader and followers, although not small, was certainly not so wide as the gap facing today's newly industrializing countries. Finland and Portugal, the poorest European economies in 1870, had a GDP per capita which was one third that of Great Britain, although for per capita manufacturing output the gap was considerably larger (some 6 to 8 times).

12 In Western Europe, the coefficient of variation of GDP per capita remained stationary, at 0.31, between 1870 and 1900 and fell to 0.25 by 1913.

13 Williamson, *op. cit.*, p.294.

14 See B. Supple, "The State and industrial revolution 1700-1914", in C. Cipolla (ed.), *The Fontana Economic History of Europe,* Vol. III - *The Industrial Revolution* (London: Fontana, 1973); and R. Kozul-Wright "The myth of Anglo-Saxon capitalism", in H.-J. Chang and R. Rowthorn (eds.), *The Role of the State in Economic Change* (Oxford: Oxford University Press, 1995).

15 See P. Bairoch and R. Kozul-Wright, "Globalization myths: Some historical reflections on integration, industrialization and growth in the world economy", *UNCTAD Discussion Paper*, No.113, Geneva, March 1996.

16 C. Freeman, "New technology and catching-up", *European Journal of Development Research*, Vol. I, No.1, 1989; and J. Campbell *et al.*, *Governance of the American Economy* (Cambridge: Cambridge University Press, 1991).

17 As Felix (*op. cit.*, p.65) has shown, although this was an era of stable prices and exchange rates, it was not one of cheap capital; short- and long-term interest rates were higher and more volatile than in 1946-1970. During 1880-1914 only 12 countries remained permanently on the gold standard, and most of them had embarked on a period of sustained growth and industrial transformation prior to their entry; see M. Panic, *European Monetary Union: Lessons from the Gold Standard* (London: Macmillan, 1993).

18 See Kenwood and Lougheed, *op. cit.*, pp. 137-140; D. Senghaas, *The European Experience: A Historical Critique of Development Theory* (Leamington Spa: Berg Publishers, 1985), chap. 3; on Argentina and Mexico in this period see C. Marichal, *A Century of Debt Crises in Latin America* (Princeton, N.J.: Princeton University Press, 1989).

19 This was particularly true of the British colonies, because of the greater dependence of British manufacturing exporters on their colonial markets; see P. Bairoch, *Economics and World History: Myths and Paradoxes* (Harvester: London, 1993), pp.72-79 and pp. 88-92.

20 See D. Ben-David and D. Papell, "Slowdowns and Meltdowns: Postwar Growth Evidence from 74 Countries", *CEPR Discussion Paper*, No. 1111 (London: Centre for Economic Policy Research, 1995).

21 Indeed, from the discussion of global dynamics in the 19th century it is evident that divergence has been the stronger trend for well over a century. This is also the conclusion of a recent study, which estimates that the ratio of GDP per capita of the richest to that of the poorest country has risen from 8.7 in 1870 to 38.1 in 1960 and 51.6 in 1985. The dispersion of global income (as measured by the standard deviation of the log of per capita income), which was between 0.51 and 0.71 in 1870, rose to 0.87 in 1960 and to 1.03 in 1985. See L. Pritchett, "Divergence Big Time", *World Bank Policy Research Working Paper,* No. 1522 (Washington, D.C.: The World Bank, 1995).

22 Data on per capita income in terms of purchasing power parity used in this chapter are taken from the Penn World Tables. Their unique feature is that expenditure entries are denominated in a common set of prices in a common currency so that real international quantity comparisons can be made between countries and over time. For further information see R. Summers and A. Heston, "The Penn World Table (Mark 5): an expanded set of international comparisons, 1950-1988", *The Quarterly Journal of Economics*, Vol. 106, 1991.

23 For a further discussion of the measurement of world income distribution see R. Korzenwiewicz and T. Moran, "World economic trends in the distribution of income, 1965-1992", *American Journal of Sociology*, Vol. 102, No.4, 1997. A comprehensive picture of global income distribution must, of course, take into account the distribution both among and within countries. However, according to this study, the general picture of world income distribution and changes therein does not significantly alter if the distribution within countries is also included.

24 The assessment of the absolute gap among countries and their comparative welfare conditions depends on how per capita income is measured - i.e. whether in constant or current prices or at market

exchange rates or (as above) purchasing power parity (PPP). While PPP provides a better indicator of welfare conditions, the more generally used yardstick of GNP per capita at market exchange rates provides a better indicator of the command that inhabitants of different countries have "over the human and natural resources" of each other. See G. Arrighi, "World Income Inequalities and the Future of Socialism", *New Left Review*, No. 189, 1991. However, the choice of measurement does not appear to influence the overall trends.

25   The number of small island economies in the group of economies moving into the top quintile is notable and, in part, explains why the number of countries in that quintile was larger in 1990 than in 1965.

26   The list of countries covered in this analysis consists of the OECD members as at the end of 1973, other than Turkey (i.e. the 12 countries of the European Economic Community, Australia, Austria, Canada, Finland, Japan, New Zealand, Norway, Sweden, Switzerland, United States).

27   The coefficient of variation with respect to productivity fell from 0.43 in 1950, to 0.21 in 1973 and 0.17 in 1992.

28   See W. Baumol, "Productivity growth, convergence and welfare: What the long- run data show", *The American Economic Review*, Vol. 76, 1986; B. De Long, "Productivity growth, convergence and Welfare: comment", *ibid.*, Vol. 78, 1988; S. Dowrick and D-T. Nguyen, "OECD comparative economic growth, 1950-85: Catch-up and convergence", *ibid.*, Vol.79, 1989; and S. Dowrick, "Technological catch-up and diverging incomes: Patterns of economic growth, 1960-1988", *Economic Journal*, Vol. 102, 1992.

29   On these trends see D. Dollar and E. Wolff, *Competitiveness, Convergence and International Specialization* (Cambridge, MA: MIT Press, 1993); S. Broadberry, "Local Convergence of European Economies during the Twentieth Century", paper presented at seminar on Comparative Historical National Accounts for Europe in the 19th and 20th Centuries, University of Groningen, Netherlands, 1994; E. O'Leary, "Productivity Convergence: A Study of European Union Countries at the Aggregate, Sectoral and Industry Levels, 1960 to 1990" (Ph.D. thesis, Cork: National University of Ireland, 1995); R. Rowthorn, "Productivity and American Leadership", *The Review of Income and Wealth*, Series 38, No. 4, Dec. 1992; and J. Andrés, J.E. Bosca and R. Doménech, "Main patterns of economic growth in OECD countries", *Investigaciones Economicas*, Vol. XIX, No. 1, Jan. 1995.

30   For the entire period 1960-1990 the rate of convergence for the 12 countries has been 1.5 per cent for productivity and 0.9 per cent for income. However, the figures drop to 1.2 per cent and 0.1 per cent, respectively, for 1970-1990.

31   Ireland joined in 1973, Greece in 1981 and Spain and Portugal in 1986.

32   See O'Leary, *op. cit.*, pp.175-191.

33   See B. Walsh, "Stabilization and adjustment in a small open economy: Ireland, 1979-95", *Oxford Review of Economic Policy*, Vol. 12, Autumn 1996; E. O'Malley, "Industrial policy in Ireland since 1920", in J. Foreman-Peck (ed.), *A Century of Industrial Policy* (forthcoming from the Oxford University Press).

34   See IMF, *World Economic Outlook* , May 1997, table 17.

35   See , for example, Sachs and Warner, *op cit.*; and D. Ben-David and A. Rahman, "Technological Convergence and International Trade", *CEPR Discussion Paper*, No.1359 (London: Centre for Economic Policy Research, 1996).

36   There are serious methodological problems associated with such international comparisons; see R. Levine and D. Renelt, "A sensitivity analysis of cross-country regressions", *The American Economic Review*, Sept. 1992; and for a satirical illustration of the limits of such studies, see H. J. Wall, "Cricket v Baseball as an Engine of Growth", *Royal Economic Society Newsletter* (London), July 1995.

37   See L. Pritchett, "Measuring outward orientation in LDCs: Can it be done?", *Journal of Development Economics*, Vol.49, 1996.

38   The theoretical foundations of *dynamic* gains from free trade are indeed controversial. See, for example, D. Rodrik, *Has Globalization Gone too Far?* (Washington, D.C., Institute for International Economics, 1996), p. 30; and the articles on international competitiveness in *Oxford Review of Economic Policy*, Vol. 12, Autumn 1996. On the notion of a virtuous trade-growth circle see the "General study of exports of manufactures and semi-manufactures from developing countries and their role in development" in *Proceedings of the United Nations Conference on Trade and Development*, Vol. IV - *Trade in Manufactures* (New York: United Nations, 1964).

39   For recent reviews see S. Edwards, "Openness, trade liberalization, and growth in developing countries", *The Journal of Economic Literature*, Vol. XXXI, No. 3, 1993; D. Greenaway, "Liberalizing trade through rose-tinted glasses", *The Economic Journal*, Vol. 103, 1993; D. Greenaway and D. Sapsford, "What does liberalization do for exports and growth", *Weltwirtschaftliches Archiv*, Vol. 130, No. 1, 1994; and S. Sharma and D. Dhakal, "Causal analysis between exports and economic growth in developing countries", *Applied Economics*, Vol. 26, 1994.

40   For more detailed discussions see *TDR 1994* and *TDR 1996*.

41   D. Ben-David, "Equalizing exchange: Trade liberalization and income convergence", *Quarterly Journal of Economics*, Vol. 108, 1993.

42   Extending the analysis to a wider range of countries, including some developing countries with which there were close trade links, confirms a positive association between trade and convergence for countries that were already developed in 1960. See D. Ben-David, "Trade and Convergence among

Countries", *CEPR Discussion Paper*, No.1126 (London: Centre for Economic Policy Research, 1995).

43 The idea of factor price equalization is an impeccable - if controversial - legacy of conventional trade theory. A number of attempts have recently been made to defend a fairly traditional rendition of this argument, most notably by A. Wood in his *North-South Trade, Employment and Inequality: Changing Fortunes in a Skill-Driven World* (Oxford: Clarendon Press, 1994). However, most assessments have sacrificed theoretical correctness for a more pragmatic mix of traditional static forces and more dynamic ones; see R. Findlay, "Modelling global interdependence: Centers, peripheries and frontiers", *The American Economic Review*, May 1996.

44 See E. Leamer and J. Levinsohn, "International trade theory: The evidence", in G. Grossman and K. Rogoff (eds.), *Handbook of International Economics*, Vol. III (Amsterdam: Elsevier, 1995).

45 See H. Gremmen, "Testing the factor price equalization theorem in the EC: An alternative approach", *Journal of Common Market Studies*, Vol. 24, 1985; and A. Van Nourik, "Testing the factor price equalization theorem in the EC: A comment", *ibid.*, Vol. 26, 1987.

46 Exchange rate movements have complicated a direct comparison of wage trends in different countries. However, since 1980, when the real manufacturing wage in dollar terms was $15.97 in Germany, $15.64 in the United States, $14.26 in the United Kingdom and $6.76 in Japan, real wages have risen strongly in Germany and Japan (32 per cent and 35 per cent, respectively), risen moderately in the United Kingdom (by 21 per cent) and fallen in the United States (by 5 per cent).

47 S. Davies, "Cross-country patterns of change in relative wages", *NBER Macroeconomics Annual, 1992* (Cambridge, MA, and London: The MIT Press, 1992).

48 E. Paus and M. Robinson, "The implications of increasing openness for real wages in developing countries, 1973-90", *World Development*, Vol.25, No.4, 1997. This is also the conclusion reached for the OECD countries by Dollar *et al., op. cit.*

49 S. Claessens, M. Dooley, and A. Warner, "Portfolio Capital Flows: Hot or Cool?", *World Bank Discussion Paper*, No. 228 (Washington, DC: The World Bank, 1993), p.22.

50 M. Blomstrom *et al.*, in "What explains developing country growth?" *NBER Working Paper*, No.4132 (Cambridge, MA: National Bureau of Economic Research, 1994), do find such a causal link. On the other hand, a study by A. Dutt, "Direct foreign investment, transnational corporations and growth: Some empirical evidence and a North-South model", in R. Kozul-Wright and R. Rowthorn (eds.), *Transnational Corporations and the Global Economy* (London: Macmillan, 1997), finds no evidence of causation.

51 See E. Borensztein *et al.*,"How does foreign direct investment affect economic growth?", *NBER Working Paper* No.5057 (Cambridge, MA: National Bureau of Economic Research, 1995), where the threshold is linked to the level of human capital.

52 See S. Lall, "Industrial strategy and policies on foreign direct investment in East Asia", *Transnational Corporations*, Vol.4, No. 3, Dec. 1995; B. Aitken *et al.*, "Wages and foreign ownership: A comparative study of Mexico, Venezuela and the United States", *Journal of International Economics*, Vol. 40, 1996.

53 This is discussed in greater detail in *TDR 1996*, with reference to South-East Asia. For a discussion of these issues in the context of the information technology industry see P. Evans, *Embedded Autonomy* (Princeton, N.J.: Princeton University Press, 1995).

54 See J. Kregel, "Capital flows : Globalization of production and financing development", *UNCTAD Review, 1994* (United Nations publication, Sales No. E.94.II.D.19), New York and Geneva, 1994.

55 M. Feldstein, and C. Horioka, "Domestic Savings and International Capital Flows", *Economic Journal*, Vol. 90, No. 2, 1980; see also M. Baxter, and M. Crucini, "Explaining Savings-Investment Correlation", *The American Economic Review*, Vol. 83, No. 3, 1993.

56 See A. Dean, M. Durand, J. Fallon, P. Hoeller, "Saving Trends and Behaviour in OECD Countries," OECD Department of Economics and Statistics, *Working Paper*, No. 67, June 1989, p. 73. This weakening may simply reflect policy coordination failures and the associated trade and fiscal imbalances in some of the major OECD countries rather than the way in which capital resources are allocated internationally.

57 M. Feldstein, "The Effects of Outbound Foreign Direct Investment on the Domestic Capital Stock", *NBER Working Paper*, No. 4668 (Cambridge, MA: National Bureau of Economic Research, March 1994). These results should be interpreted cautiously since they rely on netting the coefficients for outward and inward FDI flows. While the former are statistically significant in most of the regression estimates, the latter generally are not and have frequently been of the wrong sign, which could imply that FDI leads to a decrease in global investment.

58 *Ibid.*, p. 16.

59 See G. Epstein, "International Profit Rate Equalization and Investment: An Empirical Analysis of Integration, Instability, and Enforcement", in G. Epstein and H. Gintis (eds.), *Macroeconomic Policy After the Conservative Era* (Cambridge: Cambridge University Press, 1995).

60 *TDR 1987*, Part One, chap. II, sect. B, introductory text.

61 For the evidence on the effect of profits on investment and the effect of unemployment on profits see A. Glyn, "Does Aggregate Profitability *Really* Matter?", to be published in *Cambridge Journal of Economics*, Sept. 1997.

Chapter III

INCOME INEQUALITY AND DEVELOPMENT

A. Introduction

In recent years there has been increasing concern about trends in income distribution. This concern is rooted in fears that globalization and greater play of market forces are somehow accentuating inequalities at the national level. But against these fears, it has been suggested that integration into the world economy can actually resolve the apparent trade-off between growth and equity. In this respect the East Asian experience is often cited; in those countries rapid and sustained growth has supposedly been combined with low and declining inequality thanks to market-friendly, outward-oriented policies.[1]

This chapter presents evidence on patterns and trends in income inequality and discusses why growth is sometimes associated with rising and sometimes with falling inequality. The next chapter focuses on the relationship between trade and financial liberalization and specific components of inequality - wage differentials, wage and profit shares in value added, agricultural incomes and interest incomes.

The thrust of these chapters is analytical rather than normative; questions of justice and equity are not broached.[2] Equally, the analysis is not concerned with poverty *per se*. Maintaining minimum socially adequate levels of consumption of the poor is certainly a serious social challenge for governments. However, it is the spending behaviour of the rich and the deployment of income from their capital assets which is of central importance for the rate of investment and growth. Moreover, preventing the development of a polarized society through the hollowing-out of the income share of the middle class and a rising gap between the richest and poorest groups in society is important for political stability. All three problems present policy dilemmas and deserve attention.

B. Personal income distribution: recent evidence

A major difficulty facing all research on income distribution, particularly in developing countries, is the availability of reliable and comparable data.[3] This section draws on a recently compiled data set which has gathered more than 2,600 income distribution observations from various primary and secondary sources, and filtered them to give "high quality data", which include 682 observations from 108 countries.[4] This material, supplemented where necessary by data from other sources, provides information on Gini coefficients and income shares of population quintiles (see box 6) for a large number of countries and also enables some analysis to be made of long-term

Box 6

INCOME DISTRIBUTION AND THE MEASUREMENT OF INEQUALITY

Analyses of income distribution within a country are founded on two general approaches. The first focuses on the functional distribution of income, i.e. the share of national income accruing to different factors of production. Classically, the basic division of national income is between wages (paid to labour), profits (the reward to capital) and rent (income from land). But it is possible to differentiate further by sector, location, and mode of production, distinguishing, for example, workers and capitalists in rural and urban areas, the self-employed and other workers in urban areas, and subsistence and commercial farmers. The second approach focuses on the personal (or size) distribution of income, i.e. a description of how much income is received during a given period by individual recipient units within a given population. The recipient units are generally households or individuals. In the latter case, estimates of household incomes are adjusted by household size (sometimes using an adult-equivalent scale) to give household income per capita (or per equivalent individual). [1]

Whilst analysis of factor incomes is based on national accounting data, the basic data for analyses of personal income distribution are obtained from household surveys. Three main sources of income are usually considered to calculate gross incomes available to households: (1) wages and salaries of employees and income from self-employment; (2) "property income", which includes interest, rents and dividends, but excludes retained corporate profits; and (3) current transfers, comprising social security benefits, pensions and life insurance annuity benefits, and other current transfers. Capital gains are usually excluded from consideration, but attempts are made to include income in kind, which ideally should cover fringe benefits from employment (which can be important in rich countries), production for own consumption (particularly important in agrarian societies), and the imputed rent received by homeowners. Net household income (or disposable household income) is calculated by deducting direct taxes and social security and pension fund contributions from the gross figure.[2]

Personal income distribution statistics provide a measure of the living standards of individuals and households. They are regarded as a measure of personal welfare, on the assumption that welfare is derived from personal consumption and that income during a period represents potential consumption and thus potential welfare. The measure is nevertheless only a partial one, since it is concerned uniquely with "that part of total welfare which is attributable to the consumption of goods and services of the kinds which are normally sold on the market".[3] It excludes welfare derived from services provided free by government - notably for health and education. Moreover, there is an implicit assumption that income is shared out equally within households, and hence that no biases arise because of the intra-household distribution of resources. Sometimes personal income distribution statistics use household consumption expenditure rather than household income as an indicator of living standards and welfare. Expenditure data are regarded as more accurate than income data, because there are likely to be fewer errors of under-reporting. But because of higher savings rates of upper-income groups, such statistics give lower estimates of "income inequality" than those based on income data.

The main approach to measuring income inequality focuses on the relative shares of the total income of the population received by different persons or households. One common way in which these shares are depicted graphically is using a Lorenz curve, which shows the cumulative share of the income received by cumulative shares of the population, starting from the poorest income-receiving units. From this curve simple indicators of income distribution, such as the share of the richest 20 per cent (fifth quintile) or the share of the poorest 40 per cent (first and second quintiles) in the total income of the population, can be derived. An example of a Lorenz curve is the chart, which compares income distribution in Brazil and Finland: the chart shows that in Brazil in 1989 the richest quintile received 65 per cent of the total income and the poorest 40 per cent received 7 per cent, while in Finland in 1991 the corresponding proportions were 34 per cent and 26 per cent.

The Gini coefficient is the most common statistical indicator of inequality. It is the area between the Lorenz curve and the diagonal of perfect equality and varies from 0 (maximum equality) to 1 (maximum inequality), or from 0 to 100 when expressed in per cent. The more unequal the income distribution, the greater the distance of the Lorenz curve from the diagonal, and the greater the Gini coefficient. But this index is not particularly sensitive to inequality due to extreme affluence.[4]

A second general approach to measuring inequality is to examine the absolute income levels of particular population groups (such as the poorest 40 per cent of the population and the richest 20 per cent).[5] The per capita absolute income of a particular group can be calculated by multiplying GNP per capita by the income share of that group and by dividing their population share. This procedure gives

Box 6 (concluded)

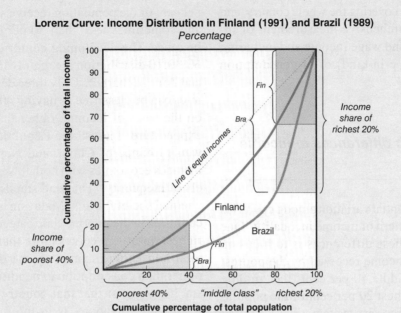

Lorenz Curve: Income Distribution in Finland (1991) and Brazil (1989)
Percentage

only a rough approximation of the absolute incomes of different groups, since the sum of personal incomes as measured by household surveys is less than GNP. But it provides a useful complement to statistics based on relative shares. For example, falling shares of certain population groups, including of course the poorest, are not necessarily associated with declining absolute incomes when an economy is growing. Also, absolute income statistics can indicate whether or not there is an increasing absolute income gap between the rich and the poor.

The axiomatic basis for income inequality statistics is that the measure should satisfy the criterion that when an income transfer is made from a richer to a poorer income-recipient unit there is a decrease in the index of inequality (and vice versa). This condition is not necessarily satisfied when polarization occurs, and thus increasingly a distinction has been made between inequality and polarization. An income distribution can be said to be more polarized when the distribution is more "spread out" from the middle, so that there are fewer persons or households with middle-level incomes. Alternatively, polarization may refer to a situation in which there is increasing bimodality in the income distribution in the sense that the frequency of middle-level incomes declines and the frequency of either higher- or lower-level incomes increases. New statistics are being derived to measure this phenomenon,[6] but polarization can at a simple and intuitive level be detected if the gap between the rich and the poor is increasing.

[1]   Throughout this Part of the *Report*, the term "personal income distribution" is used interchangeably to refer to the distribution of income among households or among persons. Some analysts, however, reserve this term for the latter type of distribution and refer to the former as "household income distribution".

[2]   Guidelines for collecting and preparing income distribution statistics are summarized in United Nations, *Provisional Guidelines on Statistics of the Distribution of Income, Consumption and Accumulation of Households*, Statistical Papers, Series M, No. 61, New York, 1977.

[3]   H. Lydall, "Effects of Alternative Measurement Techniques on the Estimation of the Inequality of Income", *World Employment Research Working Paper*, No. 2-23/100 (Geneva: ILO, 1981), p. 11.

[4]   For a discussion of the sensitivity of various measures of inequality, including the Gini coefficient, to extreme poverty, extreme affluence, and other forms of inequality, see D. Champernowne, "A Comparison of Measures of Income Distribution", *Economic Journal*, Vol. 84, 1974.

[5]   This was a central method adopted by the World Bank in the 1970s (see H. Chenery *et al.*, *Redistribution with Growth* (New York and Oxford: Oxford University Press, 1974)).

[6]   It has been shown that it is possible for redistributive transfers from richer to poorer households to coincide with increased polarization. Also, in the transition to a bimodal distribution, it is possible for the income share of the, say, middle 30 per cent of the population to decrease while the share of the middle 60 per cent increases, and on this basis it has been concluded that analyses which seek to measure polarization using quintile shares "are unable to detect the phenomenon they claim to be studying". Various measures of polarization have been suggested to deal with such problems; see M.C. Wolfson, "When Inequalities Diverge", *The American Economic Review*, Vol. 84, No. 2 *(Papers and Proceedings)*, May 1994.

trends in some developing countries in Latin America and East Asia. All the data are derived from household surveys, which are based on representative samples covering the whole country, and they attempt comprehensive measurement of incomes (going beyond wage income and including estimates of income-in-kind) or of consumption expenditure.[5]

1. North-South differences in income inequality

There is substantial variation among countries in terms of their pattern of income inequality. One way of depicting these differences is to focus on the share of total income received by the poorest 40 per cent, the middle 40 per cent (the "middle class"), and the richest 20 per cent of the population.[6] As these shares vary systematically a broad classification of countries can be made according to their pattern of inequality (see chart 8). At one end of the scale, it is possible to identify a number of highly unequal societies, in which the richest 20 per cent of the population receives around 60 per cent of total income, the middle class 30 per cent, and the poorest 40 per cent a mere 10 per cent of the total. In such "60:30:10" societies, the average income of the poorest 40 per cent of the population is only a quarter of the national average, and the average income of the richest 20 per cent is four times greater than that of the middle class, and 12 times greater than that of the bottom 40 per cent. At the other end of the scale, there are a few "low inequality" societies in which the share of total income of the middle class exceeds that of the richest 20 per cent. In between, a repeated pattern is for the richest 20 per cent of the population to receive around 40 per cent of total income, the middle class the same share, and the poorest 40 per cent only about 20 per cent. In these "40:40:20" societies, the average income of the middle class is equal to the national average, and the average income of the richest 20 per cent is just double that of the middle class, and four times greater than that of the poorest 40 per cent.

In most developed countries there is a "40:40:20" pattern - or the income share of the middle class is greater than that of the richest quintile. The only exceptions are Australia, Ireland, New Zealand and the United States, in which the share of the richest quintile has recently been 44-46 per cent of total income.

A few developing countries have 40:40:20 societies, but most are high-inequality countries or in an intermediate category, where the richest 20 per cent of the population receive sometimes more, and sometimes less, than 50 per cent of the total income. The developing countries which have a 60:30:10 distribution are mainly in Latin America and Africa (chart 8). Only three developing economies can be classified as having 40:40:20 societies on the basis of income, rather than consumption expenditure, shares: the Republic of Korea, Taiwan Province of China, and Nepal.[7] East Asia includes economies with both lower and higher levels of inequality. Thailand stands out as a highly unequal society, whilst Malaysia is one of the nine countries in the intermediate category in which the richest quintile receives more than 50 per cent of total household income. Some data on income, rather than consumption expenditure, for Indonesia also suggest that that country too, like Hong Kong and Singapore, is in the intermediate category.[8]

Overall, this pattern confirms the continuing existence of a major difference between developing and developed countries which was identified over 40 years ago by Kuznets:

> The former [developing countries] have no "middle" classes: there is a sharp contrast between the preponderant portion of the population whose average income is well below the generally low country-wide average, and a small top group with a very large relative income excess. The developed countries, on the other hand, are characterized by a much more gradual rise from low to high shares, with substantial groups receiving more than the high countrywide income average, and the top groups securing smaller shares than the comparable ordinal groups in underdeveloped countries.[9]

A more precise view of the North-South divide in terms of distribution of the national income can be gained if the relationship between income inequality and GNP per capita is examined. Using a GNP per capita of $3,000 (in 1987 prices) to mark off developing countries from the developed market economies for the 74 countries for which data are available (a threshold which separates low-income, lower-middle income and most upper-income developing countries from richer countries), it is apparent that:

(i) Income inequality is greater in the developing countries, except for the very poorest, than in the richer countries;

Chart 8

RECENT PATTERNS IN PERSONAL INCOME DISTRIBUTION IN 92 COUNTRIES

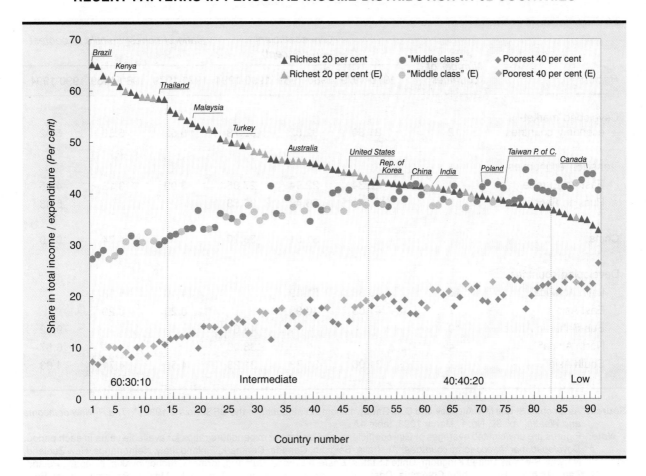

60:30:10 societies	Intermediate societies		40:40:20 societies		Low inequality societies

		Share of richest 20 per cent			
	> 50 per cent	< 50 per cent			

(1) Brazil	(15) Honduras	(28) Hong Kong	(51) Kyrgyzstan	(74) *Germany*	(84) *Latvia*
(2) South Africa	(16) Dominican Rep.	(29) Nigeria (E)	(52) Rep. of Korea	(75) *Taiwan P. of China*	(85) *Netherlands*
(3) Guatemala	(17) Nicaragua (E)	(30) Bolivia (E)	(53) Ghana (E)	(76) *Hungary*	(86) *Luxembourg*
(4) Zimbabwe (E)	(18) Colombia	(31) Uganda (E)	(54) *Lithuania*	(77) *Czech Rep.*	(87) *Ukraine*
(5) Kenya (E)	(19) Malaysia	(32) Jordan (E)	(55) *France*	(78) *Slovenia*	(88) *Spain (E)*
(6) Chile	(20) Sri Lanka	(33) Bahamas	(56) *Japan*	(79) *Denmark*	(89) *Belgium*
(7) Lesotho (E)	(21) Puerto Rico	(34) Singapore	(57) *Bulgaria*	(80) *Russian Fed.*	(90) *Canada*
(8) Panama	(22) Ecuador (E)	(35) Algeria (E)	(58) China	(81) *Italy*	(91) *Finland*
(9) Mexico	(23) Philippines	(36) *Australia*	(59) *Norway*	(82) *Romania*	(92) *Slovakia*
(10) Botswana (E)	(24) Costa Rica	(37) Tunisia (E)	(60) *Moldova*	(83) *Belarus*	
(11) Guinea-Bissau (E)	(25) Peru (E)	(38) Mauritania (E)	(61) *Greece (E)*		
(12) Senegal (E)	(26) Turkey	(39) Morocco (E)	(62) India (E)		
(13) Thailand	(27) Madagascar (E)	(40) Bangladesh	(63) Egypt (E)		
(14) Venezuela		(41) *Estonia*	(64) *United Kingdom*		
		(42) U.R.Tanzania	(65) Indonesia (E)		
		(43) Jamaica (E)	(66) *Portugal*		
		(44) *New Zealand*	(67) Kazakhstan		
		(45) *Ireland*	(68) Lao P.D.R (E)		
		(46) Niger (E)	(69) Pakistan (E)		
		(47) *United States*	(70) Nepal		
		(48) Côte d'Ivoire (E)	(71) *Poland*		
		(49) Mauritius (E)	(72) *Sweden*		
		(50) Viet Nam (E)	(73) Rwanda (E)		

Source: UNCTAD secretariat calculations, based on a data set compiled by Deininger and Squire, *op. cit.* (see also text).

Note: The chart is based on the most recent data reported for each country. These are for 1987 or later, except for Botswana (1986), Bangladesh (1986), France (1984), Germany (excluding the new Länder, 1984), Luxembourg (1983), Japan (1982), Nepal (1984) and Rwanda (1983). Countries are ordered in the chart and the list according to the shares of the richest 20 per cent of the population. The suffix (E) indicates that distribution data for the country concerned are for consumption expenditure shares which, owing to savings, are lower than the income shares used for the other countries.

Table 33

INCOME INEQUALITY SINCE 1970, BY REGION

Region[a]	Number of countries	Gini coefficient (in per cent)			Ratio of richest quintile to poorest		
		1970-1979	1980-1989	1990-1994	1970-1979	1980-1989	1990-1994
Developed market-economy countries	12	31.60	32.02	32.78	5.59	5.56	6.02
Transition economies							
Eastern Europe	4	22.34	22.94	27.85	3.09	3.13	4.05
Russian Federation[b]			26.40	30.53			5.08
China			31.51	36.20		4.74	6.10
Developing countries							
Latin America	10	49.86	51.39		14.46	15.58	
East Asia	7	41.08	40.98		8.29	8.20	
Sub-Saharan Africa[c]	10			44.64			9.52
North Africa[c]	4			38.03			6.57
South Asia[c]	2	31.06	31.73	31.28	4.56	4.71	4.63

Source: As for chart 8, and M.V. Alexeev and C.G. Gaddy, "Income Distribution in the USSR in the 1980s", *The Review of Income and Wealth*, Vol. 39, No. 1, March 1993, table 4A.

Note: Figures are unweighted averages of Gini coefficients and income or expenditure ratios for available years in each period.

a *Developed market-economy countries:* Australia, Belgium, Canada, Denmark, Finland, Italy, Netherlands, New Zealand, Norway, Sweden, United Kingdom, United States; *Eastern Europe:* Bulgaria, former Czechoslovakia, Hungary, Poland; *Latin America:* Brazil, Chile, Colombia, Costa Rica, Dominican Republic, Guatemala, Mexico, Panama, Puerto Rico, Venezuela; *East Asia:* Hong Kong, Malaysia, Philippines, Republic of Korea, Singapore, Taiwan Province of China, Thailand; *sub-Saharan Africa:* Ghana, Guinea-Bissau, Kenya, Mauritius, Niger, Nigeria, Senegal, Uganda, United Republic of Tanzania, Zimbabwe; *North Africa:* Egypt, Jordan, Morocco, Tunisia; *South Asia:* India and Pakistan.

b The Gini coefficient for 1980-1989 is for the former Russian Soviet Socialist Republic and relates to 1988 only.

c Calculations are based on consumption expenditure and measured inequality is hence not directly comparable with other regions, for which measures are based on income data.

(ii) The variance in inequality is greater among the developing than the developed countries;

(iii) The main difference in the pattern of inequality between developing countries and the developed countries is that the richest 20 per cent of the population receives a much higher proportion of total income in the developing countries than in the developed, whilst the middle 40 per cent receives a much lower proportion. Differences between developing countries and richer countries in shares of the bottom 40 per cent are less marked.

These patterns are apparent for both income and consumption expenditure data, but they are sharpest for the former.

2. Global trends

Regional trends in income inequality are summarized in table 33. On the basis of the Gini coefficient it is evident that so far in the 1990s income inequality has increased sharply from relatively low levels in the former socialist countries of Eastern Europe and also in China. Greater inequality is also evident in Latin America in the 1980s. The ratio of the average incomes of the richest to those of the poorest quintiles of the population was over 15:1 in those countries. The ratio is also particularly high in Africa, considering that it is based on expenditure data.

These regional averages mask different country trajectories in inequality. From all available evidence, it is apparent that there were widespread tendencies for inequality to increase during the 1980s.[10] Estimates for 16 developed market economies show that inequality was rising in nine of them. The rise was modest in Belgium, the Netherlands and Germany (a 1-2 percentage point increase in the Gini coefficient) and somewhat greater in Australia, Japan, Sweden, United States and, especially, the United Kingdom. Of the former socialist countries of Eastern Europe, where inequality has increased sharply against the background of shrinking overall income, the Gini coefficient rose by 10 points between 1987 and 1993 in Bulgaria, by over 5 points in Romania, and by between 2 and 5 points in Poland, Hungary and the Czech Republic.

While there was a pronounced tendency for inequality to increase in Latin America during the debt crisis of the 1980s, the subsequent recovery has not been sufficient to reverse this tendency, largely because of sharp changes in policy stance that are discussed in the next chapter. Thus, comparing the Gini coefficient in 1979-1981 with that in 1989-1990, it is apparent that it was higher in the later period in Argentina (Buenos Aires), Brazil, Chile, Panama, and Venezuela (but in Colombia it was lower). The coefficients were relatively stable in Uruguay and Mexico. The latest available statistics on the distribution of income among urban households show that, although there was some improvement, the income shares of the richest 20 per cent of the urban population remained higher in the early 1990s than the early 1980s in Argentina, Brazil, Costa Rica, Mexico, Panama, and Venezuela. Unambiguous declines in inequality are apparent in Uruguay and Bolivia (table 34).

In Africa, it is possible that in some countries there has been a process of "equalizing downwards" across much of the personal income distribution as monetary sectors have contracted relative to subsistence sectors, real wages have fallen and consumer demand for the goods and services of urban informal sector activities has declined. In this process, the rural-urban gap, measured in terms

Table 34

INCOME DISTRIBUTION AMONG URBAN HOUSEHOLDS IN LATIN AMERICA IN VARIOUS YEARS SINCE 1979

(Percentage)

| Country | Year | Share of | | |
		Poorest 40 per cent	Richest 20 per cent	Richest 10 per cent
Argentina[a]	1980	17.4	45.3	30.9
	1986	16.2	48.7	34.5
	1994	13.8	51.1	34.2
Bolivia	1989	12.1	54.3	38.2
	1994	15.1	51.5	35.4
Brazil	1979	11.8	56.0	39.1
	1987	9.8	60.8	44.3
	1993	11.8	58.7	42.5
Chile	1987	12.7	56.1	39.6
	1994	13.4	55.6	40.4
Colombia	1980	11.0	58.8	41.3
	1986	13.1	51.4	35.3
	1994	11.6	57.2	41.9
Costa Rica	1981	18.9	40.1	23.2
	1988	17.2	43.3	27.6
	1994	17.4	43.5	27.5
Guatemala	1986	12.5	52.0	36.4
	1989	12.0	53.5	37.9
Honduras	1990	12.3	55.0	38.9
	1994	13.3	52.5	37.2
Mexico	1984	20.2	41.2	25.8
	1989	16.3	51.3	36.9
	1994	16.8	49.6	34.3
Panama	1979	15.5	45.9	29.1
	1986	14.3	48.9	33.0
	1994	13.8	51.6	37.4
Paraguay[a]	1986	16.4	48.9	31.8
	1994	16.2	49.8	35.2
Uruguay	1981	17.7	46.4	31.2
	1986	17.8	48.3	33.6
	1994	21.7	40.0	25.4
Venezuela	1981	20.1	37.8	21.8
	1986	16.2	45.1	28.9
	1994	16.7	46.4	31.4

Source: ECLAC, *Statistical Yearbook for Latin America and the Caribbean, 1996 Edition* (United Nations publication, Sales No. E/S.97.II.G.1).

a The metropolitan area only.

Table 35

RECENT CHANGES IN INCOME DISTRIBUTION AND PER CAPITA GNP IN SUB-SAHARAN AFRICA

Country	Scope of survey	Year	Gini coefficient[a] (Per cent)		Average annual growth of real GNP per capita[b] (Per cent)
Côte d'Ivoire	National	1985	41.2	44.6	-3.77
		1988	36.9	34.6	
Ethiopia	Rural	1989		40.8	..
		1994		45.1	
Ghana	National	1988	35.9	40.9	1.39
		1992	33.9	40.8	
Kenya	Rural	1981		50.8	-0.31
		1992		55.6	
Mauritius	National	1986	39.6		6.11
		1991	36.7		
Nigeria	National	1986	37.0	38.1	1.09
		1993	37.5	43.5	
Uganda	National	1989	33.0		0.87
		1992	40.8		
United Republic of Tanzania	Rural	1983		53.5	1.14
		1991		76.7	

Source: The source indicated for chart 8, and also C. Jayarajah, W. Branson and B. Sen, *Social Dimensions of Adjustment: World Bank Experience, 1980-1993* (Washington, D.C.: The World Bank, 1996).
   a Figures in the second column for the Gini coefficient are from the second source indicated.
   b From the first to the second year shown.

of the ratio of wage earners' incomes to incomes of farmers on small holdings, has disappeared. An example of "equalizing downwards" is Côte d'Ivoire (see table 35). By contrast, large increases in the Gini coefficient for household expenditures are evident in Uganda, and also in Nigeria according to some estimates. A tendency which is apparent in Kenya, United Republic of Tanzania and Ethiopia is increasing rural inequality.

Turning to Asia, it is apparent that the crude stereotype of East Asia as a zone of "low and decreasing inequality" is a misleading description not only because some of the countries have relatively high levels of inequality, but also because inequality has increased in many parts of East Asia in the 1980s. There was an increase in Hong Kong during 1986-1991 and a particularly sharp one in Singapore during 1979-1983, though it was moderate thereafter. Inequality appears to have been increasing in Taiwan Province of China since 1980, and in the Republic of Korea since the late 1980s. In Thailand the strong upward trend towards greater inequality which started in the mid-1970s, following the shift towards a more export-oriented strategy, continued in the 1980s. Declining inequality is apparent in Indonesia and the Philippines and also, during 1979-1987, in Malaysia, though in that country the downward trend may not have continued in the 1990s. In South Asia, Sri Lanka stands out as a country in which inequality has continued to rise.

3. Growth and inequality

From the available data set it is possible to trace the evolution of income inequality in 16 developing economies[11] since the late 1960s or early 1970s. Trend analysis indicates no clear relationship between per capita income and inequality. Economies such as those of Taiwan Province of China and Thailand grew relatively rapidly, but inequality increased in the latter case but not in the former. Similarly, growth was slow in both Sri Lanka and the Philippines, but while inequality rose significantly in the former country, it fell in the latter.

The share of total income received by the poorest 40 per cent of the population declined during this period in 11 of the 16 countries, but at a very slow rate. Their absolute per capita income fell only in Venezuela, which is also the only country of the 16 in which there was a downward trend in real GNP per capita over the entire 20-year period. For eight of the nine countries in which the growth of real GNP per capita is statistically significant, the growth in incomes of the poorest 40 per cent is also statistically significant, confirming their dependency on economic expansion for an increase in their income. In Chile and Thailand, in particular, increased inequality has not been associated with the absolute immiseration of the poorest groups thanks to rapid growth. But the main feature of the results is perhaps not these statistical relationships, but rather the finding that the real incomes of the poorest 40 per cent of the population grew by less than $12 per annum (in constant 1987 prices), or declined over this period, in 13 of the 16 countries, the exceptions being the Republic of Korea, Malaysia and Taiwan Province of China.

Trend analysis can be usefully supplemented through analysis of changes in inequality and GNP per capita during shorter episodes of change.[12] One way in which inequality analysts now do this is by focusing on "spells" of change. For each country, a "spell" of distributional change is defined as the time between two comparable and consecutive household surveys. For example, a country for which income distribution data are available in three household surveys (1973, 1980 and 1987) enables analysis to be made for two "spells" (1973-1980 and 1980-1987).

Table 36 shows the results of such analysis for 22 countries, using income rather than consumption expenditure data, which together provide information on 94 spells of change. It is apparent that inequality increases with growth as often as it decreases.[13] But when the sample is broken up into episodes of change during two different periods, distinguishing the period up to and including 1980 and that from 1980 onwards, a major shift is apparent. First, inequality increases in only 42 per cent of the total spells of change in the first period, but in the second it increases in 64 per cent of the total spells. Second, inequality increased in only 17 out of 39 spells in which growth in GNP per capita occurred in the period 1965-1980, but from 1980 to 1995 inequality increased in 19 out of 29 such spells. For spells in which decline in GNP per capita occurred (which are fewer in number) there is also a shift, in the sense that decline was much more likely to be associated with increasing inequality after 1980 than before.

The sample on which these relationships are based was necessarily determined by the availability of data,[14] but the findings suggest that the growth-inequality relationship changed in the 1980s in ways which imply that growth is now more unequalizing.

4. The changing relative positions of income classes

A more detailed view of how inequality is changing in developing countries can be obtained by examining trends over time in the income shares of the richest 20 per cent, the middle 40 per cent, and the poorest 40 per cent. The charts in the annex to this chapter[15], showing trends for 24 countries since the 1960s, indicate that:

• A recurrent pattern of distributional change in the 1980s was an increase in the income shares of the rich, which was almost invariably associated with a fall in the income shares of the middle class;

• For many countries this was a reversal of trends before 1980, which involved the middle class gaining income shares whilst the rich lost shares.

The countries in which divergence between the rich and the middle classes occurred in the 1980s are diverse. They include Bangladesh (post-1977), Brazil (post-1986), Sri Lanka (post-1973), Mexico

Table 36

RELATIONSHIP BETWEEN GROWTH PERFORMANCE AND CHANGES IN INCOME INEQUALITY IN DEVELOPING COUNTRIES, 1965-1995

Spells associated with:	1965-1980		1980-1995		1965-1995	
	No. of spells	Per cent of total	No. of spells	Per cent of total	No. of spells	Per cent of total
Positive GNP growth per capita						
Inequality increasing	17	40	19	49	40	43
Inequality decreasing	22	51	10	26	39	41
Negative or no GNP growth per capita						
Inequality increasing	1	2	6	15	8	9
Inequality decreasing	3	7	4	10	7	7
Total	43	100	39	100	94	100

Source: As for chart 8.

Note: The countries (and number of spells of change) covered for 1965-1995 are: Bangladesh (6); Brazil (11); Chile (3); Colombia (5); Costa Rica (5); Dominican Republic (1); Gabon (1); Guatemala (2); Honduras (1); Malaysia (4); Mexico (3); Panama (3); Philippines (3); Puerto Rico (2); Republic of Korea (10); Singapore (2), Sri Lanka (4), Taiwan Province of China (10); Thailand (6); Trinidad and Tobago (2); Turkey (2); Venezuela (8). The sum of the spells of change for the periods 1965-1980 and 1980-1995 is less than the number for 1965-1995, because some spells of change were omitted in partitioning the data set. Countries for which data were only available for one period - Turkey, Trinidad and Tobago, Guatemala and the Dominican Republic - were omitted. Spells of change which began before 1980 but ended after 1980 were also omitted, except for Bangladesh (1978-1981), Costa Rica (1977-1981), and Thailand (1975-1981), which were classified as 1965-1980; and Puerto Rico (1979-1989), Venezuela (1979-1981) and Sri Lanka (1979-19781), which were classified as 1980 and onwards. For Taiwan Province of China data after 1976 (which are reported annually) are included as three-year averages.

(post-1977), Panama (post-1980), Venezuela (post-1978), Guatemala (post-1978), Singapore (post-1978), Thailand (post-1975), and United Republic of Tanzania (post-1976). Of the eight cases for which data are available for both the 1970s and the 1980s, there is a reversal from increasing convergence to increasing divergence between the rich and middle classes in six, which was particularly marked in Sri Lanka, Panama and Venezuela. A similar shift also occurred in Hong Kong around 1980, and in India a trend of rich-middle convergence in the late 1980s was reversed after 1990, though it is not clear whether this represents a new trend.

An important feature of these patterns of divergence is the scale of change, in terms of the magnitude of the gap in income shares between the richest 20 per cent and middle class. From table 37, it can be seen that in Thailand, for example,

the gap between the income shares of the richest quintile and the middle class increased from 12 percentage points in 1975 to 28 in 1992, as the richest group increased their share of total income from 48 per cent to 58 per cent and the income share of the middle class fell from 36 per cent to 30 per cent. The extent of change is such that some countries are transforming from 40:40:20 societies into intermediate societies in which the richest quintile receives 50 per cent of the total available income of households, the middle class 36 per cent and the poorest two quintiles 15 per cent; and some intermediate societies, such as Thailand in 1975, are transforming into 60:30:10 societies. For some societies in Latin America with very high income inequality the reversal from rich/middle-class convergence to divergence halted a shift towards a pattern in which the richest quintile received 50 per cent of total income, and re-established an earlier pattern of a very unequal distribution.

Table 37

PERIODS OF INCOME DIVERGENCE AND CONVERGENCE BETWEEN THE RICHEST QUINTILE AND THE MIDDLE CLASS IN SELECTED DEVELOPING COUNTRIES

Divergence (Income share of middle class falling and share of richest quintile rising)				**Convergence** (Income share of middle class rising and share of richest quintile falling)			
Country	Period	Change in gap[a]	Size of gap[b]	Country	Period	Change in gap[a]	Size of gap[b]
Bangladesh	1977-1986	+11	+12	Colombia	1978-1991	-7	+21
Brazil	1982-1989	+13	+38	Rep. of Korea	1980-1988	-3	+4
Chile	1971-1989	+19	+37	Malaysia	1976-1989	-6	+20
Mexico	1977-1989	+10	+29	Turkey	1968-1987	-16	+14
Panama	1980-1989	+11	+28	Chile	1989-1994	-5	+32
Sri Lanka	1973-1987	+13	+19	Indonesia	1976-1993	-3	+2
Thailand	1975-1992	+16	+28	Pakistan	1979-1991	-4	0
Venezuela	1979-1990	+16	+18	Hong Kong	1971-1991	-4	+14
Rep. of Korea	1969-1980	+9	+7	Costa Rica	1977-1989	-7	+14
India	1990-1992	+4	+4	Philippines	1965-1988	-9	+19

Source: As for chart 8.
  a From beginning to end of period (percentage points).
  b The share of the richest quintile minus the share of the middle class (percentage points) in the final year.

A second important feature of these patterns is the degree of synchronization in the timing of distributional changes in countries with very different economic structures and cultures. Synchronized shifts can be taken as an indicator that income inequality trends are increasingly being influenced by forces common to all the countries, i.e. forces which are global in character, and not just by particular national circumstances. Precise identification of changes is difficult as the household surveys on which the distributional data are based are not conducted on an annual basis and are for different years in different countries. But it is apparent that in many countries a turning-point from rich-middle class convergence to divergence occurred during the late 1970s and early 1980s, a period when the external environment of developing countries changed considerably. The reversal may also reflect a common domestic policy response to the changed circumstances.

Of the other cases which are depicted in the annex, the Republic of Korea and Chile both exhibit a pattern of increasing divergence between the rich and middle-class income shares during certain periods. However, in both instances there is a reversal in the opposite direction to that observed in the majority of cases. The income divergence is marked in Chile, where from 1971 to 1989 the gap between the shares of the rich and the middle class increased from 18 to 37 percentage points, as the income share of the richest 20 per cent increased from 52 per cent to 63 per cent of total income, whilst that of the middle class declined from 34 per cent to 27 per cent. In the Republic of Korea the share of the middle class in 1969 was actually 2 percentage points greater than that of the richest quintile, but by 1980 the share of the latter was 7 percentage points greater than that of the middle class. There was a change to convergence between the rich and the middle class in Chile from 1989 to 1994 and in the Republic of Korea from 1980 to 1988 (see also table 37).

As regards the other countries in the annex to this chapter, Costa Rica and Taiwan Province of China also show signs of divergence in income shares, particularly since 1985, but it is the poorest 40 per cent that loses shares to the rich, and to the rich and middle class, respectively. A similar pattern, though much less pronounced, is also apparent in Puerto Rico, with a shift from the 1970s to the 1980s. Tendencies towards rich/middle-class income convergence are apparent in Turkey, Malaysia, the Philippines, Indonesia, and Pakistan, but more so in Turkey than in the other four countries; indeed, the tendency may have been reversed in Malaysia. A characteristic which these five countries have in common is a large Moslem population.[16] Colombia and Jamaica also show tendencies for rich and middle-class incomes to convergence.

The above patterns of change are also evident from a spell-of-change analysis of income shares of different quintile groups, i.e. changes between consecutive surveys. Table 38 classifies patterns of changes in inequality into four basic categories and two sub-categories, showing the frequency of occurrence of these patterns of change before and after 1980, distinguishing between developed and developing countries, and singling out Latin America and East Asia among the developing countries. The patterns of change distinguished are:

Type 1: Share of richest 20 per cent increasing, share of middle class declining, and

    (a) share of poorest 40 per cent rising, or
    (b) share of poorest 40 per cent falling;

Type 2: Share of richest 20 per cent falling, share of middle class rising, and

    (a) share of poorest 40 per cent rising, or
    (b) share of poorest 40 per cent falling;

Type 3: Share of richest 20 per cent and middle class falling;

Type 4: Share of richest 20 per cent and middle class rising.

A number of conclusions can be drawn from table 38:

- The main pattern of change in both developed market economies and developing countries is either type 1 or type 2. It is rare for both the richest quintile and the middle class to be gaining or losing shares together;

- The share of the richest quintile increased more frequently after 1980 than before, particularly in developing countries. In developed market economies, the share of the

richest quintile increased during 46 per cent of the spells of change up to 1980 and 49 per cent from 1980 onwards, while in the developing countries the corresponding increases were 45 per cent and 62 per cent, respectively. The pattern of change in Latin America and East Asia shows a striking similarity. In Latin America, the richest quintile gained in 33 per cent of the spells up to 1980 and 55 per cent of the spells from 1980 onwards; in East Asia the increase was from 50 per cent to 67 per cent. However, unlike East Asia, in Latin America this shift involved a reversal from rich/middle class income convergence in the 1965-1980 period (61 per cent of the spells) to a rich/middle class divergence from 1980 onwards (55 per cent of the spells);

- In developed countries, whenever the richest quintile increased their share and the middle class lost ground (type 1 change), the poorest 40 per cent also tended to lose ground. In developing countries, this pattern is also apparent, though it was more marked in the 1970s, particularly in East Asia;

- In developed countries, whenever the middle class gained ground and the richest quintile lost income shares (type 2 change), the poorest 40 per cent also tended to gain income shares. But in the developing countries, when the middle class gained ground, the poorest 40 per cent were just as likely to gain as to lose income shares in the 1970s, while in the 1980s they were more likely to lose;

- There is a major difference between Latin America and East Asia concerning the changing position of the bottom 40 per cent. In Latin America, this group gained shares in 44 per cent of the spells up to 1980, but in only 30 per cent of the subsequent ones. In East Asia, they gained shares in 41 per cent of the spells up to 1980, but this proportion increased to 44 per cent thereafter.

The findings of this spell-of-change analysis, like that which focuses on growth and inequality, reflect the experience of the countries for which data are available. However, the results suggest that by focusing only on poverty much analysis of the experience of the 1980s has missed some crucial changes which have taken place in income distribution in developing countries, namely: (i) the

Table 38

PERSONAL INCOME DISTRIBUTION IN 1965-1995, BY REGION: FREQUENCY OF OCCURRENCE OF DIFFERENT TYPES OF CHANGE

Type of change				*Number of spells*							
Direction of change of income share of the:				Developed market economies [a]		Developing countries [b]					
						All regions		Latin America		East Asia	
	richest 20 per cent	*middle class*	*poorest 40 per cent*	1965-1980	1980-1995	1965-1980	1980-1995	1965-1980	1980-1995	1965-1980	1980-1995
1(a)	Up	Down	Up	4	1	5	10	3	4	2	5
1(b)	Up	Down	Down	19	27	15	12	3	7	8	4
Total 1	Up	Down	Up/Down	23	28	20	22	6	11	10	9
2(a)	Down	Up	Up	23	22	12	3	4	2	6	0
2(b)	Down	Up	Down	10	14	11	8	7	5	4	2
Total 2	Down	Up	Up/Down	33	36	23	11	11	7	10	2
3	Down	Down	Up	6	6	2	3	1	0	1	3
4	Up	Up	Down	9	12	1	4	0	1	1	3
5	No change			2	1	0	1	0	0	0	1
Others [c]				6	3	0	1	0	1	0	0
Total				79	86	46	42	18	20	22	18

Source: As for chart 8.
   a The countries covered (and number of spells) are: Australia (8); Canada (19); Denmark (3); Finland (10); Germany (5); Ireland (2); Italy (11); Japan (16); Netherlands (8); New Zealand (11); Norway (7); Sweden (13); United Kingdom (26); United States (26).
   b Those listed in table 36, with the addition of Hong Kong (3 spells in each period).
   c Cases where either the share of the richest quintile or of the middle class stays constant while that of the other changes.

increasing share of the richest 20 per cent of the population; and (ii) the declining share of the middle class. Indeed, what may be the main story of the 1980s is that trends of the 1970s, when a relatively richer middle class was emerging, were reversed. It is this group that appears to have been hardest hit in relative terms in the 1980s. In situations of economic decline, the implications of decreasing shares of the middle class are not necessarily as serious as declining shares for the poorest 40 per cent. But the withering of the middle class - and the reinforcement of a pattern of society in which there is a small rich group at the top and a very thin layer of middle class, and the bottom 40 per cent of the population have average incomes about one third to one half of the national average - has important socio-political and economic implications which in the long run are probably more significant for the consumption standards of the poor.

C. Inter-country differences in income inequality

The evidence examined in the previous section indicates that there are important differences among countries in the degree of income inequality, not only between countries at different levels of economic development, but also among those at similar levels. While in general income inequality is greater in developing than in developed countries, there are also significant differences within the developing world.

Why income inequality is greater in some countries than in others is one of the most difficult and intriguing questions for economic analysis. The traditional answer that enjoyed a certain degree of consensus sought to explain these differences in terms of how income distribution changed in association with economic development. According to this view, pioneered by Simon Kuznets, income inequality increases in the early stages of development and then decreases. Under this so-called "inverted-U" hypothesis, income inequality can be expected to be greater in the middle-income countries than in both the least developed countries and the industrialized countries. Underlying this approach is the idea that the economic development process involves a transition from a low-productivity agrarian economy to a high-productivity industrial one. Income inequality tends to rise in the process of industrialization not only on account of earnings differentials between agriculture and industry, but also because of the increased importance of industrial incomes, which are distributed less equally than agricultural incomes. However, as industry takes over and average incomes rise, earnings differentials associated with productivity differences will fall. Consequently, a turning-point will be reached after which income distribution improves as the level of income rises. On this view, therefore, growth is first unequalizing, then equalizing.

An analysis of various forces influencing income distribution in different phases of economic development is undertaken in the subsequent section. Here an assessment is made of the extent to which inter-country differences in income distribution can be attributed to differences in levels of development, and of whether other factors also need to be taken into account.

Evidence based on cross-country analysis of the relationship between per capita income and inequality broadly confirms the existence of the inverted-U pattern in which inequality is lowest in low-income and high-income countries and highest in middle-income countries, although a number of studies failed to establish such a relationship.[17] The evidence analysed above also points to a systematic relationship between inequality and per capita income, particularly when the former is measured in terms of the income shares of the richest quintile and the middle class.

Nevertheless, there can clearly also be considerable variations in income distribution among countries at similar per capita income levels. Attention has been focused on a number of factors in cross-country studies to explain these variations.[18] Although these factors are often closely correlated with income, they are also strongly influenced by policy choices.

The first set of such factors identified in cross-country studies relates to the production structure. Since earnings are usually closely linked to productivity, large productivity differences among different sectors of an economy can be expected to yield a high degree of income inequality unless they are corrected through redistributive policies. Indeed, this is one of the main ideas underlying the original Kuznets thesis. However, there need not be a one-to-one correspondence between average per capita income and inter-sectoral differences in productivity. Therefore, other things being equal, the greater the duality in the structure of production associated with a given average per capita income, the greater the degree of inequality. Indeed a number of studies have found evidence of a close correlation (though not necessarily a linear relationship) between income inequality and a number of variables reflecting the extent of duality, such as the proportion of wage labour in the total labour force, the share of agriculture in GDP, and the share of primary goods in exports.

A second factor explaining inter-country variations in inequality is population growth. Although the latter generally declines as per capita income rises, there are still considerable variations in population growth rates among countries at similar income levels. Generally, inequality has been found to be greater where population growth is faster. There may be various reasons for this relationship. One is that the dependency burden can be higher for poorer income groups, because of the observed tendency for fertility rates to decline with rising income and education. Another is that faster population growth slows the rate of labour absorption (other things being equal) and thereby reduces the share of labour income in output.

It is generally agreed that one of the most important factors underlying inequality is the level of and access to education. There is a two-way link. On the one hand, an unequal distribution of income tends to prevent the poor investing in education and acquiring skills. As discussed at greater length in chapter V below, this can be a serious impediment to growth. On the other hand, an unequal distribution of educational opportunities leads to greater inequality in income distribution by widening skill and productivity gaps in the working population. In this respect, too, there are considerable variations among countries at similar income levels. In most cross-country studies higher levels of secondary school enrolment are associated with lower levels of inequality. Differences in education are also among the most important factors explaining inequality in labour income within countries. For instance, a recent study of 10 Latin American countries for the 1980s attributed about 25 per cent of inequality among workers' incomes to differences in educational levels, with factors such as sex, ethnic origin, age, occupation, and firm size explaining the rest.[19]

It should, however, be noted that a higher average level of educational attainment is not necessarily associated with less educational inequality. Indeed, according to one estimate educational inequality increases until the average duration of schooling of the labour force reaches about 6.8 years, when further expansion of education is associated with declining inequality. The average educational attainment in most developing countries is below this threshold level,

particularly in sub-Saharan Africa and South Asia.[20] If the above threshold were to hold generally, then educational expansion in all these cases could be associated with increasing educational inequality, particular if emphasis is placed on secondary and higher education, rather than on the education of people without any schooling.

The focus on education highlights the crucial importance of ownership of assets for income distribution. However, inequality in the distribution of human capital is not the only, or even the principal, determinant of income inequality. Distribution of material wealth, and hence of value added between labour and property-owning classes, is equally and even more important. Indeed, large income inequalities are often associated with considerable concentration of material wealth, particularly in developing countries. Exclusive focus on education and human capital thus permits only a partial understanding of the factors influencing distribution in market economies. More importantly, as discussed in chapter V below, it also has the effect of delinking the analysis of growth from that of distribution, for the behaviour of the capitalist class is central to capital accumulation and technical progress, on which the real incomes of both property owners and workers depend.

Just as for incomes, there are considerable variations among countries at similar income levels in the distribution of wealth. Evidence from OECD countries shows that wealth inequality tends to be much higher than income inequality. Gini coefficients of household wealth distribution (ranging from 0.65 to 0.71 in the United Kingdom, Germany, France, Canada, Sweden and Australia, and coming close to 0.80 in the United States and 0.52 in Japan in the 1980s) are considerably above those for income distribution. Although roughly comparable in terms of wealth inequality, Australia has distinctly higher, and Sweden distinctly lower, income inequality than the United Kingdom. However, within individual countries concentration of wealth and of income tends to move together; for instance, in the United States household wealth held by the richest 1 per cent fell from 44 per cent in 1929 to 20 per cent in 1972, but rose to 34 per cent in 1992. Income inequality followed a similar path, dropping significantly in the postwar period, but rising sharply during the past two decades.

There is little information on the distribution of wealth in developing countries. However, data on land ownership show that it was highly concen-

Table 39

INEQUALITY OF LAND DISTRIBUTION IN SELECTED DEVELOPING COUNTRIES AND REGIONS

Country/region		Year/period	Gini coefficient of land distribution
Latin America			
Peru		1961	0.95
Venezuela		1961	0.94
Argentina		1970	0.87
Colombia		1960	0.87
Brazil		1960	0.85
Uruguay		1966	0.83
Asia			
India		1953-1954	0.69
		1961-1962	0.58
		1971-1972	0.59
Indonesia		1973	0.56
Pakistan		1972	0.52
Philippines		1971	0.52
Taiwan Province of China		1960-1961	0.47
Thailand		1978	0.46
Bangladesh		1977	0.45
Middle East and Mediterranean			
Iran (Islamic Republic of)		1960	0.62
Turkey		1960	0.61
Africa			
Botswana	(Traditional holdings)	1968-1969	0.50
Côte d'Ivoire	(Traditional sector)	1973-1975	0.42
Kenya	(Registered smallholdings)	1969	0.55
Malawi	(Smallholdings)	1968-1969	0.41
Mozambique	(Traditional sector)	1970	0.42
	(Modern sector)	1970	0.81
Nigeria	(Northern farm crops)	1963-1964	0.43
	(Eastern farm/tree crops)	1963-1964	0.56
	(Western farm/tree crops)	1963-1964	0.40
Somalia	(Five districts)	1968	0.55
Zambia	(Commercial sector)	1970-1971	0.76
Ghana	(All holdings)	1970	0.64

Source: R.M. Sundrum, *Income distribution in Less Developed Countries* (London and New York: Routledge, 1990); D. Ghai and S. Radwan, "Agrarian change, differentiation and rural poverty in Africa: A general survey", in D. Ghai and S. Radwan (eds.), *Agrarian Policies and Rural Poverty in Africa* (Geneva: ILO, 1983).

trated in Latin America in the 1960s compared to most other countries and regions (table 39). A study on the Republic of Korea suggests that financial assets could well be more unequally distributed than real assets. In the late 1980s, it is estimated that the Gini coefficients in that country for such assets were 0.77 and 0.60, respectively (as against 0.40 for income). At that time 43 per cent of the wealth was owned by the richest 10 per cent of the population.[21]

The effect of wealth distribution on income inequality can be expected to be stronger in developing countries. Indeed, evidence suggests that for such countries there is a positive and rather strong relationship between the distribution of operational land holdings and income inequality.[22] On the other hand, property incomes appear to constitute a much larger share of total personal income in developing countries than elsewhere. While in the 1980s and early 1990s such incomes ranged from 7 per cent to 16 per cent in Canada, Australia, New Zealand and the United Kingdom, estimates put them as high as 21 per cent in urban Colombia in 1967, 25 per cent in Taiwan Province of China in 1968, and over 20 per cent in Chile in more recent years.[23] An important reason for this contrast (discussed in greater detail in chapter V) is that, while in industrial countries property incomes tend to be retained in corporations and pension funds, in developing countries they are more likely to accrue to households. Comparatively high shares of property income in personal incomes magnify the effects of wealth inequality on income inequality.

It is also generally agreed that socio-political variables are important determinants of equality. In that respect, attention is often drawn to the low level of inequality in the former socialist countries. Again, as noted above, inequality appears to be low, given their GNP per capita, in some countries with a large Moslem population. It has also been suggested that income inequality is lower in rich countries because "societal tolerance for income inequality" is lower. The level of income inequality is seen from this perspective as a social choice which countries make within their structural limits.[24]

It should be noted that these factors offered to explain inter-country differences in income inequality are derived from a comparative static analysis which compares various characteristics of different countries at different levels of development, and hence makes no attempt to describe how inequality may change in the process of national development. This issue is taken up in the following section, where various forces operating on income distribution in different phases of development are discussed.

D. Surplus labour, growth and income inequality

1. Forces making for greater or lesser inequality

While it is very difficult to account fully for inter-country differences in income inequality, it is virtually impossible to construct a single model to describe how income distribution evolves in the course of economic development. Consequently, attention will be focused on a number of key forces that tend to operate on personal income distribution through their effects on various functional categories of income at different phases of development, with the aim of shedding some light on the possible causes of changes that have occurred during recent decades, and on the way policy has influenced these changes.

In societies with surplus labour, which may take the form of open unemployment, underemployment or disguised unemployment in a multiplicity of low-productivity activities, a necessary condition for declining inequality is that demand for labour should increase. But whether increased employment is sufficient to reduce inequality depends on a host of other factors.

For surplus labour to be absorbed, employment opportunities must expand faster than the labour force. Both the rate and labour-intensity of economic growth are thus important. But the population growth rate also affects the speed with which surplus labour is absorbed. If economic and demographic conditions are favourable, a turning-point can be reached at which the surplus labour is fully absorbed and the labour force is fully and productively utilized.[25] Before that point, changes in income distribution depend on what happens to wages and productivity. If real wages remain constant while employment is expanding and labour productivity is rising, income inequality can be expected to increase.

Initially, much of the surplus labour is in agriculture, and earnings in that sector set a lower limit to real wages in the modern sector. Therefore, how real wages move in the modern sector as surplus labour is absorbed depends very much on productivity and earnings in agriculture. Because of disguised employment, output in agriculture can be kept constant while labour input is reduced. Thus, a transfer of labour to industry would raise average labour productivity, and hence earnings, in agriculture. However, if labour absorption is slow and output per hectare remains constant, then agricultural earnings would remain sluggish and real wages in the modern sector can be kept stable despite increased employment. Under these conditions, income distribution is likely to worsen as surplus labour is absorbed, for reasons which also underlie the inverted-U hypothesis. Although average earnings of labour in the economy as a whole would increase as employment is raised in the modern sector, the dispersion of earnings would be greater to the extent that the gap between the modern and traditional sectors remains large. Furthermore, profits would increase relative to wages. The implication of all this is that a process of industrialization, wherein agriculture considerably lags behind industry, can be expected to result in a significant worsening of income distribution. Furthermore, the slower the pace of accumulation and job creation in industry, the longer the persistence of inequality.

Income distribution can worsen even when agricultural earnings and industrial real wages are both rising. This may happen not only because real wages in industry lag behind productivity growth, but also because inequality in agriculture increases as earnings in different segments of the sector expand at different rates. How far they do so depends, in large part, on the nature of agricultural development. If it is broad-based, benefiting large segments of the rural population, then the forces making for greater equality will be strengthened. In this respect, greater equality in the initial distribution of land would certainly be a key factor. However, the labour intensity of agricultural development also plays an important role. If labour is released faster than it can be productively absorbed by industry, then the surplus labour would simply be transferred from rural areas to the urban informal sector, exerting a downward pressure on real wages.

Once the surplus labour is fully absorbed, growth would slow down and be restricted to what can be attained through increases in the labour force and in productivity. At this point the labour market would tighten, creating forces making for greater equality. Sustained growth of real wages depends on continuous upgrading to technology- and skill-intensive products. Such a process can again lead to greater inequality if there are shortages of skilled labour. However, without upgrading, there is a danger that real wages will need to fall in order to ensure competitiveness with newly emerging low-cost producers. If rapid investment and technological progress enhance labour productivity and ensure competitiveness while education policies continuously upgrade skills, rapid wage growth can be sustained and in such circumstances income inequality may start to decline.

Changes in income distribution are also a function of the strength of the underlying tendency towards increasing inequality that is inherent in the relationship between wealth accumulation and income inequality. This tendency is rooted in the simple fact that wealth created through industrialization and accumulation tends to be concentrated in the hands of the rich, constituting the basis for greater income inequality. The degree of concentration of wealth, and hence its effects on distribution, in turn, depends on how far the initial stages of development led to inequality.

These considerations suggest that policies can play a key role in changes in income distribution. In the early stages of labour absorption, agricultural policies, as well as policies designed to accelerate accumulation in industry, greatly influence both the speed with which the surplus labour is absorbed and the pattern of income distribution. Industrial, education and manpower policies gain added importance as the economy moves up the technology ladder.

2. The experience

The sequence of changes in an economy with labour surplus described above is stylized. But the operation of various forces, some making for greater inequality and others making for less, is apparent in the recent experience of three groups of countries: first, those which passed the turning-point at which labour surplus is absorbed, and have also upgraded their production structure (e.g. Japan and the first-tier NIEs); second, those which have been successfully absorbing the surplus labour through sustained and rapid growth, but so far without significant industrial upgrading (e.g. Chile, Malaysia, Mauritius and Thailand); and third, those which have not been able to sustain rapid growth and absorb surplus labour. The last group contains the vast majority of developing countries, although there is considerable difference among them in the degree of industrialization achieved. In a number of them, notably the middle-income countries, the surplus labour is primarily in the urban sector, while in others it is largely in rural areas, although urban unemployment and underemployment can still be significant.

Changes in the pattern of income distribution vary considerably in the earlier stages among the countries in the first two groups, in large part because of differences in their initial distribution of wealth and the policies pursued for agricultural development and industrial accumulation. The most successful East Asian economies, namely Japan during its high-growth period and the first-tier NIEs, started with a substantial labour surplus.[26] Both Taiwan Province of China and the Republic of Korea were typical of most developing economies in that the surplus was in rural areas; in Japan many people returned to the primary sector after military demobilization, while in Hong Kong and Singapore there were high levels of urban unemployment and underemployment.

In Japan, income inequality increased from 1953 until the early 1960s, when full employment was reached, largely because of divergent income trends for agricultural and non-agricultural households and because the share of profits rose in industry. After the turning-point, income inequality decreased as both of these trends were reversed. The precise timing of the turning-point is less clear in the Republic of Korea, but it appears to have been in the second half of the 1970s. The country started with a relatively equal income distribution due in large part to a high degree of equality in land ownership. There was little change in overall income inequality, as measured by the Gini coefficient, during 1964-1970; the shares of the richest quintile and the middle class declined slightly, while that of the bottom 40 per cent rose (see annex).

However, income inequality rose sharply thereafter until 1976, principally because real wage growth, though rapid, lagged considerably behind productivity growth. The labour market tightened in the second half of the 1970s, when there was a phenomenal growth in real wages, closely tracking rising labour productivity growth. Starting in 1980, the share of the poorest 40 per cent rose at the expense of the richest 20 per cent, while that of the middle class was constant. Demand for skilled labour increased considerably because industrial upgrading started before full employment had been reached. However, wage differentials both between college and high school graduates and between college and elementary school leavers fell from 1976 onwards after rising in the earlier period, thanks in large part to education policies.

The full employment turning-point was passed in Taiwan Province of China earlier than in the Republic of Korea, in the late 1960s. Income distribution improved significantly in the 1950s, but in most of the following decade it changed little largely because equalizing and unequalizing forces were broadly in balance. The share of agricultural incomes declined rapidly, and there was a significant rise in non-agricultural property income. However, inequality declined considerably within agriculture. Furthermore, the falling share of agriculture took place in the context of a rapid transformation of the sector, which constantly raised productivity and hence the lower limit of industrial wages. Real wages in rural industries, which absorbed an important part of the surplus labour, indeed rose, whereas they remained relatively stable in urban industries. After the turning-point, the decline in inequality in non-agricultural income on account of a strong rise in real wages and labour share reinforced the continuing downward trend in inequality in agriculture, underlying a steady rise in the share of the middle classes (see the annex to this chapter).

The experience of Taiwan Province of China in the 1950s highlights the importance of agricultural policies for income distribution in the early stages, where much greater attention was paid than in the Republic of Korea to an early modernization of agriculture. A combination of price, investment and support policies was used in order to generate rapid and broad-based agricultural growth as well as a large surplus for accumulation in industry. At the beginning a land reform was implemented, reducing farm rents, which had been the main mechanism of agricultural surplus transfer; tenants became owner-cultivators and landowners were encouraged to become involved in industrial development. Government policies caused the domestic terms of trade to move sharply against farmers, but agricultural output expanded rapidly, by 78 per cent from 1952 to 1964, and output per worker and farm household income per capita increased by about 35 per cent and 10 per cent, respectively.[27] Productivity and production increases were founded on public investment, particularly in irrigation and flood control, introduction of new seed varieties, increased application of fertilizer, and diversification introduced through government-supported research agencies. As earlier in Japan, both yields and labour input per hectare rose in rice cultivation. Productivity improvements did not therefore displace labour initially, and in consequence agricultural expansion contributed to the absorption of surplus labour. Both rich and poor farmers participated in the expansion. Moreover, farm incomes of poorer households were supplemented through employment in rural industries. The net result was a substantial reduction in income inequality, which available statistics suggest was the sharpest experienced by the economy since the war, with the Gini coefficient dropping from 0.55 in 1953 to 0.32 in 1964.[28]

This pattern of increasing labour intensity with increasing labour productivity is of wider relevance for all East Asia, since it is intrinsic to the nature of wet-rice agriculture. Indeed, in Java surplus labour is now being absorbed in rural areas through shifts from marginal low-earning activities to rice cultivation, coinciding with the growth in formerly marginal off-farm activities, which are becoming more lucrative with the expansion of rice production and public investment in infrastructure. This pattern of change appears to explain how low-income rural groups in Indonesia have been able to increase their incomes, although the turning-point has not been reached and there is not as yet any strong upward pressure on rural wages.[29]

Again, the contrasting experiences of Thailand and Malaysia clearly show that agricultural policies can play a key role in determining whether growth in the early stages of development is equalizing or unequalizing. In the first country, agriculture has been neglected even though over 60 per cent of the labour force is still engaged in that sector. Agricultural growth has been based in particular on extension of the area under cultivation through the opening up of new lands, often forest land designated as reserves. Labour pro-

ductivity is very low, and value added per worker in agriculture is estimated to have fallen between 1971 and 1991; in the latter year it was less than one tenth that of industry. In Malaysia, by contrast, opening up of new land has also been an important mechanism of agricultural growth, but the process was more carefully managed, founded on government-sponsored programmes of agricultural investment and productivity growth, and linked to the New Economic Policy (1971-1990) which aimed to increase the asset ownership of indigenous Malays. In 1991, value added per worker in agriculture was three times higher than in Thailand, and the labour productivity gap between industry and agriculture was much smaller.[30] Growth has been less unequalizing in Malaysia (see the annex to this chapter), though the overall pattern, which in contrast to Thailand was slightly downward until the mid-1980s, obviously reflects various other influences, including a policy of asset redistribution towards the indigenous Malays and the greater importance of public sector employment.[31]

As noted above, even though neglect of agriculture can be unequalizing, it does not follow that agricultural growth as such is always equalizing. Indeed, an important feature of various episodes of agro-export booms in Latin America and Africa is their effect of widening inequality among farmers, especially where plantations and peasant production coexist, but also among smallholders. An example is Malawi, where there is marked dualism between the estate sector and smallholder sector, but also significant differentiation within the latter. The economy grew rapidly in the 1970s on the basis of agro-exports, but the Gini coefficient among smallholder families more than doubled.[32] In Latin America, although smallholders do have some labour and management advantages, their ability to adopt new crops and techniques is restricted by factors such as unfavourable input and output prices compared to large-scale producers, high transaction costs and limited access to credit. These can lead to land concentration in which small-scale producers sell up, as seen during the recent agro-export boom in Chile founded on fruit production. Unequalizing agricultural growth, together with the existence of a sizeable surplus of labour, may account for the increased share of the richest quintile in Chile at the expense of the middle 40 per cent in the earlier years of expansion in the 1980s, while subsequent tightening of the labour market appears to have been an important factor in the improvements in the 1990s (see annex).[33]

While most developing countries have not been able to sustain rapid growth so as to absorb their surplus labour, they have nevertheless had episodes of rapid growth. As in the above examples, changes in income distribution were of varying patterns during such periods according to the balance of various forces in different countries, and it is not possible to make generalizations. Nevertheless, it appears that in economies where the surplus labour was in urban areas, growth was often associated with a narrowing of the rich-middle class gap, with no significant relative improvement at the bottom. One plausible explanation is that growth was neither sufficiently rapid nor sufficiently labour-intensive to absorb the surplus labour, which consequently remained in the informal sector. Since formal and informal labour markets are often segmented, the existence of a large population of urban poor does not always influence wage movements in the formal sector and hence the distribution between the top (richest) quintile and the middle class.

The evidence presented above suggests that in general in economies with considerable surplus labour, inequality tends to widen when growth collapses. Increased unemployment and reduced real wages often lead to shrinking income shares of the middle classes. The urban and rural poor, the bottom 40 per cent, are generally less affected in relative terms than the middle class by contraction of economic activity, because they are not properly integrated into the formal economy; they often rely on self-employment, which provides some protection against sharp declines in incomes. This is particularly the case for those who depend primarily on subsistence agriculture. As noted above, in such cases, economic declines can even coincide with a rise in the share of the poor engaged in the subsistence sectors. By contrast, where the poor are concentrated in urban areas, their incomes tend to decline with activity in the formal economy because of their greater dependence thereon.

In many middle-income countries with considerable surplus labour, particularly in Latin America, the deteriorating relative position of the middle classes vis-à-vis the richest quintile since the early 1980s reflects the influence of a number of factors. That their income share should fall when growth collapsed is hardly a matter for surprise, but it also fell when growth remained positive, though moderate, because measures taken to attain a swift and sizeable payments adjustment, such as devaluations and cuts in investment, had serious consequences for real wages and employment. This is perhaps an important reason for the observed shift in the relationship between growth and inequality discussed above. Another reason relates to policies and explains why the subsequent recovery did not result in a reversal of the relative position of the middle classes; the drastic turnaround in economic policies, particularly the liberalization of trade and finance, appears to have changed the balance of forces in favour of those making for greater inequality - an issue which is taken up in the following chapter.

E. Conclusions

The evidence examined above shows that it is very difficult to make generalizations about how income distribution changes with economic development. Perhaps one of the few definite conclusions that can be drawn is that none of the countries that successfully closed the income gap with the advanced industrial countries in the postwar period, namely Japan and the first-tier NIEs, has a very high degree of inequality. It is difficult to venture beyond this conclusion, since a number of countries at much lower levels of industrialization and development have income distribution as equal as and even more equal than the successful late industrializers. Moreover, contrary to a widespread perception, income distribution did not constantly improve throughout the industrialization process in these successful countries.

The balance of forces appears to be weighted towards those making for greater income inequality during the initial stages of labour absorption. However, increasing inequality is not inevitable, much depending on agricultural policies. In Japan, the Republic of Korea and Taiwan Province of China agricultural growth was founded on land reform, which resulted in a relatively equal initial asset distribution. Policies in Japan and Taiwan Province of China resulted in a widely shared agricultural growth which played a key role in maintaining a relatively stable income distribution in earlier periods of industrialization. By contrast the Republic of Korea experienced sharply rising income inequality.

In general, during the phase of labour absorption there is a tendency for profits to rise as real wages lag behind productivity. If profits are not reinvested, the growth process will slow down and inequality may persist. An important aspect of policy must thus be to ensure that profits are saved and invested to create jobs and new wealth, rather than consumed. As discussed in chapter V, in this respect there are considerable variations among developing countries, and successful countries stand out by their high savings and investment from profits, stimulated by policies discussed in chapter VI.

The balance of forces making for more or less inequality after the full absorption of surplus labour depends on a host of factors, including manpower policies and industrial upgrading. Carefully designed industrial policies can prevent pressures from building up on wages as a result of the emergence of low-cost competitors by facilitating industrial upgrading. An adequate and increasing supply of educated labour can prevent skill shortages leading to widening wage differentials at this point. As examined in detail in *TDR 1996*, the first-tier NIEs have been generally successful on both fronts, whereas the second-tier NIEs still lag considerably behind.

Again, evidence does not support the view that outward orientation is associated with greater income equality. Inequality in a number of countries in East and South-East Asia with very strong export orientation is as high as or even higher than in countries which have relied on domestic markets and import substitution. A careful examination of the East Asian experience finds no support for the notion that improved equality was associated with a switch from import substitution to export-oriented development policies. As examined in detail in *TDR 1996,* this distinction makes little sense in East Asia, where export promotion was combined with import protection so as to accelerate accumulation and productivity growth. As the late Michael Bruno put it, commenting on the findings of cross-country studies linking employment performance with outward-orientation:

> The good outward-looking performers ... had a good employment record not necessarily because of a preference for exports over import substitution. Most likely they did better because their general macro-policy stance (fewer stop-go policies, etc.) and other conditions (e.g. foreign exchange availability) helped them grow more rapidly and thus absorb their labour force.[34]

Policies seeking to determine the form, speed and timing of integration into the world economy have certainly played a key role in managing the growth-distribution linkages in the first-tier NIEs both during the earlier stages of surplus labour absorption and in the subsequent period of upgrading. In none of the economies was economy-wide trade and financial liberalization undertaken before surplus labour was absorbed; nor was sector-specific exposure of the domestic market to foreign competition undertaken before attaining significant productivity growth and learning. These countries indeed never resorted to the kind of abrupt shifts in trade and financial policies implemented in recent years in some developing countries.

Evidence strongly suggests that while rapid growth does not guarantee improvement in income distribution, economic decline is usually associated with greater inequality. In countries where there is a sizeable surplus labour delinked from the formal economy, decline tends to be associated with a squeeze of the middle classes, as happened widely during the 1980s. However, the relationship between growth and equality appears to have undergone a major transformation in a number of countries, where there has been no tendency for rising inequality to be reversed despite some recovery in the 1990s. This phenomenon appears to be closely related to a sudden shift in policies giving much greater role to market forces.

These economies characterized by surplus labour may now require even more rapid growth than in the past in order to improve distribution. The challenge is to put in place policies to accelerate capital accumulation and productivity growth and shift the balance of forces towards those making for less inequality. Their policy environments differ in three respects from the first-tier NIEs, rendering this challenge particularly difficult to meet. Firstly, in Latin America a large proportion of the surplus labour is urban, and in Africa both urbanization and population growth rates are very high. Second, in both continents ownership of and access to land is highly concentrated and educa-tional attainments are very unequally distributed. Finally, the "big bang" approach to liberalization in many of these countries seems to have changed the balance of forces in favour of those making for greater inequality without generating any additional stimulus to growth. ■

Notes

1   On outward orientation see A. O. Krueger, *Trade and Employment in Developing Countries*, Vol. 3 - *Synthesis and Conclusions* (Chicago and London: University of Chicago Press, 1983); M. Schiff and A. Valdés, *The Political Economy of Agricultural Pricing Policy*, Vol. 4 - *A Synthesis of the Economics in Developing Countries* (Baltimore and London: Johns Hopkins University Press for the World Bank, 1992). For a discussion of East Asia as an example of rapid growth with equality, see *The East Asian Miracle: Economic Growth and Public Policy* (New York: Oxford University Press for the World Bank, 1993); and also N. Birdsall, D. Ross and R. Sabot, "Inequality and Growth Reconsidered: Lessons from East Asia", *The World Bank Economic Review*, Vol. 9, No. 3, 1995. On the relationship between trade and distribution, see F. Bourguignon and C. Morrison, *External Trade and Income Distribution* (Paris: OECD Development Centre Studies, 1989); M. Ahluwalia, "Inequality, Poverty and Development", *Journal of Development Economics*, Vol. 3, No. 4, Dec. 1976; G. Papanek and O. Kyn, "Flattening the Kuznets Curve: The Consequences for Income Distribution of Development Strategy, Government Intervention, Income and the Rate of Growth", *Pakistan Development Review*, Vol. 26, No. 1, 1987; and A. Wood, *North-South Trade, Employment and Inequality: Changing Fortunes in a Skill-driven World* (Oxford: Clarendon Press, 1994).

2   For the relationships between ethical principles and income distribution, see D. Lal, "Distribution and Development: A Review Article", *World Development*, Vol. 4, No. 9, 1976; and A.K. Sen, *Inequality Revisited* (Oxford: Clarendon Press, 1992); and for an alternative approach to social justice, see G. Rodgers, C. Gore and J.B. Figueiredo (eds.), *Social Exclusion: Rhetoric, Reality, Responses* (Geneva: International Institute for Labour Studies, 1995).

3   On these problems see W. Van Ginneken, "Generating Internationally Comparable Income Distribution Data: Evidence from the Federal Republic of Germany (1974), Mexico (1978) and the United Kingdom (1979)", *The Review of Income and Wealth*, Series 28, No. 4, 1982; A Berry, "On Trends in the Gap Between Rich and Poor in Developing Countries: Why we Know so Little", *ibid.*, Series 31, No. 4, 1985; A. Berry, "Evidence on the Relationships among Alternative Measures of Concentration: A Tool for the Analysis of LDC Inequality", *ibid.*, Series 33, No. 4, 1987.

4   For a description of this statistical material see K. Deininger and L. Squire, "A New Data Set Measuring Income Inequality", *The World Bank Economic Review*, Vol. 10, No. 3, 1996. The complete data set can be accessed through the Internet (http://www.worldbank.org/html/prdmg/grwthweb/growth-t.htm).

5   Some of the distribution statistics relate to households, while others relate to persons, and incomes are reported either gross or net. No attempt is made to adjust for these differences in the present analysis.

6   Throughout this chapter, the term "middle class" is used to refer to the 40 per cent of the population with incomes between the richest 20 per cent and the poorest 40 per cent.

7   Because of higher savings in upper income groups, inequalities in consumption expenditure are generally less than those in income. Some of the developing countries classified as intermediate or "40:40:20" societies on the basis of expenditure data may therefore be "60:30:10" or intermediate societies, respectively, if their classification could be made on the basis of income data.

8   According to Indonesian national survey data, the Gini coefficient for household consumption expenditure per capita was 0.34, 0.38 and 0.33 in 1976,

1978 and 1981, respectively; for income per capita it was 0.47, 0.47 and 0.44 in 1976, 1978 and 1982, respectively. See A. Booth, "Income Distribution and Poverty", ch. 10 in A. Booth (ed.), *The Oil Boom and After: Indonesian Economic Policy and Performance in the Suharto Era* (Oxford: Oxford University Press, 1991).

9   S. Kuznets, "Economic Growth and Income Inequality", *The American Economic Review*, Vol. XLV, No. 1, March 1955, p. 22.

10   This section draws on A.B. Atkinson *et al., Income Distribution in OECD Countries: Evidence of the Luxembourg Income Study*, OECD Social Policy Studies No.18 (Paris, 1995); B. Milanovic, "Income, Inequality and Poverty during the Transition: A Survey of the Evidence", *MOCT: Economic Policy in Transitional Economies*, Vol. 6, No. 1, 1996; O. Altimir, "Income Distribution and Poverty through Crisis and Adjustment", *CEPAL Review,* No. 52, April 1994; A. De Janvry and E. Sadoulet, *Poverty, Equity and Social Welfare: Determinants of Change over Growth Spells*, Issues in Development Discussion Paper, No. 6 (Geneva: ILO, 1995); G. Psacharopoulos *et al., Poverty and Income Distribution in Latin America: The Story of the 1980s*, Latin America and the Caribbean Technical Department Regional Studies Programme, Report No. 27 (Washington, D.C.: The World Bank, 1996); R. Infante, "Labour Market, Urban Poverty and Adjustment: New Challenges and Policy Options", in G. Rodgers and R. van der Hoeven (eds.), *The Poverty Agenda: Trends and Policy Options* (Geneva: International Institute for Labour Studies, 1995); C. Jayarajah, W. Branson, and B. Sen, *Social Dimensions of Adjustment: World Bank Experience 1980-93* (Washington, D.C.: World Bank, 1996); V. Jamal and J. Weeks, *Africa Misunderstood, or Whatever Happened to the Rural-Urban Gap?* (London: Macmillan, 1993); V. Jamal (ed.), *Structural Adjustment and Rural Labour Markets in Africa* (London: Macmillan, 1995); and M. Krongkaew, "Income Distribution in East Asian Developing Countries", *Asia-Pacific Economic Literature*, Vol. 8, No. 2, Nov. 1994.

11   Bangladesh, Brazil, Chile, Colombia, Costa Rica, Malaysia, Mexico, Panama, Philippines, Republic of Korea, Sri Lanka, Taiwan Province of China, Thailand, Venezuela (income data); India and Pakistan (consumption expenditure data).

12   The importance of episodes of change in inequality analysis is stressed in A. Atkinson, "Bringing Income Distribution in from the Cold", *Economic Journal*, Vol. 107, March 1997.

13   Such a pattern is also observed by G. Fields in his "Changes in Poverty and Inequality in Developing Countries", *The World Bank Research Observer*, Vol. 4, No. 2, 1989, and "Income Distribution in Developing Economies: Conceptual, Data, and Policy Issues in Broad-based Growth", chap. 4, in M. G. Quibria (ed.), *Critical Issues in Asian Development: Theories, Experiences and Policies*

(Hong Kong, Oxford and New York: Oxford University Press, 1985).

14   For another view of the growth-inequality relationship, which covers only the 1980s and for some countries uses expenditure data and for other countries income data, see M. Ravallion and S. Chen, "What Can New Survey Data Tell us about Recent Changes in Distribution and Poverty?", *World Bank Policy Research Paper*, No. 1694 (Washington, D.C., 1996). The authors found that in developing countries "growth tends to be associated with slightly higher inequality and polarization" (p. 30), but this conclusion is only statistically robust for polarization, and there was an equal likelihood for inequality to rise or fall with growth.

15   The charts are based on data from the sources indicated for chart 8, except for the United Republic of Tanzania, where they are from H. Tabatabai, *Statistics on Poverty and Income Distribution: An ILO Compendium of Data* (Geneva: ILO, 1997).

16   This pattern requires further exploration, particularly as at their level of per capita income, countries with large Moslem populations also appear to have relatively low levels of inequality. For such an attempt, see G.A. Jekle, "*Zakat* and Inequality: Some Evidence from Pakistan", *The Review of Income and Wealth*, Series 40, No. 2, June 1994.

17   For key early contributions to the debate see I. Adelman and C. T. Morris, *Economic Growth and Social Equity in Developing Countries* (Stanford, CA: Stanford University Press, 1973); F. Paukert, "Income Distribution at Different Levels of Development: A Survey of Evidence", *International Labour Review*, Aug.-Sep. 1973; M.S. Ahluwalia, *op. cit.* For more recent discussions see S.M. Randolph and W.F. Lott, "Can the Kuznets Effect be Relied on to Induce Equalizing Growth?", *World Development*, Vol. 21, No. 5, 1993; R. Ram, "Economic Development and Inequality: An Overlooked Regression Coefficient", *Economic Development and Cultural Change*, 43, 1995; S.K. Jha, "The Kuznets Curve: A Re-assessment", *World Development*, Vol. 24, No. 4, 1996; and M. Bruno, M. Ravallion and L. Squire, "Equity and Growth in Developing Countries: Old and New Perspectives on the Policy Issues", *World Bank Policy Research Paper,* No. 1563 (Washington, D.C., 1996).

18   See, for example, H. Chenery and M. Syrquin, *Patterns of Development 1950-1970* (Oxford: Oxford University Press, 1975); M.S. Ahluwalia, *op. cit.*; J. Cromwell, "The Size Distribution of Income: An International Comparison", *The Review of Income and Wealth*, Series 23, No. 3, 1977; G. Papanek and O. Kyn, *op. cit.;* A. Fishlow, "Inequality, Poverty, Growth: Where Do We Stand?", in Michael Bruno and Boris Pleskovic (eds.), *Annual World Bank Conference on Development Economics* (Washington, D.C.: The World Bank, 1995); F. Nielsen, "Income Inequality and Industrial Development: Dualism Revisited", *American Sociological Review*, Vol. 59, Oct. 1994.

19   See Psacharopoulos *et al., op. cit.*

20   On the inequality turning-point see R. Ram, "Educational Expansion and Schooling Inequality: International Evidence and Some Implications", *The Review of Economics and Statistics,* Vol. LLXXII, 1990.

21   For wealth inequality in OECD countries, see E. Wolff, "International Comparisons of Wealth Inequality", *The Review of Income and Wealth,* Series 42, No. 4, December 1996. On the Republic of Korea see D. Leipziger *et al., The Distribution of Income and Wealth in Korea* (Washington, D.C.: The World Bank, Economic Development Institute, 1992).

22   See N.T Quan and A.Y.C. Koo, "Concentration of Land Holdings: An Empirical Investigation of Kuznets' Conjecture", *Journal of Development Economics,* Vol. 18, 1985; for a dissenting view see G. Wignaraja, "Concentration of Land Holdings and Income", *ibid.,* Vol. 29, 1988.

23   These estimates are derived from P. Saunders, H. Stott and G. Hobbes, "Income Inequality in Australia and New Zealand: International Comparisons and Recent Trends", *The Review of Income and Wealth,* Series 37, No. 1, 1991; P. Ryan, "Factor Shares and Inequality in the UK", *Oxford Economic Review,* Vol. 12, No. 1, 1996; M. Wolfson, "Stasis amid Change: Income Inequality in Canada, 1965-83", *The Review of Income and Wealth,* Series 32, 1986; G. Fields, "Income Inequality in Urban Colombia: A Decomposition Analysis", *ibid.,* Series 25, No. 3, 1979; J. Fei, G. Ranis and S. Kuo, *Growth with Equity: The Taiwan Case* (New York: Oxford University Press, 1979); and A. Guardia, "Distribución del Ingreso en Chile, 1990-1993, según la Encuesta de Hogares", *Estadística y Economía,* 10 (Santiago: Instituto Nacional de Estadística, June 1995).

24   See B. Milanovic, "Determinants of Cross-country Income Inequality: An Augmented Kuznets Hypothesis", *World Bank Policy Research Working Paper,* No. 1246 (Washington, D.C.: The World Bank, 1994).

25   The issue here is the elimination of structural unemployment. After the turning-point, the economy can still have cyclical unemployment, owing to fluctuations in economic activity.

26   The discussion in this subsection draws on: R. Minami, *The Turning Point in Economic Development: Japan's Experience,* Economic Research Series, No. 14, Institute of Economic Research, Hitotsubashi University (Tokyo: Kinokuniya Bookstore Co., 1973); T. Mizoguchi and N. Takayama, *Equity and Poverty under Rapid Economic Growth: The Japanese Experience,* Economic Research Series, No. 21, Institute of Economic Research, Hitotsubashi University (Tokyo: Kinokuniya Company Ltd., 1984); Moo-Ki Bai, "The Turning Point in the Korean Economy", *The Developing Economies,* Vol. 20, No. 1, March 1982; Won-Duck Lee, "Economic Growth and Earnings Distribution in Korea", chap. 4 in T. Mizoguchi (ed.), *Making Economies More Efficient and more Equitable: Factors Determining Income Distribution,* Economic Research Series No. 29, Institute of Economic Research, Hitotsubashi University (Tokyo: Kinokuniya Company Ltd. and Oxford University Press, 1991); D.-I. Kim and R.H. Topel, "Labour Markets and Economic Growth: Lessons from Korea's Industrialization, 1970-1990", chap. 7 in R.B. Freeman and L.F. Katz (eds.), *Differences and Changes in Wage Structures* (Chicago and London: University of Chicago Press, 1995); J.C.H. Fei, G. Ranis and S.W.Y. Kuo, *Growth with Equity: The Taiwan Case* (Oxford: Oxford University Press, 1979); R. Hung, "The Great U-turn in Taiwan: Economic Restructuring and a Surge in Inequality", *Journal of Contemporary Asia,* Vol. 6, No. 2, 1996.

27   As in the Republic of Korea, there was a shift from "taxing" to subsidizing agriculture in the early 1970s. For agricultural pricing policy in East Asia, see K. Anderson and Y. Hayami, *The Political Economy of Agricultural Protection: East Asia in International Perspective* (Sydney and London: Allen and Unwin, 1986); and M. Moore, "Economic Structure and the Politics of Sectoral Bias: East Asian and Other Cases", *Journal of Development Studies,* Vol. 29, No. 4, July 1993; figures cited in the text for output and income changes are taken from M. Karshenas, *Industrialization and Agricultural Surplus* (Oxford and New York: Oxford University Press, 1995).

28   See J.C.H. Fei, G. Ranis and S.W.Y. Kuo, *op. cit.*

29   For the labour-absorbing nature of agricultural growth in East Asia see S. Ishikawa, *Economic Development in Asian Perspective* (Tokyo: Kinokuniya Bookstore, 1967); and *Labour Absorption in Asian Agriculture* (Bangkok: ILO-ARTEP [Asian Regional Team for Employment Promotion], 1978). For a discussion of rural Java, see D. Mazumdar and P. Basu, "Macro-economic Policies, Growth and Employment: The East and Southeast Asian Experience", Paper No. 7, prepared under the ILO/UNDP project "Economic Policy and Employment"; C. Manning, "What has Happened to Wages in the New Order?", *Bulletin of Indonesian Studies,* Vol. 30, No. 3, Dec. 1994.

30   See D. Mazumdar and P. Basu, *op. cit.*

31   This policy aimed to increase indigenous Malays' (*bumiputra*) corporate ownership and breakdown ethnic compartmentalization of economic activities whereby Indians and Chinese dominated trade and industrial activities. A specific goal was to increase Malay share ownership from 3 per cent of total share capital in 1971 to 30 per cent in 1991, mainly by reducing the proportion owned by foreigners (from 63 per cent to 30 per cent).

32   See F. Pryor, "Changes in Income Distribution in Poor Agricultural Nations: Malawi and Madagascar", *Economic Development and Cultural Change,* Vol. 9, No. 1, Oct. 1990.

33   For the effects of agro-export booms in Latin America, see M.R. Carter and B.L. Barham, "Level

Playing Fields and *Laissez-faire*: Post-Liberal Development Strategy in Inegalitarian Agrarian Economies", *World Development*, Vol. 24, No. 7, 1996; and M.R. Carter and D. Mesbah, "Can Land Market Reform Mitigate the Exclusionary Aspects of Rapid Agro-export Growth?", *ibid.*, Vol. 21, No. 7, 1993. For analysis of a cross-over in which inequality within agriculture increases and then exceeds that in non-

agriculture, see R. Weisskoff, "Income Distribution and Economic Change in Paraguay, 1972-88", *The Review of Income and Wealth*, Series 38, No. 2, 1992.

34   M. Bruno, "Comments on 'The Relationship between Trade, Employment and Development'", in G. Ranis and T.P. Schultz (eds.), *The State of Development Economics: Progress and Perspectives* (Oxford: Basil Blackwell, 1988), p. 384.

TRENDS IN PERSONAL INCOME DISTRIBUTION IN SELECTED DEVELOPING COUNTRIES

(Shares in total income or expenditure of different population groups)

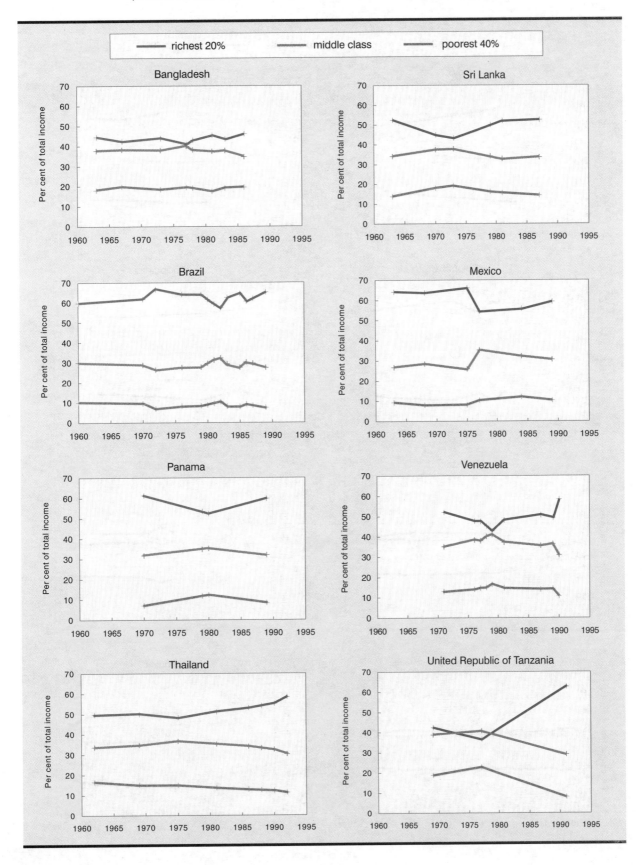

Source: As for chart 8 of the main text and also H. Tabatabai, *op. cit.*

Annex to chapter III (continued)

TRENDS IN PERSONAL INCOME DISTRIBUTION IN SELECTED DEVELOPING COUNTRIES

(Shares in total income or expenditure of different population groups)

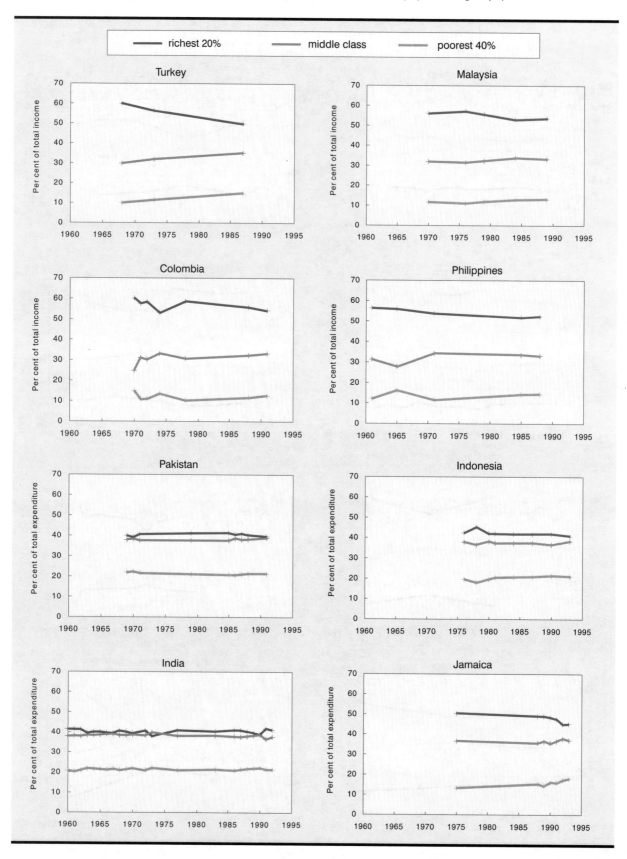

Source: As for chart 8 of the main text and also H. Tabatabai, *op. cit.*

Annex to chapter III (concluded)

TRENDS IN PERSONAL INCOME DISTRIBUTION IN SELECTED DEVELOPING COUNTRIES

(Shares in total income or expenditure of different population groups)

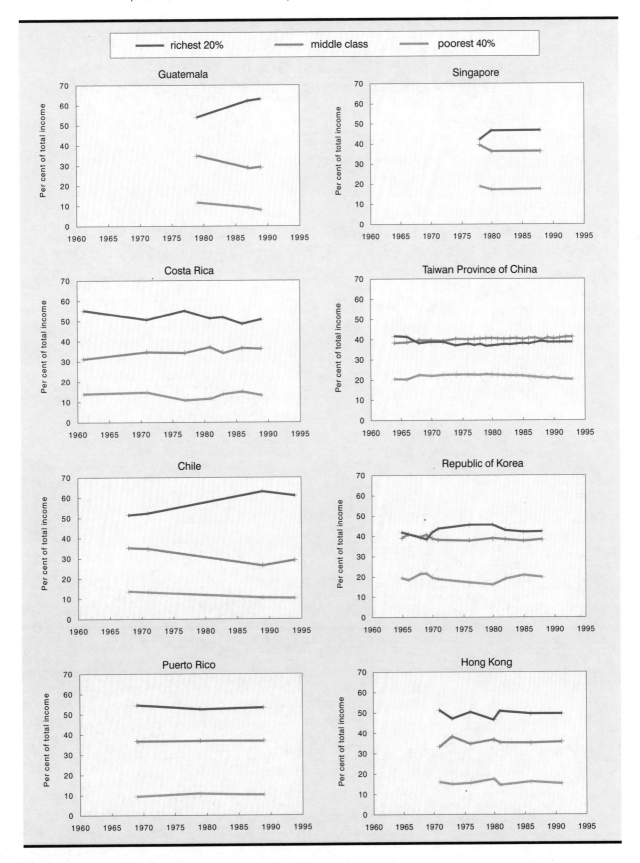

Source: As for chart 8 of the main text and also H. Tabatabai, *op. cit.*

Chapter IV

LIBERALIZATION, INTEGRATION AND DISTRIBUTION

A. Introduction

In a large number of developing countries, especially in Africa and Latin America, the debt crisis of the early 1980s and the macroeconomic adjustment and policy reforms introduced in response thereto have shaped recent trends in income distribution. As noted in chapter III above, during the 1980s income distribution in general worsened in countries where growth collapsed as a result of the debt crisis. However, in a number of countries, particularly in Latin America, the situation did not improve with recovery. With very few exceptions, inequality is now greater than before the outbreak of the debt crisis.

The debt crisis itself brought about an immediate increase in income inequality, since the short-term costs of adjustment were not shared equally by all income groups. The external trade and financial shocks created large macroeconomic imbalances, the elimination of which had a widely diverse impact on different income groups. Worsening terms of trade due to the collapse of commodity prices in the early 1980s caused foreign exchange losses for the economy as a whole, but hit commodity producers in particular, reducing their incomes. Nor did the burden of budgetary transfers, necessitated by a sharp swing in net external financial transfers brought about by cut-backs in bank lending and the hike in international interest rates, fall equally on all groups. Property incomes, on the other hand, could be more easily protected because of the exit option provided

by capital flight. The adjustment required to adapt to shrinking external resources necessitated a sharp decline in the pace of economic activity, producing significant unemployment and underemployment. As discussed in some detail in *TDR 1989*, in most countries the burden of shifts in relative prices designed to alter competitiveness, such as currency devaluations, fell disproportionately on labour incomes, as evidenced by the sharp declines in real earnings throughout the 1980s. External shocks and the adjustment process gave rise to serious distributional conflicts and rapid inflation in many debtor countries.

Many, if not all, of the immediate causes and effects of the debt crisis, as well as the dislocations caused by stabilization and macroeconomic adjustment, are now a matter of history in a number of countries. Success in stabilization has been almost unprecedented. Contrary to earlier expectations, many countries have made significant progress in normalizing their relations with international capital markets, and capital inflows in such countries have been restored at an unexpected volume and speed. Commodity prices have seen some recovery following the collapse of the early 1980s. Economic activity has picked up, albeit moderately, in most countries. However, they have not been able to reverse the deterioration in income distribution, in large part because the drastic changes that have taken place in public policy in response to the crisis have resulted in fundamental and permanent shifts in income distribution. Nowhere else has this shift been more drastic than in Latin America. As has been noted,

> ... the new modality under which the economies are functioning and the new rules of public policy involve greater income inequalities and more precarious employment situations than in the past. ... Consequently, one should not expect significant equity improvements in these countries as a consequence of stabilization and recovery. Indeed, full deployment of policy reforms and associated adjustment measures ... may still bring a medium-term increase in income inequality.[1]

The new modality and new rules are designed to give greater freedom to market forces. While they encompass a vast area of public policy, including taxation, public spending, public enterprises, labour markets, agriculture, trade, industry and finance, they seek to assign a greater role to markets primarily through a closer integration with the global economy. Accordingly, this chapter will discuss the impact of policies in two principal areas of integration, namely trade and finance, on income distribution. Attention will be focused on the evolution of wage differentials between skilled and unskilled workers, the distribution of manufacturing value added between labour and capital, the impact of agricultural price reforms on domestic terms of trade, and the sources of increases in the share of interest and other financial incomes.

B. Trade liberalization and wage inequality

The view that globalization will promote greater income equality in developing countries is based primarily on the assumption that greater integration of developing countries into the world trading system through the elimination of tariff and non-tariff barriers would benefit the poor. This view is based on the premiss that under free trade a country's production structure is shaped by comparative advantage, determined by its relative factor endowments. Thus, a country should produce and export those goods which use its most abundant domestic resources most intensively, and import those goods which require its least abundant factors. Since capital was considered to be the relatively scarce factor in developing countries, these countries would import capital-intensive goods and export goods which use land and labour more intensively. As a result, the demand for labour should rise and the demand for capital decline, causing labour incomes to improve relative to capital incomes.

According to a growing body of opinion, the increasing international mobility of capital has reduced the importance of differences in the level of capital stock in determining a country's comparative advantage, whilst the growth of trade in goods with high knowledge and skill content has increased the importance of relative endowments of skilled and unskilled labour in shaping the pattern and effects of trade. It follows that since skilled labour will be in relatively scarce supply in developing countries, their production under free trade should concentrate on agricultural and manufactured products that require unskilled labour. This would consequently increase in the relative demand for unskilled labour, which should lead to a reduction in wage inequality. Consequently, globalization is expected not only to improve labour incomes relative to capital incomes, but also to increase the incomes earned by unskilled labour relative to those earned on the human capital embodied in skilled labour.

Since the mid-1980s, a large number of developing countries have undertaken unilateral trade liberalization measures, including elimination of non-tariff barriers and sharp reductions of tariffs. Trade liberalization has gone much further in Latin America than elsewhere. Most Latin American countries which had once erected much greater barriers to imports than East Asian countries have recently gone further than the latter in dismantling such barriers. In the early 1990s, compared to East

Asia, the average and maximum tariff rates in six of the largest countries of Latin America were smaller by almost one half and two thirds, respectively, and their dispersion was considerably lower. Non-tariff barriers were quite moderate and on the whole lower than those in advanced industrial countries as well as the East Asian NIEs.[2]

Despite the theoretical prediction of reduced income inequality, the evidence from this experience of trade liberalization in Latin America on earnings differentials points in a different direction: in almost all countries that resorted to a rapid trade liberalization following the so-called import-substitution strategy of industrialization, the gap between the wages of skilled and unskilled workers has increased. A number of studies examining the behaviour of relative wages in various episodes of trade liberalization in Argentina, Chile, Colombia, Costa Rica, Mexico, and Uruguay find almost unanimous evidence of rising rather than falling wage differentials.[3] In most countries the wage gap widened while the real wages of unskilled workers actually fell and unemployment increased. Again, the increased skill premium has been associated in some cases with increases in the supply of skilled labour relative to unskilled labour. There were certainly other factors operating on wages and employment during such episodes of trade liberalization, including those linked to macroeconomic adjustment and labour market reforms. However, the evidence shows that while these factors may have also contributed to increased wage inequality in some countries, it is explained primarily by trade liberalization.

The worsening of the position of unskilled labour in Latin America has recently been noted, among others, by ECLAC:

> The distance separating the incomes of professional and technical personnel from those of workers in low-productivity sectors increased by between 40 per cent and 60 per cent in 1990-1994. This was due to the rapid improvement of the labour incomes of skilled manpower and the reduction or lack of growth in pay levels for workers not taking part in the modernization of production, who account for a large percentage of total employment.[4]

Chart 9 shows changes in earnings of three different skill groups of labour in Latin America in recent years for countries and periods for which such data are available. Of the 10 countries included in the chart, all except one experienced widening gaps between skilled workers (professional and technical workers) and unskilled workers (i.e. those in low-productivity sectors). With the exception of Chile, Costa Rica and Uruguay, real earnings of unskilled workers fell during the periods covered, with declines reaching 30 per cent in Bolivia and Brazil, and 20 per cent in Colombia and Mexico. In Bolivia and Brazil real earnings of unskilled workers fell much more than those of skilled ones. In Colombia and Mexico, declines in the earnings of unskilled workers were associated with increases in those of the skilled. In Chile the increase in the real earnings of unskilled workers during 1990-1994 (a cumulative 5 per cent) remained well below the rise in real per capita income in the same period (over 20 per cent). The earnings gap of public employees and workers in bigger firms with skilled workers also widened in most countries, though by a lower margin.[5]

Increased wage dispersion in manufacturing during the recent period of globalization is also reported by the ILO, for a sample of 30 countries in Africa, Asia and Latin America which compares average real wages over 1975-1979 with those in 1987-1991. The largest increases in wage dispersion were in Chile, Thailand, Brazil, and the United Republic of Tanzania. It was found that in about two thirds of all the countries real average wages had fallen, and that the fall was correlated with a rise in wage dispersion.[6] The economies in which wage dispersion diminished include the first-tier East Asian NIEs, where it was accompanied by significant increases in labour productivity. The only exception to diminishing wage dispersion in East Asia is Hong Kong.

A number of explanations have been offered to reconcile the increased wage inequality with the theoretical implications of the impact of comparative advantage on trade. If trade liberalization and increased capital mobility accelerate the introduction of best-practice technology in developing countries, and if the use of such technology requires specially trained labour, the increase in demand for skilled labour may lead to a widening of the wage gap. However, a fairly sizable shift in technology would be required, which should be reflected in a sharp increase in imports of capital goods as well as in an expansion of exports of skill-intensive products. Yet, the greater openness observed in Latin America has not generally been associated with a significant increase in investment and technology transfer. As analysed in greater

Chart 9

CHANGES IN EARNINGS OF VARIOUS CATEGORIES OF URBAN LABOUR IN LATIN AMERICAN COUNTRIES IN THE 1990s

(Per cent)

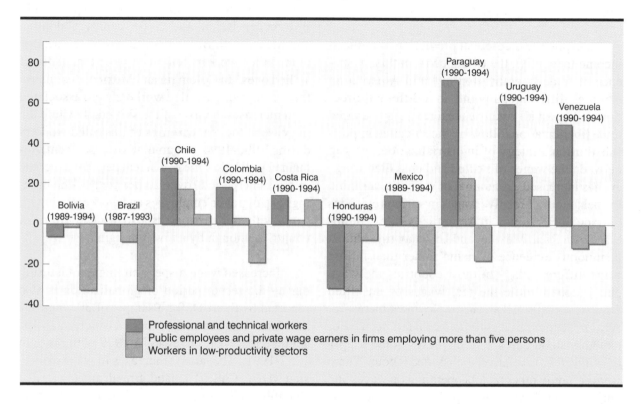

Source: ECLAC, *The Equity Gap. Latin America, the Caribbean and the Social Summit* (LC/G.1954 (CONF. 86/3)), Santiago, Chile, March 1997, table II.5.

Note: Workers in low-productive sectors include wage earners in firms employing up to five persons, own-account workers not employed in professional or technical occupations, and domestic employees.

detail in *TDR 1995*, investment in the region was sluggish even in the presence of massive inflows of capital. Moreover, much of the increase in investment was in residential construction; in 1992, for the seven major Latin American countries taken together, investment in machinery and equipment was lower than in the early 1980s.

More importantly, the observed shift in wage differentials towards skilled labour has not been associated with any relative increase in the exports of more skill-intensive products. In Chile there has been a sharp recovery in investment, but it has been accompanied by rapid growth of labour-intensive and natural resource-based exports. Productivity has strengthened as a result of the investment boom, but the export surge appears to be strongly influenced by the fact that real wages in these sectors lagged behind productivity growth. For Argentina, Chile and Colombia taken together,

the share of primary commodities plus resource-based and labour-intensive goods in total exports fell only slightly, from 89 per cent to 82 per cent, from 1985 to 1994. The decline was from 64 per cent to 58 per cent in Brazil. The only country which showed a sizable decline in the share of such exports was Mexico (from 45 per cent to 23 per cent), but what appears to be a jump from the lower skill range to the upper range in fact reflects an increase in labour-intensive, assembly-type *maquiladora* activities associated with FDI.[7]

In some instances demand for skilled labour (as measured by educational attainment) has increased relative to that for unskilled labour without a significant increase in investment to upgrade the industry and move exports towards technology-intensive products. Industries producing low-technology products have replaced less-educated with more-educated labour (including managers). This skill-upgrading may have been triggered by trade liberalization when the industries concerned were no longer able to compete with imports, and competitiveness could not be restored simply by lowering the wages of unskilled labour, but it necessitated taking on more skilled labour. There is some evidence that such a skill-biased demand shift occurred in Mexico during 1987-1993 in the traded-goods sectors.[8]

It was noted in the previous chapter that in the course of surplus labour absorption, employment of unskilled labour could be raised without an increase in real wages. Since unskilled labour-intensive activities also employ some skilled labour, absorption of unskilled labour would be associated with an increased demand for skilled labour. When the skilled labour is in short supply, this could lead to a rise in the wages of skilled labour and widening of wage inequality. That may indeed be one reason for rising wage inequality in countries such as Chile which, as already noted, have successfully been absorbing surplus labour. However, it does not explain the general experience. First, as noted above, wage differentials rose even where the supply of skilled labour increased. Secondly, and more importantly, wage differentials rose mostly in the context of falling real wages and falling employment of unskilled labour in manufacturing.

An alternative explanation of increasing wage dispersion suggests that factor supplies should be compared on a global basis. On this view, the increased competition in labour-intensive products from countries such as China, India and Indonesia, where unskilled labour is much more abundant and much less expensive, has caused the share of middle-income countries to decline in the global market for labour-intensive products, offsetting the predicted rise in relative demand for unskilled labour in such countries. Just as increased unemployment of unskilled labour and increased wage inequality in industrial countries are explained by the expansion in North-South trade in manufactures, so greater openness is said to lead to similar labour market problems in middle-income developing countries, which find it increasingly difficult to compete at home or abroad with cheaper producers. This is another way of saying that in such countries the poor suffered from trade liberalization because they were not poor enough, or because they were not sufficiently numerous. At the same time, these countries are unable to expand their skill-intensive exports because they cannot compete with industrial countries. While the effect of these two influences on wage inequality depends on their relative strengths, it is assumed that the loss of competitiveness has been greater in the less skill-intensive products, partly as a result of the presumed skill-enhancing effects of increased openness.

The emergence of low-cost producers of labour-intensive manufactures in Asia has no doubt changed the parameters in international trade for other exporters of such products, and its effect should also have been important for the first-tier East Asian NIEs, where about half of their exports consisted of such goods in the mid-1980s. However, these countries have been able to respond to the new competition by restructuring and upgrading their labour-intensive exports, and by shifting towards skill-intensive products.[9] As noted in *TDR 1996*, there was a wave of capital goods imports into the Republic of Korea and Taiwan Province of China during the 1980s as the economies were restructured toward more skill-intensive industrial activities. This upgrading took place before imports were liberalized in the second half of the 1980s. The share of labour-intensive products in the combined exports of the two economies fell from over 40 per cent in 1985 to 25 per cent in 1994, while the share of skill- and technology-intensive exports doubled, reaching over 56 per cent in 1994. In the Republic of Korea wage differentials narrowed throughout the 1980s, while in Taiwan Province of China the trend towards widening wage inequality was reversed in the latter half of the decade. In both cases, restructuring and upgrading were facilitated by increased supplies of skilled labour brought about by appropriate manpower policies. In Hong Kong, where wage inequality increased throughout the 1980s, there was little upgrading; the share of labour-intensive and primary exports fell from 60 per cent in 1985 to only 53 per cent in 1994.

It thus appears that the effect of trade liberalization on wages and income distribution differs considerably among countries, depending on the domestic and international conditions under which it is implemented. While resource endowments are certainly important in determining comparative advantage, there are also other factors that influence the degree of competitiveness of various industries. In this respect, it is important to recall the textbook argument invoked to counter the idea that low-wage countries have an unfair competitive advantage in international trade relative to high-wage countries. It is not relative wage costs, but output per head, that determines international competitiveness. Two countries with similar relative endowments of skilled and unskilled labour can have different productivity levels in any given industry, depending on their success in learning and upgrading. That the burden of low productivity often falls on labour is also recognized by the World Bank:

> Increased competition also means that unless countries are able to match the productivity gains of their competitors, the wages of their workers will be eroded. In the coming decade the most vulnerable groups are likely to be:
>
> • unskilled workers in middle-income and rich countries, ..., as they face competition from low-cost producers; and
>
> • some entire countries (especially in sub-Saharan Africa) that lack the dynamism needed to compensate for rising competition and match the efficiency gains achieved by their competitors, or the flexibility to move into other products.[10]

This is also illustrated by the data on international wage differentials in table 31. The table includes some major exporters of labour-intensive goods such as textiles and clothing. There are significant wage differences among these countries in the same industries. The Republic of Korea and Hong Kong have wages 10-15 times those in some other major exporters such as India and Indonesia, but they have been successfully competing in export markets thanks to their high productivity levels and further upgrading of these products, even though Hong Kong has been feeling the strains of greater competition from cheaper producers because of its failure to adapt as fast as the Republic of Korea. These productivity differences are not simply a reflection of relative supplies of educated labour. They are determined by the success of past industrial and trade policies, and cannot readily be altered by changes in the pattern of incentives.

Herein lies the main difference between trade liberalization in the first-tier East Asian NIEs and most other middle-income developing countries. In the former, liberalization followed the successful implementation of industrial and trade policies; protection and support were removed in large part because they were no longer needed. In the latter, on the contrary, liberalization has largely been triggered by the failure to establish efficient, competitive industries in labour-and/or skill-intensive sectors. Accordingly, the impact of increased competition brought about by trade liberalization on income distribution has been crucially different.

C. Integration and distribution between labour and capital

The recent period of globalization has not only witnessed increased earning differentials among workers in developing countries. It has also seen a shift in income distribution from wages to profits in industry.

Chart 10 shows the evolution of the share of wages in manufacturing value added for 26 developing countries since the mid-1970s. In more than half of the countries the share increased between the latter half of the 1970s and the first half of the 1980s or else remained constant. Among countries where it increased were a number of African, Latin American and Asian countries that suffered from the debt crisis. By contrast, there was a widespread fall in the average share of wages between 1980-1985 and 1985-1992, affecting all Latin American countries in the chart except Panama and also all African and Mediterranean countries. Altogether, the wage share rose in only six countries during this period, four of which are in East Asia.

These figures indicate that movements of real wages lagged behind those of labour productivity in countries outside East Asia. However, there are considerable differences among countries in the relative rates of change of the two variables. In

Chart 10

SHARE OF WAGES IN MANUFACTURING VALUE ADDED IN 26 DEVELOPING COUNTRIES

(Index numbers, 1975-1980=100)

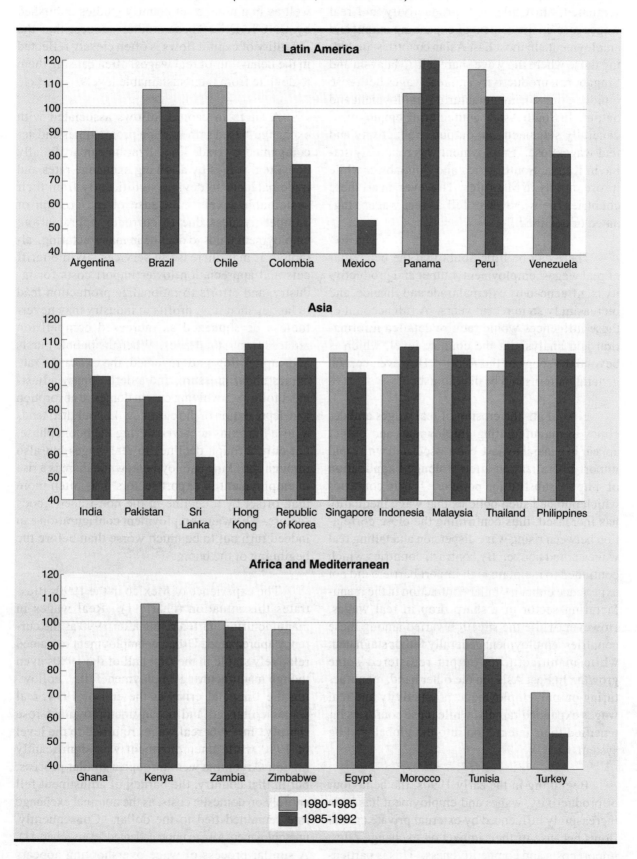

Source: ILO, *World Employment Report, 1996/97* (Geneva: ILO, 1996), table 2.

general, real wages declined in conditions of stagnant or only slow productivity growth. In particular, in all the major Latin American countries shown in the chart (other than Chile) manufacturing output and employment also fell or stagnated. In Chile both productivity and real wages rose, in the context of expanding output and employment. In most East Asian countries, including those where the wage share fell (Malaysia and Singapore), productivity and real wages both rose rapidly alongside manufacturing employment and output. In South Asia manufacturing employment generally stagnated, but output, productivity and real wages rose. Employment was relatively stable in Kenya, South Africa and Zimbabwe, while it rose rapidly in Mauritius. However, in all these countries the wage share fell as real wages stagnated or declined.[11]

There can be little doubt that the behaviour of real wages, employment, output and productivity is influenced by external trade and finance, and increasingly so in recent years. A full account of these influences would require detailed information and analysis at the country level, which is beyond the scope of this *Report*. However, certain general patterns can be distinguished.

First of all, the erosion of real wages and declines in manufacturing employment and output appear in general to have been associated with rapid import liberalization after prolonged application of import-substitution policies. It is in countries which pursued such policies that wage inequality has increased, thus confirming the close correlation between rising wage dispersion and falling real wages noted above. By contrast, countries which continued to maintain high import barriers did not experience either a similar contraction in the manufacturing sector or a sharp drop in real wages. However, while the situation varied among these countries, employment generally fell or stagnated, while manufacturing output registered some growth. In East Asia, on the other hand, manufacturing output, employment, productivity and real wages expanded rapidly, while these countries intensified their integration into the global trading system.

Beginning in the early 1990s, the behaviour of productivity, wages and employment has been increasingly influenced by external private capital flows because of their impact on exchange rates, import costs and competitiveness. This is particularly the case in Latin America, although a number of countries in Asia and Africa have also been recipients of increased capital flows. Differences among countries in their policy approach to capital flows and their macroeconomic effects have been examined in greater detail in past *TDRs* as well as in a number of country studies published by UNCTAD.[12] These studies suggest that the volatility of capital flows is often closely reflected in the behaviour of real wages, often causing them to deviate from their sustainable levels.

A surge in capital inflows associated with exchange-based stabilization programmes and accompanied by trade liberalization can artificially boost real wages by allowing exchange rates and trade balances to deviate significantly from their sustainable levels. Because of the erosion of competitiveness due to currency appreciation, employment tends to decline in manufacturing, although it may increase in services. While tariff cuts and appreciation lower import costs for industry, and efforts to rationalize production lead to labour shedding, profits in industry may nevertheless be squeezed as increased competition reduces firms' total sales. When the bubble bursts and capital flows are reversed, the exchange rate comes under pressure, and a deflationary adjustment follows, involving cuts in domestic absorption and depreciation of the currency. Labour then tends to lose the gains achieved during the boom phase, not only through declines in real wages but also through shrinking employment; while there is a rise in employment in export sectors, it is often more than offset by a decline in the non-traded goods sectors. The wage-employment configuration can indeed turn out to be much worse than before the beginning of the boom.

The experience of Mexico in the 1990s illustrates this situation (chart 11). Real wages in manufacturing started rising after 1990 as the currency appreciated. Urban unemployment remained relatively stable in the first half of the 1980s even though manufacturing employment fell.[13] Following the financial crisis at the end of 1994, real wages collapsed and urban unemployment rose sharply. In 1996, real wages returned to the level of 1990 while unemployment was significantly higher. Argentina went through a similar process, but in that country, the burden of adjustment fell entirely on domestic costs, as the nominal exchange rate remained tied to the dollar. Consequently, unemployment rose to unprecedented levels (chart 11). A similar process of wage-overshooting appears to be under way in Brazil, where manufacturing

Chart 11

ARGENTINA, BRAZIL AND MEXICO: REAL WAGES AND URBAN UNEMPLOYMENT, 1990-1996

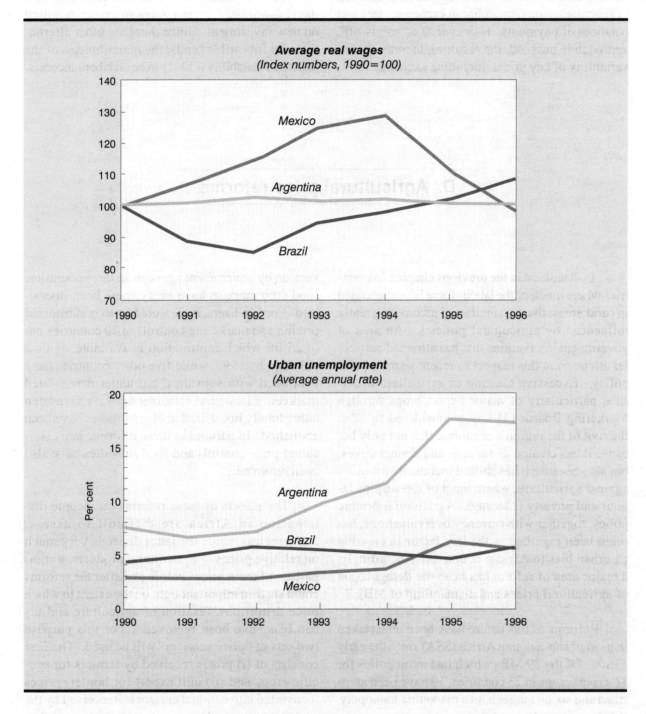

Average real wages
(Index numbers, 1990=100)

Urban unemployment
(Average annual rate)

Source: ECLAC, *Preliminary Overview of the Economy of Latin America and the Caribbean, 1996* (Santiago, Chile: United Nations publication, Sales No. E.96.II.G.13), tables A.4 and A.5.

real wages have been rising constantly alongside the appreciation of the currency and the widening trade deficits since the *Plano Real* was introduced in 1994. Although total urban unemployment has remained stable, manufacturing employment has been falling, and many of the jobs created in the urban non-manufacturing sector appear to be low-quality ones; it has also been suggested that Brazilian firms have responded to loss of competitiveness by "informalizing their labour force".[14] The crucial question is again the sustainability of this process.

As noted above, short-term capital flows may not exert a significant influence on underlying trends in investment, employment, productivity and income distribution as long as they are not allowed to generate serious instability in exchange rates and balances of payments. However, if a "hands-off" approach is pursued, the resulting increase in the variability of key prices, including exchange rates, interest rates and real wages, could adversely affect competitiveness. This in turn could be prejudicial to investment and productivity growth in industry, since the greater volatility would increase risks and raise the risk-adjusted barrier rates of return required on new investment. Since there are other alternatives for investible funds, the major burden of the increased instability is likely to be on labour incomes.

D. Agricultural price reforms

As discussed in the previous chapter, in countries where much of the labour force is concentrated in rural areas, the distribution of income is greatly influenced by agricultural policies. An area of government intervention that has attracted particular attention in this respect in recent years is price policy. Excessive taxation of agriculture in Africa, particularly of major export crops through Marketing Boards (MBs), is considered to be at the root of the region's economic ills, not only because it has created distortions and disincentives, but also because it has shifted income distribution against agriculture, where most of the surplus labour and poverty is located. Agricultural pricing policy, together with currency overvaluations, has often been regarded as the key factor in creating an urban bias in African countries. Accordingly, a major area of reform has been the deregulation of agricultural prices and dismantling of MBs.[15]

Reforms of this nature have been undertaken in most of sub-Saharan Africa (SSA) since the early 1980s. Of the 39 MBs which had monopolies for 11 export crops in 23 countries, 10 have been abolished and six no longer hold a marketing monopoly. While previously prices were set for export crops in 25 countries out of 28 for which information is available, this number has now fallen to 11. Moreover, where MBs continue in existence, their prices are now more closely linked to world prices. In North Africa, with the exception of Egypt, liberalization has generally proceeded more slowly, particularly in crops considered to be of key importance. For food crops in particular, the number of sub-Saharan countries with price controls has fallen from 15 to 2 and, except for limited inter-vention by government agencies in three countries, food crop markets have everywhere been liberalized. For fertilizers, there were formerly subsidized pricing and marketing controls in 20 countries out of 25 for which information is available, against only two by 1992, while five other countries have continued with subsidies, but under deregulated markets. Elsewhere, fertilizer markets have been either totally liberalized or else subsidies have been abolished. In parallel to these reforms, most consumer price controls and food subsidies have also been removed.[16]

The effects of these reforms on income distribution in Africa are difficult to assess. Nevertheless, since the latter depends very much on relative prices of agricultural products, a comparison of these prices before and after the reforms could shed an important light on the extent to which price distortions, taxation of agriculture and urban bias have been removed. For this purpose two sets of "price scissors" will be used. The first consists of (i) prices received by farmers for specific crops and (ii) unit export (or border) prices (converted into national currencies) received by the exporting agent. This set of price scissors makes it possible to assess the evolution of the surplus extracted by the exporting agents (i.e. MBs or private traders). It also helps to assess how the "gains" from devaluations and "losses" due to overvaluations are distributed between exporters and producers.

The second set consists of aggregate index numbers of agricultural prices, on the one hand, and of manufacturing prices, on the other, whereby

Table 40

TERMS OF TRADE OF AGRICULTURE FOR SUB-SAHARAN AFRICA AND THE WORLD, 1973-1995

Agricultural terms of trade of:	1979 (1973=100)	1985 (1979=100)	1995[a] (1985=100)
(1) Sub-Saharan Africa[b]	114.0	102.8	130.6
World			
(2) Food and beverages[c]	86.1	57.8	81.7
(3) Agricultural raw materials[c]	77.0	85.6	93.0
Ratio of sub-Saharan to world terms of trade of agriculture			
(1)/(2) Food and beverages	1.32	1.78	1.60
(1)/(3) Agricultural raw materials	1.48	1.20	1.40

Source: UNCTAD secretariat calculations, based on World Bank, *World Development Indicators, 1997* (CD Rom).
   a Preliminary estimates.
   b Unweighted mean of the ratios of the implicit GDP deflators for agriculture to those for manufactures in 13 countries (Benin, Burkina Faso, Cameroon, Côte d'Ivoire, Ghana, Kenya, Senegal, Zambia; Botswana, Burundi, Gambia, Nigeria and Sierra Leone). The deflator for total GDP was used for the five latter countries, where the share of manufactures in GDP was less than 10 per cent in 1973.
   c Ratio of the index of free market prices for each of the two groups of commodities to that of the export unit value of manufactures.

the terms of trade for the whole agricultural sector, including products sold in domestic markets, can be measured. These two series are derived as the sectoral deflators from GDP data in current and constant prices. Agricultural prices thus obtained represent prices received by producers. Movements in the agricultural terms of trade also reflect changes in the degree of the "squeeze" of farmers through backward market linkages. A comparison of the domestic terms of trade with the relative prices of agricultural and industrial products in world markets over time could help identify the origin of these movements and provide some indication as to the extent to which distortions are removed. [17]

Table 40 compares for 13 SSA countries changes in their terms of trade for agriculture with changes in the world terms of trade for agriculture, distinguishing food and raw materials, for three consecutive periods (1973-1979, 1979-1985 and 1985-1995). In all three periods world terms of trade fell for both groups of agricultural prod-

ucts, while the domestic terms of trade in SSA countries improved. As a comparison of the last two rows of the table indicates, there are no striking differences between the pre-reform and post-reform periods regarding the improvement in the domestic terms of trade in comparison with movements in world prices. From 1973 to 1979 the domestic terms of trade fell in only four countries; from 1979 to 1985 it fell in five; and from 1985 to 1995 in four. Among the 13 countries in the sample, markets for export crops are now deregulated in four (Côte d'Ivoire, Gambia, Nigeria, Sierra Leone). For this subgroup, the agricultural terms of trade fell by 3.7 per cent from 1985 to 1995. By contrast, they rose by 54.8 per cent in five countries which still had centralized price setting, under regulated or partially liberalized markets.

Table 41 compares prices received by farmers with border prices of specific commodities in major exporting countries of Africa. There can be little doubt that in such products MBs have ex-

Table 41

RATIO OF PRODUCER PRICES TO EXPORT UNIT VALUES FOR MAJOR COMMODITIES IN NINE MAJOR EXPORTING AFRICAN COUNTRIES, 1973-1994

Country	Commodity	Average ratio in:		
		1974-1979 (1973=100)	1980-1985 (1979=100)	1986-1994 (1985=100)
Cameroon	Cocoa	66.9	168.7	142.9
Côte d'Ivoire	Cocoa	88.1	136.4	163.6
	Coffee	82.5	115.5	307.1
Egypt	Cotton	93.4	149.0	88.6
Ghana	Cocoa	84.9	277.1	89.4
Kenya	Coffee	101.9	93.9	82.5
	Tea	110.0	105.6	83.7
Malawi	Tea	89.7	84.1	155.9
	Tobacco	91.0	103.8	68.3
Sudan	Cotton	109.8	93.8	169.6
United Republic of Tanzania	Cotton	106.3	148.1	16.2
	Tea	90.2	107.8	46.6
Zimbabwe	Tobacco	93.7	104.3	97.5
Average of nine countries		*93.0*	*129.9*	*116.2*

Source: UNCTAD, *Handbook of International Trade and Development Statistics*, various issues; FAO data base.
Note: The average ratio is obtained by dividing annual index numbers for producer prices by the annual index numbers for export unit values (multiplied by 100). A value above 100 indicates that between the base year and the period in question the rise in producer prices exceeded, on average, the rise in border prices, signifying a lower rate of "surplus extraction" from the producers by the exporting agent (discussed in the text).

tracted large surpluses, particularly during price booms and after devaluations. But again, the evidence shows that extended periods of currency appreciation and depressed world prices have often been associated with declining rates of surplus extraction.[18] Of the countries included in the table, Côte d'Ivoire, Egypt, Malawi and the United Republic of Tanzania are among those that have carried out reforms. Cameroon, Ghana and Kenya, on the other hand, have continued with centralized price setting and/or MBs. In the first group all except Côte d'Ivoire show a widening of price scissors since the mid-1980s, which suggests that there

have been large and even growing profit margins for private traders at the expense of farmers. The results are mixed in countries with regulated markets; they point to a pro-farmer price movement in Cameroon but increased "taxation" by MBs in Ghana and Kenya.

These results strongly suggest that, contrary to original expectations, market-based reforms have not so far had a great impact on farm income in much of Africa. A number of other studies also support this conclusion. For example, a study on Egypt before and after the deregulation of agricultural prices, based on a direct comparison of producer prices with input prices for individual crops, shows that after the price reforms, the price-cost margins declined for cotton, and widened for maize, rice and sugar cane.[19] Comparing producer prices with overall price movements, the World Bank has estimated the average domestic terms of trade for export crops for 27 SSA countries in two different periods, 1981-1983 and 1989-1991. It found that there had been an improvement in 10 countries. For countries where centralized price setting has continued, the terms of trade for export crops rose by 4.8 per cent between these two periods, whereas for countries implementing reforms there was a decline of 18.8 per cent.[20]

As discussed in the previous chapter, the early development experience of Taiwan Province of China, which is generally regarded as a key example of rapid growth with equality, shows that "taxing" agriculture through price policies can actually be compatible with high rates of agricultural growth as well as greater income equality. The recent experience of Africa shows that policies designed to remove such price distortions are insufficient to promote greater incentives and equality. The reasons are likely to vary from country to country. However, a common element underlying this failure appears to be the neglect of

serious market imperfections and shortcomings in undertaking reforms. It seems that many of the markets for export crops are dominated by a few traders. Producer prices have continued to be depressed, particularly in regions with poor infrastructure and low population density and where hungry-season food purchases of farmers lead to the interlocking of credit and product markets. Farmers in remote locations were particularly affected following the abandonment of pan-territorial pricing in a number of countries.

This is yet another example of a "big bang" liberalization without preparing the institutions and infrastructure needed for markets to perform effectively. It is true that state monopolies in agricultural markets have for many years been the single most important factor preventing the development of essential ingredients of private markets. However, most of the reforms appear to have been undertaken as if the ingredients for such markets already existed. Certainly, over time competitive forces may prevail and some of these earlier trends may be reversed. However, the present outcome could have been avoided if a gradual approach had been adopted to reforming agricultural pricing by first establishing the necessary institutional and physical basis rather than unleashing market forces in one fell swoop.

E. Debt, finance and distribution

In many developing countries, particularly the middle-income countries, there has been a rapid expansion in recent years in outstanding domestic debt relative to GDP, accompanied by an associated increase in the share of interest in the national income. Since the early 1980s interest payments on total private and government debt have been rising rapidly, reaching levels as high as 15 per cent of GDP in recent years in a number of countries. This unprecedented expansion of public and private debt and associated interest payments took place concomitantly with financial liberalization, advocated on grounds of both efficiency and equity. Liberalization was justified on the grounds that financial repression, notably the policy of

maintaining nominal interest rates below the rate of inflation, not only led to inefficiency in the allocation of resources and discouraged savings, but also redistributed wealth at the expense of savers. Since large savers are often in a position to hedge against inflation, small savers were thought to be particularly vulnerable.

Deregulation of interest rates was also accompanied by a major shift in the financing of budget deficits from central banks to the private sector. It was also argued that the privileged access of governments to central bank financing increased inequality because of its effects on inflation, and that the introduction of the discipline of private financial markets in the public sector would increase fiscal responsibility and encourage budget balance. Setting monetary growth targets was considered to be the best way to eliminate price instability. In the face of continued government deficits, meeting these targets meant that increasing amounts of debt had to be held on private sector balance sheets.

For a number of reasons, financial liberalization in many middle-income countries gave rise to a massive expansion of public and private debt. First, interest rates were deregulated under conditions of rapid inflation and depressed economic activity resulting from the debt crisis. Consequently, while nominal interest rates rose sharply and real interest rates reached double-digit figures, the financing gaps in the public and private sectors widened due to the effect of recession on revenues, and often a "Ponzi" financing pattern emerged whereby interest payments were financed by incurring new debt at very high interest rates. Second, a number of governments in highly-indebted countries, particularly in Latin America, faced net financial transfers abroad as net new borrowing fell short of interest payments. Consequently, they had to borrow at very high rates at home in order to service their external debt.

The increased public and private debt has witnessed the emergence of a new class of rentiers whose incomes depend as much on capital gains on financial assets as on interest payments. In socio-economic terms, the origin of this class appears to vary from country to country. Since most countries undergoing the development process lack the kind of viable institutional investors which dominate developed country financial markets, the main sources of finance are wealthy individuals whose activities are intermediated through the banking system. Further, large segments of the industrial and commercial classes have been attracted to borrowing and lending, and to buying and selling existing assets, as a source of income, rather than to investing in commercial or industrial ventures or construction as they normally would under conditions of "repressed finance". The attractive terms which have been offered on public debt in order to shift government financing from the central bank to the private sector has meant that low-risk, often tax-free, government bonds constitute an increasing proportion of the total investments of such rentiers. This tendency has gone so far that in some middle-income countries the corporate sector has become a surplus sector, lending directly and indirectly to the public sector.

Although the public domestic debt has risen rapidly since the early 1980s in a number of developing countries, the stock of such debt as a proportion of GDP is still small compared to the proportion in industrialized countries. For instance, in mid-1996 it was around 30 per cent in Brazil and Turkey - two countries which saw a rapid accumulation of domestic debt in the past decade - compared to 60 per cent or more in most industrial countries. However, in developing countries this debt has been accumulated over a very short period. Moreover, real interest rates in these countries are considerably higher than in the industrialized countries, often reaching double digits. Thus, real interest payments on debt tend to be much higher than in industrial countries; in Brazil and Turkey they have reached 5-6 per cent of GDP, compared to 2-3 per cent in most industrial countries.

However, as in the industrialized countries, the accumulation of debt by the public sector in developing countries has been associated with a sharp slowdown in public investment. Much of the new debt has been contracted in order to finance current spending and transfers, including interest payments, rather than investment. Indeed, public investment has often been cut in order to service debt. The combination of increased public debt and reduced public investment suggests that the debt does not correspond to an equivalent build-up of productive capacity, capable of producing additional revenues for its servicing. The burden has had to fall on ordinary tax revenues, implying a redistribution from taxpayers to holders of government debt.

The redistributional effect of government debt depends on who pays the taxes and who holds the debt and, hence, receives interest payments. In industrial countries where the taxation is progressive and government debtholding is widespread, particularly in the portfolios of pension and provident funds, the servicing of government debt through taxation may not distort income distribution. Evidence from the United States suggests that the redistributional impact of government debt may even be positive due to the progressiveness of the tax system and the dispersion of debt ownership.[21] However, this does not seem to be generally the case; for instance, there is evidence to show that the redistributional impact may have been negative in the 19th century in Great Britain.[22] Although it is difficult to estimate the precise redistributional effects of government debt in developing countries because of lack of information regarding the distribution of debt ownership by different income groups and institutions, there are strong reasons to believe that an increased government debt held primarily by the private sector aggravates inequalities in income distribution. First, in most developing countries the taxation system is highly regressive, both because of widespread evasion of taxation on non-wage incomes, and also because of heavy reliance on indirect taxes. Second, the ownership of government debt appears to be highly concentrated. For instance, in Turkey, where government debt is held primarily by banks, bank deposits are heavily concentrated in large accounts: according to one estimate, the Gini coefficient of bank deposits in Turkey in the 1980s was close to 0.7, and 60 per cent of deposits were held by 11 per cent of deposit holders.[23]

As noted above, in some countries new debt is incurred in order to meet interest payments on outstanding debt. While postponing taxation required for debt servicing, recourse to such financing tends to aggravate the problem by increasing the wealth concentration relative to GDP. Since typically real interest rates on public debt are well in excess of real growth rates, the debt/GDP ratio will rise continuously even if a Government incurs no new debt to finance its non-interest expenditures. However, this process cannot continue indefinitely, and eventually the debt will have to be serviced from tax revenues, and the tax burden will rise significantly because the stock of debt will have grown in relation to GDP.

It is generally agreed that inflation is regressive in its effects on income and wealth distribution because the rise in nominal incomes of the poor does not keep up with the rise in prices, particularly as regards the urban poor and the lower middle class. Moreover, inflation constitutes a tax on currency holdings, and such holdings amount to a greater proportion of the incomes of the poor than the rich as financial liberalization proceeds. While a shift from money printing to bond printing may benefit the poor in the former sense, it will not necessarily do so when the redistributive effects of government debt are compared and contrasted with the inflation tax on currency holdings. Such holdings do not generally amount to more than a few percentage points of GDP, and tend to decrease rapidly as inflation accelerates. Consequently, when the tax system is highly regressive and government debt ownership is concentrated, income redistributed from poor taxpayers to rich bondholders may well exceed the inflation tax that the poor

Chart 12

DISTRIBUTION OF VALUE ADDED[a] IN INDUSTRIAL FIRMS IN TURKEY, 1978-1986

(Percentage of total value added)

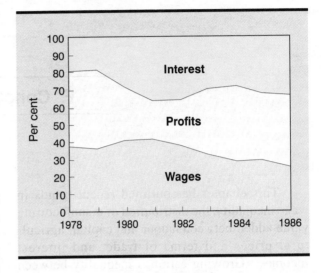

Source: Y. Akyüz, "Financial Liberalization in Developing Countries: Keynes, Kalecki and the Rentier", in G. Helleiner, S. Abrahamian, E. Bacha, R. Lawrence and P. Malan (eds.), *Poverty, Prosperity and the World Economy: Essays in Memory of Sidney Dell* (London: Macmillan Press, 1995).
a Gross value added before taxes.

would have paid under conditions of inflationary financing.

The rise in interest rates has also been a key factor in the increase in interest payments as a proportion of value added in the corporate sector. The immediate effect of financial liberalization in the 1980s was to squeeze profits by pushing up the cost of capital and transferring a greater part of corporate income to rentiers. Thus, the rise in interest rates and the share of interest in national income were initially reflected in a redistribution of property income from profits to rentiers.

However, mark-ups in trade and industry typically respond to sustained increases in interest rates in the same way as they respond to changes in other costs. Since, under financial liberalization, interest rates adjust rapidly to changes in the price level, mark-up pricing implies that the greater interest burden tends to be shifted onto labour. There is indeed evidence from some countries that the redistribution of income in favour of rentiers has been at the expense of labour. For example, in Turkey, the hike in interest rates brought about by financial liberalization in the early 1980s initially resulted in a tight profit squeeze, but the share of profits in value added recovered subsequently at the expense of wages while interest payments continued to absorb about one third of value added, against less than 20 per cent in the late 1970s (chart 12). Since interest rates on corporate debt have generally increased in the past decade, it is likely that some of the income redistributed from wages to profits in manufacturing (see chart 10) accrued to rentiers rather than industrial entrepreneurs.

F. Conclusions

This chapter has outlined recent trends in wage inequality, the distribution of manufacturing value added between labour and capital, agricultural prices and terms of trade, and interest incomes. Growing earnings inequality between unskilled and skilled workers, coupled with a declining wage share in manufacturing value added, can be expected to worsen personal income distribution in semi-industrialized countries, a tendency which could be reinforced by increases in the share of interest incomes. In more agrarian economies, these tendencies could be reinforced if the benefits of agricultural price liberalization accrue to oligopsonistic traders, and if policies to align producer prices in agriculture more closely to world prices are confounded by declines in the latter.

Trade liberalization and financial liberalization have thus strengthened some of the forces making for increasing inequality in income distribution in the short run. But the crucial issue is what will happen in the longer term. According to one view, the recent dislocations caused by trade liberalization in developing countries, including widening earning inequalities, are temporary, being the inevitable consequences of a shift from a "distorted trade regime" to free trade which will eventually be reversed as markets prevail and bring about productivity gains and upgrading. On this view, all that Governments need to do is simply to maintain free trade and facilitate this process by policies designed to increase the supply of skilled labour. Proponents of this view accordingly believe that it is possible to envisage a new kind of Kuznets curve associated with greater integration: at first inequalities increase, but subsequently they decrease.

From the analysis of the preceding chapter, it would appear that though this is a possible outcome, it is an unlikely one. It is possible because, as the first-tier East Asian NIEs have shown, declining inequalities can be achieved if a rapid rate of growth is sustained long enough to absorb surplus labour. But it is not clear that this experience can be replicated under full-scale trade liberalization, particularly if carried out with financial liberalization. As already noted in chapter II, there are fundamental differences between export promotion policies and full-scale import liberalization in their effects on the exploitation of *static* comparative advantage based on existing resource endowments and know-how, as well as on the promotion of infant industries and realization of *dynamic* comparative advantages. Moreover, there can be little doubt that such a process depends crucially on investment, and the role of governments in accelerating capital accumulation was much greater in the East Asian successes than is typically assumed in the conventional approach. In these circumstances, there are serious dangers that growth will not be sufficiently rapid, particularly since, as already noted, population in surplus labour economies is growing relatively fast. It may be very difficult to promote investment and employment and raise productivity while competing with more efficient producers. Consequently, wage inequality may well become a more permanent feature of the middle-income countries, in very much the same way as it has become in a number of major industrial countries in the past two decades.

To avoid this trap it is important to focus policy more on the issue of capital accumulation and on management of the relationship between capital accumulation and distribution. This issue is taken up in the subsequent chapters, examining first the possibility that an unequal distribution of income or a particular pattern of factor shares can lead to slower growth, and then considering the policy implications for sustaining faster growth. ■

Notes

1 O. Altimir, "Income distribution and poverty through crisis and adjustment", *CEPAL Review*, No. 52, April 1994, pp. 8 and 26.

2 See *TDR 1993*, Part Two, chap. III.

3 For discussions of these findings, see E.J. Amadeo, "The knife-edge of exchange-rate-based stabilization: Impact on growth, employment and wages", *UNCTAD Review 1996* (United Nations publication, Sales No. E.97.II.D.2); D. J. Robbins, "HOS Hits Facts : Facts Win Evidence on Trade and Wages in the Developing World", *Development Discussion Paper* No. 557, Harvard Institute for International Development, Cambridge, MA, Oct. 1996; C. A. Pissarides, "Learning by Trading and the Returns to Human Capital in Developing Countries", *The World Bank Economic Review*, Vol. 11, No. 1, January 1997; and A. Wood, "Openness and Wage Inequality in Developing Countries: The Latin American Challenge to East Asian Conventional Wisdom", *ibid.*

4 ECLAC, *The Equity Gap. Latin America, the Caribbean and the Social Summit* (LC/G.1954 (CONF. 86/3)), Santiago, Chile, March 1997, p. 60.

5 Despite the mounting evidence on the impact of trade liberalization on increased earnings inequality in Latin America, a recent IADB study reports a positive effect of trade liberalization on personal income distribution. However, no attempt is made to reconcile these findings with all this other evidence to the contrary; see J. L. Londoño and M. Székely, "Sorpresas Distributivas Después de una Década de Reformas: América Latina en los Noventa" (mimeo), IDB, February 1997.

6 *World Employment Report 1996/97* (Geneva: ILO, 1996), table 5.9 and related text.

7 See *TDR 1996*, table 32.

8 M. I. Cragg and M. Epelbaum, "Why has wage dispersion grown in Mexico? Is it the incidence of reforms or the growing demand for skills?", *Journal of Development Economics*, Vol. 51, 1996.

9 Differences in the ability of different countries to respond to increased competition in labour-intensive products are also reflected by movements in the manufacturing terms of trade. During 1979-1994 the world price of manufactured exports of developing countries fell relative to that of the skill-intensive exports from industrial countries by about 2 per cent per annum. The decline was largest in LDCs, followed by ACP, Latin American and Mediterranean countries, while it was significantly smaller in East Asia; for the Republic of Korea, the manufacturing terms of trade indeed moved favourably during that period. See *TDR 1996*, Part Two, chap. III.

10 *World Development Report 1995. Workers in an Integrating World* (New York: Oxford University Press for The World Bank, 1995), p. 58.

11 On the behaviour of output, employment, real wages and productivity in these countries see ILO, *op. cit.*, figure 5.1.

12 See UNCTAD, *International Monetary and Financial Issues for the 1990s*, Vol. VIII (United Nations publication, Sales No. E.97.II.D.5), New York and Geneva, 1997.

13 On manufacturing unemployment see Amadeo, *op. cit.*

14 G. Gonzaga, "The effects of openness on industrial employment in Brazil", *Texto Para Discussão*, No. 362, PUC-RIO, Rio de Janeiro, November 1996.

15 These views have been elaborated in a series of studies at the World Bank, including the "Berg Report" *Accelerated Development in Sub-Saharan Africa: An Agenda for Action* (Washington D.C.: The World Bank, 1981); and M. Schiff and A. Valdés, *Plundering of Agriculture in Developing Countries* (Washington D.C., The World Bank, 1992).

16 *Adjustment in Africa: Reforms, Results and the Road Ahead* (New York: Oxford University Press for The World Bank, 1993), chap. 3 and table A.9; ECA, *Economic and Social Survey of Africa, 1994-1995* (United Nations publication, Sales No. E.95.II.K.8), Addis Ababa, 1995, pp. 50-52 and 87-88.

17 Ideally this should be complemented by an analysis of movements of sectoral productivity à la Prebisch,

but this is extremely difficult for international comparisons.

18 See V. Jamal, "Surplus extraction and the African agrarian crisis in a historical perspective", in A. Singh and H. Tabatabai (eds.), *Economic Crisis and Third World Agriculture* (Cambridge University Press for the International Labour Organisation, 1993), p.77; IFAD, *The State of World Rural Poverty* (New York: New York University Press, 1992), p.83.

19 J. Baffes and M. Gautam, "Price Responsiveness, Efficiency, and the Impact of Structural Adjustment on Egyptian Crop Producers", *World Development*, Vol. 24, No. 4, 1997. These results are compatible with the movement of relative prices of Egyptian cotton shown in table 41.

20 *Adjustment in Africa* ...., tables A.9 and A.18.

21 See D. F. Vitalino and Y. E. Mazaro, "Public Debt and Size Distribution of Income" in P. Davidson and J. A. Kregel (eds.), *Macroeconomic Problems and Policies of Income Distribution* (Aldershot: Edward Elgar, 1989).

22 B. J. Moore, "The Effects of Monetary Policy on Income Distribution", in Davidson and Kregel , *op. cit.*, p. 28.

23 See Y. Akyüz, "Financial System and Policies in Turkey in the 1980s", in. T. Aricanli and D. Rodrik (eds.), *The Political Economy of Turkey. Debt, Adjustment and Sustainability* (London: Macmillan, 1990).

INCOME DISTRIBUTION, CAPITAL ACCUMULATION AND GROWTH

A. Introduction

As discussed in previous chapters, recent years have witnessed increased polarization both among countries and among various income groups and classes within countries. Rapid and steady growth in developing countries is clearly necessary to close their income gap with the advanced industrial countries and improve standards of living. There may be some scope for raising income through reallocation of existing resources, but restoring rapid growth depends in large part on raising the rate of capital accumulation.

Experience shows that while rapid growth as such may not lead to a significant improvement in income distribution in the short to medium term, it is indispensable for attaining a more balanced pattern of distribution in the longer term. More importantly, as discussed in the preceding chapters, policies can be designed so as to strengthen the forces making for greater equality while promoting growth and absorbing the surplus labour that prevails in many developing countries.

While previous chapters concentrated on the effects of growth on income distribution, this chapter examines the effects of income distribution on capital accumulation and growth. It concentrates on various channels through which personal and functional income distributions influence savings, investment and growth. Chapter VI will then discuss the role of policies and institutions in promoting growth, particularly by influencing the behaviour of classes that absorb a large share of national income, drawing on the experience of a number of developing countries, especially those in East Asia.

The next two sections examine how inequality in income distribution can slow accumulation and growth, concentrating on various channels of influence. First, it is shown that inequality can trigger political and social pressures that may eventually undermine incentives to save and invest. Second, it can reduce the average skill level of the labour force by making it harder for the poor to finance their education and that of their children.

The proposition is then examined that unequal income distribution is essential for rapid accumulation and growth because the rich save and invest a greater proportion of their incomes than the poor. It is shown that, while the rich may indeed save and invest proportionately more than the poor, the same degree of inequality among countries is often associated with different rates of accumulation, or that a given rate of accumulation is compatible with lower or higher inequality. Thus, accelerating growth does not necessarily require a greater concentration of income in the hands of the rich.

The relationship between inequality and accumulation is greatly influenced by the extent to which profits are saved and invested. An examination of sources of capital accumulation shows that corporate profits are often the principal source of investment in industry, while the contribution of voluntary household savings to productive investment is relatively small. However, the extent to which profits are saved and reinvested varies considerably among countries. It is argued that high retention and reinvestment of profits foster accumulation and growth at minimal inequality in terms of personal income distribution. What distinguishes East Asian NIEs from other developing countries is not so much an exceptionally high rate of household savings as a considerably higher propensity of corporations to save and invest from profits.

B. The political economy of distribution and growth

While the evolution of income distribution throughout the process of growth and industrialization has attracted considerable attention, the effect of income distribution on capital accumulation and economic growth has been relatively neglected. A commonly held view is that the rich save proportionately more than the poor, so that greater inequality tends to be associated with higher savings. Consequently, any attempt to redistribute income from the rich to the poor in order to alleviate poverty would be counter-productive over the longer term, since it would slow capital accumulation, income growth and job creation.

The validity and implications of this proposition are examined in greater detail in the subsequent sections. Here, attention is focused on an important aspect of the distribution-growth link which is neglected in this approach; namely, the effect of income distribution on incentives to save and invest. The traditional view assumes that propensities to save of various income groups are independent of how income is distributed among them. However, greater income inequality can reduce incentives to save and invest across the entire spectrum of income groups. Consequently, even if the rich save and invest proportionately more than the poor, a higher degree of inequality may be associated with lower aggregate savings and investment if it has a significant adverse effect on incentives.

Recent work has concentrated mainly on two possible channels through which greater inequality can reduce incentives for accumulation and growth.[1] The first is through the impact of inequality on social and political instability, and of instability on investment. Income inequality and polarization can lead to social discontent, demand for radical changes, political violence and attempts at an unconstitutional seizure of power. In particular, the absence or weakening of a relatively well-off middle class can be a major factor contributing to socio-political instability, which has an adverse effect on investment and growth. The interaction among income distribution, instability and growth may threaten to set off a vicious circle whereby greater inequality leads to increased instability and reduced growth, which in turn can lead to still greater instability. Consequently, successful redistribution policies could promote growth by reducing social and political instability, provided, of course, that they do not introduce other impediments to accumulation and technical progress.

Placing social and political instability at the centre of the analysis of the link between income distribution and investment provides an important insight into how social and economic phenomena interact. However, the link between inequality and political instability is not a mechanical one. History shows that in most societies there is at any moment in time a notion of a socially acceptable distribution of income, and hence of inequality, which is widely regarded as legitimate. It reflects a long history of class bargains and struggles over income distribution specific to each society. In other words, the degree of socially acceptable income inequality varies among societies. Although, this notion of what is acceptable changes over time as the balance of power among different classes shifts, at any particular moment it sets a limit to the extent to which income distribution and inequality can be changed in either direction without causing serious socio-political dislocations. Thus, just as a sharp deterioration in income distribution often leads to serious socio-political instability and even to a social revolution, there are also socio-political limits to policies of progressive income redistribution.

The question of legitimacy also relates to specific types and sources of income. Some sources of income are almost everywhere considered illegitimate (e.g. the profits of heroin dealers). Some are legally tolerated in some countries but not in others (e.g. interest on loans). Some are permitted by law, but may not be acceptable to all (e.g. lottery winnings). There is a whole spectrum of what might be called "legitimacy weightings" attached to different types of income. A rise in the "aggregate legitimacy index" can also cause social and political turmoil, as recently in some Central European countries.

The fundamental problem is, thus, that there are two sorts of income inequality, one unacceptable (illegitimate) and the other acceptable (legitimate), and any existing pattern of income distribution embodies both, in proportions that are hard to analyse statistically. To the extent that the inequality of income distribution reflects legitimate inequalities, it is compatible with socio-political stability.

It follows that instability would be greater where high inequality is accompanied by widespread poverty, because in that case the legitimacy of the measured inequality would be lower. Thus, social unrest and political instability can be expected to be less pronounced in economies where a given income inequality is associated with relatively high average per capita incomes and a relatively low level of poverty. For instance, the United States has as high a Gini coefficient as a number of poor countries, but does not have the political instability of many of the latter. Moreover, people often find higher inequality more tolerable if incomes are rising and poverty is diminishing. Thus, inequality does not necessarily lead to greater socio-political instability, unless it is associated with widespread poverty. By the same token, a relatively equitable income distribution may result in instability if the average level of income is low and poverty is widespread. Finally, the impact of inequality on socio-political instability and growth may vary with the nature of the political system.

These various factors shaping the effect of income distribution on political instability differ considerably from one country to another. There is some evidence of a positive correlation between income inequality and the degree of political instability, and between political instability and investment, suggesting that income inequality is harmful to growth.[2] It appears that socio-political instability exerts a greater influence on growth than the nature of the political regime itself, and that transition from dictatorships to democracy is often, but not always, associated with increased instability and less growth. However, it cannot be deduced simply from this correlation whether it is political instability that leads to slow growth or slow growth that leads to political instability. Moreover, not all studies linking political stability to growth find a significant relationship between the two.[3]

Another link between growth and income inequality is through government intervention. It is often argued that a highly skewed pattern of income distribution can generate significant social and political pressure on governments to pursue redistributive policies. Such policies can introduce serious distortions and lead to a reduction in the after-tax return on capital, thereby impeding accumulation and growth. Such outcomes can be expected to emerge more easily in democratic societies, where the poor may vote in favour of redistributive taxes that reduce incentives to invest. However, governments that are more autocratic may also be subject to similar social and political influences.

It is also argued that government intervention is linked to unequal asset distribution as well. On this view, because of imperfections in capital markets, people cannot borrow against their future earnings to finance long-term investment, and they have thus to rely on their own resources, including assets which provide collateral for loans. Unequal asset distribution can generate political pressures on governments to intervene in capital markets, leading to distortions in the allocation of resources and thereby reducing investment and growth.[4]

Political pressures arising from highly unequal income distribution can indeed lead to populist policies which harm investment and growth through their effects on macroeconomic stability or the return on investment. However, such pressures do not necessarily give rise to harmful intervention. For instance, if they lead to policies of taxing the rich to provide better public education, they may both reduce inequality and promote faster growth. Similarly, they could lead to government transfers that may help reduce criminal activities, thereby alleviating social tensions and instability, and stimulating investment and growth. There is indeed some evidence of a positive relationship between government transfers and growth. It is therefore possible that growth may be low in more unequal societies because they redistribute less, not because they redistribute more.[5]

Indeed, income inequality does not always lead to redistributive policies in favour of the poor. For instance, in most of those developing countries where income distribution is highly unequal taxation is also regressive, suggesting that the link between corrective policy action and income distribution is not automatic. In the same vein, redistributive policies are not always associated with large inequalities; for instance, despite a relatively high degree of equality in income distribution, Japan effectively pursued redistributive policies in the form of conces-

sional lending and technical support in favour of small producers both in industrial and in rural sectors in the postwar era, which also helped accelerate growth.[6]

While various political pressures generated by income inequality may adversely influence investment and growth, the considerations above suggest that the link between inequality and growth is a highly complex one. That is perhaps why empirical studies of the subject covering a number of countries have failed to demonstrate any robust relationship.[7]   In most studies either the two are found to be unrelated, or the relationship loses its significance when other variables are included.[8] Even where an inverse relationship is found, the impact of inequality on growth is rather small.[9] Nor is it possible to generalize about how different political systems influence the relationship between inequality and growth.[10]

C. Distribution, education and skill acquisition

1. Distribution and education

Another influence of income distribution on growth is through its effect on human capital formation. The degree of educational attainment has come to be considered as a crucial determinant of a country's stock of human capital, as well as of an individual's earnings capacity. Income distribution exerts an important influence on school enrolment, since the financial situation of individuals is an important determinant of their capacity to invest in education. Family income has a direct impact on that capacity because people make most of their investments in education when they are young. Families that are better off financially can more easily finance the education of their children to more advanced levels; they also tend to have lower fertility and fewer children to educate. One part of this investment consists of the direct cost of education, such as tuition fees and the cost of textbooks and other teaching material. The other, and more important, part is the opportunity cost in the form of current earnings that the family unit

forgoes. The two-way causality between income levels and investment in education points to the possibility that families on the lower rungs of the income ladder, dependent on subsistence earnings, may be caught in a low-education and low-income trap, since they cannot afford to forgo current income and invest in education.

Similarly, the distribution of wealth has a significant effect on investment in education because bequests allow current income forgone and the cost of education to be covered. The initial distribution of wealth can also have long-term effects, since investment in education allows the wealthy to obtain better-paid jobs and to bequeath more to future generations. Moreover, wealthy individuals may form a club which provides private education with a bias towards advanced education for a few rather than basic education for all. Education also provides them with greater exit options by equipping them with skills that enable them to obtain more remunerative employment abroad. Hence, the manner in which society stratifies largely determines who has access to education, what skills are accumulated and, therefore, the future distribution of income and wealth. Initial inequality in income and wealth distribution can create a low-skill-low-income trap for the poor, while for richer families these variables are constantly on the increase.[11] The combination of low skills and low income also tends to be perpetuated, since differences in socio-economic status between families in which children are raised lead to differences in their achievements as students. Consequently, groups or neighbourhoods in deep poverty have great difficulties in overcoming their initial circumstances because their state of poverty tends to be self-perpetuating.

In linking asset distribution and investment in education, recent work has emphasized the role of assets (noted above) in providing collateral for loans. While there is some evidence that land ownership is a determinant of educational attainment, and that there is a negative correlation between the degree of inequality in initial land distribution and subsequent growth,[12] the precise mechanism linking the two is not clear. On this view, the relationship between land distribution and growth should be especially strong in low-income countries, but this is not always the case. The fact that a number of developing countries with egalitarian land distribution have experienced slow growth (e.g. India, Islamic Republic of Iran, Mali, the Philippines, Senegal and Uganda) suggests that the link between asset distribution and growth depends on a host of other factors, including incentives for individuals to invest in skill acquisition and the provision of public education. More importantly, it does not appear that using land as collateral for educational loans is a common practice in developing countries. Commercial banks are usually unwilling to extend credits to small farmers since farmland is a difficult collateral to handle. It is usually specialized state-owned banks that fulfil this role, but the credits they extend are rarely for purposes other than agricultural activities. It is therefore more likely that land ownership influences investment in education as a source of income rather than as a collateral for credits.[13]

The argument that an individual's or family's capacity to invest in education depends on their own incomes and assets assumes that there is no provision of free education and/or of public credit schemes to cover the costs involved. The provision of government finance for education is required because the value to society of investment in skill acquisition exceeds its value to the individual; it creates positive externalities which are not captured by the individual concerned. As already noted, educational subsidies for the poor are one of best redistributive policies because they not only help attain greater equality, but also promote growth.

2. Employment, investment and skill acquisition

Investment in education depends not only on the ability of the individual to afford the costs involved, but also on the incentive to do so. The incentive is there if the future flow of income can be expected to rise in consequence. That in turn depends on wage differentials between better educated and less educated labour, and on the probability of finding employment that adequately rewards the skills achieved. In order for higher wages for better educated labour to provide an adequate incentive for investment in education, the wage differential should be large enough to compensate for the costs incurred throughout the investment period. There is strong evidence of such a differential in developing countries. Moreover, it seems to widen as educational levels increase; the difference between the wages of workers with secondary and primary education tends to exceed that between workers with primary education and those with no schooling.[14]

The probability of finding employment compatible with increased skills arising from investment in education, and also the extent of wage differentials between better and less educated labour, depend very much on the demand for skilled labour. But in many developing countries, lack of such demand and widespread unemployment among labour with primary or secondary education, or employment of such labour in low-paid jobs not commensurate with their education and skills, is as important an impediment to an individual's or family's investment in education as their ability to afford it.

On the other hand, too fast an expansion of the educated labour force out of line with industrial growth can also be problematic. The high level of education in the early 1960s in the Republic of Korea is often remarked on, but it has also been reported that in 1964, when the per capita income was about $100 and one in every 289 citizens was in college, college graduates were competing for jobs as municipal streetsweepers despite a tradition against manual labour. A major policy goal of the Government in the early 1960s was to reduce college enrollments by a third.[15] Unemployment among secondary school leavers has also been important in Malaysia.[16]

Demand for skilled labour depends very much on the level of technological development reached, and rises at a pace determined by the speed with which the economy moves up the technology ladder. Since the latter depends on the rate of capital accumulation, investment and technological change are the two most important determinants of the demand for skilled labour. Thus, rapid accumulation and technological change stimulate investment in education by creating high-wage jobs and thereby the ability to finance such investment.

Moreover, capital accumulation, technological upgrading and job creation play a key role in raising the quantity and quality of skilled labour by allowing workers to acquire and develop skills through on-the-job training and learning by doing. From the point of view of workers, incentives to enrol in industrial training programmes are similar to those for schooling. At the same time, the training may benefit employers by developing specialized job-related skills and raising productivity. The acquisition of such skills is a benefit to society as a whole; they can be transferred to other firms or industries while their costs are firm-specific. If skilled labour is attracted by higher wages elsewhere in the economy or abroad, the firm will need to match these levels in order to retain it, thereby incurring additional costs. That is why firms may be reluctant to undertake costly training. One way to overcome this problem is through the public provision of training facilities. A direct subsidy to a firm, linked to the labour force and skill formation, often provides a better alternative.

It is sometimes argued that FDI may also be an important means of skill acquisition because the skill content of production associated with it tends to be higher than that of domestic production. However, the extent to which these benefits spill over to the local economy depends on how strong the linkages are between TNCs and domestic producers and on indigenous capabilities to allow such linkages to develop. Indeed, evidence suggests that positive and significant spillovers occur only when the capability and technology gaps between domestic and foreign firms are moderate. In countries where such linkages are lacking, there are significant skill and wage differentials between foreign and domestic enterprises.[17]

Training and learning by doing during an individual's career are important aspects of human capital formation. For jobs requiring moderate levels of skill, they can indeed be much more effective than providing basic education. In most developing countries, skills acquired through apprenticeship in artisan workshops are often considered superior to those resulting from primary and even secondary education. Thus, the fact that individuals from poor families cannot invest much in formal schooling does not always mean that they are totally excluded from skill acquisition. At higher levels of technology, post-school skill acquisition through learning by doing and training is often an integral part of an individual's skill level, and much training in manual and managerial skills is of an on-the-job nature. General training provided by schools improves adaptability and learning capacity and is an essential complement to on-the-job industrial learning; it is especially vital to an agenda of technological upgrading. However, its contribution to industrialization depends crucially on capital accumulation and job creation.

Chart 13 plots educational attainment in a number of countries against the skill intensity of their exports. Educational attainment is measured by the average number of person-years of schooling of the population aged 15 and above, whereas the share of a country's skill- and technology-intensive goods in its total exports is used as a proxy for the skill intensity of the country's production.[18] Any interpretation of the chart needs to take account of the fact that some of the skill- and technology-intensive exports of a number of countries, such as Malaysia, Mexico and Thailand, have very high skill- and technology-intensive import contents, since a high proportion of such exports comes from assembly operations.[19] Moreover, certain non-traded services can be very skill-intensive. If these sectors are excluded, there results an underestimation of the skill-intensity of production in economies such as those of Hong Kong and Singapore, where the provision of services is important.

However, even allowing for these considerations, chart 13 lends support to the hypothesis that educational attainment is a necessary but not a sufficient condition for skill-intensive production. All countries with a high share of skill-intensive exports also have a relatively high educational attainment, while the evidence for countries such as

Chart 13

SKILL AND TECHNOLOGY INTENSITY OF EXPORTS, AND LEVEL OF EDUCATIONAL ATTAINMENT IN SELECTED COUNTRIES IN THE 1990s

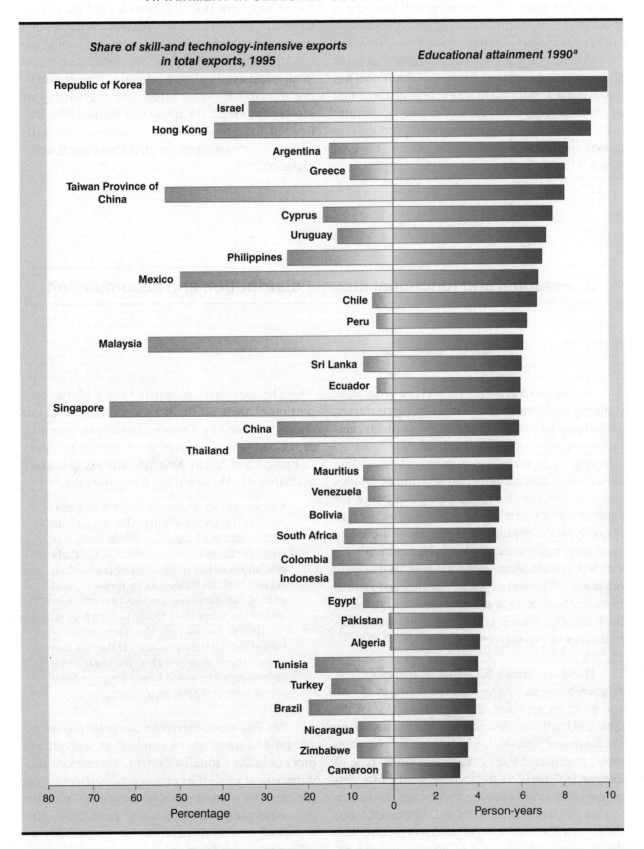

Source: R.J. Barro and J.W. Lee (1996), "International Measures of Schooling Quality", *The American Economic Review*, Vol. 86, No. 2, 1996; United Nations, *Commodity Trade Statistics* tapes.

a Average number of person-years of schooling of the population aged 15 and above.

Argentina, Chile, Peru and Uruguay suggests that relatively high educational attainment does not automatically translate into skill-intensive exports. These countries have educational attainments as high as East Asian NIEs, but their skill intensity is much lower. By contrast, Brazil and Tunisia have lower educational attainment than those NIEs, but their skill intensity is considerably higher. Almost all countries where high educational attainment has translated into skill-intensive exports are those that have sustained a rapid pace of capital accumulation, technological upgrading and productivity growth over many decades, most notably the East Asian NIEs.

These considerations strongly suggest that even when greater equality in income and/or wealth distribution does succeed in stimulating greater investment in education, it will not necessarily also create sufficient skilled jobs to reward the expectations of all who have so invested. Whether that goal can be reached depends on the pace of accumulation and technical progress. Since investment in physical assets plays a crucial role in stimulating demand for education and the supply of job-related skills, the impact of income distribution on the acquisition of education and skills depends very much on its effect on capital accumulation.

D. Personal and functional income distribution and accumulation

As discussed in the previous chapter, notwithstanding significant differences among countries, a relatively large share of national income in capitalist societies accrues to a relatively small minority. It is, therefore, primarily the spending behaviour of this minority that determines savings and accumulation. This is particularly true for developing countries, where incomes of a large majority of the population are barely sufficient to meet their basic needs, and provides the basis for the view in mainstream economic analysis that there is a trade-off between income equality and growth because the rich have a higher savings ratio than the poor. This view is consistent with various formulations of private savings behaviour.[20]

However, unlike the standard analysis of the relation between savings and the incomes of rich and poor, an approach different from that of the classical tradition (described in box 7) focuses on the functional distribution of income - i.e. between rents, profits and wages. Each functional type of income is defined as the income source of a particular class: landowners earn rents, capitalists earn profits and workers earn wages. In this analysis, the propensity to save out of profits is greater than the propensity to save out of wages, so that a redistribution of income in favour of profits would raise aggregate savings at any given level of income.

The idea that capitalists save a higher proportion of their profits than workers save out of wages was used by Keynes to justify the working of the capitalist system of the nineteenth century in Europe and North America, already discussed in chapter II. He described the system thus:

> Europe was so organized socially and economically as to secure the maximum accumulation of capital. While there was some continuous improvement in the daily conditions of life of the mass of population, society was so framed as to throw a great part of the increased income into the control of the class least likely to consume it. ... Herein lay, in fact, the main justification of the capitalist system. If the rich had spent their new wealth on their own enjoyments, the world would long ago have found such a regime intolerable.[21]

On this view, therefore, inequality is an essential feature of the accumulation and growth process in the capitalist system. Investment provides social as well as economic justification for the concentration of an important part of national income as profits in the hands of a small minority. It indeed acts as a social tax on profits that restricts their use for personal consumption of the capitalists, and thus makes for lesser inequality in consumption than income. Thus, unlike the "so-

Box 7

GROWTH AND DISTRIBUTION IN THE CLASSICAL AND KEYNESIAN TRADITIONS

A common feature of the classical and Keynesian theories of economic growth is that both link the accumulation process to the functional distribution of income. According to both Ricardo and Marx, profits not only constitute an incentive for investment, but also are the only source of capital accumulation. Over the long term, wages tend to remain at the subsistence level, although they may fluctuate in the short term. Ricardo explained this in terms of the "Malthus Law", while Marx attributed it to the existence of a "reserve army" of unemployed workers. In both approaches the interaction between accumulation and profits sets off a cumulative downward process whereby accumulation leads to a decline in profits which, in turn, slows accumulation. In Ricardo this happens because diminishing returns in agriculture raise wage costs in industry, increasing agricultural rent at the expense of industrial profits. Marx argued that the increase in capital deepening (rising "organic composition of capital") associated with accumulation reduces the mass of surplus extracted from workers per unit of capital, thereby lowering profits and slowing accumulation.

The class perspective also dominates the Keynesian approach to income distribution and growth. However, unlike the classical political economists, this approach sees a mutually reinforcing interaction between profits and accumulation. This interaction was first formulated by Keynes and Kalecki in the 1930s, in the context of short-term income determination, and subsequently by Kaldor in the 1950s, in the context of accumulation and growth. Assuming that the propensity of capitalists to save out of profits is greater than that of workers to save out of wages, and that prices respond to aggregate demand faster than wages, it was shown that the share of profits in national income was positively related to the investment rate and inversely related to the propensity to save out of profits. If workers do not save at all, profits are determined entirely by the spending of the capitalists; thus, "workers spend what they earn, capitalists earn what they spend". If capitalists invest aggressively, aggregate savings and the aggregate savings ratio will be greater as income is redistributed from low-saving workers to high-saving capitalists. By contrast, in an economy where investment is sluggish and/or workers are parsimonious, the share of profits in income tends to be lower.

If workers save, however, they also earn property income (dividends or interest) as they invest their savings and accumulate wealth. This was the basis of a further refinement of the theory in the 1960s. Under these conditions, the shares of wages and profits (but not the shares of workers and capitalists) in national income are independent of the savings rate of workers.

However, all this depends on the assumption that nominal wages would not respond to a rise in prices brought about by increases in investment and aggregate demand. When they do, the redistribution-growth process hits an inflation barrier, as was emphasized by the Cambridge economist Joan Robinson. If there is a limit to how much the absolute level of wages can fall, then inflation sets in whenever investment exceeds the level compatible with the minimum acceptable wage rate, setting a limit to how much the share of profits and, with it, the aggregate savings rate can rise.

cial instability view" discussed in the previous section, here social cohesion and stability depend not so much on the distribution of income as on the way the rich dispose of their incomes. Inequality can be tolerated if it is associated with accumulation and "continuous improvement in the daily condition of the mass of population".

However, higher propensity to save from profits than from wages does not necessarily imply that aggregate savings and investment rise with inequality in personal income distribution. Although some empirical studies find a positive correlation between income inequality and aggregate savings, these results are not robust to different specifica-

Chart 14A

LOW-INCOME COUNTRIES: INCOME SHARES OF THE RICHEST QUINTILE IN TOTAL PERSONAL INCOME, AND PRIVATE INVESTMENT AS A SHARE OF GDP, 1970-1994

(Percentage)

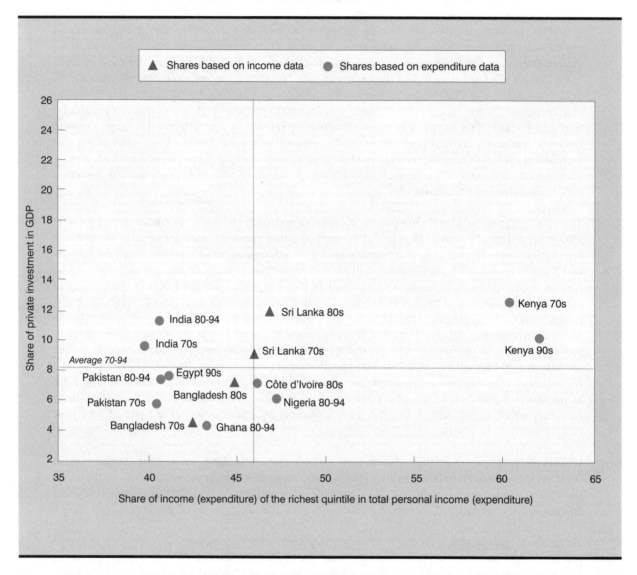

Source: F.Z. Jaspersen, A.H. Aylward and M.A. Sumlinski, *Trends in Private Investment in Developing Countries*, IFC Discussion Paper No. 28 (Washington, D.C.: The World Bank, 1995); dataset compiled by K. Deininger and L. Squire (see note 4 to chapter III).

tions and for different country groups. A recent study using the "high-quality" distribution data (discussed in chapter III) for 52 countries, finds no support for the hypothesis that income inequality affects aggregate savings, either in developing or in industrialized countries.[22]

Charts 14 A and B plot the share of private investment in GDP against the share of the richest quintile in the distribution of personal incomes (expenditures) for a number of low-income and middle-income developing countries, for the 1970s and for 1980-1994, for which data are available.[23] There are considerable differences among countries in the relationship between inequality, as measured by the concentration of income (expenditure) in the richest quintile, and the share of private investment in GDP. On average, both investment

MIDDLE-INCOME COUNTRIES: INCOME SHARES OF THE RICHEST QUINTILE IN TOTAL PERSONAL INCOME, AND PRIVATE INVESTMENT AS A SHARE OF GDP, 1970-1994

(Percentage)

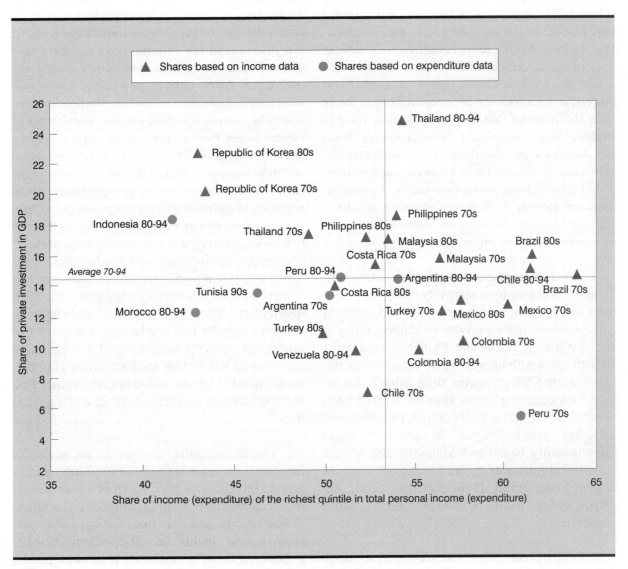

Source: See chart 14A.

and income shares of the richest quintile are low in low-income countries (chart 14A). However, it should also be noted that in almost all low-income countries the distribution data refer to personal expenditures rather than incomes, and hence show less concentration. In this group the share of the richest quintile varies from 40 per cent to 50 per cent of total personal income (expenditure) in almost all the countries included in the chart, while

the private investment ratio ranges from 4.5 per cent of GDP (Ghana in 1980-1994 and Bangladesh in the 1970s) to 12 per cent (India, Sri Lanka and Kenya in the 1970s). In Kenya the share of the top quintile is considerably higher than in other low-income countries, apparently because there is a high degree of concentration of privately owned land; one estimate puts the Gini coefficient for land distribution in that country at 0.72.[24]

Among the medium-income countries, the share of the richest quintile exceeds 50 per cent of total personal income (expenditure) in a large majority of countries, while private investment rates range from around 5 per cent (Peru in the 1970s) to 25 per cent of GDP (Thailand during 1980-1994) (chart 14B). A number of countries with similar investment ratios have widely different concentration ratios. Again, some countries with similar patterns of income distribution have sharply different private investment ratios. In most Latin American countries the investment ratio is lower than the average, but the concentration ratio is higher. Some South-East Asian countries, notably Malaysia and Thailand, have concentration ratios comparable to Latin America, but considerably higher private investment ratios. Indonesia, and even more so the Republic of Korea, also have high private investment ratios, but much lower income concentration ratios.

Private investment/income concentration configurations appear to be relatively stable over time. Two middle-income countries show significant improvements in their private investment ratios in the past decade (Chile and Thailand), associated in both cases with increases in the share of the top quintile. In Chile, however, the decline in the income concentration ratio appears to have been reversed in the 1990s, while the private investment ratio has continued to rise. In some other countries (notably Brazil and Malaysia) the private investment ratio was higher and income concentration lower during 1980-1994 than during the 1970s, but the extent of change was much more moderate.

In interpreting these inter-country variations in the relationship between distribution and investment it is important to bear in mind that there is not a one-to-one correspondence between the distribution of income between wages and profits and among persons. To what extent a high share of profits in value added would be associated with a high degree of inequality in personal income distribution depends on a host of factors. First of all, wages are not always the most important type of labour income in developing countries. In those in the early stages of industrial development, and particularly where agriculture is the principal economic activity, proprietor incomes of small landowners, artisans and shopkeepers, and income from self-employment in the formal and informal sectors, can be more important than wage incomes. They often accrue to the poorest segments of the

population, while wages are earned by people in the middle of the income range. Again, in such economies ground rent, rather than profits, can be the dominant form of property income.

Secondly, the extent to which a high share of profits results in high inequalities in personal incomes depends on the distribution of capital assets. For instance, in the extreme (and unlikely) case where capital is equally distributed among the population, the personal income distribution would be totally independent of the distribution of value added between wages and profits. Ownership of capital assets by workers emerges at a relatively advanced stage in the process of industrialization and development, often in the form of contractual savings in institutions such as pension funds. When workers, in addition to their wage income, obtain income from such assets, the wage-profits distinction no longer coincides with that between workers' and capitalists' incomes, and a redistribution between wages and profits would not necessarily be associated with large changes in personal income distribution. Moreover, both theory and empirical evidence suggest that workers save more out of profits and profit-related incomes than from wages (see chapter VI), so that a redistribution of profits from capital to labour would not necessarily lead to a considerable decline in aggregate private savings.[25]

Finally, personal incomes do not add up to functional incomes because an important part of private incomes (such as the contractual savings mentioned in the preceding paragraph) is retained in institutions, and thus does not appear as personal income. In this connection a distinction has to be made between insurance premiums paid by employees to private pension funds, which are treated as household incomes and savings; and payments into public social security schemes, which are treated as income taxes.[26] Since government pension schemes are traditionally much more common than private schemes in developing countries, much of the institutional savings of households take place before labour incomes are paid out. More importantly, retained corporate profits are not included in personal incomes. If profits are largely retained, a high share of profits in value added is not necessarily associated with high inequality in personal incomes; a greater equality in personal income distribution may simply reflect a higher propensity to retain profits rather than a lower share of profits in value added. Thus, a high share of profits in value added can coexist with a high or a low degree of inequality in personal income distribution, depending on the propensity of corporations to retain profits for investment. For any given profit share in value added, a higher propensity to save and invest by corporations would generate not only a faster growth, but also a more equal personal income distribution.

There can be little doubt that the importance of corporate retentions tends to increase with economic development and industrialization. For this reason, international comparisons of income distribution often lead to an overestimation of the difference in inequality between developing and developed countries, since corporate business and retained profits are less important in the former. However, it should also be noted that in developing countries with per capita income of $300 or more, companies already play an important role, often in the modern sector, and their retained profits can constitute an important share of value added.[27] Consequently, the extent to which profits are retained in corporations can also influence the comparison of personal income inequality among developing countries.

The inter-country variations in the relationship between personal income distribution and capital accumulation also suggest that, unlike Keynes's description of capitalism in 19th century Europe and North America, economic and social life in developing countries is not always so organized "as to secure the maximum accumulation of capital". Indeed, the extent to which the rich save and invest their incomes in productive assets appears to vary considerably among countries and plays a key role in relative economic performance.

Property income, including rents and profits, constitutes the principal source of earnings of the rich. There is no direct evidence on savings and investment by the recipients of such incomes in developing countries. For a small number of such countries data exist on the contribution of retained corporate profits to capital formation, and these will be examined in the following section. A procedure that makes it possible to study a larger number of developing countries, as well as other income than profits received by the rich, is to compare the share of the richest quintile in personal income distribution with aggregate private invest-

ment, drawing on the data presented in charts 14 A and B. In developing countries most of the private investment can be expected to be undertaken, directly or indirectly, by this income group, although it may be financed in part by savings of persons below this income level or by transfers from abroad. The share of private investment in GDP is thus only a proxy measure of the extent to which the rich use their incomes for investment. The richest quintile can also be expected to embrace all major recipients of property income, including profit earners and rentiers.

As noted in chapter III, for some countries the data on personal income distribution is based on shares in consumption rather than in income. In such cases, which include most low-income countries, the ratio of the share of private investment in GDP to the share of the richest quintile (i.e. the accumulation/concentration ratio, or ACR) is an indicator of the extent to which the rich spend their incomes on investment rather than personal consumption. Even when the distribution data refer to personal incomes, the ACR measures the same relationship, since the evidence presented in the subsequent section suggests that property-owning classes save primarily through corporate retentions, and use their personal incomes mainly for consumption.

In charts 15 A and B developing countries are ranked according to their ACRs for the 1970s and for 1980-1994, respectively. The successful East Asian countries are generally at the top of the list, followed by North African, Latin American and sub-Saharan African countries. The ranking of countries is much the same in both periods, with the notable exception of Chile and Peru, which move significantly up the scale in the latter period.

For the reasons noted above, the ACR is only a proxy for measuring how the property-owning classes allocate their incomes between consumption and investment. However, the ranking of countries by the ACR broadly conforms to that by the contribution of corporate profits to capital accumulation and growth, discussed in the next section. It thus confirms that success in growth and industrialization depends very much on how the capitalist class divides its income between the two types of expenditure.

Chart 15A

SELECTED DEVELOPING COUNTRIES: ACCUMULATION/CONCENTRATION RATIO[a], 1970-1979

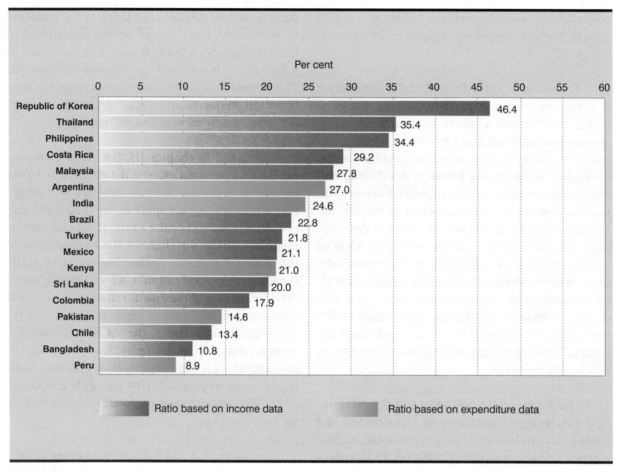

Source: See chart 14A.
   a Share of private investment in GDP expressed as a percentage of the share of the richest quintile in total income or consumption.

E. Profits and accumulation

Both theory and evidence suggest that capital accumulation in industry is financed primarily by savings out of profits, and such savings generally take the form of corporate retentions rather than household savings from dividends. Capitalists save primarily through undistributed corporate profits, while personal dividends are largely devoted to consumption. Shareholders tend to make allowance for undistributed profits in their saving decisions, since such retentions increase the mar-

ket value of corporations and hence the wealth of the shareholders, which, in turn, stimulates personal consumption.[28]   However, the marginal propensity to consume out of retained earnings is smaller than the marginal propensity to consume out of distributed income, so that an increase in corporate saving is not compensated by an equivalent decrease in household savings. Therefore, household and enterprise savings are not perfect substitutes; corporate retentions raise total savings

SELECTED DEVELOPING COUNTRIES: ACCUMULATION/CONCENTRATION RATIO[a], 1980-1994[b]

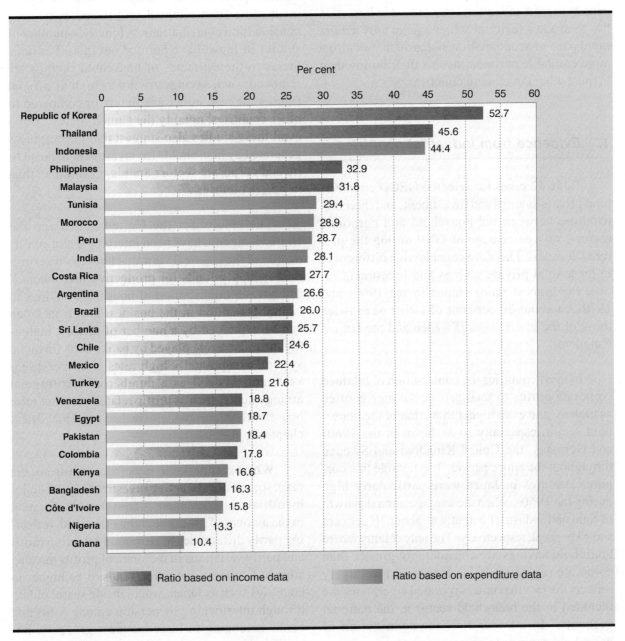

Source: See chart 14A.

a Share of private investment in GDP expressed as a percentage of the share of the richest quintile in total income or consumption.

b The ratios for the Republic of Korea, the Philippines, Malaysia, Costa Rica, Brazil, Sri Lanka, Turkey, Bangladesh and Côte d'Ivoire are for 1980-1989; those for Tunisia, Egypt and Kenya are for 1990-1994.

out of profits and are the main reason for the existence of a higher propensity to save from profits.

The decision of corporations as to what proportion of profits should be retained is not independent of their decisions on investment. Over the long term, a high rate of corporate retention is almost always associated with a high rate of corporate investment. In this sense, a high propensity to retain profits is an indication of a strong accumulation drive and corporate dynamism. This dynamism and the division of profits between savings and consumption vary considerably from one country to another, and play a crucial role in the overall pace of accumulation and industrialization. It is also an important determinant of inequality in personal income distribution. Indeed, greater propensity to save and invest from profits in East Asia has been a key factor in achieving not only a more rapid pace of accumulation and growth, but also a more equitable personal income distribution than in most other developing countries.

1. Evidence from industrial countries

Table 42 gives for selected OECD countries total private savings and investment, and their distribution between the household and corporate sectors, as a percentage of GNP during the past three decades. There are considerable differences in these total private savings and investment ratios; the highest ratios (Japan in the 1960s and 1970s, at about 30 per cent of GNP) were twice those of the lowest ones (Sweden and the United Kingdom).

In most countries the contribution of retained corporate profits to total private savings is often as high as, and even higher than, that of the household sector, especially so in Japan in the 1960s and Germany, the United Kingdom and Sweden throughout the entire period. It is notable that corporate savings in Japan were particularly high during the 1960s, when the average annual growth of total and industrial output was about 10 per cent and 13 per cent, respectively. The only country where household savings are considerably greater than corporate savings is Italy. However, this largely reflects the fact that unincorporated enterprises are included in the household sector in the national accounts. In all countries, the contribution of household savings to corporate capital formation is less than that of retained corporate profits.

It is generally recognized that, for a number of reasons, national income data tend to overstate the contribution of households to productive investment, and that, if appropriately measured, "pure" household savings would be much smaller.[29] A study on the United States for the period 1947-1991 found that household gross savings did not significantly exceed household gross capital formation. In cumulative terms the latter was equal to 99.8 per cent of household gross savings, while gross savings by enterprises exceeded their gross

capital formation in all but 11 of those 45 years.[30] Similarly, a study on the United Kingdom for 1952-1984 found that, when properly measured, voluntary household savings were just sufficient to meet household investment. Enterprise investment came from retained profits and mandatory pension fund contributions.[31] Finally, a number of studies in Japan have pointed out that, if various biases in the estimates of household savings are removed, such savings are not as high as official figures suggest, either absolutely or compared to other countries, notably the United States. However, these studies also suggest that the surpluses generated by households for investment in the public and corporate sectors are bigger in Japan than in other countries.[32]

The results for the United States and the United Kingdom have been interpreted as a confirmation of the classical view that household savings do not supply funds for productive investment.[33] The greater contribution of household savings to capital formation in the business sector in Japan can be explained by a number of factors, including the greater role played by banks in its financial system, exceptionally high rates of corporate investment, as well as a number of institutional arrangements, such as profit-related pay, that raise household savings, which are discussed in the next chapter.[34]

While corporate savings from profits are the main source of productive investment in the major industrial countries, there is considerable variation in the amount of investment thus financed, reflecting partly differences in corporate retention ratios and partly variations in the share of profits in value added. Corporate retention tends to be higher in countries such as Japan, where inside shareholding through interlocking ownership among firms and banks belonging to large business groups is important, than in the Anglo-American system, where widespread individual shareholding and active secondary markets result in considerable pressures on corporate managers to distribute dividends; according to one estimate, individuals in Japan owned only 20 per cent of total shares in 1987, as opposed to 65 per cent in the United States.[35] However, since depreciation allowances account for a large proportion of gross corporate profits, inter-country differences in corporate gross savings rates are relatively small.

The share of gross profits in gross value added varies considerably (table 43). However, there is

Table 42

PRIVATE SAVING AND INVESTMENT AS A PERCENTAGE OF GNP IN SELECTED OECD COUNTRIES

Country/sector	1960-1970		1971-1980		1981-1990	
	Saving	*Investment*	*Saving*	*Investment*	*Saving*	*Investment*
United States						
Total	17.7	16.1	19.1	17.3	19.4	16.9
Households	9.2	7.1	10.7	7.5	10.3	7.0
Corporate	8.5	9.0	8.4	9.8	9.1	9.9
Japan						
Total	28.3	30.7	30.4	28.2	26.2	23.6
Households	13.3	8.0	17.9	10.3	14.9	7.5
Corporate	15.0	22.7	12.6	17.9	11.3	16.1
Germany						
Total	21.1	22.7	20.4	19.5	20.8	17.6
Households	6.9	..	8.7	..	7.9	..
Corporate	14.2	..	11.8	..	12.9	..
France						
Total	..	..	22.2	21.8	18.8	17.3
Households	..	..	13.6	10.0	9.8	7.4
Corporate	..	..	8.6	11.8	9.0	9.9
United Kingdom						
Total	14.8	14.7	15.3	15.7	15.5	15.7
Households	5.4	3.0	6.1	3.9	5.9	4.9
Corporate	9.4	11.7	9.2	11.8	9.6	10.8
Italy						
Total	26.0	16.8	31.2	16.6	28.1	17.7
Households	..	..	24.5	7.2	21.7	9.9
Corporate	..	..	6.6	9.4	6.4	7.8
Sweden						
Total	..	..	14.3	17.0	15.0	16.6
Households	..	..	4.9	4.5	3.0	3.3
Corporate	..	..	9.4	12.5	12.0	13.3

Source: OECD, *National Accounts*, various issues.

considerable variation among countries in the relationship between the share of gross profits and that of corporate savings as a proportion of GDP, partly because of differences in various charges on gross operating surplus, such as corporate taxes and interest payments, and partly because of differences in the propensity of corporations to retain profits.[36]

Table 43

PROFIT SHARES IN SELECTED OECD COUNTRIES[a]

(Percentage)

Country	1960	1973	1980	1990
United States	30.9	28.8	32.1	37.2
Japan	50.1	46.7	42.0	43.4
Germany	40.8	32.7	29.0	31.9
France	..	35.1	30.4	38.8
United Kingdom	31.7	31.8	31.3	36.2
Italy	..	34.1	45.3	47.7
Sweden	..	32.5	29.0	31.1

Source: OECD, *Historical Statistics*, various issues.
a Gross operating surplus (as defined in note 36 to the text) as a percentage of gross value added in industry, transport and communication.

2. Corporate savings in developing countries

The orthodox analysis of industrialization and growth in developing countries typically concentrates on household savings and explains savings performance in terms of macroeconomic fundamentals. Such explanations are also given for East Asian economies, such as those of the Republic of Korea and Taiwan Province of China, where domestic savings rose at unprecedented rates, from less than 10 per cent of GDP in the 1950s to more than one third in the 1990s.[37] According to this view, macroeconomic stability, together with the exceptional efficiency of those economies in using their physical and human resources, gave rise to rapid accumulation and growth which, in turn, resulted in a rapid increase in the savings rate.[38]

Clearly, economic growth exerts a positive influence on savings, but it is less clear how savings and macroeconomic stability are related. The causality may indeed run in the reverse direction; often a high rate of saving is needed to maintain a high rate of accumulation without running into inflation and balance of payments difficulties. On the other hand, evidence on the relationship between growth and stability shows that "low inflation and small deficits are not necessary for high growth, over even quite long periods".[39] More important, while rapid income growth is essential for savings to rise, since it also allows consumption to rise, income growth is not translated automatically into higher savings growth. For instance, the average savings rate in some of the middle-income countries of Latin America failed to show a significant increase from the 1960s to the 1980s despite a relatively rapid growth of per capita income. During 1968-1977 in Brazil, for example, GDP grew at an average rate of 7.5 per cent per annum, but the gross domestic savings ratio was constant at around 20 per cent of GDP and the ratio of private savings at around 16 per cent.[40]

This emphasis on household savings is one of the main reasons why the high savings rates in East Asia have not been properly understood. UNCTAD research on East Asia has taken a different route and concentrated on the link between profits and savings. It has revealed that the success of East Asian industrialization has depended very much on the role of government intervention in accelerating capital accumulation and growth, and that government policy achieved this objective by animating the investment-profits nexus that is constituted by the dynamic interactions between profits and investment: profits are simultaneously an incentive for investment, a source of investment and an outcome of investment. This thesis was based on three basic propositions. Firstly, high rates of investment played a major role in the exceptionally rapid growth of successful East Asian economies and this investment was, after an initial period, supported by high rates of domestic saving. Secondly, profits increasingly became the main source of savings and capital accumulation. Thirdly, government policy accelerated the process of capital accumulation by creating rents and pushing profits beyond what could be attained under free-market policies. Some evidence was provided in *TDR 1994* and *TDR 1996* in support of these propositions.[41] This section introduces additional evidence from the region and compares it with other developing countries for which data are available, and relates profits and savings to income distribution.

Data on sectoral savings and investment are not readily available for developing countries, and hence it is not easy to account for the respective roles of corporate and household savings in inter-country differences in capital accumulation. Table

Table 44

SECTORAL SAVINGS AND INVESTMENT IN SELECTED COUNTRIES
(Percentage of GDP)

Country	Period	Households		Business		Memo item: Profit shares in manufacturing[a]
		Savings	Investment	Savings	Investment	
China	*(1982-1986)*	12.5	5.5	14.1	22.1	..
Republic of Korea	*(1980-1984)*	10.3	5.3	8.3	20.0	74.1
Malaysia	*(1980-1986)[b]*	19.7	2.9	9.1	16.3	70.3
Taiwan Province of China	*(1980-1984)*	13.7	..	12.0	..	..
Thailand	*(1981-1983)*	10.4	3.6	8.7	13.2	75.8
Japan	*(1960-1970)*	13.3	8.0	15.0	22.7	..
Philippines	*(1983-1985)*	10.0	1.0	3.3	10.2	80.3
India	*(1978-1982)*	16.6	10.0	1.9	3.1	52.7
Colombia	*(1980-1984)*	8.6	5.1	5.4	10.4	80.3
Ecuador	*(1980-1984)*	9.6	5.0	3.6	11.1	63.5
Paraguay	*(1980-1984)*	5.9	..	1.8	..	..
Peru	*(1980-1984)*	16.7	..	4.2	..	81.0
Uruguay	*(1980-1984)*	9.2	..	3.3	..	73.7
Venezuela	*(1980-1984)*	3.8	..	3.2	..	75.0
Cameroon	*(1980-1984)*	4.4	0.4	9.2	18.7	63.0
Côte d'Ivoire	*(1974-1978)*	4.1	3.0	3.3	12.3	73.0
Tunisia	*(1980-1984)*	6.7	4.3	5.9	20.4	53.0
Turkey	*(1977-1981)*	12.1	4.5	3.9	16.1	74.5

Source: UNCTAD secretariat estimates, based on national and international sources; World Bank, *World Development Report*, various issues.

a Manufacturing value added less total gross earnings of employees.

b Average of the three years 1980, 1985 and 1986.

44 assembles data from various sources on corporate and household savings and investment in a number of developing countries for the late 1970s and early 1980s, as well as corresponding data for Japan for the 1960s. These figures are not based on a common methodology and their margin of error is likely to be large, since the difficulties noted above in obtaining accurate estimates of household and corporate savings are even more serious for developing countries. Moreover, they do not all refer to the same period, or reflect long-term tendencies.

Even allowing for these problems, however, table 44 strongly suggests that the exceptional savings-investment performance of East Asian economies has been due not so much to household as to corporate savings. Compared to most other developing countries, the East Asian NIEs have significantly higher business savings, while their

Box 8

COMPULSORY SAVING SCHEMES IN SINGAPORE AND MALAYSIA

Singapore is the only country among the first-tier NIEs where household savings account for a large proportion of gross domestic investment. A large part of these savings is accumulated in the Central Provident Fund (CPF) established in 1955 as a compulsory social security programme. The contribution rates were initially set at 5 per cent of the employee's remuneration and a matching contribution of another 5 per cent by the employer. These rates were gradually raised to 25 per cent by the mid-1980s. They were subsequently lowered, but the total contributions by employers and employees never fell substantially below 40 per cent. Use of these funds by the employees is allowed primarily to purchase housing built by a public Housing Development Board or, to a lesser extent, to finance education, but otherwise the participants have a limited ability to withdraw their balances, even upon retirement. A very large proportion (about 95 per cent) of the Fund is invested in government securities. The contribution of gross CPF savings to gross national savings rose from around 10 per cent in the second half of the 1960s to over 20 per cent in the second half of the 1970s. At its peak in 1985, CPF contributions amounted to 36 per cent of gross national savings or almost 15 per cent of GNP. This state-managed fund is run extremely efficiently: in 1990, its administrative costs amounted to 0.5 per cent of total contributions, against 15 per cent in the privately-run Chilean scheme. Moreover, it is distributionally progressive: workers earning less than a specified minimum wage are exempt from contributions while deriving benefits.

In Malaysia, an important part of household savings appears to consist of forced or contractual savings, accumulated in the Employees Provident Fund, established in 1951. Total contributions to the Fund amount to 20 per cent of the wage bill, of which 11 per cent is paid by employers and 9 per cent by employees. These funds are directed primarily towards financing long-term development projects initiated by the public sector, although recently they have been increasingly invested in private sector assets. As in Singapore, withdrawals are allowed for housing purposes. The reserves of the Fund stood at over 45 per cent of GDP in 1994.

household savings are not exceptionally high, except in Malaysia and Singapore, where they are due mainly to compulsory saving schemes (see box 8). On average, business savings as a proportion of GDP are almost three times higher than in other developing countries, whereas the difference in household savings is much smaller. To put it differently, on average the business sector in East Asia appears to save 7 percentage points of GNP more than the business sector in other developing countries for which data are available, and the East Asian investment ratio is also higher by a similar margin.

The contrast between the East Asian NIEs and Latin American economies for which the data are available is particularly striking. For the Latin American countries, the average corporate savings ratio as a proportion of GDP is almost a quarter that of East Asian NIEs. Since the share of profits in Latin America is no less than in East Asia

(see also chart 16), this suggests that the low rate of accumulation in Latin America is not the result of insufficient capacity to generate investible resources, but of the high propensity to consume of property-owning classes. Moreover, this feature is not of recent origin; it was already noted as far back as the 1950s in respect of Chile:

> The percentage of net undistributed profits in total net profits was remarkably low in Chile throughout the period [1940-1954]; companies tended to distribute much the greater part of their increase in earnings. ... The extremely low estimates of national savings, despite the high ratio of both profits and dividends to the national income, are thus to be explained by the high propensity to consume of the capitalist classes.[42]

It was estimated that the capitalist class in Chile spent on personal consumption more than two

Chart 16

SHARE OF PROFITS IN MANUFACTURING VALUE ADDED, AND SHARE OF THE TOP QUINTILE IN TOTAL PERSONAL INCOME, 1970-1992: A COMPARISON FOR SELECTED DEVELOPING COUNTRIES

(Percentage)

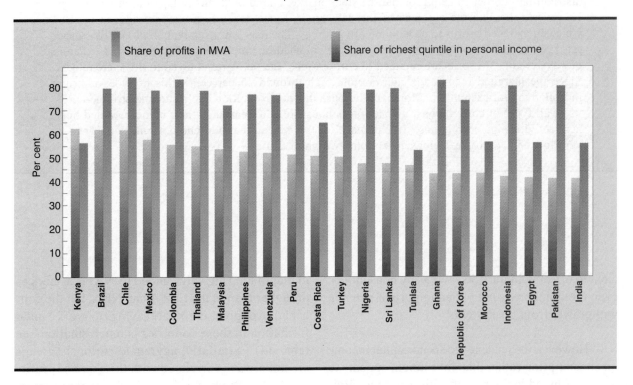

Source: World Bank, *World Development Report*, various issues; K. Deininger and L.Squire, *op. cit.* (see chart 14A).

thirds of their gross income, or three quarters of their net income - i.e. after tax, absorbing more than 20 per cent of national resources, as opposed to less than 8 per cent in the United Kingdom:

> In comparison to other countries, the luxury consumption of the property-owning classes appears to take up an altogether disproportionate share of national resources, part of which would be automatically released for investment purposes if a more efficient system of progressive taxation were introduced and/or if effective measures were taken to encourage retention of profits by enterprises.[43]

From the mid-1970s to the mid-1980s private savings in Chile never reached even 10 per cent of GDP. In the past decade, however, they have risen sharply, exceeding 20 per cent in the first half of the 1990s. This increase in private savings was a major factor in the recovery of the national sav-

ings rate, which has averaged some 26 per cent since 1990 - a very high rate in Latin America even though modest by East Asian standards. While reliable data on the respective contribution of the household and corporate sectors are not available, it is generally agreed that much of this rise in private savings has been due to corporate retentions. Some estimates indeed put corporate savings as high as 20 per cent of GDP- a level exceptional even by East Asian standards. Whatever its actual value, there can be little doubt that corporate savings are now the main source of capital accumulation in Chile. Adoption of the kind of policies advocated by Kaldor three decades ago, together with a strong investment drive in the traded goods sectors, appears to have played a major role in this respect (box 9). By contrast, the contribution of private pension funds to the rise in Chilean national savings is relatively small (around 3.2 per cent in the first half of the 1990s, compared to 2 per cent in the 1980s) and, on some estimates, not suffi-

Box 9

TAX REFORM AND CORPORATE SAVINGS IN CHILE

Taxation of corporate profits in Chile during the 1970s was designed to encourage dividend distribution in order to help promote the stock market and allow firms to tap household savings. However, following the outbreak of the debt crisis, a new tax reform was introduced in 1984 which encouraged profits to be kept in corporations. The new law effectively replaced the corporate tax with an income tax. A 15 per cent tax is levied on corporate profits, but is in the nature of a tax credit. If profits are retained in corporations, the tax is reimbursed to the shareholders. Since the marginal income tax rate is quite high (around 45 per cent), this provides a strong incentive to profit retention. Moreover, because this tax exemption applies to undistributed profits of all types of corporations, it encourages households to rearrange their unincorporated business activities in corporations. It is perhaps for this reason that household savings appear to be very low and corporate savings exceptionally high in Chile.

cient to offset voluntary dissavings by households, even though there is not yet an important pension withdrawal from the system.[44]

However, the tendency to spend capital income on consumption rather than investment appears to have continued in the rest of Latin America. Evidence available for a number of Latin American countries (Colombia, Ecuador, Paraguay, Peru, Uruguay and Venezuela) suggests that in the early 1990s the recipients of property and entrepreneurial income consumed, on average, more than 85 per cent of their incomes, and such spending absorbed up to 40 per cent of national income.[45] Despite many reforms and the end of the debt crisis, for the region as a whole the ratio of gross private investment to GDP during the 1990s has been even lower than during the difficult period of the 1980s.

3. Profits, savings and distribution

To what extent do variations among developing countries in the importance of corporate savings reflect variations in the share of profits in value added? Cross-country evidence shows that the correlation between the two is weaker in developing countries than in mature industrial economies, suggesting significant variations in corporate retention ratios among the former. In countries such as Colombia, Peru, Philippines, Tunisia, Turkey, Uruguay and Venezuela, the share of gross profits

in manufacturing value added (MVA) is as high as or higher than in the East Asian NIEs, but the contribution of gross corporate savings to gross capital formation in these countries is much smaller (see table 44). Similarly, aggregate national savings are not always correlated with the share of profits in MVA. There can be little doubt that factors other than the propensity to save from profits play an important role in differences in the extent to which corporate profits are retained for investment, including variations in the burden of interest charges on corporate debt, the level of corporate taxation and depreciation allowances. As discussed in the next chapter, most of these factors are influenced directly by government policy.

The previous section has shown that a high share of profits in value added may be associated with greater or smaller inequality in income distribution, depending on the extent to which profits are retained in corporations. Chart 16 compares the share of profits in MVA with the share of the richest 20 per cent in personal income distribution in 1980-1992 for countries for which data are available. The relationship between income equality and profit shares is indeed rather weak. A number of countries with similar profit shares have widely different income concentration ratios. In Kenya, Costa Rica, Tunisia, Morocco and Egypt profit shares are all lower than the average for the countries in the table, but the income concentration ratios vary considerably, from 62 per cent in Kenya to about 40 per cent in India.

More important, some East Asian NIEs, such as the Republic of Korea and Indonesia, have profit shares as high as Latin American countries, but they have considerably lower income concentration ratios. These differences can be explained, at least partly, in terms of corporate retentions, since, as noted above, retained profits are not included in personal incomes. A similar functional distribution of income between wages and profits results in a more equal distribution of personal incomes in East Asia than in Latin America, to a large extent because a much greater proportion of profits is retained and reinvested in corporations in the former than in the latter. To put it differently, a more equal personal income distribution in East Asia is a reflection of higher corporate savings rather than lower profits.

The difference between East Asian NIEs and other developing countries in the degree of equality of income distribution and the concentration of income at the top narrows down significantly if undistributed profits are added to household incomes. It is common practice to impute these to the top quintile in studies seeking to derive internationally comparable income distribution measures.[46] The same procedure can also be applied to East Asian NIEs since, unlike for land, there is no evidence that corporate ownership of capital assets is particularly evenly distributed in these countries. For instance, contrary to conventional wisdom, wealth is highly concentrated in Japan. It was estimated that during the early 1970s the top income decile held almost one half of total private wealth and that in 1988, the richest quintile had stock holdings that were nearly 14 times greater than that of the poorest.[47] Again, as noted in chapter III, the Gini coefficient for the distribution of financial assets in the Republic of Korea in 1988 was as high as 0.77. Comparable estimates are not available for other countries, but it is notable that this ratio is higher than the Gini coefficient of the distribution of bank deposits in Turkey noted above (0.70), where such deposits account for a large proportion of household financial assets.

If it is assumed that the sum total of personal incomes falls short of GDP only by the amount of retained corporate profits, a measure of the adjusted share of the richest quintile can be estimated for a number of countries for the early 1980s by adding such profits to the personal incomes of that quintile. Clearly, for all countries this measure is higher than the share of the top quintile in personal income, but more so for East Asian NIEs because of higher retained corporate profits. The inclusion of retained profits narrows the difference between the latter countries and other developing countries. For example, the richest quintile income shares in the first half of the 1980s would rise from 42.7 per cent to 48.1 per cent in the Republic of Korea and from 42.0 per cent to 48.6 per cent in Indonesia. They would rise from 57.4 per cent to 59.7 per cent in Colombia; from 47.2 per cent to 48.9 per cent in Venezuela; from 47.4 per cent to 49.1 per cent in Côte d'Ivoire; and from 53.2 per cent to 55.0 per cent in Turkey.

When the share of profits in value added is high, even if profits are retained and invested, wealth concentration will increase over time with the accumulation of capital unless the initial distribution of corporate ownership is relatively equal. In other words, the relatively benevolent effect on present income distribution is obtained by a worsening of the distribution of wealth, which will certainly influence income distribution in the future. The question then arises how to avoid such an outcome without slowing down accumulation and growth. A redistribution from profits to wages over time as incomes rise can prevent a worsening of income distribution without slowing accumulation, provided that household savings gradually replace corporate savings. That is what appears to have happened in Japan in the past three decades: corporate savings as a proportion of GDP fell alongside the share of profits (in gross value added) and the increase in household savings largely made up for the decline (tables 42 and 43). As discussed in the next chapter, certain factors appear to have played an important role in this process. Reliance on excessive profits (rent creation) needed to build up infant industries gradually declined as industrialization progressed. The fall in the share of profits in value added coincided with the development of the bonus system, which promoted household savings. ∎

Notes

1   For a discussion of these channels see T. Persson and G. Tabellini, "Growth, distribution and politics", *European Economic Review*, No. 36, 1992; A. Alesina and D. Rodrik, "Distributive Politics and Economic Growth", *The Quarterly Journal of Economics*, Vol. CIX, No. 2, May 1994; A. Alesina and R. Perotti, "The Political Economy of Growth: A Critical Survey of the Recent Literature", *The World Bank Economic Review*, Vol. 8, No. 3, 1994; T. Persson and G. Tabellini, "Is Inequality Harmful for Growth?", *The American Economic Review*, Vol. 84, No. 3, June 1994; A. Alesina and R. Perotti, "Income distribution, political instability, and investment", *European Economic Review*, Vol. 40, 1996.

2   The evidence is based on cross-country regressions, where instability is measured in terms of an index combining the number of politically motivated assassinations, the number of people killed as a result of domestic mass violence, the number of *coups d'état*, and a variable indicating whether the country is a democracy (free competitive elections) with universal franchise, a semi-democracy (some form of elections, with severe restrictions on political rights), or a dictatorship. For details see Alesina and Perotti, "Income distribution, political instability, and investment", *op. cit.*

3   For one such study that failed to find such a relationship see Douglas Hibbs, *Mass Political Violence: A Cross-Sectional Analysis* (New York: Wiley and Sons, 1973).

4   See O. Galor and J. Zeira, "Income Distribution and Macroeconomics", *Review of Economic Studies*, Vol. 60, 1993; M. Bruno, M. Ravallion and L. Squire, "Equity and Growth in Developing Countries", *Policy Research Working Paper* No. 1563, World Bank, Jan. 1996; and K. Deininger and L. Squire, "New Ways of Looking at Old Issues: Inequality and Growth" (mimeo), World Bank, Washington, D.C., July 1996.

5   See, for example, G. Saint Paul and T. Verdier, "Education, democracy and growth", *Journal of Development Economics*, Vol. 42, 1993; G. Saint Paul and T. Verdier, "Inequality, redistribution and growth: A challenge to the conventional political economy approach", *European Economic Review*, Vol. 40, 1996; and X. Sala-i-Martin, "Transfers", *Working Paper* No. 4186, National Bureau of Economic Research, Cambridge, MA, 1992.

6   See K. Goto, K. Hayashi, and K. Tsuji, "The 'East Asian Miracle' as Intellectual Public Property", in

UNCTAD, *Proceedings of the International Conference on East Asian Development: Lessons for a New Global Environment, Kuala-Lumpur, Malaysia, 29 February - 1 March 1996* (a forthcoming United Nations publication).

7   The procedure is typically to examine whether initial inequality exerts a negative influence on subsequent growth, often over two or three decades. The data used generally include both developing and developed countries. As noted in chapter II, such growth regressions suffer from a number of serious methodological shortcomings.

8   See J.D. Sachs and A.M. Warner, "Natural Resource Abundance and Economic Growth", *Working Paper* No. 5398, National Bureau of Economic Research, Cambridge, MA, Dec. 1995; A. Fishlow, "Inequality, Poverty and Growth: Where Do We Stand?", in M. Bruno and B. Pleskovic (eds.), *Annual World Bank Conference on Development Economics* (Washington D.C.: The World Bank, 1995); and Deininger and Squire, *op. cit.*

9   For instance, according to one study, if in 1960 the Republic of Korea had had Brazil's level of inequality, Korean per capita income in 1985 would have been lower by 15 per cent, representing a loss of about two years' growth (N. Birdsall, D. Ross, and R. Sabot, "Inequality and Growth Reconsidered: Lessons from East Asia", *The World Bank Economic Review*, Vol. 9, No. 3, 1995, p. 496. It is, however, noted that there is also an indirect effect of inequality on growth through lower investment in education). See also G.R.G. Clarke, "More evidence on income distribution and growth", *Journal of Development Economics*, Vol. 47, No. 2, 1995.

10 In some studies (e.g. Persson and Tabellini, *op. cit.*), income inequality is found to be bad for growth only in democracies, while in others (e.g. Alesina and Rodrik, *op. cit.*, and Clarke, *op. cit*), no difference could be detected between democracies and other regimes. Yet, according to another study, the link between initial income inequality and subsequent growth is much weaker in democracies (Deininger and Squire, *op. cit.*).

11 See R. Bénabou, "Human capital, inequality, and growth: a local perspective", *European Economic Review*, Vol. 38, 1994.

12 Deininger and Squire, *op. cit.* See also Bruno, Ravallion and Squire, *op. cit.*

13 However, in the studies mentioned above, the correlation between land and income distribution is

weak, possibly because the income-earning capacity of land depends on a host of factors, including its quality and agricultural policies, which are not accounted for in such studies. A plot of land which does not earn much income does not provide a good collateral.

14 See, for example, *World Development Report, 1995* (New York: Oxford University Press for the World Bank, 1995), p. 39.

15 See I. Adelman and S. Robinson, *Income Distribution Policy in Developing Countries: A Case Study of Korea* (Oxford University Press, 1981).

16 See D. Mazumdar, *The Urban Labour Market and Income Distribution: A Study of Malaysia* (Oxford University Press, 1981).

17 See UNCTAD, *World Investment Report, 1995* (United Nations publication, Sales No. E.95.II.A.9, New York and Geneva, 1995), chap. III; A. Kokko, R. Tansini and M. C. Zejan, "Local Technological Capability and Productivity Spillovers from FDI in the Uruguayan Manufacturing Sector", *Journal of Development Studies*, Vol. 32, 1996; and B. Aitken, A. Harrison, and R.E. Lipsey, "Wages and foreign ownership. A comparative study of Mexico, Venezuela, and the United States", *Journal of International Economics*, Vol. 40, 1996.

18 For the definition of skill-intensive goods see *TDR, 1993*, Part Two, chap. IV, sect. B.

19 See *TDR 1996*, Part Two, chap. II, sect. C.3.

20 For a review of these formulations and their implications for the relationship between inequality and savings see K. Schmidt-Hebbel and L. Servén, "Income Inequality and Aggregate Saving. The Cross-Country Evidence", *Policy Research Working Paper No. 1561*, World Bank, Washington, D.C., Jan. 1996.

21 J. M. Keynes, *The Economic Consequences of the Peace* - Vol. II of *The Collected Writings of John Maynard Keynes* (third edition) (London: Macmillan, 1971), p. 11.

22 See Schmidt-Hebbel and Servén, *op. cit.*, which also contains a survey of the empirical studies on the relationship between savings and income distribution.

23 The private investment figures include FDI and hence overestimate domestic investment. Deducting FDI from these figures would, however, result in an underestimation of domestic investment since FDI includes purchase of existing assets as well as greenfield investment.

24 See A. R. Khan, "Reversing the Decline of Output and Productive Employment in Rural Sub-Saharan Africa", *Issues in Development, Discussion Paper No. 17*, ILO, Geneva, 1997, table 5.

25 L. O. Taylor, "Saving out of Different Types of Income", *Brookings Papers on Economic Activity*, No. 2, 1971; and E. Malinvaud, "Pure Profits as Forced Saving", *Scandinavian Journal of Economics*, Vol. 88, No. 1, 1986.

26 A. Dean, M. Durand, J. Fallon, and P. Hoeller., "Saving Trends and Behaviour in OECD Countries", *Working Paper No. 67*, OECD, Paris, June 1989, p. 79.

27 See J. Lecallion, F. Paukert, C. Morrisson and D. Germidis, *Income Distribution and Economic Development. An Analytical Survey* (Geneva, ILO, 1984), p. 50.

28 See Malinvaud, *op. cit.*.

29 For a discussion of this issue see R. Ruggles, "Distinguished Lecture on Economics in Government. Accounting for Saving and Capital Formation in the United States, 1947-1991", *Journal of Economic Perspectives*, Vol. 7, No. 2, Spring 1993; and A. Dean *et al.*, *op. cit.*

30 Ruggles, *op. cit.*

31 C. Pitelis, *Corporate Capital. Control, Ownership, Saving and Crisis* (Cambridge: Cambridge University Press, 1987).

32 See C. Y. Horioka, "Is Japan's Household Saving Rate Really High", *Review of Income and Wealth*, Series 41, No. 4, Dec. 1995, and the references therein.

33 See F. Guy, "Correspondence: Unhooking Household Saving and Business Investment", *Journal of Economic Perspectives*, Vol. 9, No. 2, Spring 1995. The results are also taken as further evidence against the orthodox theory that household and enterprise savings are perfect substitutes.

34 On corporate investment, savings and leverage see A. Singh, "Savings, Investment and the Corporation in the East Asian Miracle", Study No. 9 prepared for the UNCTAD project on "East Asian Development: Lessons for a New Global Environment", sponsored by the Government of Japan (Geneva: United Nations, March 1996).

35 J. Bauer and A. Mason, "The Distribution of Income and Wealth in Japan", *Review of Income and Wealth*, New Series, 38, No. 4, December 1992, p. 419.

36 Gross operating surplus is defined as gross value added *minus* compensation of employees *minus* indirect taxes paid by the producer net of subsidies received. By contrast corporate savings are calculated as gross operating surplus *minus* various charges, including particularly corporate taxes and interest on debt, *minus* dividends; see T.P. Hill, *Profits and Rates of Return* (Paris: OECD, 1979).

37 For the evolution of savings in East Asia see *TDR 1996*, table 31.

38 See, for example, *The East Asian Miracle* (New York: Oxford University Press for The World Bank, 1993). The claim of exceptional productivity is highly controversial. For a summary of various views see Y. Akyüz and C. Gore, "The Investment-Profits Nexus in East Asian Industrialization", *World Development*, Vol. 24, No. 3, 1996; and Singh, *op. cit.*

39 S. Fischer, "The role of macroeconomic factors in growth", *NBER Working Paper* No. 4565, 1993, p. 21.

40 See M. R. Agosin, "Savings and investment in Latin America", *UNCTAD Review, 1995* (United Nations

publication, Sales No. E.95.II.D.23), New York and Geneva, 1995.

41 This approach was subsequently further developed in Akyüz and Gore, *op. cit.*

42 N. Kaldor, "Economic Problems in Chile", *Essays on Economic Policy II* (London: Duckworth, 1964), p. 256.

43 *Ibid.*, p. 266.

44 See M. R. Agosin, G. Crespi and S.L. Letelier, "Explicaciones del Aumento del Ahorro en Chile" (mimeo), IDB, Washington, D.C., August 1996; and G. Palma, "Whatever happened to Latin America's savings? Comparing Latin American and East Asian savings performances", Study No. 6 prepared for the UNCTAD project on "East Asian Development: Lessons for a New Global Environment", sponsored by the Government of Japan (Geneva: United Nations, March 1996). While agreeing on the importance of corporate savings, these studies give different figures for the division of private sav-ings between the household and corporate sectors. The corporate savings are obtained as a residual and thus depend on the figure adopted for house-hold savings. On the other hand, while the above studies give a negative figure for household sav-ings for 1983-1985, according to a flow-of-funds study this sector had a financial surplus during that period; see P. Honohan and I. Atiyas, "Intersectoral Financial Flows in Developing Countries", *Working Paper, WPS 164*, March 1989, World Bank, Washington, D.C., p. 32.

45 These estimates are based on CEPAL national ac-counts data; see Palma, *op. cit.*

46 See Lecallion *et al., op. cit.*; and Wouter van Ginneken and Jong-goo Park, *Generating Internationally Comparable Income Distribution Estimates*, A World Employment Programme Study, ILO, Geneva, 1992, pp. 4-8.

47 See Bauer and Mason, *op. cit.*

Chapter VI

PROMOTING INVESTMENT: SOME LESSONS FROM EAST ASIA

A. Introduction

As noted in the previous chapter, accumulation and growth depend largely on the spending behaviour of the classes that take a very large share of national income, particularly the capitalist class. Historical and cultural factors play an important role in the emergence of a dynamic capitalist class with a high propensity to save and invest from profits. It was also noted that income distribution itself can have an important influence on incentives to save and invest. However, experience shows that government policies play a key role in promoting "animal spirits" among business, not only by securing certain basic conditions such as political and economic stability and property rights, but also through appropriate use of fiscal, financial, industrial and trade policy tools and institutional arrangements that enhance the effectiveness of government intervention.

This chapter discusses the key policy instruments and institutions used in the East Asian countries in animating the investment-profits nexus and attaining a rapid pace of growth and industrialization without widening inequality. The next section examines the policies and institutions designed to encourage savings and investment from profits, and is followed by a discussion of specific policies aimed at discouraging luxury consumption, focusing on how trade and development strategies can be designed to link investment and production to exports rather than domestic consumption. The final section examines the role of profit-related pay in reconciling distributional and growth objectives. While the chapter draws primarily on the East Asian experience, comparisons are also made with other countries.

B. Animating the investment-profits nexus

All the East Asian governments have generally succeeded in guaranteeing certain basic conditions for investment by maintaining political stability, ensuring the respect of property rights and creating a pro-investment macroeconomic climate. "Pro-investment" is a better description of East Asian macroeconomic policies than "stable" or "low inflation", because some of these governments were willing to tolerate a fair degree of inflationary pressure for the sake of boosting investors' confidence. Moreover, consumption was sacrificed in preference to investment when more restrictive measures were considered necessary for the achievement of national economic goals. However, central to sustaining the momentum of industrialization in the most successful economies in the region has been the pursuit of policies designed to promote profits and to provide incentives to private firms to invest in productive capacity and productivity, and to compete aggressively for a greater market share.[1]

This was done in two major ways. Firstly, fiscal instruments were used to increase corporate profits and to encourage retentions in order to accelerate capital accumulation. Fiscal incentives included specific instruments targeting directly corporate profits and investment, such as tax breaks and special depreciation allowances. Legislation allowed firms to put aside reserve funds against risks and exempted funds from taxation, making it possible to defer tax payments on profits. Such policies also played a catalytic role, since banks were more willing to make loans for investment qualifying for accelerated depreciation allowances.

Secondly, trade, financial and competition policies raised profits above levels that would have been attained under free-market conditions, thus creating rents. State-created rents, indeed, were more vital than fiscal incentives in boosting profits and promoting investment. They were created through a combination of selective protection, controls over interest rates and credit allocation, and managed competition, including the encouragement of mergers, the coordination of capacity expansion, restrictions on entry into specific industries, screening of technology acquisition, and the promotion of cartels for specific purposes such as product standardization, specialization and exports.[2] As a result, domestic prices were allowed to deviate from international ones. This was particularly true in Japan, during the catch-up period, and of the Republic of Korea and Taiwan Province of China - the three economies where the international competitiveness of national firms was steadily built up and industrial deepening proceeded furthest.[3]

The low interest rate policy was particularly important to firms as they built up internal funds. Similarly, the rationing of credit, through such mechanisms as "window guidance" in Japan, also played an important role in raising returns on investment and hence internally generated funds by preventing excessive expansion of productive ca-

pacity.[4] Thus, credit rationing was not just used as an instrument for "picking winners"; it also enabled rent creation and capital accumulation to take place. Together with competition policy, it was also used in the coordination of investment decisions so as to prevent the "investment race" among large oligopolistic firms from going so far as to lead to falling profits and hence falling investment.[5]

Rents were also created by protectionist measures, but an important feature of these rents was that they were often linked to export performance. The most lucrative form of rent provided by the Government of the Republic of Korea consisted of profits from sales on domestic markets made possible by protection that was conditional on export performance. In Taiwan Province of China rent creation was linked to exporting by tying the allocation of import licences to export performance, a practice which ensured that "those getting the windfalls (rents) from importing scarce commodities are at the same time contributing to the economic success of the country by exporting".[6]

Most of the fiscal instruments and rent-creation measures were applied, in a deliberately concerted way, to specific industries at particular moments in time. However, they have not just reallocated given resources among various sectors, but have also significantly increased the overall rate of accumulation in a number of ways. Firstly, in promoting investment in industries with greater potential for learning, scale economies and productivity growth, the policies served to raise the average rate of return on investment, and hence total profits, thereby stimulating capital accumulation. Secondly, the overall rate of capital accumulation was raised as the result of forward and backward linkage effects that these favoured sectors generated for the rest of the economy. Finally, the policies also contributed to growth by easing key macroeconomic constraints on capital accumulation, including particularly the balance of payments constraint on capital goods imports.

A number of factors account for the successful management of rents in East Asian NIEs in accelerating capital accumulation and growth compared to other developing countries that pursued similar policies. First, the rents were achievable through productive activities which served broad national interests, and governments acted to close off non-productive channels of wealth accumulation. Second, the provision of fiscal subsidies and the realization of rents were related to performance standards. Significantly, the reciprocity between government support and private sector performance entailed a faster rate of capital accumulation and growth. This was not only because support was often provided in exchange for higher investment, but also because better export performance as a measure of the quality of investment necessitated faster accumulation in order to raise competitiveness through adaptation of new technology, scale economies, learning and productivity growth. By contrast, in many other developing countries where similar policies were pursued, reciprocity between government support and private sector performance was not assured, and earning high incomes did not always depend on productive investment. In such countries the outcome has been a combination of a high share of profits in national income with a low propensity to save and invest from profits, and a highly unequal personal income distribution.

There can be little doubt that the characteristics of the business community as well as government policies play a crucial role in the process of capital accumulation. As one commentator has pointed out describing Japan during the catch-up period, "the success of guidance from above was only made possible by dynamism in industrial circles".[7] Government policy contributed to that dynamism and accelerated the process of capital accumulation by animating the investment-profits nexus through creating rents and pushing profits and investment beyond what could be attained under free-market conditions.

Effective implementation of such policies in East Asian NIEs depended crucially on building appropriate public and private institutions.[8] Creation of a strong bureaucracy based on the principles of meritocracy, continuity and insulation from day-to-day political pressures played a major role in establishing an effective government-business network needed to ensure reciprocity. Formal and informal links with peak business organizations, as well as sectoral ties, were instrumental in the design, implementation and coordination of policy measures.

A corporate structure based on large, diversified business groups and concentration of ownership in the hands of a small number of inside investors, together with a close relationship and interlocking ownership with banks, has allowed enterprises to take a long view and hence to establish a pattern of corporate governance which has not been pressured by considerations of short-term profit goals. Such forms of business organization and ownership provided especially effective institutional arrangements under conditions of scarce endowment of capital, entrepreneurship and skill and of inadequate and imperfect information. They helped overcome coordination problems in investment decisions; facilitate exchange of information and reduce risks and uncertainties surrounding investment projects; internalize economies of scope and realize interrelated investment opportunities by encouraging firms to create externalities for each other as well as provide cross subsidies in financing infant industries and R&D.[9] Similarly, the internal capital market organized within banks and firms served to reduce the borrower's risk and to lower the cost of investment and the rate of return required by investors to undertake investment.[10]

C. Control over luxury consumption, trade and industrialization

1. Luxury consumption

Given that the distribution of capital ownership is usually highly unequal, and that savings out of profits take place mainly through corporate retentions, the coexistence of a high share of profits in value added with a highly unequal personal income distribution suggests a low propensity to save and invest by the rich. This phenomenon is much more widespread in developing countries than the coexistence of high profits with low personal income inequality. There is thus good reason to believe that the rich in developing countries do not always save and invest a large proportion of their incomes, but spend them on goods and services that by many developing country standards can be considered luxury consumption. They also have a greater tendency to consume goods with high import contents, which, besides emphasizing consumption over savings, has also the effect of leading to a tighter balance of payments constraint on accumulation and growth.

Most countries, whether developing or developed, place few or no constraints on luxury consumption. A policy of controlling luxury consumption has been adopted only by a relatively limited number of countries since the Second World War, and sometimes for only limited periods. Examples include certain restrictions on travel abroad in Western Europe in the immediate postwar years, the efforts of the socialist countries of Eastern Europe to give second place to luxuries in their pursuit of more egalitarian social structures, and the determination of some East Asian economies to increase savings and accelerate capital formation. The corresponding policies have been introduced and subsequently relaxed during various stages of development or, in Western Europe, during the postwar recovery.

There is a popular perception that some countries are more prone to engage in luxury consumption than others, and that this makes a difference to the country's economic performance. These tendencies can be clearly seen from table 45 with respect to passenger car ownership, which is a typical luxury good in the sense that it neither fulfils a basic need nor can be afforded by most people in at least the developing countries. The table provides some snap-shot statistics on car ownership for selected developed and developing countries in mainly the early stages of their development. It shows that some countries had a much smaller fleet of cars in relation to population than others at the same level of development (as denoted by per capita GDP in constant 1985 dollars). For instance, the Republic of Korea in 1984 had one third of the number of cars per 1,000 inhabitants that France had in 1950, although real per capita was roughly the same in both countries at around $4,000. Likewise, in 1989 it had the same number of cars per 1,000 inhabitants as Turkey in 1992, even though its real per capita income was one and a half times greater than that of Turkey at the time. Germany, Japan and the Republic of Korea stand out as having an exceptionally low level of car consumption compared to that of other countries in their early stages of development or postwar recovery. At the other extreme, there are countries such as South Africa, Brazil and Malaysia where car ownership has been exceptionally high

for their incomes from the very early stages of development.

In some countries car ownership has grown broadly in tandem with per capita income. For example, it has grown fast in Malaysia and Thailand, but so also has per capita real income. In other countries, however, the stock of cars has risen relatively much faster. For example, although Argentina's real per capita income remained unchanged at around $5,000 during 1965-1989, the number of cars per 1,000 persons rose from 41 to 133 from the beginning to the end of the period. Likewise, Chile, Egypt and Turkey initially had relatively low levels of car consumption, but these levels subsequently increased more rapidly than per capita income. The years of economic crisis of the 1980s only served to brake temporarily the growth of car ownership, which has spiralled in some countries that have recently adopted economic liberalization measures. In the Republic of Korea car ownership rose very slowly until the mid-1980s; the pace accelerated subsequently, but remained slower than that of per capita income growth.

Another indicator of luxury consumption for which international data are readily available is foreign tourism expenditure. Although they cover only the last two decades, they give a similar picture to that of car ownership. It is, however, striking that per capita expenditure on foreign travel in the Republic of Korea has shot up since 1988, when restrictions on such travel were lifted. It therefore seems that underconsumption, at least in foreign travel, had been due as much to restrictive policies as to any intrinsic tendency to save rather than consume by the country's higher-income groups. Import controls were one of the main restrictive measures adopted in that country to discourage or prevent luxury consumption during the initial phase of growth and development. They ranged from outright import bans on goods such as luxury cars or fur coats to a combination of quantitative restrictions, prohibitive tariffs and foreign exchange rationing in which priority was given to importers of capital goods and intermediate inputs. There was a surge in the import especially of luxury goods when controls were relaxed in 1986. Imports of fur-skin products, for example, were 40 times greater in value in 1995 than in 1986 and of tobacco products more than 300 times greater, as opposed to 4.5 times for manufactured imports as a whole.

Both Japan and the Republic of Korea instituted various domestic taxes that discriminated

Table 45

DIFFERENCES IN CAR OWNERSHIP AT COMPARABLE LEVELS OF PER CAPITA INCOME

(Number of cars per 1,000 of population in year or period specified)

Per capita GDP[a] around		Germany	France	Austria	Italy	Japan	Republic of Korea	Thailand	Malaysia	Indonesia	Turkey	Egypt	Argentina	Brazil	Chile	Mexico	South Africa
$1,000	Year					1950[b]	1963-64	1962-63	1955[b]		1950	1964		1950[b]	1950[b]	1950[b]	
	Cars					<1	1	2	<8	4	1	3		<6	<7	<7	
$2,000	Year					1955	1973	1979	1969-70	1990-91	1966-67	1992[c]		1967-68	1950[b]	1950[b]	1953
	Cars					2	2	9	22	8	3	20		20	<7	<7	35
$3,000	Year			1950-51	1951-52	1960	1978	1989	1977		1976-84			1972-73	1961-76	1963	1970-90
	Cars			9	10	5	5	21	39		12-19			29	7-27	14	65-95
$4,000	Year	1951	1950	1956	1958	1963-64	1984	1992[c]	1981-87		1992[c]		1950-54	1978-91	1987	1970	
	Cars	16	36	27	30	15	12	24	61-91		37		17-19	64-80	49	23	
$5,000	Year	1954-55	1956	1960	1961	1966	1987		1990				1965-89		1992[c]	1977-78	
	Cars	33	69	57	48	29	20		104				41-133		60	49	
$6,000	Year	1958-59	1961	1964	1966	1968	1989									1980-91	
	Cars	62	133	97	121	52	37									63-91	
$7,000	Year	1962-63	1964	1968-69	1968-69	1969-70	1990-91										
	Cars	116	182	157	169	76	56										
$8,000	Year	1966-67	1967	1971-72	1972-73	1972											
	Cars	175	236	186	238	118											

Source: UNCTAD secretariat estimates, based on national and international sources.

Note: It was not always possible to identify a single year as the point when a country reached a given level of income. In some instances an average for two years has been used. In others, where income passed a certain threshold in one year but fell below it subsequently, the number of cars is given as a range for the period between the year when the country first passed the threshold and the year after which per capita income did not fall below the threshold again.

a In constant 1985 dollars at purchasing power parities.

b The relevant income level was reached before the earliest year for which car data are available.

c Income did not reach this threshold until the last year for which the data are available, but was less than 10 per cent below it.

between consumer goods in terms of how "luxurious" they were deemed to be. In Japan 10 adjustments were made to the list of luxury goods during 1945-1987, each reflecting transitions in consumption norms as the country became more prosperous and living standards and expectations rose. Various such adjustments were also made in the Republic of Korea before 1977, when the commodity tax regime based on the Japanese model was replaced by a VAT system that taxed luxury goods far more heavily than other consumer goods.

Credit control was another allocative measure utilized by the Republic of Korea to deter luxury consumption. The loans made by the government-influenced banking system tended to favour production and investment in sectors accorded greater priority. Few, if any, consumer loans were available through the banking system. By the mid-1990s, however, well-established manufacturers themselves began to make credit available to their customers. Car manufacturers, for example, established specialized financing companies for this purpose.

The Governments of the Republic of Korea and other East Asian countries also publicly exhorted wealthy persons to show self-restraint in luxury consumption. The appeals sought to remind them of the harsh working and living conditions that the majority of the population had to endure during those early years of development and growth. These campaigns also had the effect of creating a valuable sense of sharing and solidarity in the population.

2. Production and exports

Many of the goods that are treated in developing countries as luxury items, such as motor cars and consumer durables, are precisely those that have driven, especially through their strong backward linkages, modern industrial development in the advanced economies. They involve industries that typically employ mass production technology based on the use of dedicated capital equipment, where the achievement of scale economy is critical for cost efficiency. This poses an important challenge to developing countries in designing infant industry promotion programmes for such industries.

Typically, the domestic market in developing countries is too small to enable producers to reach a minimum scale of efficiency. This problem is further exacerbated by the tendency of consumers to want variety in markets such as cars, which leads to a proliferation of models, often produced at below the minimum efficient scale, as in many Latin American countries.[11] At the same time, the scope for exporting is limited by their inability to compete with more efficient producers in the industrial countries. The response to this problem in many developing countries has been to provide trade protection or subsidies to allow them to survive.

Expanding domestic consumption may overcome the problem of minimum efficient scale in countries with relatively large domestic markets, but is not necessarily a solution in the long run. For one thing, expanding the demand for such consumer goods ahead of income would lead to a fall in savings. For another, financing the imports needed for their production would depend on primary export earnings or foreign borrowing, neither of which may increase as fast as domestic production of the goods.

East Asian countries such as Japan and, subsequently, the Republic of Korea have succeeded in resolving this dilemma by focusing on a strategy of export-led growth while at the same time discouraging luxury consumption. In some industries it proved possible to channel domestic production towards exports relatively easily. For instance, during the early 1980s, when the domestic consumption of furs was virtually banned, the Republic of Korea exported fur-skin products on a large scale, becoming one of the world's leading exporters of these luxury goods. In other instances, however, the industries needed to develop first on the basis of domestic markets before they became globally competitive. In some such cases, the consumption of domestically produced luxury goods was initially encouraged in the Republic of Korea in order to enable the infant industries concerned to gain experience and attain minimal scale efficiency on the basis of the relatively large domestic market. To that end, the VAT rate on certain technology-intensive products, such as VCRs, was set at an initially low rate during 1982-1986, with the expressed intention to raise it to 16 per cent in 1986, 28 per cent in 1987 and 40 per cent in 1988.

It was thus a judicious combination of government policies that encouraged producers of luxury goods to export and discouraged domestic consumption of such goods, thereby stimulating domestic capital formation and enabling corporations to achieve the necessary economies of scale and quality standards to compete globally. Emphasis on exports to advanced country markets has also had the benefits of providing a further spur to domestic producers in respect of productivity and of quality control. Here again the Republic of Korea provides a good illustration. After an initial learning period based on the domestic market, that country's passenger car industry increased exports much faster than production, thanks to its competitiveness in global markets and the adoption of measures to discourage domestic car consumption. As may be seen from table 46, the experience of that country in this respect differed considerably from the more common experience of many other developing countries, where transnational corporations jumped import barriers by establishing local plants to produce for domestic consumption rather than export. Mexico provides an illustration of another sort. There much of the assembly operations is for the export of cars to the United States, but the operations are carried out by subsidiaries of TNCs rather than by domestic firms; moreover, they have a very high import content and low domestic value added.

Entry restrictions were instrumental in the Republic of Korea in encouraging potential investors to build large factories. Other measures for achieving and maintaining sufficient economies of scale included government-induced mergers of firms operating at sub-optimal levels of produc-tion, forcing firms to withdraw from the market where too many of them were competing in too small a market, and arranging negotiated segmentation of markets to accommodate efficiently two or more producers having distinct comparative advantages.

Since the key to success in solving this dilemma was attaining competitiveness and raising exports rapidly, measures were taken to increase productivity in industries that were regarded as of key importance in the export drive. The measures included the establishment of standards for industries producing parts and components, the provision of fiscal incentives for training and R&D, the suspension of anti-trust legislation where large technological agglomerations were necessary, and the dissemination of information on international "best practice" methods and technologies. Policies were also pursued that facilitated, where their effects were considered beneficial, the operations of TNCs.

Thus, a combination of restrictions on luxury consumption and the promotion of exports was crucial in raising savings, investment and productivity so as to attain rapid industrialization and competitiveness in a variety of technologically advanced product fields. This success was in no small measure made possible by the careful sequencing, phasing and control by government authorities of the pace at which the production, export and domestic consumption of luxury goods occurred.

D. Profit-related pay, distribution and accumulation

A factor that has played a key role in reconciling growth and distributional objectives in East Asia is the bonus system, first adopted in Japan and subsequently in the East Asian NIEs. By linking an important part of labour compensation to company performance and promoting stability of employment, this system has served to attain greater equality in income distribution while at the same time promoting higher savings by workers and higher investment by firms.

1. Extent and nature of the bonus system

Profit-related pay is practised in a number of countries both in East Asia and elsewhere under different institutional arrangements. A widely used scheme is profit-sharing, whereby workers receive, in addition to their wages and salaries, a predetermined share of the profits of the enterprise concerned. Such formal profit-sharing arrange-

Table 46

VEHICLE PRODUCTION AND TRADE: MEXICO, BRAZIL, ARGENTINA AND THE REPUBLIC OF KOREA, 1976-1996

(Thousands of units)

Year	Mexico				Brazil				Argentina				Republic of Korea [a]		
	Total production	of which for export	Imports	Export share (Per cent)	Total production	of which for export	Imports	Export share (Per cent)	Total production	of which for export	Imports	Export share (Per cent)	Total production	of which for export	Export share (Per cent)
1976	..	..	..	..	..	..	..	..	..	..	..	..	27	1	2.1
1977	..	..	..	..	..	..	..	..	..	..	..	..	44	5	11.5
1978	..	..	..	..	..	..	..	..	..	..	..	..	87	17	19.0
1979	..	..	..	..	..	..	..	..	..	..	..	..	114	19	16.5
1980	490	18	0	3.7	1165	157	0	13.5	282	4	0	1.3	57	15	25.6
1981	597	14	0	2.4	781	213	0	27.2	172	0	0	0.2	69	17	25.0
1982	473	16	0	3.3	859	173	0	20.2	132	3	0	2.4	95	14	15.0
1983	286	22	0	7.9	896	169	0	18.8	160	5	0	3.3	122	16	13.5
1984	358	34	0	9.4	865	197	0	22.7	167	4	0	2.5	159	49	30.8
1985	459	58	0	12.7	967	208	0	21.5	138	1	0	0.6	265	119	45.1
1986	341	72	0	21.2	1056	183	0	17.3	171	0	0	0.2	457	299	65.3
1987	395	163	0	41.2	920	346	0	37.6	193	1	0	0.3	793	535	67.5
1988	513	173	0	33.8	1069	320	0	30.0	164	2	0	1.0	872	565	64.7
1989	641	196	0	30.6	1013	254	0	25.0	128	2	0	1.4	872	347	39.8
1990	821	277	0	33.7	914	187	3	20.5	100	1	0	1.1	897	340	37.9
1991	989	351	0	35.4	960	193	28	20.1	139	5	17	3.7	1158	379	32.7
1992	1081	383	6	35.4	1074	342	45	31.8	262	17	65	6.3	1307	428	32.7
1993	1080	472	3	43.7	1391	332	97	23.8	342	30	65	8.8	1593	573	36.0
1994	1097	575	56	52.4	1581	378	218	23.9	409	38		9.4	1806	648	35.9
1995	931	779	17	83.6	1629	263	369	16.1	285	48	72	16.7	2086	944	45.3
1996	1211	971	30	80.2	1813	306	224	16.9	313	109	134	34.8			

Source: M. Mortimore, "Dimensions of Latin American Integration: the NAFTA and MERCOSUR Automobile Industries" (mimeo), ECLAC, Santiago, Chile, 1997; and K.H. Lee, *Hankook Jadongcha Sanup ui Baljun Kwajung* (The Development Process of the Korean Automobile Industry) (in Korean), Seoul, Kia Economic Research Institute, 1995.

a No data are available for imports.

ments are typical of the profit-related pay schemes in developed countries, in particular those of OECD.[12] They are often encouraged by tax concessions, and applied after a threshold level of profits. Payment may be made in cash or shares. When in cash, the payment may be made immediately or after a certain period. A special instance of deferred payment is where profit-sharing is used to allow workers to accumulate retirement funds, as in North America. In the share-based system employees acquire shares in the company free or on preferential terms. These are often company-wide incentive schemes which do not depend on individual performance, although eligibility to participate usually varies with length of service.

In East Asia profit- and performance-related pay is particularly widespread in Japan, where the tax and social security systems encourage bonus payments. While the law requires such payments to be made with an interval of at least three months between them, in practice bonuses are paid twice a year. The Republic of Korea has an almost equally developed bonus system, where such payments are encouraged by favourable treatment in the social security system. The payments are made four times a year, and consequently the amounts can be altered more rapidly according to business conditions. In other economies, such as China, Taiwan Province of China and Singapore, the bonus system is also widely practised, although its importance in terms of workers covered and the share of such payments in total remuneration in the latter two appears to be somewhat more limited than in Japan and the Republic of Korea.

The bonus system in Asia differs from profit-sharing schemes in North America and Europe in a number of important respects. First, formal agreements for the distribution of a pre-determined portion of profits are much less common, and there is often an important discretionary component, particularly in Japan. According to a survey made by the Ministry of Labour in 1983, only one third of all firms in Japan paying bonuses had formal arrangements. Moreover, only three quarters of such arrangements were linked to profits, and the rest were payments made on the basis of value added or the volume of production or sales. Even formal profit-sharing agreements often include provisions for discretionary payments. Similarly, enterprises have been given considerable freedom in the implementation of the incentive pay system in China since it was introduced in the mid-1980s. Detailed information is not available for other

Asian countries, but formal agreements seem to be more common in the Republic of Korea, although not to the same extent as in the profit-sharing schemes of OECD countries. However, there appears to be a move in the region towards the kind of flexible pay system practised in Japan.[13]

While the discretionary component of the bonus system weakens the sensitivity of bonus payments to changes in profits, it introduces considerable flexibility into corporate management and promotes greater interaction between labour and capital, which often leads to cooperative arrangements. In Japan, for instance, in unionized firms negotiations over bonus payments are conducted separately during *Shunto* (Spring Wage Offensive) and on the basis of a different set of considerations. While the current level of profits is an important element in setting bonuses, other factors are also important, including firms' plans for expansion or job creation. This appears to be the case in the Republic of Korea, too. For instance, the labour union at Daweoo Electronics recently announced that it would voluntarily give up part of the bonus payments, amounting to half a month's wage, and accept a wage freeze for the year, in order to help the company expand investment in new areas of business and stabilize employment.[14]

Thus, the bonus system in East Asia does not simply provide a rule for labour compensation, but is a component of a broader labour-capital interaction whereby the interests of the workers are reflected in company decisions. This is certainly an important reason for greater corporate loyalty in East Asia. Bonuses also provide an important incentive for work effort and have been shown to have a significant positive effect on productivity in the Republic of Korea.[15] Although bonuses are determined by the collective performance at the firm level, social ostracism and peer pressure help to solve the individual incentive problem, since co-workers can easily monitor each other's efforts.[16]

A second important difference is that, while the overall significance of profit-sharing schemes in labour compensation is fairly limited in most industrialized countries, the bonus system in many East Asian countries has a wider coverage and accounts for a substantial part of total pay. In Japan it was initially limited to white-collar workers in large firms, but since the 1950s it has spread widely to cover blue-collar workers and has begun to account for a growing portion of total pay.[17] By the early 1980s, almost all workers in firms with

Chart 17

BONUSES AS A PERCENTAGE OF WAGES IN JAPAN AND THE REPUBLIC OF KOREA

(Percentage)

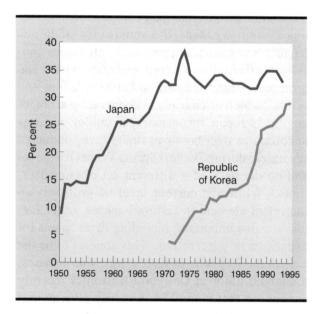

Source: Ministry of Labour, Republic of Korea, *Occupational Wage Survey*. Ministry of Labour, Japan, *Monthly Labour Statistics*.

at least 30 employees were receiving bonuses. The bonus/wage ratio rose from about 10 per cent in 1950 to over 40 per cent in the mid-1970s, declining somewhat and stabilizing at around 33 per cent thereafter; thus, in the early 1980s about a quarter of total labour remuneration took the form of bonuses. In the Republic of Korea the bonus system also covers almost all workers in firms with 30 employees or more. Its development was started later than in Japan; the bonus/wage ratio rose from around 5 per cent in the early 1970s to 15 per cent in the mid-1980s. There has been a further sharp increase since the late 1980s, and the ratio has now reached a level similar to that in Japan (see chart 17).

There are no systematic data for other countries in the region. In China, the share of bonus payments in total labour compensation appears to have increased considerably after the mid-1980s, and this may have been a key factor in the rise of the share of labour in total factor payments in various branches of industry. Available evidence suggests that in Taiwan Province of China bonus payments amounted to some 15 per cent of total

labour compensation in the 1970s, and it seems that this proportion has been maintained in more recent years.[18] In Singapore the system includes annual bonus and annual wage supplements; in 1989 about 90 per cent of workers seem to have received some form of bonus. In manufacturing, such payments represented about 11 per cent of wages in 1988.

2. The bonus system, distribution and accumulation

The bonus system clearly has implications for income distribution both among workers and between labour and capital, as well as for savings and capital accumulation. However, these implications have been little explored in studies on the bonus system, and empirical evidence is scarce. What follows is a brief description and discussion of various characteristics of the system and their relevance to distribution and growth.

A number of features of the bonus system in East Asia appear to widen, rather than narrow, income differentials among workers. In Japan the share of bonus in total remuneration tends to be higher for workers who receive higher wages; bonuses account for a greater proportion of pay for white-collar than for blue-collar workers. The share is also positively correlated with the size of firm and the length of continuous service, factors that play a major role in wage determination in Japan (see table 47). In the Republic of Korea, too, the share of bonus in total pay is higher in larger than in smaller firms, for white-collar workers than blue-collar workers, and for male workers than female workers (see table 48). The variation of bonuses with firm size appears to be responsible for the large inter-industry wage differences in Japan and the Republic of Korea by international standards.[19]

While the bonus systems in Japan and the Republic of Korea tend to widen earnings differentials in some respects, they tend to promote equality in others. Despite the large inequalities among different groups of workers noted above, wages are much the same for all workers within the same gender and age groups, irrespective of education and occupation. The close correlation between the share of bonus in total pay and length of service suggests that bonuses promote skills based on learning-by-doing, as well as corporate

Table 47

SHARE OF BONUS IN TOTAL LABOUR COMPENSATION IN JAPAN IN 1983, BY SIZE OF FIRM, LENGTH OF EMPLOYMENT AND TYPE OF OCCUPATION

(Percentage)

	Size of firm *(number of employees)*							
	10-99		*100-999*		*1,000 or more*		*All firms* [b]	
Years of service [a]	White-collar	Blue-collar	White-collar	Blue-collar	White-collar	Blue-collar	White-collar	Blue-collar
1-9	17.5	15.3	21.6	19.3	24.1	21.4	21.3	17.9
10-19	20.8	18.1	25.5	22.3	27.8	23.5	26.0	21.8
20-29	20.7	18.7	27.4	23.0	31.2	24.8	29.1	23.1
30 and more	20.4	18.7	28.1	23.4	31.1	26.0	29.2	24.0
All workers	18.8	15.8	24.7	20.6	28.6	23.4	25.7	20.2

Source: J. Suruga, "Bonus system and flexible wages" (in Japanese), *Nihon Rodo Kyoukai Zashi*, March 1987.

Note: White-collar: administrative, office, technical workers; blue-collar: production workers.

a Years of continued employment in the firm.

b With at least 10 employees.

loyalty. Development of such skills is certainly conducive to better income distribution when opportunities to develop such skills are widely available.

In one important respect the bonus system promotes greater equality among workers since, in as much as it imparts intra-firm wage flexibility, it stabilizes employment at the firm level. This result is attained through an internally organized labour market within firms and by linking pay to firm-specific conditions, rather than to market-clearing wage formation based on the kind of "flexible labour market" advocated by orthodox analysis. Consequently, its implications for the distribution of income and jobs among workers are quite different from a system where wages and employment change in response to labour market conditions.

In a system where hiring and firing is relatively costless, contraction in business activity often results in workers being laid off. Consequently, while some workers are fully employed and earn going wages, others are without jobs or pay. By contrast, the bonus system rations work more or less uniformly at times of contraction. Indeed, one of the main features of the Japanese labour market is the flexibility of working hours. Compared to the other major developed economies, the market is characterized by considerable fluctuations in working hours and very little fluctuation in the number of people employed.[20] Japanese firms tend to vary working hours and with them overall pay, rather than employment, when adjusting to demand fluctuations, promoting what is known as "life-time" employment. When obliged nevertheless to reduce employment, they tend first to cut down on fresh recruitment, then send existing workers to subsidiary firms in the business group, call for voluntary resignations after that, and discharge and lay off workers only as a last resort and with great reluctance. This certainly leads to a better income distribution among workers than a system where part of the labour force is unemployed and part is gainfully employed.

Until the mid-1980s adjustment of employment to variations in business conditions was more widespread in the Republic of Korea than in Japan,

Table 48

SHARE OF BONUS IN TOTAL LABOUR COMPENSATION IN THE REPUBLIC OF KOREA IN 1995, BY SIZE OF FIRM, TYPE OF OCCUPATION AND GENDER

(Percentage)

Firm size (Number of employees)	White-collar workers		Blue-collar workers		All workers
	Male	*Female*	*Male*	*Female*	
10-99	15.9	14.7	11.7	9.8	13.0
100-299	24.0	20.6	19.0	16.4	20.6
300-499	27.4	24.9	23.7	21.1	24.8
500 or more	33.6	31.9	31.6	28.9	32.0
All firms[a]	24.9	20.8	21.8	18.0	22.4

Source: Ministry of Labour, *Monthly Labour Statistics* (various issues).
   a With at least 10 employees.

but less than in other developed economies. Despite similarities with Japan in the bonus system, variable working hours and permanent employment were not important features of the Republic of Korea, where the average length of continuous employment was only four years in 1989, compared to almost 11 years in Japan. Although in the previous decade aggregate employment was fairly stable in the economy as a whole, the employment pattern has become more like that of Japan; since 1987, adjustment of employment has become more rigid, while working hours have become more flexible. It is also notable that increased stability of employment has coincided with a steep rise in real wages and increased power of the unions.[21]

The wage flexibility brought about by the bonus system is crucially different from the labour market flexibility underlying the conventional analysis. As discussed in greater detail in *TDR 1995*, when there is a chronic demand deficiency and structural unemployment, greater labour market flexibility simply turns open unemployment into disguised unemployment, characterized by low-pay, low-productivity occupations, particularly in the services sector, and leading to wide earnings differentials, as has been observed in some industrial countries since the early 1980s. Intra-firm flexibility not only helps to maintain a high level of employment in high-productivity jobs by promoting investment through the channels explained

below, but also allows firms to adjust to shocks such as loss of international competitiveness due to currency appreciations or the emergence of low-cost producers, without creating hysteresis in the labour market whereby unemployment leads to a deterioration of skills, rendering workers increasingly less employable. Indeed, intra-firm wage flexibility has certainly played an important role in the Japanese adjustment to shifts in international competitiveness since the mid-1980s without triggering massive unemployment. Under such a system, a persistent excess supply of labour may at least partly be absorbed by intra-firm work-sharing arrangements through cuts in working hours. Such a response is certainly more equitable than leaving some workers without jobs and pay and consigning others to low-wage occupations.

More importantly, the bonus system contributes to high employment and better income distribution through its effect on productivity and investment. As noted above, this system tends to raise productivity by promoting incentives for greater work effort and corporate loyalty. Bonus payments from increased corporate revenues not only serve to stabilize the distribution of value added between labour and capital incomes, but also raise profits and corporate investment. Higher investment, in turn, helps to maintain a high level of employment, contributing to a better income distribution.

The bonus system promotes higher employment and better income distribution also by increasing the propensity to save from personal income. There is, indeed, a striking correlation between the household savings rate and the bonus/wage ratio in Japan (chart 18).[22] The correlation is somewhat weaker in the Republic of Korea, but bonuses are an important element in household savings in that country too.[23]

Since bonuses are paid as a lump sum at periodic intervals, they are at the disposal of firms in the interim as interest-free funds. From the workers' point of view such suspended payments may constitute involuntary savings and involuntary deferred consumption, in view of their limited access to consumer credit. In any event, the propensity to save from such temporary and transitory incomes tends to be higher than for regular incomes. Similarly, consumption decisions are often the creatures of habit, and change only slowly in response to changing incomes. Evidence suggests that in Japan household consumption has a stable relationship to wage income, while the bonuses are considered a convenient supplementary source of savings. Thus, the marginal propensity to consume bonus income during 1969-1980 was estimated to be about 0.5, compared to that for regular income of about 0.7.[24] The bonus system accordingly appears to be one of the reasons why household savings have been relatively high and rising in the East Asian NIEs.

It was noted above that even if corporations in the major East Asian economies retain a large proportion of their profits, their investment still exceeds their savings by a large margin because of high "animal spirits". If household savings were not sufficient to close the corporate savings gap, the outcome would be inflation. The result would be to reduce the corporate savings gap by generating forced savings through a redistribution of income from wages to profits, with attendant consequences for income distribution, as well as by reducing corporate investment. Thus, high household savings promoted by the bonus system help reconcile greater equality with rapid growth by reducing the inflationary pressures that are usually associated with a process of rapid accumulation. ∎

Chart 18

LABOUR BONUSES AND HOUSEHOLD SAVINGS IN JAPAN, 1958-1978

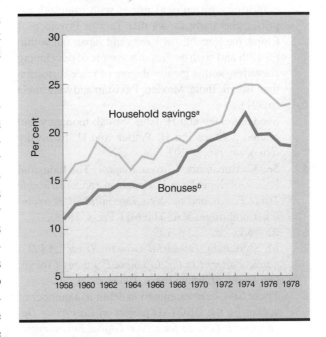

Source: Ishikawa and Ueda, *op. cit.* (see text, note 17).
a As a percentage of disposable household income.
b As a percentage of total labour compensation (wage plus bonus).

Notes

1 Certain aspects of these policies were discussed briefly in *TDR 1994*, Part Two, chap. I, sect. G.

2 See A. Amsden, *Asia's Next Giant; South Korea and Late Industrialization* (New York: Oxford University Press, 1989); A. Amsden and A. Singh, "Concurrence dirigée et efficacité dynamique en Asie: Japon, Corée du Sud, Taiwan", *Revue Tiers-Monde*, Vol. 35, No. 139, July-September, 1994; M.J. Peck and S. Tamura, "Technology", in H. Patrick and H. Rosovsky (eds.), *Asia's New Giant: How the Japanese Economy Works* (Washington, D.C.: The Brookings Institution, 1976); and R. Wade, *Govern-*

ing the Market: Economic Theory and The Role of Government in East Asian Industrialization (Princeton, NJ: Princeton University Press, 1990).

3   This has also been demonstrated by the World Bank in *The East Asian Miracle ....* In respect of the conformity of national prices with international prices, the study shows that Taiwan Province of China, the Republic of Korea and Japan fall within the fifth and sixth deciles of a sample of developing countries, with a greater degree of price distortion than Brazil, India, Mexico, Pakistan and Venezuela (p.301).

4   See G. Ackley and H. Ishi, "Fiscal, monetary and related policies", in H. Patrick and H. Rosovsky (eds.), *op. cit.*, p. 205.

5   See K. Yamamura, *"Caveat Emptor:* The Industrial Policy of Japan", in P. Krugman (ed.), *Strategic Trade Policy and the New International Economics* (Cambridge, MA: The MIT Press, 1988).

6   R. Wade, *op. cit.*, p. 129.

7   M. Shinohara, *Industrial Growth, Trade and Dynamic Patterns in the Japanese Economy* (Tokyo: University of Tokyo Press, 1982), p. 23.

8   These have been examined in detail in a number of studies for the UNCTAD project on *East Asian Development: Lessons for a New Global Environment*, sponsored by the Government of Japan (Geneva: United Nations, March 1996). See in particular study No. 2, by Tun-jen Cheng, S. Haggard and D. Kang, "Institutions, economic policy and growth in the Republic of Korea and Taiwan Province of China"; study No. 9, by A. Singh, "Savings, investment and the corporation in the East Asian Miracle"; and study No. 10, the report by the UNCTAD secretariat to the Kuala Lumpur Conference.

9   See T. Yanagihara, "Economic System Approach and its Applicability" in T. Yanagihara and S. Sambommatsu (eds.), *East Asian Development Experience* (Tokyo: Institute of Developing Economies, 1997).

10   See A. Singh, *op. cit.*; and Y. Akyüz, "Financial Liberalization: The Key Issues", in Y. Akyüz and G. Held (eds.), *Finance and the Real Economy*, ECLAC, Santiago, Chile, 1993.

11   See M. Mortimore, "Dimensions of Latin American Integration: the NAFTA and MERCOSUR Automobile Industries", (mimeo), CEPAL, Santiago, Chile, 1997.

12   For a survey of these schemes see *OECD Employment Outlook* (Paris: OECD, July 1995), chap. 4 - "Profit-sharing in OECD countries".

13   See ILO, *World Labour Report 1992* (Geneva: ILO, 1992), pp. 64-65.

14   *Chosun Ilbo*, 7 March 1997.

15   B. Lee and Y. Rhee, "Bonuses, unions and labour productivity in South Korea", *Journal of Labour Research*, Vol. 17, No. 2, 1996.

16   See M. Okuno, "Corporate loyalty and bonus payments : an analysis of work incentives in Japan", in M. Aoki (ed.), *The economic Analysis of the Japanese Firm* (Amsterdam: North Holland, 1984).

17   T. Ishikawa and K. Ueda, "The bonus payment system and Japanese personal savings", in M. Aoki (ed.) *The Economic Analysis of the Japanese Firm* (Amsterdam: North Holland, 1984).

18   M. Shinohara, *Industrial Growth, Trade and Dynamic Patterns in the Japanese Economy* (Tokyo: University of Tokyo Press, 1982).

19   See A. Krueger and L. Summers, "Efficiency wages and inter-industry wage structure", *Econometrica*, Vol. 56, 1988.

20   See T. Tachibanaki, *Wage Determination and Distribution in Japan* (Oxford: Clarendon Press, 1996). It is estimated that, over 1970-1983, the variability of employment, as measured by the standard deviation, was more than twice as high in the United States as in Japan, while variability of working hours was lower by 25 per cent (p. 225).

21   See J.-I. You, "Changing capital-labour relations in South Korea", in J. Schor and J-I. You (eds.), *Capital, the State and Labour: A Global Perspective* (Aldershot: Edward Elgar, 1995); and J-H. Lee, "Ways to improve wage structure in order to increase wage flexibility" (in Korean), *Korea Development Research*, Vol. 16, No. 1, 1994.

22   See also M. Shinohara, *Industrial Growth, Trade and Dynamic Patterns in the Japanese Economy* (Tokyo: University of Tokyo Press, 1982).

23   See T. Mizoguchi, *A Statistical Analysis of the Consumption Function* (Tokyo: Iwanami, 1964); M. Shinohara, "The puzzles of savings rate" (in Japanese), *Chochiku Jiho*, No. 127, 1981; and *Industrial Growth, Trade and Dynamic Patterns ....* See also Ishikawa and Ueda, *op. cit.*

24   Ishikawa and Ueda, *op. cit.*

UNITED NATIONS CONFERENCE ON TRADE AND DEVELOPMENT

Palais des Nations
CH-1211 GENEVE 10
Switzerland

Selected UNCTAD publications

Trade and Development Report, 1995

United Nations publication, Sales No. E.95.II.D.16
ISBN 92-1-11-2384-4

Part One		Global Trends
	I	The World Economy: Performance and Prospects
	II	International Financial Markets and the External Debt of Developing Countries
	Annex	Impact of the Naples terms

Part Two		Rethinking Economic Policies
	I	Convergence of Growth, Inflation,and Unemployment in the North
	II	The Invisible Hand, Capital Flows and Stalled Recovery in Latin America
	III	Systemic Risk and Derivatives Markets: Selected Issues

Part Three			Unemployment and Interdependence
	I		The Issues at Stake
	II		Trade, Technology and Unemployment
	III		The Labour Market, Capital Formation and Job Creation
	IV		Policies for Full Employment
	Annex	I	A Simulation Model of North-South Trade and Unemployment
	Annex	II	The Dynamics of Service Sector Employment
	Annex	III	Disguised Unemployment in the North

Trade and Development Report, 1996

United Nations publication, Sales No. E.96.II.D.6
ISBN 92-1-112399-2

Part One		Global Trends
	I	The World Economy: Performance and Prospects
	II	International Capital Markets and the External Debt of Developing Countries

Part Two		Rethinking Development Strategies: Some Lessons from the East Asian Experience
	I	Integration and Industrialization in East Asia
	II	Exports, Capital Formation and Growth
	III	Responding to the New Global Environment

Annex	Macroeconomic Management, Financial Governance, and Development: Selected Policy Issues

International Monetary and
Financial Issues for the 1990s

Volume VI (1995)

United Nations publication, Sales No. E.95.II.D.7

ISBN 92-1-112375-5

Manuel R. Agosin, Diana Tussie
and Gustavo Crespi
  Developing Countries and the Uruguay Round: An Evaluation and Issues for the Future
Dani Rodrik
  Developing Countries After the Uruguay Round
Ann Weston
  The Uruguay Round: Unravelling the Implications for the Least Developed and Low-Income Countries

Volume VII (1996)

United Nations publication, Sales No. E.96.II.D.2

ISBN 92-1-112394-1

John Williamson
  A New Facility for the IMF?
Ariel Buira and Roberto Marino
  Allocation of Special Drawing Rights: The Current Debate
Chandra Hardy
  The Case for Multilateral Debt Relief for Severely Indebted Countries
Azizali F. Mohammed
  Global Financial System Reform and the C-20 Process
Raisuddin Ahmed
  A Critique ot the World Development Report 1994: Infrastructure for Development
Dipak Mazumdar
  Labour issues in the World Development Report: A Critical Assessment
Ann Weston
  The Uruguay Round: Costs and Compensation for Developing Countries

Volume VIII (1997)

United Nations publication, Sales No. E.97.II.D.5

ISBN 92-1-112409-3

G. K. Helleiner
  Capital Account Regimes and the Developing Countries
Rudi Dornbusch
  Cross-Border Payments Taxes and Alternative Capital-Account Regimes
Guillermo Le Fort V. and Carlos Budnevich L.
  Capital-Account Regulations and Macroeconomic Policy: Two Latin American Experiences
Louis Kasekende, Damoni Kitabire and Matthew Martin
  Capital Inflows and Macroeconomic Policy in Sub-Saharan Africa
Yung Chul Park and Chi-Young Song
  Managing Foreign Capital Flows: The Experiences of the Republic of Korea, Thailand, Malaysia and Indonesia
Devesh Kapur
  The New Conditionalities of the International Financial Institutions
Aziz Ali Mohammed
  Notes on MDB Conditionality on Governance
Matthew Martin
  A Multilateral Debt Facility - Global and National
Peter Murrell
  From Plan to Market: The World Development Report 1996 - An Assessment

UNCTAD Review, 1995

United Nations publication, Sales No. E.95.II.D.23
ISBN 92-1-112391-7

Mehdi Shafaeddin
The impact of trade liberalization on export and GDP growth in least developed countries
Thomas Ziesemer
Economic development and endogenous terms-of-trade determination: Review and reinterpretation of the Prebisch-Singer thesis
Robert Rowthorn
A simulation model of North-South trade
John Eatwell
Disguised unemployment: The G7 experience
Ajit Singh
The causes of fast economic growth in East Asia
José María Fanelli and Roberto Frenkel
Micro-macro interaction in economic development
Manuel R. Agosin
Savings and investment in Latin America
Alfred Maizels and Theodosios B. Palaskas
The Common Fund and the behaviour of the ten "core" commodity prices
Andrew Cornford
Risks and derivatives markets: Selected issues
Ernesto Tironi
Some lessons from the Uruguay Round: Reflections of a developing country trade negotiator

UNCTAD Review, 1996

United Nations publication, Sales No. E.97.II.D.2
ISBN 92-1-112406-9

Edward J. Amadeo
The knife-edge of exchange-rate-based stabilization: Impact on growth, employment and wages
Theodosios B. Palaskas and Trevor Crowe
The effect of financial and fundamental factors on the behaviour of commodity futures prices
E.V.K. FitzGerald
Intervention versus regulation: The role of the IMF in crisis prevention and management
J.A. Kregel
Some risks and implications of financial globalization for national policy autonomy
David Felix
Financial globalization versus free trade: The case for the Tobin tax
Andrew Cornford
The Tobin tax: Silver bullet for financial volatility, global cash cow or both?

******

These publications may be obtained from bookstores and distributors throughout the world. Consult your bookstore or write to United Nations Publications/Sales Section, Palais des Nations, CH-Geneva 10, Switzerland, fax: 41 22 917 0027, e-mail, unpubli@un.org, Internet: http://www.un.org/publications; or from United Nations Publications, Two UN Plaza, Room DC2-853, Dept. PERS, New York, N.Y. 10017, U.S.A., telephone: 1 212 963 83 02 or 1 800 253 96 46; fax: 1 212 963 34 89, e-mail: publications@un.org.

UNCTAD series on East Asian Development:
Lessons for a New Global Environment

Study No. 1   Yilmaz Akyüz
New trends in Japanese trade and FDI: Post-industrial transformation and policy challenges

Study No. 2   Tun-jen Cheng, Stephan Haggard and David Kang
Institutions, economic policy and growth in the Republic of Korea and Taiwan Province of China

Study No. 3   Yoshihisa Inada
The economic impact of regional integration with special reference to APEC

Study No. 4   K.S. Jomo
Lessons from growth and structural change in the second-tier South-East Asian newly industrializing countries

Study No. 5   S.C. Kasahara
The role of agriculture in the early phase of industrialization: Policy implications from Japan's experience

Study No. 6   Gabriel Palma
Whatever happened to Latin America's savings? Comparing Latin American and East Asian savings performances

Study No. 7   V.R. Panchamukhi
WTO and industrial policies

Study No. 8   Robert Rowthorn
East Asian development: The flying geese paradigm reconsidered

Study No. 9   Ajit Singh
Savings, investment and the corporation in the East Asian Miracle

Study No. 10   *UNCTAD secretariat Report* to the Conference on East Asian Development: Lessons for a New Global Environment, held in Kuala Lumpur (Malaysia), 29 February to 1 March 1996.

******

Copies of the above studies may be obtained from the Editorial Assistant, UNCTAD, Division on Globalization and Development Strategies, Palais des Nations, CH-1211 Geneva 10, Switzerland (telephone: 41 22 907 5733; fax: 41 22 907 0274, e-mail: nicole.winch@unctad.org).

UNCTAD Discussion Papers

No. 94, Jan. 1995	XIE Ping	Financial services in China
No. 95, Jan. 1995	William W.F. CHOA	The derivation of trade matrices by commodity groups in current and constant prices
No. 96, Feb. 1995	Alexandre R. BARROS	The role of wage stickiness in economic growth
No. 97, Feb. 1995	Ajit SINGH	How did East Asia grow so fast? Slow progress towards an analytical consensus
No. 98, April 1995	Z. KOZUL-WRIGHT	The role of the firm in the innovation process
No. 99, May 1995	Juan A. DE CASTRO	Trade and labour standards: Using the wrong instruments for the right cause
No. 100, Aug. 1995	Roberto FRENKEL	Macroeconomic sustainability and development prospects: Latin American performance in the 1990s
No. 101, Aug. 1995	R. KOZUL-WRIGHT & P. RAYMENT	Walking on two legs: Strengthening democracy and productive entrepreneurship in the transition economies
No. 102, Aug. 1995	J.C. DE SOUZA BRAGA M.A. MACEDO CINTRA & Sulamis DAIN	Financing the public sector in Latin America
No. 103, Sep. 1995	Toni HANIOTIS & Sebastian SCHICH	Should governments subsidize exports through exportcredit insurance agencies?
No. 104, Sep. 1995	Robert ROWTHORN	A simulation model of North-South trade
No. 105, Oct. 1995	Giovanni N. DE VITO	Market distortions and competition: The particular case of Malaysia
No. 106, Oct. 1995	John EATWELL	Disguised unemployment: The G7 experience
No. 107, Nov. 1995	Luisa E. SABATER	Multilateral debt of least developed countries
No. 108, Nov. 1995	David FELIX	Financial globalization versus free trade: The case for the Tobin Tax
No. 109, Dec. 1995	Urvashi ZUTSHI	Aspects of the final outcome of the negotiations on financial services of the Uruguay Round
No. 110, Jan. 1996	H.A.C. PRASAD	Bilateral terms of trade of selected countries from the South with the North and the South
No. 111, Jan. 1996	Charles GORE	Methodological nationalism and the misunderstanding of East Asian industrialization
No. 112, March 1996	Djidiack FAYE	Aide publique au développement et dette extérieure: Quelles mesures opportunes pour le financement du secteur privé en Afrique?
No. 113, March 1996	P. BAIROCH & R. KOZUL-WRIGHT	Globalization myths: Some historical reflections on integration, industrialization and growth in the world economy
No. 114, April 1996	R. TANDON	Japanese financial deregulation since 1984
No. 115, April 1996	E.V.K. FITZGERALD	Intervention versus regulation: The role of the IMF in crisis prevention and management
No. 116, June 1996	Jussi LANKOSKI	Controlling agricultural nonpoint source pollution: The case of mineral balances
No. 117, Aug. 1996	José RIPOLL	Domestic insurance markets in developing countries: Is there any life after GATS?
No. 118, Sep. 1996	Sunanda SEN	Growth centres in South East Asia in the era of globalization
No. 119, Sep. 1996	Leena ALANEN	The impact of environmental cost internalization on sectoral competitiveness: A new conceptual framework
No. 120, Oct. 1996	Sinan AL-SHABIBI	Structural adjustment for the transition to disarmament: An assessment of the role of the market
No. 121, Oct. 1996	J.F. OUTREVILLE	Reinsurance in developing countries: Market structure and comparative advantage
No. 122, Dec. 1996	Jörg MAYER	Implications of new trade and endogenous growth theories for diversification policies of commodity-dependent countries
No. 123, Dec. 1996	L. RUTTEN & L.SANTANA-BOADO	Collateralized commodity financing, with special reference to the use of warehouse receipts
No. 124, March 1997	Jörg MAYER	Is having a rich natural-resource endowment detrimental to export diversification?
No. 125, April 1997	Brigitte BOCOUM	The new mining legislation of Côte d'Ivoire: Some comparative features
No. 126, April 1997	Jussi LANKOSKI	Environmental effects of agriculture trade liberalization and domestic agricultural policy reforms
No. 127, May 1997	Raju Jan SINGH	Banks, growth and geography

＊＊＊＊＊＊

Copies of the **UNCTAD Discussion Papers** may be obtained from the Editorial Assistant, UNCTAD, Division on Globalization and Development Strategies, Palais des Nations, CH-1211 Geneva 10, Switzerland (telephone: 41 22 907 5733, fax: 41 22 907 0274, e-mail: nicole.winch@unctad.org).